MEDIA
AND
TERRORISM

MEDIA AND TERRORISM

by :

Niranjan Dass

MD Publications Pvt Ltd
New Delhi
www.mdppl.com

Published by
MD Publications Pvt Ltd
"MD House", 11, Darya Ganj,
New Delhi-110002
Ph. : +91-11-41563325, 41562846
E-mail : **contact@mdppl.com**
Website : **www.mdppl.com**

ISBN : 978-81-7533-108-2

PRICE : Rs. 1095.00

Published and Printed by
MD Publications Pvt Ltd at Printext,
D2/149A, Jeewan Park, Uttam Nagar, New Delh.

PREFACE

The analysis proceeds with the investigation of some of the earlier analytical efforts that contributed to the general confusion over the concept of Media and Terrorism. A critique of nonproductive attempts to define terrorism through the identification of perpetrators and their causes is offered, and an evaluation is made of the usefulness of the many typologies of terrorism that exist in the literature.

An overview of the employment of terrorism as an instrument of politics is presented. Of continuing and current interest is the employment of terrorism by national liberation movements and ideologies. In a world-order system functioning under the threat of nuclear holocaust, a natural progression away from open warfare has precipitated a movement toward state support and sponsorship of international terrorism.

A significant amount of the literature involves the investigation of the causes of terrorism. Lack of agreement on a definition of the concept of terrorism has resulted in chaos, whereby acts of terrorism are attributed to literally every known source of violence. Few have chosen to address the basic question of why a specific individual or group chooses to commit a terrorist atrocity instead of utilizing another form of political protest. A limited discussion focuses directly on the issue of why a decision may be taken to employ terrorism in the pursuit of political goals.

To perform a quantitative analysis of the relationship between media coverage of terrorist atrocities and the success of terrorists, this analysis first identifies and investigates the functions of terrorism and the applicable functions of the media.

An attempt is made to clarify the nature of the terror that political terrorists seek to impart to a target audience. At issue is the transmission of terrorist violence, inflicted upon symbolic victims, to the target audience by the exploitation of the free press in a democratic society. A clear concept of the relationship among terrorist violence, the media, and the political power of the terrorists is extremely important. The dependence of international terrorists upon the media to transmit terror is addressed. The effectiveness of the transnational flow of information is equated with the ability of the media to influence the public's perception of terrorism. The relevance of the news media's selection of labels and terminology when covering terrorism is examined, along with the communicative techniques involved in the intentional or unintentional dissemination of terrorist propaganda.

The responsibilities of a democratic society's media in the reporting of terrorism are emphasized, with attention to the problems of the contagion of terrorist violence, the close association of members of the media with terrorists during the gathering of information, and the tactical errors committed by members of the media on and away from the scene of terrorist atrocities. A challenge is offered to the general assumption in the literature that the relationship between the media and the terrorists is symbiotic. At issue is whether the benefits derived by both are in balance over the long term. Research of problems that can be quantified and analyzed normally yields recommendations as well as conclusions. Alternative resolutions to the problems usually emerge during the analytical process. The problem posed to democratic societies by the exploitation of their media by terrorists is an exception to that generalization.

Thanks to Mr. Pranav Gupta of **MD Publications Pvt Ltd,** New Delhi, who supported me fully for completing this book.

Niranjan Dass

CONTENTS

1

Terrorism, Politics and Media

Introduction

One should also note that throughout history wars of national liberation and self-determination have been fought by "guerrillas" without recourse to terrorism. Unfortunately, in the literature and in circles where political terrorism is a necessary topic of discussion, many frequently make the mistake of equating terrorism with guerrilla warfare. Wilkinson cautions, "there are quite clear differentiae between the intent, aims and psychological effects of terrorism and those of other forms of violence such as the collective violence of riots and revolutionary uprisings and conventional war." As previously stated, one should proceed cautiously when labeling political violence as terrorism. The repeated theme of this analysis is that terrorism exists only when a unique form of violence, unacceptable to civilized societies, is employed.

Assuredly, some guerrilla movements have at times employed some variety of terror as a weapon. However, terrorist tactics can, and should, be distinguished from guerrilla tactics in general. Wilkinson has provided three basic elements to utilize in examining unconventional warfare to determine whether it is terroristic in nature: "the aims of its perpetrators, their modus operandi in deploying particular forms of violence upon the victims, and the target audience." He urges further examination of the particular form of violence as to whether it (1) is indiscriminate in the selection of victims, (2) appears arbitrary and unpredictable, (3) does not provide for noncombatant status or the other rules of warfare, (4) observes no moral constraints on weaponry or tactics, (5) justifies any means to achieve its ends, (6) regards extreme violence as inspirational and the most effective means available, (7) regards vengeance as a moral necessity, and (8) justifies the use of terror to avoid the greater evil represented by the enemy.

Analysts of political terrorism are well advised to use Wilkinson's descriptive elements when investigating national liberation movements in order to determine whether their active members are guerrillas or terrorists. Such analysis would likely show that some national liberation movements have indeed employed terrorism at various points. However, in only a few instances of a history filled with national liberation movements has the employment of terrorism contributed significantly to successful "liberation." The Irgun and Stern Gang's terror campaign against the British during the Palestine Mandate is the notable exception, along with the limited success of the Palestine Liberation Organization. It can be argued that those successes did not result from the employment of terrorism in isolation, but by its combination with other less violent political endeavors. Those nationalist movements that relied solely or principally on terrorism to achieve their goals have, for the most part, failed. Most notable examples are the Basque Homeland and Freedom (ETA) in Spain and the Provisional Irish Republican Army (PIRA) of Northern Ireland.

An evaluation of the forms of political violence employed by national liberation movements also includes a comparison of the French Resistance during World War II and the later FLN terrorist campaign to "liberate" Algeria. Although German civilians were well within reach of the French underground, they were apparently not normally targeted. France was, of course, eventually liberated and restored as a democratic state, whereas the indiscriminate slaughter of French nationals by Ben Bella's terrorists eventually yielded the undemocratic, despotic state of Algeria. In contrasting terrorist campaigns to national liberation movements, Benjamin

Netanyahu has noted that the means employed by terrorists reveal their true objectives: "Those who deliberately butcher women and children do not have liberation in mind. The choice of means indicates what the true ends are."

Ideologies and Terrorism

Along with the basic human motivations for self-identification and community, beliefs based on social or economic systems, on religions, or on other deeply held convictions have also been identified as sources of political violence that have sometimes led to terrorism. For example, Netanyahu identified Islamic radicalism and communist totalitarianism as two movements that have gained international prominence since World War II while providing a basis for the intensification of terrorism: "Both legitimize unbridled violence in the name of a higher cause, both are profoundly hostile to democracy, and both have found in terrorism an ideal weapon for waging war against it." While one can accept or reject Netanyahu's observation on the basis of personal convictions and interpretation of evidence, it is instructive to review these two movements as examples of how terrorism can be utilized as a political instrument.

Terrorism and Soviet Foreign Policy

The Soviet Union regularly employed terrorism as an instrument of foreign policy. Extensive evidence has been documented and is available through numerous Western sources. A sharp increase in the level of Soviet-sponsored terrorism began in the 1960s and was the result of a synthesis of several factors. Two of the most important were:

1. Khrushchev's peaceful coexistence, followed by the era of détente, called for low-risk foreign policy alternatives for the global expansion of Soviet influence.
2. The turbulent political atmosphere of the 1960s provided opportunities for the Soviets to disrupt the domestic stability of several Western nations.

Khrushchev's adaptation of the communist ideology at the 20th Party Congress laid the groundwork for a foreign policy that included terrorism as an integrated instrument. Nuclear weapons had negated the inevitability of war, and the communist victory would now be achieved by intensifying the class struggle in capitalist nations, and by worldwide support for every just war of national liberation. The doctrine that developed from Khrushchev's version of the ideology seemed to be directed toward ensuring that both class struggles in the capitalist nations and wars of national liberation in the Third World did, in fact, occur. The violence of terrorism was utilized as a means to bring about the occurrence and/or intensification of those class struggles and those wars of national liberation.

The strategy that evolved for intensifying class struggles proved to be support of whatever violent disruptive forces existed, or could be developed, in targeted capitalist societies. Soviet support, in terms of training and weapons, flowed through surrogates to groups already waging campaigns of political terror against Western regimes. Soviet surrogates sought out, encouraged, organized, trained, and armed violent groups that were spawned by the social conflicts of the 1960s. With peaceful coexistence and the spirit of détente calling for the avoidance of direct confrontation, the Soviets discreetly directed activities through surrogates. Direct control of targeting was neither desired nor required. It was not desired because terrorist violence in the West dare not be attributable to Moscow. It was not required because it was quite sufficient to simply train, organize, and equip the terrorists and allow their innovation to do the rest.

The Soviet strategy for supporting wars of national liberation involved creating a political base for expansion in the target area, then sending aid, advisers, weapons, and money under an elaborate cover of propaganda. Terrorist violence was inflicted to ensure that a sufficient level of conflict arose requiring the prospective client, either the old or the new regime, to request Soviet military assistance. The troops, normally surrogate but sometimes Soviet, were there and ready to assist. The terrorists in these scenarios were normally indigenous groups, but they were trained, equipped, and organized by the Soviets directly or through their surrogates.

Soviet foreign policy and terrorism in the Middle East. The documented evidence shows that the Soviets were often directly involved in training and equipping international terrorists. However, their preferred mode of operation was indirectly through surrogates, and their major effort was through the Palestinians in the Middle East. The Middle East was of vital importance to the Soviets.

Proximity to their border invoked national security concerns. Ports and airfields in the Mediterranean area would have greatly enhanced the Warsaw Pact war-fighting capability versus NATO. Further, key members of the NATO alliance depended heavily on the oil resources of the Middle East. The foreign policy instruments of military aid and diplomacy had produced less-thanfavorable results with the area's unstable, sometimes erratic Islamic regimes. With Moscow's regional influence apparently based on the oilrich Arabs' desire for Soviet weapons to oppose the perceived Zionist threat, it was in the Soviet Union's best interests to pursue a foreign policy that would ensure continued fear and hatred between the region's Arabic and Jewish populations. The homeless Palestinians were the precise tool for that task, and extensive Soviet efforts in training and equipping the Palestinians are well documented.

The results of a Soviet foreign policy to create a continued state of low-intensity conflict via Palestinian terrorists were highly successful. In spite of limited U.S. mediation success at Camp David, peace did not come to the Middle East. While the Egyptians became somewhat less hostile and fearful toward Israel, Iraq and Syria, armed with the latest weapons technology, kept the region in a high level of tension. As a bonus for the Soviets, the United States has been forced to pay high economic and political costs for support of Israel. Paradoxically, Israel's reprisals against Soviet-surrogate Palestinian terrorists resulted in the destruction of the adjacent pro-Western state of Lebanon. The Western Judeo-Christian democracies have not been able to cope with the Lebanese situation, and it remains for the Soviets' Islamic client, Syria, to reconstruct the nation in the presence of a strong Iranian-backed terrorist movement.

Coups in South Yemen and Ethiopia allowed Moscow to establish an early military presence that could have ensured wartime control of the Persian Gulf and the eastern approaches to the Suez. When the South Yemen regime embraced communism following the 1978 coup, the Soviets had also successfully encircled conservative Arab states friendly to the United States. Within South Yemen, Soviet terrorist facilities were established that could have threatened the stabilization of the Arab states bordering the Persian Gulf when deemed appropriate by Moscow. International in scope, the South Yemen terrorist facilities were manned by Soviet surrogates from

Eastern Europe, Cuba, and Libya, along with thousands of Palestinians.

Soviet foreign policy and terrorism in Western Europe. The Soviets also used Palestinian surrogates effectively throughout Western Europe. Their efficient support of Red Brigades terrorists in Italy in the 1970s almost brought that major NATO member to its knees. Lacking support from Eurocommunists, Moscow developed a Western European network of terrorist groups that proved effective in disrupting the domestic tranquillity of the NATO partners when the Soviet Union deemed it opportune. In the north, Soviet support through Libyan surrogates ensured continued terrorist activities by the Provisional IRA, which tied down thousands of British troops. In the south, the fragile democracy of Spain was challenged by increasingly severe attacks by the Soviet trained and equipped ETA, with Spanish membership in NATO at stake. While Soviet-sponsored terrorism did not threaten the existence of any Western European member of the NATO alliance, the timely employment of terrorism proved more useful to the Soviets in affecting their domestic activity than did the Western European communist parties. Therefore, Soviet employment of terrorism in Western Europe could be viewed as successful in relative terms as to what they achieved through other means.

Soviet foreign policy and terrorism in North Africa. Moscow's bid for ports and airfields in the Mediterranean area was enhanced by its partnership with Libya. Satisfying Qadhafi's desire for military aid resulted in an alliance for terrorism that saw the worldwide deployment of Libyan surrogates as well as development of extensive terrorist facilities in Libya. Qadhafi was most useful in relaying Soviet support to the Muslim rebels in Southeast Asia, especially in the southern Philippines. The vulnerable Philippine democracy was caught between the Communist New People's Army (NPA) in the north and the Muslim separatist rebels in the south, where 85 percent of the Philippine armed forces were often tied down. Obviously the costs to the United States for its Pacific outpost increased considerably.

Libyan support for the Polisario guerrillas was directed toward the gradual replacement of Morocco's regime with one more pro-Soviet. Soviet airfields and ports in Morocco, coupled with facilities in Angola, could create severe difficulties for NATO resupply through central and southern Atlantic sea lanes. A rim of pro-Soviet regimes along the southern shores of the Mediterranean could seriously threaten the southern flank of NATO.

Soviet foreign policy and terrorism south of the Sahara. After their early economic failures in Africa south of the Sahara, the Soviets seemed content to hold on to strategically important Angola while ensuring that Western influence on the continent would be costly. As demonstrated by repeated Western failures in the region, that policy proved successful. Through the African National Congress (ANC) and the South-West Africa People's Organization (SWAPO), the Soviets attempted to develop clients that could eventually come to power in a region from which the United States imports extensive amounts of strategic raw materials. While Moscow politically supported the ANC and SWAPO, Soviet surrogates trained and equipped their armed terrorist branches.

Soviet surrogates in the Western Hemisphere. Keenly aware of both sides of the balance-of-power equation, the Soviets adroitly targeted for destabilization those areas with the highest potential cost for the opposing superpower. The Soviets' first client in the Western Hemisphere, Cuba, proved to be extremely costly, and apparently discouraged them from fully supporting another. Moscow instead discounted part of the expense of Cuba by utilizing Castro's armed forces and intelligence services. Under KGB tutelage, an impressive number of international terrorists graduated from Castro's terrorist training facilities. Their exploits and successes throughout the Caribbean, Central and South America, and Western Europe are well documented. While the United States obviously pursued its role as the major regional power, Soviet-orchestrated destabilization of the southern half of the Western Hemisphere exacted a heavy political and economic toll on Washington.The lack of a challenge to Soviet-sponsored terrorism. Ample evidence shows that Moscow did not always succeed in disguising its support for terrorism. Documents captured in Lebanon and uncovered in Western Europe, along with numerous Western intelligence reports, clearly show the roots of international terrorism reaching deep into the Soviet Union. The question remains why the Western powers did not call more attention to this obvious violation of the principles of peaceful coexistence and the spirit of détente. For Western European regimes, the answer was simple and direct: the Soviets had skillfully woven a strong Arab participation into their terrorist network. Even though Western European authorities often apprehended Moscow's surrogate terrorists, they normally stopped short of effective punitive measures for fear of provoking those Islamic Arab nations upon whom they were energy-dependent. In the case of the United States, the Soviet support of international terrorism was ignored by an American regime, media, and public interested in not disturbing the era of detente. By discreet employment of surrogates, and by agreeing to a few antiterrorist treaties of common economic interest, such as the prevention of hijackings, the Soviets were able to maintain a lofty separation between their status as a superpower and the reality of their perpetration of terrorist violence at the international level.

Islam and Terrorism

Muslims constitute one-seventh of the world's population, are a majority in some forty-three countries, and are a significant minority in others. There is generally little popular awareness in the West of the basic tenets of Islam, and only minimal appreciation of the role of Islam in politics, law, and society. For Americans, the activities of Islam in Iran and elsewhere in the Middle East are in contrast to at least three American traditions and beliefs:

1. The separation of religion and politics, basic to the U.S. version of democracy, is challenged by Islam's combination of church and state.
2. Americans tend to believe that Islam has been a barrier to socioeconomic progress in Islamic countries.
3. Americans tend to believe that secular nationalism is a stage through which developing nations must pass, and, at least in some Muslim states, Islam has not been overpowered by secularism.

The West is traditionally viewed by fundamentalist Muslims as responsible for the downfall of Islam. The recent resurgence of Islamic fundamentalism has given new life to a radical version of the faith that partitions the world into Muslims and infidels, and calls for Muslims to convert the infidels to Islam, to subjugate them, or to destroy them. Contemporary terrorism has given that resurgence a means of radical expression.

Islam is a politicized religion. Muhammad was a ruler as well as a religious leader, promulgating laws while enforcing and adjudicating them, levying taxes and raising armies and making war and peace. All of those functions have a part in the Quran (Koran), the Holy Law of Islam.

Within Islamic law, tradition, and history, violence has two forms: (1) conflict against external enemies and (2) conflict against internal enemies. The conflict against external enemies is the violent struggle between the worlds of Islam and the infidels. It can be ended only by the death, conversion, or subjugation of the unbelievers. This external conflict is conducted by rules of war contained in Islamic law, which, at least by some interpretations, do not condone terrorist atrocities.

The internal conflict involves the use of violence to defend God's state against those who have violated it. This was demonstrated in the seventh century when the third caliph of Islam, the Caliph Uthman, was killed by the Shiite faction. They regarded the Caliph as a tyrant in violation of God's law, and his execution as the will of God. The Sunni faction regarded the Shiites as murderers that should be prosecuted under the law. Out of this internal conflict emerged Shiite radical groups. They combine Islam and terrorism in a tradition that began with the eleventhcentury Assassins in the north of Iran. Shiites under the leadership of Hasan-i Sabbah were dedicated to the killing of the enemies of Islam.

The terrorism of the Shiites has endured for centuries, expressing the frustrations within a society undergoing dramatic change. It terrorized many regimes, and its offspring has now emerged in the Middle East as perhaps the most important terrorist threat of this century. The same tradition of violence and terror is continued today by the followers of the late Ayatollah Khomeini: "God is our goal, the Prophet is our leader. The Koran is our Constitution, struggle is our way. Death in the service of God is the loftiest of our wishes. God is great, God is great."

A predecessor of Khomeini led the Shiite Muslim Fedayeen-i Islam in terrorist attacks against the Russians and the British in Iran in the late nineteenth century. Their descendants attempted to assassinate the Shah in 1948, and later provided the core around which the Ayatollah Khomeini grouped his followers in their successful revolution to return fundamental Islam to Iran.

The martyrdom of Caliph Ali's son, Husayn, at Karbala in A.D. 680, after an unsuccessful Shiite rebellion against the Umayyad Caliph Yazid, was the paradigm for the 1970s revolution. Shiism provided the ideological framework and Ali Shariati (1933-1977) was the ideologue. The mosques provided the focus, and Khomeini was the spokesman.

Shiite Islam is a religion of protest. "To kill and get killed for Allah, that's the message of Ruhollah." As explained by Schlagheck, in a religious society where crime is punished by amputation and stoning, "it is consistent with Shiite beliefs to use violence, physical struggles, jihad, martyrdom, and even death to combat the enemies of Islam."

The Ayatollah's followers view Western influence as the major enemy of Islam. They firmly believe that they are emerging from an era in which their culture and values were corrupted by Western infidels. Their defense of Islam involves the destruction of the Western influence, by whatever means available. One of those principal means has clearly been the formation and support of terrorist groups to promote the violent Shiite version of Islam throughout the Middle East.

The employment of terrorism within and outside of Iran has become a trademark of Khomeini's revolution. In 1981 Khomeini followers liquidated the Marxist Mujahdeen opposition in Iran by killing more than six thousand of its members. In camps in Qom and Tehran, the regime began the training of thousands of entaharis (commandos) for suicide attacks. Fundamentalist groups in the Philippines, Malaysia, Turkey, and Pakistan, as well as those in the Middle East, were recipients of a massive propaganda campaign. Egypt's President Anwar Sadat was assassinated by followers of the Ayatollah. When the 1982 Israeli invasion of Lebanon produced a power vacuum and chaos, hundreds of Iran's Revolutionary Guards were sent into the Bekaa Valley to organize and train Shiite terrorist groups, among those the Islamic Jihad, the Islamic Amal, Hizballah, and Al Da'awa. By 1983, the capability of those groups was being demonstrated by the suicide bombings of the U.S. embassy in Beirut and the U.S. Marine Corps barracks at the Beirut airport, as well as attacks on French military installations. In 1984, Islamic fundamentalist terrorist tactics were expanded to include hostage taking, and in 1985 terrorists hijacked TWA Flight 847. After Islamic fundamentalist terrorists kidnapped and tortured to death the U.S. embassy's political attaché, William Buckley, the Reagan administration made secret arms sales to Iran that led to the release of two other hostages. After the disclosure of the Iran-contra affair, the kidnappings continued.

The terror campaign of the Islamic fundamentalists in Lebanon could be judged a success, with the withdrawal of Western military forces and the sharp reduction of Western influence. Although Lebanon today is essentially destroyed and can no longer effectively function as a state, the Shiite factions in Lebanon are in a considerably stronger position than are their Christian or other Islamic sect competitors.

Threatened by the exportation of Khomeini's revolution, other Arab regimes in the Middle East must deal with instability from within and terrorism from without. As per John Esposito's conclusion: "To the extent that incumbent governments fail to satisfy the political and economic needs of their societies and to pursue a path of modernization which is sensitive to their Islamic heritage, they will remain in a precarious position in which stability is based more often than not on authoritarian rule and force."

The Ayatollah Khomeini's plan for the escalation of terror. The escalation of Iranian-sponsored terrorism in the Middle East is examined in a recent academic publication that includes a document, reportedly smuggled out of Iran to Britain, containing the classified minutes of a 26 May 1984 meeting of Iranian government leaders, wherein they decided upon the creation of a brigade-size terrorist unit to attack targets throughout the Middle East.

The Ayatollah Khomeini's comments to the meeting reportedly included: All the rulers of Islamic countries are servants of foreigners and have left the entire Islamic heritage in the hands of foreigners. We have to spread Islam everywhere, and in this path we have given a great deal of blood, and we will give more act according to your religious duties. Whatever is necessary to destroy them must be carried out.

Remarks in the document by the Iranian Minister for National Guidance included: "It is not possible for us to directly confront this enormous force that is supported by the superpowers. It has been decided that the strike force which at present is composed of a few groups of 10-20 people each, who are currently serving in the Lebanon should be increased to the size of a brigade."

Remarks by the shadowy leader of the terrorist brigade, Mirhashem, included:

We have at present a number of dedicated groups who have, to the outside world, become known as suicide groups. These groups are by themselves inadequate. It has been decided to select dedicated religious and fully committed candidates from all combat organisations for carrying out unconventional warfare in enemy territory. The target countries are Saudi Arabia, Kuwait, United Arab Emirates and Bahrain. Hashamite Jordan. France and other countries who will try and confront the Islamic Republic. There is no way that we can bring them to their knees unless we are able to inflict relentless blows on them from within.

A few months after the Iranian regime's conference on escalating terrorism, an "open letter" appeared that apparently constituted the operational charter of Hizballah. Hizballah emphatically claimed to be directly linked to and receive guidance from Iran. It claimed responsibility for destroying the Marine Corps barracks at the Beirut airport, and included the United States, NATO, and France in its list of enemies, while calling for the "obliteration" of Israel.

In the year following the Tehran decision to expand its sponsorship of terrorism, Shiites operating out of Lebanon began to imitate George Habash's Popular Front for the Liberation of Palestine (PFLP). They perpetrated the hijacking of TWA Flight 847 in June 1985, and blew up a Jordanian airliner at Beirut in the summer. Tehran's Islamic Jihad in Lebanon also sent messages to the U.S., British, and French embassies in Cairo and Jakarta warning of retaliatory attacks against their embassies, diplomats, citizens, and property throughout the world for their participation in a multinational force in Beirut.

Addressing the Fletcher School of Law and Diplomacy in 1985, CIA Director William Casey identified the goals and intensity of Iran's sponsorship of international terrorism: "Tehran uses terrorism as a major element of its ongoing campaign to export the Iranian revolution throughout the Muslim world and to reduce Western influence. In 1983 we identified as many as 50 terrorist attacks with a confirmed or suspected Iranian involvement. We believe that agents working out of Iranian Embassies and Islamic cultural or student centers in several European nations will continue to attempt operations in Western Europe in the near future."

Tehran and the international network of terror. While the Iranian regime has capitalized on the expertise of Shiite terrorist groups already in existence in Lebanon, it remains to be seen if it can develop a training infrastructure and organization as efficient as that which the Soviets developed with Palestinian elements. For example, on 23 May 1990, the nations of North and South Yemen merged to re-form a united Yemeni state. During the twenty-seven years of separation, the Marxist government in the south had suffered from an increasingly difficult economic situation. Pressure from Arab neighbors to oust the Soviet influence was sufficient by May 1990 to provide a unanimous vote by the South Yemen legislative body to merge with the North. North Yemen has moved more toward fundamentalist Islam in the last few years, and the acceptance by the South to merge was not unanimous because of the recognition of women's rights, which had emerged under the Marxist regime. Whether the terrorist training facilities of South Yemen, which had accommodated the Palestinians and the international network, will now become facilities for the training of radical Shiite groups is a question of some concern to moderate Arab neighbors as well as to Western interests in the Middle East.

Tehran's motivation for the sponsorship of international terrorism differs considerably from that of Moscow's in the 1960s. However, if it is able to develop a network at the same pace as the Soviets, then the 1990s could see the escalation of an already severe problem in the Middle East. As per the preceding quote from the former director of the Central Intelligence Agency, it would seem that the Iranians already have the nucleus of an international terrorist organization in place in Western Europe. Also, Iranian leaders were quoted as saying that "one thousand suicide bombers poised to strike were in the United States."

State Sponsorship and Support of International Terrorism

During the eras of peaceful coexistence and détente, states desiring to employ political violence apparently sometimes chose to utilize a discreet mode of terroristic violence rather than to commit directly to warfare by proxy. Neil Livingstone and Terrell Arnold have outlined the advantages of terrorism as a political instrument for both weak and powerful states:

Small, weak states have discovered that it can greatly increase their political clout, and plagued as they are by resource shortages, they are not likely to abandon terrorism as a political and military tool. Larger, stronger states, by contrast, have discovered that terrorist proxies can help them achieve their national objectives without the risk attendant to other forms of warfare and without the protracted delays characteristic of the bargaining table.

The violence perpetrated by a state's surrogate terrorists is designed to create an atmosphere of fear in a target population, with the intent of forcing the target government to pursue a course of action favorable to the state sponsoring and/or supporting the attack. Terrorism as defined in this analysis the employment of a unique form of political violence is precisely the instrument to elicit such a response. The atrocity committed is of a horrifying nature and attracts the international media. The media coverage, utilizing modern technology, is so spectacular and intense that the desired goal of creating an atmosphere of fear in the target population is quickly and efficiently achieved. If the target government does not select the response option desired by the sponsoring/supporting state, another atrocity is perpetrated. The atrocities might be short-lived and intense like the 1983 Iran-sponsored bombing of the U.S. Marine barracks at the Beirut airport, which prompted the withdrawal of U.S. military forces from Lebanon or they may be of a continuing agonizing nature like the long ordeal of the Western hostages seized in Lebanon by Iran-sponsored groups attempting to bring external pressure upon Western governments for various concessions.

United States Secretary of State George Shultz addressed the challenge of state-supported terrorism in 1984 at the Johnathan Institute's second Conference on International Terrorism in Jerusalem: "Terrorists and those who support them have definite goals; terrorist violence is the means of attaining those goals. Our response must be two fold: we must deny them the means but above all we must deny them their goals. . . . In many countries, terrorism would long since have passed away had it not been for significant support from outside."

Sponsorship or Support

Scholars and politicians alike use the terms sponsorship and support interchangeably when addressing state involvement in international terrorism. More rigorously examined, support of terrorism indicates actions on behalf of a state to provide a means of support to an existing group of terrorists. Sponsorship indicates a deeper relationship with the state in the formation and organization of the group itself, as well as further support. So defined, the term support apparently applies to Moscow's actions on behalf of those terrorist groups in Western Europe that emerged during the turbulence of the 1960s. The term sponsorship could be exemplified by the actions of Tehran, wherein it has taken an active part in the formulation and organization of terrorist groups in Lebanon and throughout the Middle East.

Conclusions about State Support and Sponsorship of Terrorism

Truth, mutual trust, serious and strict solidarity exists only amongst a dozen or so individuals who form the sanctus sanctorum of the society. All the others must serve as blind tools, exploitable material in the hands of these dozen men with real solidarity.

The application of the full force of available military power as an instrument of politics becomes necessarily constrained within a world system where nuclear weapons are available. War as an option for resolving political confrontations may become further unlikely as technological advances make nuclear weapons even more effective, and more states become members of the nuclear weapons club. Michael Mandelbaum has postulated that, the more heavily armed each side is, the more deadly would be the war, and perhaps the less likely that it would be risked.

The first forty years of a world system dominated by the threat of nuclear holocaust witnessed the increasing employment of low levels of violence, often perpetrated through surrogates, by states intent upon expanding their influence upon the world order. As recognized by Richard Feinberg, the developing world has proved to be a fertile, alternative battleground where the Great Powers can wage a shadow war by proxy, and where each can seek to spread its own influence and deny or disrupt its opponent's ambitions. Both democratic and authoritarian states have conducted warfare by proxy in attempts to dominate lesser-developed regions for example, the United States and the contras in Nicaragua, and the Soviet Union and Cuban troops in Angola. As the states in lesserdeveloped regions become more developed and move into alliances with stronger states, or form coalitions of their own, the prospects of success through proxy warfare become less. For example, the ASEAN pact served to lessen the Muslim separatist threat to the Philippines, as Malaysian cooperation contributed to the disruption of Qadhafi's material support of the separatist rebels on Mindanao. Perhaps more important, technological advances in weaponry have degraded the ability to prevent escalation of proxy war to general war, and states contemplating proxy warfare face increased risks of losing control of the situation. For example, as demonstrated by Saddam Hussein's SCUD missile attacks on Israel during the Persian Gulf conflict, the possession of long-range weapons of mass destruction by Third World nations seems to pose significant problems in constraining conflicts to local areas.

With total war becoming unthinkable, and proxy warfare increasingly risky and unproductive, the eras of peaceful coexistence and détente have seen the implementation of terrorism as an important instrument of international politics. By nature of its execution and strategy, political terrorism, rigorously defined, is useful only against liberal societies. Its effectiveness as a political instrument depends upon its ability to create an atmosphere of fear within a target population to the extent that the population will force the target government to follow a course of action desired by the state sponsoring or supporting the perpetrator.

The creation of an atmosphere of fear has, in the last thirty years, depended on the media as the instrument through which the terror of atrocities is transferred to a target population. With the media's technological capability to reach and penetrate a target audience increasing rapidly and with the media's potential for exploitation by international terrorists, the increasing efficiency of terrorism as a political instrument can be expected to become even more attractive for state sponsorship and support.

As the liberalization progresses of states and regions formerly closed by communism, the field for possible political terrorism will increase proportionally. The old hatreds of the early 1900s are already emerging in Eastern Europe. While those nations, and the nationalistic groups within them, are not immediately militarily capable of making demands upon their neighbors, the appeal of sponsoring campaigns of terror in support of their politics could likely be very tempting. Almost all of them had apparats employed by the Soviets to train, equip, and support their surrogate terrorists. They could again be put into operation for nationalistic or other causes.

Summary

The employment of terrorism as an instrument of politics began in biblical times. In recent decades, it has been employed principally in support of nationalism, ideologies, and religious radicalism. During eras of peaceful coexistence and détente, it has been supported by developed states as a means of political violence short of warfare, and sponsored by developing states as a means of achieving political successes against more powerful opponents. Under the constraint of nuclear weapons, with the efficiency of political terrorism increasing and its range of applicability widening, it can be expected that some states may choose to employ or perhaps to increase their sponsorship and support of international terrorism.

2

Political Terrorism and the Media

Introduction

The proposals to prevent exploitation can be categorized as (1) recommendations for preventive action to be taken before an atrocity occurs, and (2) damage-minimization policies to be followed during and after an atrocity. Livingstone's specific recommendations exemplify the preventive category:

If the media would announce guidelines restricting the use of material produced by terrorists the incentive for terrorists to produce videotapes could be eliminated. If the media make public statements on record of their positions and their efforts to control terrorism, it will be far more difficult for them to explode later in an orgy of media coverage following a major terrorist incident.

The damage-minimization category was illustrated by recommendations from psychologist Preston Horstman at a conference of the RadioTelevision Directors Association. They included (1) withholding identification of the terrorists, (2) denying terrorists live coverage, (3) avoiding the publication of terrorist communiques, and (4) portraying the terrorists and their atrocity as despicable.

Also within the damage-minimization category, Bassiouni suggests that the media establish a pool for coverage of a terrorist atrocity. Such a procedure could lessen the competition and aggressive search for scoops that usually lead to media magnification of the violence. The media pool concept was employed by coalition forces during the Persian Gulf conflict, and perhaps lessons learned by both the authorities and the media during that sensitive period will strengthen Bassiouni's proposal. He has further recommended the creation of a media council to supervise and coordinate voluntary restraints on media activities as terrorist atrocities are occurring. Charles Fenyvesi also envisioned the formation of a media council to declare news media emergencies and prevent the endangerment of lives, with media employers holding their individual members responsible for conforming to the council's rulings.

The response by media executives to such damage-minimization proposals has not been overly enthusiastic. Some have suggested that no special policies are required. As observed by the president of NBC News, "We hire sensible people tell them to be careful and it works out okay. Every once in a while, it doesn't." Those remarks were made in 1977, two years before the media's extensive coverage of the seizure of the American embassy in Tehran. During that 444-day episode, a decision by NBC prompted the resignation of one of its journalists, Fred Rowan. NBC had agreed to televising a five-minute harangue by an Iranian spokeswoman in exchange for an interview with a hostage. Rowan accused his employers of "irresponsible journalism," trying unsuccessfully to get NBC to air a two-minute interview with a State Department spokesman on the same telecast.

Cross-National Comparative Analysis Study Approach

A cross-national comparison of four major Western democracies seriously threatened by political terrorism during the last three decades affords an opportunity to observe the problems with terrorist manipulation of the media and some attempted solutions. The democratic governments of Italy, the Federal Republic of Germany, and the United Kingdom have experienced strong internal threats and have been accommodated by a cooperative media. The experience of the United States is unique, in that an internal threat has been minimal while the external threat from international terrorists has been significant. Further, the U.S. media have chosen an adversarial role in relation to the government.

A comparative analysis should preview the societal environment in which the various national media have functioned in order to understand and evaluate their actions. At issue would be (1) the historical experiences of the state in terms of the nature of the threat from political terrorism, (2) the countermeasure policies to terrorism that have evolved within the state, (3) the role of the media, and (4) the relationship that has emerged among the government, the press, and the public with regard to the media's coverage of terrorism.

As an introduction to the comparison of cases, a brief review of responses by various regimes and societies to political terrorism might prove beneficial. From the historical perspective, Wilkinson has assembled five categories: (1) submission, (2) soft-line approach, (3) tough-line approach, (4) counterterror and ruthless repression, and (5) counterterror against foreign-based terrorists. The example of Lebanon has shown that when a government faced with intensifying terrorist attacks is submissive and fails to take necessary measures for internal defense, the people take the law into their own hands with a vicious cycle of terror and counterterror that leads to civil war. Jenkins's survey at Rand has shown the results of soft-line approaches, with 79 percent of the terrorists worldwide evading punishment for their crimes. The iron-fist policies of the Israeli Likud coalition toward the Palestinians have demonstrated the harsh measures of the tough-line approach. The death squads in Argentina exemplify a counterterror approach, while the tsar in Russia is the classic example of ruthless repression. Lastly, Israel has employed counterterror against foreign-based terrorists with attacks outside its borders, with limited tactical success and high political costs.

Along with a consideration of the historical experiences of a state and the current threats of political terrorism against it, identification of countermeasure policies employed by the state establishes the framework through which the actions of the media can be evaluated. Observation of the resulting relationship among the press, the public, and the government contributes to an understanding of the appropriateness of the media's coverage.

Emergence of the Modern Terrorist Threat

The dramatic increase in terrorism across Western Europe in the 1960s has been attributed to many factors, including (1) a contagion effect from protests in the United States against the Vietnam conflict, (2) empathy with emerging guerrilla movements in Latin America, and (3) the internationalizing of Palestinian terrorism. As related earlier, the expansion of terrorism in the West was nurtured by the Soviets, directly and through surrogates. The Palestinians funneled substantial Soviet support to various terrorist organizations across the continent and were ably assisted by the efforts of Qadhafi and Castro.

With Western Europe plagued by a sharp increase in the intensity and severity of terrorist attacks during the 1970s, public opinion polls there showed a steady progression of support favoring the statement, "Our present society must be valiantly defended against all subversive force"; likewise, there was decreasing support for the statement: "Our society must be gradually improved by reform." By 1977, the polls also indicated that the public favored capital punishment for terrorists, with military reprisals where possible and even assassination of terrorist leaders.

The rapidity with which an adroitly managed campaign of political terror can challenge a staunch democracy was demonstrated after the 1977 kidnapping and murder of West German industrialist HannsMartin Schleyer by RAF terrorists. A public opinion poll taken by EmnidInstitute disclosed that 61 percent of the Germans surveyed felt helpless against terrorism.

Evolution of the Terrorist Threat in The United Kingdom

The major terrorist challenge to the United Kingdom comes from the Provisional Irish Republican Army (PIRA), which was created in 1969 when nationalists advocating violence broke away from Marxist leadership in the official Irish Republican Army (IRA). The IRA had formed as a terror organization in 1922 at the end of Ireland's civil war. While the official IRA continued with some 200 members in 1982, it has apparently not engaged in terrorism since 1972.

In the late 1960s, the Northern Ireland Civil Rights Association (NICRA) staged peaceful demonstrations in an effort to call attention to what it perceived as discrimination against Catholics in Northern Ireland. Violence broke out when the organization was opposed by militant Protestants, and in August 1968, further public demonstrations by the NICRA were banned. When continued NICRA demonstrations violated the ban, Royal Ulster Constables used violent methods to disperse marchers. When a January 1969 Catholic civil rights march from Belfast to Londonderry was attacked by Protestants, the Royal Ulster Constabulary did not offer protection. With charges that the police were favoring the Protestants during the upsurge of violence that followed, the Provisional wing broke away from the official IRA with a pledge to protect the Catholics.

By 1982, active terrorist membership in the PIRA numbered about 300. The group had also formed a political wing called the Provisional Sinn Fein (PSF). In 1974, the Irish Republican Socialist Party also split away from the official IRA and formed its own terrorist wing, the Irish National Liberation Army (INLA). By 1982, the INLA had some fifty active terrorists.

The Catholic terrorist organizations were countered by Protestant terrorist groups like the Reverend Ian Paisley's Ulster Protestant Volunteers, the Ulster Defense Association, the Ulster Freedom Fighters, and the Ulster Volunteer Force. When British troops were deployed by the U.K. government to quell the violence, they also became targets of the terrorism that engulfed Northern Ireland.

Violence erupted on a large scale in 1972, with the PIRA bombing of a British Army officers' mess in Aldershot. The death toll from political violence had increased sharply from 13 in 1969 to a peak of 467 killed and nearly 5,000 injured in 1972. Between 1970 and 1984, an average of 160 people were killed each year.

The PIRA and INLA have links with the international terrorist network. Originally anti-Moscow, the PIRA became leftist in the 1970s. It committed itself to "demolish the Quisling Regime in the Free State of Ireland and the colonial regime in the Northern war zone." The Soviets evidently preferred to deal with the PIRA through their Libyan and PLO surrogates. In the early 1970s, the PIRA developed close ties with the Palestinian Black September hard-core terrorists. In May 1972, George Habash and Wadi Haddad brought the PIRA into the inner circle of the international terrorist network at the Baddawi summit meeting in Lebanon. In July 1972, Habash's PFLP signed a formal "Declaration of Support" for the IRA. PIRA terrorists had been trained in Palestinian terrorist camps in Jordan as early as 1969. In 1971, arms from Czechoslovakia intended for the PIRA were intercepted in Amsterdam. Soviet RPG-7 rocket launchers were supplied to the IRA in 1972. Libya has been an important supporter of the PIRA with funds, arms, and volunteers. In March 1973, the S.S. *Caudia*, captained by PIRA commander Joe Cahill, was stopped by the Irish Navy. It carried five tons of Soviet-bloc arms from Qadhafi for the PIRA. In the late 1970s, Qadhafi was contributing $5 million per year to the PIRA. The North American Irish National Aid Committee, which normally contributes about $100,000 per year, collected $250,000 for the PIRA during the first half of 1981 when Bobby Sands, elected Member of Parliament and PIRA activist, died in prison from a hunger strike.

With significant external support, the PIRA has shown no signs of agreeing to a cease-fire or settlement. When the Fitzgerald Plan was proposed in 1979, it responded with the murder of Lord Mountbatten. Both the PIRA and INLA terrorist organizations now operate with secure cellular structures. Their international capability was adequately demonstrated by a March 1987 attack on a British Army on the Rhine officers' club in West Germany. Red Army Faction German terrorists supplied the stolen car for the bomb, Iranian terrorists supplied the explosives, and the PIRA parked it outside the club during a Friday night party. Thirty-eight people were injured, mostly West German guests.

United Kingdom's Legislative Response to Terrorism

Antiterrorism laws in the form of the Civil Authorities (Special Powers) Act have existed in the United Kingdom since 1922. That act, in effect all all levels of authority, enables the Minister of Home Affairs, or Royal Ulster Constabulary officers, to "take all such steps and issue all such orders as may be necessary for preserving the peace and maintaining order." The special powers authorized include internment without public trial, detention of any person for forty-eight hours for questioning, search and seizure of property without warrant, search and arrest of persons without warrant, censorship of printed material, and dispersion of public assemblies.

While those 1922 provisions had been infrequently employed since the violence that accompanied the partitioning of the island subsided, Northern Ireland's prime minister asked Parliament to resume the internment of suspected terrorists in 1971. During the first six months after his request was granted, 2,357 persons were arrested and 598 interned. Parliament continued with further legislation to broaden the 1922 statute, including the Northern Ireland (Emergency Provisions) Acts of 1973, 1975, and 1978 and the Prevention of Terrorism (Temporary Provisions) Acts of 1974 and 1976. As demonstrated by these excerpts from the Emergency Provisions Act of 1973, the powers granted were broad, extensive, and potentially controversial:

1. There may be trials without jury for certain offenses.
2. Constables may arrest without warrant persons suspected of terrorism.
3. Members of Her Majesty's forces may arrest without warrant persons suspected of committing, or intending to commit, any offense.
4. The unauthorized collecting, recording, or publishing of information about the police or Her Majesty's forces that could be useful to terrorists is unlawful.
5. Illegal organizations include the Irish Republican Army, Sinn Fein, and the Ulster Volunteer Force.

With over 15,000 British soldiers deployed in Northern Ireland in 1974, the PIRA increased its terrorist activities in England. Westminster and the Tower of London were bombed in the summer, and in the fall, 21 persons were killed and 180 injured in the bombing of two pubs in Birmingham. Parliament responded with the Prevention of Terrorism Acts of 1974 and 1976, which (1) outlawed the PIRA and banned public displays of support for it, (2) extended the previous Northern Ireland emergency powers throughout the United Kingdom, and (3) allowed for the deportation of suspected terrorists. The November 1974 Act was passed without debate.

In 1975, the Special Powers Act of 1922 was modified to allow imprisonment without trial through the authority of the Northern Ireland government. Trial by jury was also suspended with the institution of the "Diplock Courts," named after the judge who recommended the procedure. In 1979, police detained 857 persons under the Provisions of Terrorism Act, as compared with 622 the previous year. From 29 November 1974 to 31 December 1979, about 4,600 people were detained.

The outpouring of legislation in the United Kingdom against a significant terrorist threat can best be evaluated as per Miller's observation that elected legislators "keep an ear to the ground listening to the political footsteps of the public." Further, when the electorate is threatened by the extremes of terrorist violence, "legislatures can seldom be expected to uphold a libertarian view of the law."

To some extent, Ireland has supported the United Kingdom's policies against terrorism in Northern Ireland. The Republic of Ireland's antiterrorism laws date from 1920. Its legislation likely poses greater restrictions on civil liberties than that of any other Western democracy. The 1939 Offenses Against the State Act was amended in 1972 to establish special criminal courts for terrorist threats to the state, with three judges and no jury. Further, an individual alleged to be a member of the outlawed PIRA has to prove his or her disassociation. A statement by a senior police officer is considered sufficient proof to establish an accused as a member of the PIRA. The Irish Criminal Law Jurisdiction Act of 1975 covers crimes committed outside the republic. A similar law passed in the United Kingdom is perhaps a modest beginning of increased legal cooperation with Ireland. While the Republic of Ireland does not allow extradition for political offenses, the Irish Constitution, Article 29.3, does state, " Ireland accepts the generally recognized principles of international law as its rule of conduct in its relations with other States."

U.K. Media and Legislative Restraints

In those countries where terrorist atrocities occur on a frequent basis, strong public attention is apparently given to terrorist exploitation of the media. Such has been the situation in the United Kingdom since 1972. Cooperation between the government and the media has been attempted, but the results have apparently been less than completely satisfactory. A number of provisions from the Prevention of Terrorism Acts of 1974 and 1976 could be applied to the media's coverage of terrorism. However, such was not the case until the election of the Thatcher government in May 1979. Thatcher's Conservative government often threatened the news media with the application of antiterrorist legislation and, on occasion, exerted that authority.

The INLA registered one of its most significant interruptions of the British domestic political scene with the car-bomb murder of opposition spokesman Airey Neave inside the House of Commons's underground parking lot. When BBC later broadcast an interview with a disguised INLA terrorist who claimed a connection with the murder, Thatcher directed the attorney general to investigate a possible BBC violation of the 1974 Prevention of Terrorism Act. After viewing the broadcast, she was strongly critical of the BBC: "I am appalled. It reflects gravely on the judgment of the BBC."

Public opinion in the United Kingdom was apparently supportive of Thatcher's criticism. The Lord Mayor of London said: "What a pity it is when an institution like the BBC puts someone who claims to have assisted in the murder of Airey Neave on the box and gives him a platform."

The Bishop of Chester made a poignant plea for more responsibility on the part of the British news media: "What is the limit of responsibility. If I am aware of the identity of a person who has committed a serious crime, am I not required as a citizen to inform the appropriate authorities? If I pay money to a self-confessed traitor and murderer in order to gain a supposedly valuable news-story, am I not myself a traitor and guilty of 'aiding and comforting' the enemy?" BBC's ethics were also criticized by Lord Chalfont: "The excuse that it was a 'newsworthy event,' and therefore in some way excluded from the normal canons of human behaviour, is symptomatic of the state of moral and intellectual confusion which the organs of public communication consistently display on the subject of terrorism."

In the face of this sharp criticism, the BBC attempted to justify its actions. Director-General Ian Trethowan presented the BBC view: "We believe that the public has the common sense and stability to judge very accurately the character of the people they are seeing. We do not believe that a BBC interview with the INLA will worsen by one iota that central problem of Northern Ireland: the inability of two communities to reach rational settlement of their problems."

However, the BBC was forced to retreat later when Mrs. Thatcher challenged the broadcast of a "Panorama" television program that was to include scenes taped at PIRA roadblock in Northern Ireland. The broadcast was canceled and two BBC editors were reprimanded.

These confrontations between the Conservative government and the media occurred in spite of two previous agreements between law enforcement officials and the news media. After a freelance radio reporter was involved in the 1975 kidnap and murder of a girl in England, a conference had been held between senior law enforcement officials and national and international media executives. While the conference was in session, another kidnapping occurred. During this event, the media agreed to a voluntary news blackout and the girl was eventually released unharmed. While the arrangement was at best a "gentlemen's agreement," the Home Office incorporated it into its campaign against terrorism. Britain's fifty-one chief constables were advised in August 1976 that terrorist activities could produce situations wherein it might become necessary to request the media not to publish certain information until the situation could be rectified.

A second agreement was reached in March 1979 between the BBC and the New Scotland Yard. After a BBC broadcast portraying corruption in the law enforcement system, the Metropolitan Police had sought a formal contract with the BBC for the right to review in advance BBC broadcasts that concerned them. After nine months of high-level negotiations, a written agreement was reached to govern BBC broadcasts of information that the Metropolitan Police considered sensitive or affecting national security or similar concerns.

It has been suggested that perhaps the BBC has avoided more stringent government controls in its reporting of terrorism by accepting "mediated intervention, in which spokesmen in the sphere of politics have defined the permissible limits, and these conceptual orientations have been picked up and reproduced within the media." Wilkinson objected to the Home Secretary's pressure on the BBC Board of Governors that resulted in the banning of a documentary called, "At the Edge of the Union." While the program would have included an interview with an alleged PIRA terrorist leader, Martin McGuinness, Wilkinson believed the program contained a strong message on the futility and horror of extremist violence. His principal objection was the ban by Mrs. Thatcher and Mr. Brittan without first reviewing the program's content: "I too want to prevent, so far as possible, the hijacking and manipulation of the media by the terrorists. But the proper way to do this in a democracy is to encourage the mass media to develop and enforce their own voluntary guidelines and self-restraint in terrorism coverage. Any introduction of censorship, in whatever guise, plays into the hands of enemies of democracy."

The BBC has established guidelines similar to those published by CBS in the United States. In addition, there is a formal procedure established to ensure adherence to those guidelines. At state-owned BBC radio and television, stories concerning terrorism are checked through several levels of management to ensure compliance. Such a procedure is not new in the United Kingdom. During World War II, "D-notices" (defense notices) were provided by the government to editors to prevent publication of stories harmful to national security. Following this tradition, independent television firms and newspapers as well as the BBC have cooperated with Scotland Yard in limiting the disclosure of information concerning investigations of terrorist attacks. Such cooperation by media management has brought occasional criticism from journalists. BBC reporters staged a worldwide twenty-four-hour strike in 1985 against their board of governors' decision to ban the documentary, "At the Edge of the Union." Other programs banned by the BBC board included"24 Hours" in 1971, "The Scottish Connection" in 1976, and "The City on the Border" and "A Bridge of Sorts" in 1978.

Not unlike the U.S. media, British journalists are extremely competitive. They have produced a contested study that concludes that attempted government control of the news media has resulted in public mistrust with regard to coverage of domestic terrorism and has prevented the public from fully understanding the violence in Northern Ireland. However, unlike the U.S. media, members of the British press must frequently walk streets in their own country that are littered with the aftermath of terrorist atrocities. Perhaps this contact with the stark reality of terrorism constrains somewhat their objections to close cooperation with the government in matters of national security and their coverage of terrorism. Media objections have been limited, and there has been no outcry from a British public, endangered by terrorist attacks, about denying terrorists publicity by restraining the press.

Balancing Democratic Principles and Terrorist Countermeasures in the U.K.

The British public, subjected to terrorist atrocities for more than twenty years, have accepted seemingly controversial antiterrorist legislation as necessary for the preservation of law and order. American professor Barton Ingraham has observed: "What is surprising if not shocking to the foreign observer in the light of English history in the preceding century is the alacrity with which the English surrendered practically the totality of their cherished liberties to the discretion of Government officials during an emergency." Ingraham's statement apparently disregards the democratic process of representative legislation by which the English citizens "surrendered" their liberties. It would seem that American journalism professor Walter Jaehnig has more correctly summarized the United Kingdom's experience as demonstrating that, when a society has been exposed to a long and vicious campaign of political terrorism, "The state will place its highest priority upon protecting itself, despite its expressed concerns about both the professional responsibility of the news media and the protection of civil liberties."

It is important to note the special characteristics of the emergency legislation enacted by the British government during a time of serious terrorist threats to its citizens. In his review of the antiterrorism legislation enacted by Parliament, Crozier noted, "It is very important to make it clear that any emergency legislation that is introduced, including detention without trial, is temporary in nature and will be revoked as soon as possible." Crozier further noted four provisions that were important to the acceptance and success of the United Kingdom's emergency legislation:

(1) draft laws must be easy to understand; (2) the purpose of the emergency legislation is to control an insurgent group that has demonstrated its absolute disdain for the law; (3) all "war measures" must be closely monitored and reviewed periodically; and (4) all laws must be effective and applied equally to all."

Perhaps an overriding factor in the relatively amiable relationship among the British public, press, and government has been a phenomenon recognized by Miller: "Even when legislation exists to restrict the media, democratic social and political norms can prevent the laws' implementation."

Summary

The conflict in Northern Ireland has defied resolution. PIRA and INLA terrorists, with external support, have threatened U.K. targets both internally and abroad. To the extent that the interest of communist sources in creating difficulties for the United Kingdom can be perceived as having declined, it could be noted that the total capacity of those political terrorist organizations could also have declined. Unfortunately, this decline could possibly be offset in the future by external support from sources opposed to British Middle East foreign policy and U.K. participation in the Persian Gulf conflict. The extremism generated by the deep religious cleavage in Northern Ireland indicates a continuing threat of terrorist violence to the domestic tranquility of the United Kingdom.

The onset of violence in Northern Ireland, the government of the United Kingdom has focused on legislative processes to develop and formalize countermeasures. The policies that have emerged are generally moderate, and while some legislative edicts have provided for the restraint of some personal liberties and democratic procedures, one must note that those edicts were imposed through normal democratic legislative processes. With the continuation of PIRA and INLA terrorist attacks into the 1990s, it is apparent that earlier legislated countermeasures have not effectively suppressed terrorism, although declining trends in fatality rates do indicate improvement since the mid-1970s. The U.K. experience demonstrates that the nature of the threat is perhaps the dominant factor in evaluating the challenge of political terrorism to a democracy.

The role of the media. The actions of the BBC in challenging the Thatcher government have demonstrated that a public-subsidized press is not necessarily a government-controlled press. The government appears to have exerted pressure and prevailed in those confrontations only when they have been supported by public outcry. Cooperative agreements reached among the public-subsidized media, the independent media, and the government have been openly publicized and have apparently not drawn significant objection from the media or the public. Compared to the U.S. press, the British subsidized and independent media both appear to be relatively cooperative with government administrations. Previous wartime experience has been credited with the adoption of this cooperative role. When directly challenged by the Conservative government's enforcing of antiterrorist legislation to prevent certain BBC broadcasts, some members of the British press did display their independence by a one-day strike. That demonstration was relatively limited and apparently occurred only once in the two decades following the onset of terrorist violence in Northern Ireland.

The relationship among government, press, and public. The extensive body of antiterrorism legislation that exists in the United Kingdom is a demonstration of public support for the countermeasure policies that have emerged. That legislation has included restraints on the media in the coverage of terrorism, to the extent that it can literally prohibit publication of information on the outlawed PIRA or INLA. However, during the first fifteen years that current antiterrorism legislation has been in effect, the executive branch has only occasionally chosen to invoke its authority by restraining the media in the broadcast of a few specific programs. Only on one occasion did that result in a meaningful protest from the media.

In sum, after more than twenty years of combating a significant domestic terrorist threat supported by external interests, the United Kingdom has adequately demonstrated that countermeasures against terrorism, including restraints on the media's sensationalizing of terrorists and their atrocities, can be applied, and will be accepted by the public, when those countermeasures are developed and implemented through normal democratic legislative processes. The United Kingdom's emergency legislation, including that which restrains the press, has withstood the test of time. Democracy has continued to thrive in the United Kingdom, as has its "bridled" media.

Emergence of Contemporary Terrorism in West Germany

Modern political terrorism in the Federal Republic of Germany originated with the general dissatisfaction of the Socialist Student Organization with the constitutional left in the early 1960s. The grand coalition of the Social Democratic Party (SPD) with the Christian

Democratic Union (CDU) and Christian Social Union (CSU) offered a fundamental challenge to radical student groups. Ulrike Meinhof, as editor of the radical publication *Konkret*, expressed frustration with what was considered a lack of movement toward ambitious reforms: "All Leftists have run over to the Right to boil the common pot and cook in it; there is nothing but one anger, one hatred, one lament and the exclusion, the hereticising, the bedevilment of what remains has sired a kind of Left. A 'New Left' as it calls itself, so as to doubly signal its appearance."

The new left, with its formal designation as the Extra-Parliamentary Opposition (APO), disintegrated in 1968 and some of its members opted for terrorism as a strategy to pursue political goals. Horst Mahler, an original member of the Baader-Meinhof Gang and a founder of the Red Army Faction, expressed frustration with the failure of the APO to gain acceptance in the West German formal political system:

It can only be termed deeply frustrating to recognize the necessity of a revolution with growing clarity and yet be unable to know who and where the revolutionary class, in other words the beneficiaries of this upheaval itself, actually are. How easily can such a state of affairs lead to a mood of desperation! From this point, via a completely abstract identification with the liberation struggles in the Third World, the further course led to out-and-out adventurous concepts.

The Baader-Meinhof Gang committed its first terrorist atrocity in 1968 with the firebombing of a Frankfurt shopping center. It stated that to attack was to "prevent the voice of the Extra-Parliamentary Opposition from not being able to find a hearing."

From its inception Baader-Meinhof, which later evolved into the Red Army Faction, considered itself Marxist-Leninist and a part of the "worldwide revolutionary movement." Since 1977, it has concentrated its efforts against the "world's two main imperialistic powers," the United States and West Germany. Specific targets have been U.S. military personnel and facilities, NATO activities, and West German elites.

While Mahler and Meinhof directly linked their atrocities to a political ideology, the motivation of Andreas Baader and some of their other colleagues was more directly related to a cult of violence.

Radicals dedicated to revolution, they resorted to "systematically and repeatedly breaking the law," so that the masses would be "weaned from obedience." After being trained by Dr. George Habash's PFLP in 1970 in Lebanon and Jordan, they adopted the name of Rote Armee Fraktion and robbed numerous banks to finance their operations. They stole 11.6 million Deutsche Marks between 1970 and 1978. They armed themselves by stealing weapons from NATO facilities.

The RAF made six serious bomb attacks in May 1972 across West Germany, at Frankfurt, Munich, Augsburg, Hamburg, Karlsruhe, and Heidelberg. Following tips from the frightened German public, authorities arrested six key members of the group—Baader, Meinhof, Meins, Raspe, Ensslin, and Müller. Within a year, the group had regained its strength with strongholds in Frankfurt, Hamburg, and Amsterdam, and had set as is primary goal the freeing of its imprisoned leaders. However, the group was again penetrated and demolished by German and Netherlands authorities in February 1974. It rebuilt for a third time in 1975 and switched to more violent tactics with the murder of officials and diplomats.

In April 1975, RAF terrorists seized the West German embassy in Stockholm and murdered the military and commercial attaches. Their principal demand was for the release of their jailed colleagues. However, security forces overpowered the attackers and they were also imprisoned.

In November 1976, the arrest of two lawyers, Siegfried Haag and Roland Mayer, at an autobahn checkpoint produced evidence that the RAF had again reformed. Despite the imprisonment of its leader, Haag, the RAF was strong enough to commit several atrocities in 1977, including the murder of Attorney General Siegfried Buback and his guards, the murder of banker Jurgen Ponto, and the kidnapping and murder of Hanns-Martin Schleyer after his guards had been killed.

The operational history of the RAF is unique in that its imprisoned leaders were able to continue to direct the activities of the organization through lawyer contacts. The lawyers, who linked those in prison with their operating colleagues, also recruited other young lawyers. By 1979, one of the three main groups of the organization was composed entirely of lawyers. Into the 1980s, the

RAF was concentrated in Hamburg, Baden-Württember, Hessen, and Berlin. It numbered about 150 members, about 25 of whom were active terrorists. More than half of the operatives were women.

The 2nd June Movement lacked the clear political goals and consistency of the RAF, but its tactics were apparently more effective. In 1975, 2nd June kidnapped Christian Democrat leader Peter Lorenz in Berlin and succeeded in exchanging him for the release of five of their imprisoned colleagues, who were given safe conduct to South Yemen. Authorities were successful in suppressing 2nd June activities after the Lorenz kidnapping, but four female members of the group escaped from a West Berlin prison in 1976. In 1978, four members of 2nd June were arrested in Bulgaria and extradited to West Germany.

The Revolutionary Cells (RZ) have received less publicity than the RAF and 2nd June. However, they were responsible for twenty bombings and incendiary attacks between 1973 and 1979, in which several people were killed. Unlike the RAF and 2nd June, the RZ does not operate entirely underground. The majority of its members are unknown to authorities. The RZ organization consists of small groups of three to five members who consider themselves "off-hours" terrorists. They lead normal lives participating in left-wing politics and make "anti-imperialist" and "anti-Zionist" terrorist strikes at U.S. and Israeli targets mainly in West Germany. They have developed links to the PIRA as well as to Palestinian terrorist groups.

Three main terrorist groups were operating in West Germany during the 1980s—the left extremist Red Army Faction, the Revolutionary Cells, and the neo-Nazi Hepp-Hexel organization. Although a right extremist group, the neo-Nazi Hepp-Hexel organization professes an antiimperialist ideology. Founded in 1982, its atrocities are mainly aimed at U.S. military personnel and facilities. It views the United States as occupying West Germany, with the West German government an alien regime imposed upon the Germans. Having undergone training by the PLO in Lebanon, its members also are concerned with attacking Israeli targets.

Considerable support for German terrorist groups has come from the Soviet bloc and from the Palestinians. Crozier has cited Moscow's support for Baader-Meinhof and specifically for Klaus Rainer Rohl and his wife, Ulrike Meinhof: "The Baader-Meinhof

Gang was secretly subsidized by the East Germans, whose Ministry of State Security is under the control of the KGB." Rohl and Meinhof were both "secret members of the Communist party from 1956 to 1964, and Rohl received about $250,000 (some sources say $400,000) in subsidies through East Berlin and Prague."

The Baader-Meinhof Gang, and later the RAF, received continual support from the East German secret police in the form of training, arms and ammunition, money, and false papers and identity cards. After a 1975 car accident in Belgium, police found documents revealing the existence of a KGB center in Vienna, working to "enliven" terrorist formations in West Germany, Italy, Belgium, the Netherlands, and France. Alexander Benyaminov, head of the Soviet delegation to the U.N. International Atomic Energy Agency, was reportedly in charge.

All the hard-core members of the RAF were trained by Palestinians in the South Yemen camps. German terrorists took part in Palestinian atrocities, such as the kidnapping of the OPEC oil ministers by the Carlos organization in 1975. In return, the Palestinians gave operational support to German terrorists, such as the diversionary hijacking to Mogadishu of a Lufthansa airliner during the RAF's kidnapping and murder of German industrialist Hanns-Martin Schleyer.

Speaking at an international seminar on terrorism in Tel Aviv in 1979, the director of the West Germany Department for Defense of the Constitution, Hans-Josef Horchem, noted that, between January 1970 and April 1979, thirty-one people had been murdered by terrorists in Germany, including three diplomats, four justice officials, and nine policemen. Ninety-seven had been injured in terrorist bombings and shootings, and 163 were taken hostage. Terrorists had committed ten cases of arson, twenty-five bombings, and thirty bank robberies with losses estimated at DM 5.4 million.

Prompt Response to Terrorism by West Germany

Unlike the United Kingdom, terrorism in West Germany in the 1960s and 1970s was not anchored in historic nationalism or religious conflict. The new-left ideology and terrorism of Baader-Meinhof began in the 1960s with no government countermeasures in existence. The initial concentration of atrocities was against political figures and institutions and against prosperous industrialists. This selection of targets perhaps proved somewhat derogatory to the terrorists' success, in that the endangerment of the elite likely created a sense of urgency in the development of countermeasures. There were, however, sufficient atrocities committed against random targets to create an atmosphere of fear in the general public.

For the first twenty years after the formation of the Federal Republic of Germany, the ruling coalition of the CDU and the CSU had stressed domestic security as its most prominent electoral theme. In May 1968, the West German government drafted emergency legislation to deal with growing student unrest and demonstrations, which were considered a leftist threat. The Bundestag passed the emergency measures by a vote of 384 to 100, with 1 abstention. The first antiterrorism legislation was enacted in December 1971, with stiffer prison sentences for hijackers and kidnappers. For example, a minimum penalty of five years' imprisonment was imposed for the hijacking or attack of an aircraft. If manslaughter occurred during such an event, ten years became the minimum sentence. By the 1976 elections, numerous attacks upon the elite had brought terrorism to the fore as a challenge to domestic security and a critical political issue.

After Interior Minister Hans-Dietrich Genscher's attempt to negotiate with Black September terrorists at the 1972 Olympic Games in Munich failed, conflict developed between Bonn and Munich. The West German government then accelerated the establishment of a countermeasures program that included creation of the antiterrorist unit *Grenzschutzgruppe* 9, composed initially of six units of thirty members each. Thoroughly trained in terrorist tactics, psychology, and differing modes of combat, GSG-9 units were deployed around the Federal Republic. An elaborate computerized intelligence system was also developed to combat terrorists.

Also in 1972, the powers of the Office for the Protection of the Constitution were expanded to allow for the observation of politically motivated anticonstitutional activities. Other countermeasure legislation included the *Radikalenerlass* (Radicals Ordinance) of 1972, which requires that all prospective employees of the FRG civil service indicate if they have ever been affiliated with any extremist organization. By August 1977, about a half million Germans had been checked. The government also moved to increase airport security and established telephone hotlines to encourage the public to participate by informing on terrorists.

Bonn was embarrassed in February 1975 when the government's "Grand-Crisis Committee" conceded to 2nd June Movement demands for the release of five jailed terrorists in exchange for kidnapped CDU West Berlin mayoral candidate Peter Lorenz. In April, Chancellor Schmidt described the Holger Meins Commando attack upon the West German embassy in Stockholm as, "the gravest challenge our constitutional state has faced in its 26 years of history."

The FRG parliament reacted with antiterrorism legislation that included increased prison terms for terrorists. In view of the RAF's demonstrated success in conducting operations through the legal counsels for their imprisoned leaders, legislation was enacted that forbade one attorney to defend several clients accused of terrorism. Additionally, a defense attorney suspected of involvement in a defendant's crime could be excluded from the trial. It was also made possible to conduct a trial with the accused not present, as in the case of a hunger strike by the defendant. Laws also were made to control written communication between a defense lawyer and a client accused of terrorism, to provide separation panels between lawyers and accused terrorists during meetings, and to prevent contact between defense lawyers and accused terrorists when such contact was deemed to be involved with an escape.

In January 1976, the Anti-Constitutional Advocacy Act provided for prosecution of those who publicly advocated or encouraged others to "commit an offense against the stability and security of the Federal Republic." The *June 1976 Anti-Terror Law* outlawed the formation of terrorist associations and increased the penalties for membership. Laws that permitted detention without trial, as well as fines and imprisonment for publishing terrorist manuals, were also written in 1976. A 1978 law allowed the search of all apartments within an apartment block when residents of one apartment were suspected of involvement with terrorism.

Evolution of Media Cooperation with the West German Government Until 1975 Bonn had normally attempted negotiations with terrorists and frequently granted concessions. Horchem indicates that a demonstrated government policy is a decisive factor for terrorists considering the commission of atrocities. He regards Chancellor Schmidt's firm stance during the 1975 seizing of the West German embassy in Stockholm (which followed the government's earlier capitulation to 2nd June Movement terrorists' demands for the release of prisoners in exchange for the life of Peter Lorenz) as a contributing factor to the cessation of terrorist atrocities for the following eighteen months.

Horchem is adamant in his belief that the media can either seriously undermine or credibly support a firm policy by the government. He cites as a positive example the kidnapping of Hanns-Martin Schleyer in 1977, in which the initial terrorist demands included media broadcasts of prisoner releases and a videotape of Schleyer. During the two months of Schleyer's captivity, the RAF provided numerous videotapes and photographs to the media, along with ultimatums and communiqués. However, "the West German press conducted itself with remarkable restraint," denying the RAF the publicity upon which it had planned. Practically no mention was made in the press of the fact that the RAF was demanding the release of its leaders in exchange for Schleyer's life. Additionally, a disinformation tactic was coordinated between authorities and the press to mislead the terrorists about efforts to release their leaders.

During the sixty-day standoff between the RAF and Bonn, a Palestinian terrorist group attempted to aid the RAF in breaking the silence of the media by hijacking a Lufthansa airliner to Mogadishu, Somalia. Continuing their firm stance, the West Germans dispatched a GSG-9 unit that successfully stormed the airliner and rescued the hostages after the terrorists had murdered the captain. Apparently realizing that the government was not going to capitulate and release their jailed leaders, the RAF terrorists murdered Schleyer. Four of the jailed leaders committed suicide in Stuttgart-Stammheim prison when they learned of the rescue at Mogadishu.

In 1986, close cooperation between the government and the media was again demonstrated when West German security forces captured a Lebanese terrorist who had participated in the 1985 hijacking of TWA Flight 847 to Beirut. When the international media announced that the United States would seek extradition of the terrorist, other Shiite terrorists promptly kidnapped two West Germans in Beirut and demanded an exchange. The West German government and media then cooperated on a news blackout of the extradition proceedings that denied the Beirut kidnappers vital information and allowed negotiations between the United States and the Federal Republic of Germany to proceed without interruption.

Cooperation between the media and the government in West Germany did not automatically commence with the emergence of terrorism. West German ZDF Television Washington correspondent Dieter Kronzucker has described the evolution of media cooperation with West German authorities. He observed that the 1970 killing in Guatemala of a German ambassador taken hostage by the FAR drew sympathy from the West German press because of the poor social and economic conditions in Guatemala. At that time, Latin American guerrillas were reportedly regarded as romantic revolutionaries by some of the West German press. However, when terrorists began kidnapping prominent Germans in the Federal Republic, the mood changed. After the 2nd June Movement demanded, and received, live coverage by both TV networks of the release of its jailed members in exchange for the life of Peter Lorenz, Kronzucker noted: "This changed a lot of the minds of my fellow colleagues. It was the start of cooperation between the government and many journalists."

A challenge emerged to media cooperation with the government as a result of the Schleyer kidnapping and murder. Pridham has reported that the media's cooperation in restricting coverage initiated a controversy over the principle of informing the public, which was later magnified when government mistakes made during the search for Schleyer came to light, including ignoring a tip that might have saved Schleyer. Nevertheless, Chancellor Schmidt was able to capitalize on the success of the Mogadishu rescue. He was characterized by the press as "After Mogadishu: The Admired German." He used his popularity to increase government antiterrorist measures. This included a concentrated attempt to use the media to apply psychological pressure on the terrorists, and to more fully inform the public about increasing security measures.

Public Support of West Germany's Countermeasures

The German public has been most supportive of its government's antiterrorist policies, which have been complemented by a cooperative media. The people were genuinely frightened by the terrorist atrocities. In the midst of the Schleyer affair, a public opinion poll showed that 67 percent favored a return to the death penalty. In May 1975, an Allensbach poll had shown that 69 percent of the West Germans would accept limitations on their personal freedoms for the sake of combating terrorism; by March 1978, another Allensbach poll showed 90 percent of the population believing that West Germany was threatened by terrorism. By the end of 1978, an Infas poll also showed that 83 percent thought terrorism would increase.

There were, of course, a few voices raised in dissent. The degree of self-censorship practiced by the West German media led noted author Heinrich Böll to comment: "The media have become so careful, that the laws don't actually have to be changed."

The West German government displayed a great deal of political expertise early in the war against terrorism by encouraging participation by the public. Photographs of known terrorists were widely distributed, and hotlines were made available for reporting suspicious activity. The direct participation of a German public in law enforcement can be regarded as part of their political culture. In their 1963 classic, The Civic Culture, surveys by Gabriel Almond and Sidney Verba found the Germans more politically informed and considerably prouder of their nation than the citizens of the United States, the United Kingdom, Italy, or Mexico. Motivated by a genuine fear of terrorism, politically aware of the situation, and concerned with protecting their nation, the German people united in their time of national stress. Self-restraint on the part of the news media and the public's cooperation with government antiterrorist policies, including actual participation in the identification and reporting of terrorists, enabled German authorities to suppress terrorist organizations that held potential for rapid expansion. As reported by Schlagheck:

The antiterrorist emergency laws and other state policies have been very well received by the German public. No election has raised the issue of overreacting to terrorism and thereby imperiling democracy; to the contrary, the German public has supported government efforts to end terrorism and "restore law and order."

Summary

The atrocities committed by terrorist organizations against West German targets commencing in the late 1960s were equally vicious and intense as those committed by the PIRA and the INLA against the United Kingdom. However, the roots of the West German terrorist groups were not anchored in such extremism as that inspired by the religious cleavage in Northern Ireland. The leftist ideology upon which the principal terrorist movements were based did not find support in a prosperous and expanding West German democracy. Consequently, lacking internal support in the face of effective countermeasures, and with external support from communist sources lessening, the political terrorist threat in West Germany was declining or largely suppressed by the late 1980s.

The first terrorist challenges to the postWorld War II West German government were external groups, predominantly in Latin America, which enjoyed some early sympathy from the German public and press. Consequently, an early policy of negotiation emerged. When the threat became internal and more intense, negotiation policies were replaced by a more firm stance by the executive branch, which was in turn augmented by legislative actions to provide for more staunch countermeasure policies. By the late 1970s, a balance of effective legislation and firm executive response against terrorism had been achieved.

The role of the media. The West German media during the 1960s to 1980s was a mix of some public-subsidized broadcast media and an increasing number of independent newspapers and other publications. Early in the threat period they demonstrated a vulnerability to terrorist exploitation not unlike the highly competitive U.S. media. However, after the kidnapping of Peter Lorenz in February 1975, during which both Bonn and the television news media were made to look powerless, the West German press evidently chose to pursue a supportive role against political terrorism. The guidelines, media-government agreements, and detailed legislation on media coverage of terrorism that emerged in the United Kingdom were not forthcoming in the Federal Republic, although some portions of the 1976 Anti-Constitutional Advocacy Act could have been enforced to constrain the media's coverage of terrorism if it had been deemed necessary.

The relationship government, press, and public. The West German public proved highly supportive of increasingly firm antiterrorist legislation and policies. Perhaps a strong postwar motivation for personal security dominated their beliefs and actions. This was certainly reflected in the political platforms of the successful parties. The public evidently readily accepted the self-restraint the media demonstrated in the coverage of terrorism. The West German news media reported on terrorist atrocities as they were occurring, however, as demonstrated during the Schleyer affair, their reporting was relatively carefully designed to avoid exploitation by terrorists and was positively supportive of the efforts of law enforcement agencies in combating terrorism. While terrorist organizations still exist in West Germany, the unification of public, media, and government in opposition has sharply limited their activities and will likely continue to do so in the future, the reunification process of a divided Germany that is likely to enhance the possibility of increased economic and social dissatisfaction and political violence notwithstanding.

Terrorism and Italy's Multiparty Democracy

Carlo Pisacane was an Italian socialist who died in an attempt to rally the peasantry of southern Italy against the Bourbons in 1857. In his Political Testament he noted the precedence of the propaganda of deeds over the propaganda of ideas: "The propaganda of the idea is a chimera. Ideas result from deeds, not the latter from the former conspiracies, plots and attempts are the series of deeds by which Italy proceeds to her goal."

Pisacane's forecast for violent domestic politics in Italy seemed to hold after World War II. Terrorism came from the right as well as the left. The right was initially viewed by the Allies as a stabilizing influence. It was strongly anticommunist and contained the core of bureaucrats, judiciary, and military personnel inherited by the new regime from twentyone years of fascist dictatorship. Terror from the right emerged with an extreme right-wing party, the Italian Social Movement (MSI). The strategy of its 1968 leader, Giorgio Almirante, was "combining the double-breasted suit with the club." He attempted to ensure the survival of the MSI in Italy's parliament by aligning with the Monarchist Party while simultaneously giving support to neofascist violence.

Furlong has attributed the beginning of what he terms the first phase of post-1968 Italian violence to the right wing. A 12 December 1969 bombing of the National Agricultural Bank at the Piazza Fontana in Milan killed seventeen persons. Anarchists Pietro Valpreda and Giuseppe Pinelli were arrested. Pinelli died shortly thereafter when he fell from a window at Milanese police headquarters. It took nine years to process the case, during which time Valpreda was acquitted and two neofascists were convicted in absentia, in the midst of accusations of security forces involvement in right-wing terrorism. After an abortive *coup d'état* in December 1970, right-wing extremists continued with bomb attacks against political targets through the end of 1973.

Terror from the left gained prominence with the initiation of Red Brigades violence in Milan in August 1970. Leaders Renato Curcio and Margherita Cagol emerged from a group called the Sinistra Proletaria. Their early 1970s attacks were more symbolic than spectacular, with the destruction of automobiles of known neofascists and industrialists. Occasionally they would conduct a heavily publicized kidnapping, with a "proletarian trial" followed by the release of the victim. It has been estimated that more than 12,000 terrorist acts occurred in Italy between 1969 and 1980.

In Furlong's second phase of Italian terrorism, violence increased dramatically, from 422 terrorist attacks in 1974, to 628 in 1975, to 1,201 in 1976, to 2,127 in 1977, and 2,395 in 1978. Declaring its strategy to "strike at the heart of the state," the Red Brigades strove for maximum political impact with such atrocities as the kidnapping of Public Prosecutor Mario Sossi in Genoa in April 1974, the murder of Genoa's Chief Magistrate Francesco Coco in June 1976, and the kidnapping and murder of Aldo Moro, leader of the Christian Democratic Party (DC) in March 1978. The Red Brigades apparently united with other Western European terrorist groups against NATO, with their kidnapping of U.S. Army General Dozier in 1982.

During the terror decade of the 1970s the most important political issue in Italy was the entry of the Communist Party (PCI) into the government. The PCI policy toward the Red Brigades and other similar groups was not to consider them as leftist organizations but rather as perpetrators of violence akin to the neofascists.

Like the Soviet Union, the Red Brigades viewed the Italian Communist Party's merger with the Italian political system as a betrayal of communist ideology. The Red Brigades described its terrorist attacks as a version of a class war in which it was the leader of the proletariat's armed struggle:

The Red Brigades are not the Communist Party of Combat, but an armed vanguard which works inside the metropolitan proletariat for its construction. While we affirm that BR and Party of Combat are not identical, we affirm with equal clarity that the armed vanguard must "act as a Party" from the very beginning.

The Red Brigades received considerable support from the Soviet bloc, most of which was relayed to them through the PLO. Grenades, antitank mines, explosives, machine guns, and Strella missiles were passed through the Palestinians to the Red Brigades, and its leaders were trained in Palestinian camps in Jordan in 1970. Substantial numbers of Italian terrorists were also trained at the Czechoslovakian Karlovy Vary camp. Significant quantities of Soviet-bloc weapons were delivered to the Red Brigades from Prague, by way of Hungary and Austria.

Italy's Political Response to Red Brigades Terror

Furlong notes that it took Italian political parties "at least five years to alert themselves seriously to the problem of terrorism." In describing the Italians' long suffering from terrorism, Furlong explains:

Major failings in the response to terrorism have been the deliberate manipulation of organised political violence to satisfy short-term goals goals that have been predominantly electoral but that have also been concerned with the formation of alliances within and between parties and, more broadly, the continued underestimation by politicians and senior civil servants of the capacity of clandestine groups to strike politically significant targets and of their intention to do so. The Italian state has been attempting to "ride the tiger."

The Christian Democratic Party used terrorist attacks to discredit the parties of the left. The PCI was initially pressed into a defensive stature on questions of internal security. The disclosure of information linking government security forces with neofascists, and increased political power from election victories, allowed the PCI to move to a more offensive position on internal security, and the major parties could then finally agree on antiterrorism strategies.

Before 1974, the DC advocated stronger law enforcement measures while the Socialist Party (PSI) and the PCI looked for reform and democratization of the *Carabinieri* (national police). In 1949, DC ministers had refused to demilitarize the police. Their view was that the major function of the police was maintaining public order rather than the pursuit of criminals. Hence, the *Corpo delle Guardie di Public Sicurezza* (local police) were ill equipped to combat the overwhelming intensity of terrorist attacks in the 1970s. The lack of a coordinated response to terrorism in Italy was sarcastically noted by Leonardo Sciascia:

The central error of the Red Brigades consists precisely in believing that they can succeed in striking at the heart of the State. The heart of the Italian State does not exist. Neither, any longer, does its brain. And it is that which paradoxically is its strength or at least its capacity to resist.

Italy's criminal code that existed in 1969 had its roots in the fascist era. Article 270 outlawed organizers and members of subversive associations, while Article 306 penalized those who became involved with armed groups for the purpose of overthrowing the state. With such pervasive powers already in effect, Leonard Weinberg and William Eubank have noted that "it is not surprising that Italian legislators did not react immediately to the onset of terrorism by enacting a wholly new set of emergency measures. The state already had what it needed to fight it."

After bomb attacks in Brescia and Bologna in 1974, the General Inspectorate for Action Against Terrorism and Armed Bands was formed to allow greater coordination of the police and the Carabinieri. A special unit to combat the Red Brigades was also created under Carabinieri General Carlo Alberto dalla Chiesa. Both of these units were later disbanded and their functions placed under the Defense Information Service (SID) in 1976. As a result of the Aldo Moro kidnapping, a June 1978 administrative decree again formed a special antiterrorist group from various law enforcement agencies, with General dalla Chiesa at the head. His success against Red Brigades terrorists gained for him the support of all major parties and his reappointment in August 1979.

Legislation accompanied the improvement of antiterrorist law enforcement organization. The Reale Law of May 1975 contained provisions for all forms of violence against the state. More severe sentences for terrorists, restrictions on bail, arrest without formal warrant, and increased law enforcement authority to search were included. Article 1 imposed mandatory confinement for those awaiting trial for terrorist acts. The police were also granted broader authority involving the apprehension of suspected terrorists. When those powers brought forth protests about the endangerment of civil liberties, a national referendum in June 1978 (after the murder of Aldo Moro) substantially sustained the laws. July 1977 amendments to the Reale Act included controls on the use of firearms and explosives. After the murder of Aldo Moro, further amendments allowed interrogation without the presence of defense lawyers and increased penalties for kidnapping. The *Carabinieri* and the local police also formed special antiterrorist assault teams. U.S. General James Dozier was rescued from the Red Brigades by one of those teams known as the teste di cuoio (leather heads).

When Red Brigades terrorists reacted to the introduction of the even broader December 1979 Urgent Measures for the Protection of the Democratic Order and Public Security Act by murdering four magistrates, their atrocities likely served to encourage wider public agreement with the imposition of even harsher policies. The draft 1979 emergency measures were passed in 1980 and later upheld by a national referendum in 1981.

While slow to get underway, Italy's legislative actions against terrorism have been rated by some as the toughest in Europe. As per Friedlander's observations, legislation enacted by the Italian parliament in February 1980, authorizes warrantless searches and wiretaps in a pre-Watergate fashion, permits Italian police to arrest and hold suspects for forty-eight hours without notifying anyone, allows accused terrorist actors to be detained for up to twelve years without trial, encourages the questioning of suspects outside of the presence of a lawyer, and mandates a life sentence for anyone convicted of murdering policemen, judges, attorneys, witnesses, and union officials.

A study of Italian elections from 1968 to 1979 has shown that the political parties "were rewarded when they were perceived in the electorate and elsewhere as opposed to political violence and punished when they were viewed however dimly as somehow linked to terrorism."

The eventual realization by the multiparty leadership that the growing terrorist threat was overwhelming the state's law enforcement capability, dalla Chiesa's leadership in the reorganized law enforcement structure, supportive legislation inspired by the Moro atrocity, and a judicial system that refused to be intimidated by the campaign of terror ultimately resulted in the suppression, but notably not the destruction, of the Red Brigades.

Enlightenment of the Italian Media

In the splintered Italian multiparty political system, where shifting coalitions have produced power changes at the rate of almost one new government per year, the Italian news media have become political pawns. Attempting to prosper in a democratic free-market environment, segments of the free press have sought to align their interests with political power groups and have been drawn into Italy's political morass.

Il Tempo correspondent Marino de Medici chose these words to describe the Italian news media: "It has been a political propagandist, effectively employed by political parties. Journalists are politicians. In Italy we are political participants."

In the early days of the Red Brigades violence, the Italian press tended to glamorize their attacks. In this regard, the media were merely reflecting the insincerity of the political parties toward political violence. As the atrocities of the Red Brigades worsened, the Italian news media initially sensationalized the brutality. With the hideous murder of the popular leader Aldo Moro in 1978, the media and the public abruptly realized the extent of the terrorist threat. The press responded to the public outcry within the deglamorization of the Red Brigades. As noted by Weinberg and Eubank, "there was an increasing tendency to depict their acts as ones of senseless bestiality, devoid of serious political content." Italy's successful suppression of their terror quickly followed.

Correspondent de Medici noted that there was an initial sympathy in the Italian press for the Red Brigades, and the Red Brigades capitalized on that sympathy with clever exploitation. However, "when a picture of a judge appeared with the entire transcript of his 'interrogation' by the Red Brigades, people finally began to ask. What did this have to do with the people's right to know?"

Summary

The nature of the threat. Post-World War II violence in Italy originated with neofascist groups and other right extremists with connections to legalized political parties. The emergence of the leftist Red Brigades began a decade of terror for Italy in the 1970s. The Red Brigades had its roots in Italy's universities, which allowed a base for rapid expansion. As it became more violent, it gained external support from Soviet sources critical of the integration of the Italian Communist Party into the Italian political system, and who likely viewed the Red Brigades as an instrument with which to threaten Italy's domestic tranquility and NATO's southern flank. At the height of the violence in 1978, Italy was enduring more than six terrorist attacks a day. Italy's public, press, fragmented political system, law enforcement agencies, and judiciary finally united to overcome the threat, but the Red Brigades has been suppressed, not destroyed. With the decline of external support from communist sources, its capability has been significantly reduced. However, Italy's participation in the coalition forces during the Persian Gulf crisis could result in increased support for the Red Brigades from radical Middle East sources.

Countermeasures to terrorism. A fragmented multiparty system and a disorganized law enforcement system delayed an effective national response to the 1970s terror in Italy. While the 1974 formation of a special antiterrorist law enforcement agency and 1975 antiterrorist legislation marked the beginning of political cooperation to oppose the threat, it was likely the 1978 murder of Aldo Moro served as the catalyst to unite Italy against the Red Brigades.

Increasingly harsh legislation followed that now marks Italian antiterrorist laws as among the toughest in Europe.

The role of the media. Immersed in the splintered politics of Italy, the media initially romanticized the Red Brigades and likely conjured a measure of public acceptance of its early, low-level violence. As the violence turned terroristic, the Italian press found itself discredited before the public by the skillful manipulation and exploitation of the Red Brigades. Apparently the shocking murder of Aldo Moro and several judicial figures in the late 1970s motivated members of the Italian media to disentangle themselves from the terrorists and become more supportive of the surging unification movement to suppress the Red Brigades. However, the nature of Italy's splintered multiparty political system appears to have been conducive to an equally splintered news media with tendencies to participate in the political process. The ultimate opposition of the Italian media to the Red Brigades could be only an aberration, and is likely not an indication of future Italian media unity against terrorist exploitation.

The relationship of government, press, and public. Public outrage over the seemingly always more hideous atrocities committed by the Red Brigades was likely a potent motivational force behind the strict antiterrorist legislation finally enacted. While Italian politics demonstrates the difficulties with the formulation and implementation of effective policies in a democratic multiparty system, it also demonstrates that, when threatened to an extreme extent, the system could respond sufficiently to ensure its own survival. It also seems likely that public sentiment was important in influencing the media to limit their exploitation by the Red Brigades and become more sympathetic to the seriously threatened state. The Italy of the 1970s is a disturbing example, and a stern warning, of how dangerous a terrorist campaign can become when it is waged in an environment of an indecisive government, an exploitable media, and a vulnerable public.

The historical experience of the state with terrorism is evidently an important factor in determining counterterror policies and the media's role. When the level of threat is sufficient, countermeasure policies will emerge and restraints on the media will be self-imposed or willingly accepted by both the press and the public.

The case of the United Kingdom emphasizes the importance of the originating source of political violence. When terrorism erupts from cleavages within, especially from deeply held religious convictions and loyalties, the problem of suppression may be overwhelming. The U.K. experience demonstrates a democratic response of immediate and extensive legislation to combat the threat. It also shows that the media can be coopted to contribute to countermeasures even in a volatile and emotional environment. It is important to view the cooperation of the media in the United Kingdom in terms of their personal exposure to the terrorist threat, and the relatively less competitive nature of a combined public-subsidized and private media.

The case of the Federal Republic of Germany indicates that the public can be an important force in the suppression of terrorism. Along with support for countermeasure policies and active participation in the apprehension of terrorists, the West German public's opinion was an important force in encouraging the media to resist exploitation by the terrorists. As evidenced in the Federal Republic in the early 1970s, when terrorist exploitation of the media reaches a level of absurdity, and the citizenry experiences a certain level of threat from terrorists, public pressures on the legislative and executive institutions contribute to restraining the media. As per the United Kingdom, the West German case vividly illustrates that (1) media exploitation can be restrained during a terrorist campaign without damaging the democracy, and (2) where terrorist exploitation of the media is restrained, terrorism declines.

Italy has demonstrated the vulnerability of a multiparty democratic system to terrorist attack. When the initial reaction of fiercely competitive parties is to use the occurrence of political violence to their own electoral advantage, countermeasures are slow to develop. However, Italy's experience has also shown that when the democratic institutions of law enforcement and judiciary stand fast, the nation can endure until the political parties come into line and unite against the terrorist threat. Like the United Kingdom and West Germany, Italy is another example that there is a threshold at which the threatened public will no longer tolerate terrorist exploitation of its media, and changes will be brought about. In the United Kingdom the media were restrained mostly by legislative and executive pressure; in the Federal Republic, they were restrained by themselves and by public opinion; in Italy, media restraint was mostly self-imposed in response to public outcry.

Very importantly, the United Kingdom, the Federal Republic of Germany, and Italy demonstrate that terrorist exploitation of the media can be reduced without destroying democracy, and such restraint on the media is normally accompanied by a decline in terrorism.

3

Political Violence and Terrorism

Introduction

The New York Times is the primary news outlet analyzed in this chapter. The Times was selected for several reasons. First, it offers what is arguably the most complete foreign affairs coverage of any American newspaper. Because the research design used in this project is as sensitive to what is not covered as it is to what is, The Times' reputation for thoroughness makes it the newspaper least likely to offer confirmation of the model's expectations.

Secondly, The Times reputation must be taken into consideration. Its alleged liberal bias, if true, makes confirmation of the legitimation model unlikely. If it is as critical and even biased against conservative policies and politics as is often claimed, The New York Times would seem least likely to accept the conservative Reagan and Bush administrations' line about terrorism.

A third reason for focusing on The Times is its leadership role in American journalism. Along with The Washington Post, The Los Angeles Times and more recently Cable News Network, The New York Times is often the newspaper other news media use to structure and prioritize their own news coverage. It is equally influential among the political elite, often serving as a kind of back-channel communication link between political players.

In short, while the sample used in this study is obviously not a random sample of U.S. news media coverage of political violence, a random sample of The New York Times is arguably better in the sense that it is the newspaper with the greatest number of resources and degree of independence.

Research Design

The research design distinguished two general types of news stories: Initial and Follow-up. The initial news report is simply the very first New York Times account of some violent incident. As the term implies, follow-up coverage is any and all subsequent coverage of a violent incident first covered in one of the initial stories. Because of the common concern that terrorist are able to capture and hold the attention of journalists with violence, I was particularly interested to learn something about the dynamics and characteristics of those violent events which do indeed receive more extensive coverage.

To accomplish this sort of inquiry, initial news reports of political violence appearing in The Times on sample dates were found first. Next, a search was made for all follow-up coverage for each initial story. In this way two groups of stories were eventually produced: Those initial stories which were followed-up and those which were not.

Secondly, patterns in the use of the term's "terrorist" and "terrorism" were noted for both those stories which were followed-up and those which were not. In this way several questions were addressed: What seems to account for the difference in devotion of newspaper space to violence? Which violence is referred to as terrorism and why? What is the relationship between the use of the terror terms in news accounts of violence (terrorists, terrorism), the type of violence, and the extent of coverage? Are terror stories more likely to be prominently displayed in the news? And most importantly, what is the typical source of the use of the terror terms? Are reporters on their own using terror terms to describe some of the violence or are sources using these terms turned to by reporters? We will find that in the process of the use of these descriptive terms, "terrorism" is defined in news accounts of violence. Some violence is understood to be terrorism and/or done by terrorists while other violence is not.

Variables

The research design attempted to capture as much of the complexity of the news reports as possible. Information concerning twenty-one variables was recorded for each story. At the heart of the coding procedure was the collection of information regarding four central variables: "label," "action," "target," and "source." These variables may be put in the form of a question:

Who (label) did what (violent action) to whom (target of violent action) according to whom (source of these descriptive terms)? "Source" is the person or agency specifically responsible for the violent action or label characterization of the actors or perpetrators of the violence specified in the article. In other words, "source" is the specific origin of the characterization of the violence described in the article. In some cases, reporters are themselves responsible for the use of the characterization. When sources were other than reporters, they could be either "hostile" or "friendly" according to their national or group origins. For the specific time period under review, hostile sources are sources from the Soviet Union and Eastern European nations, Sandinista controlled Nicaragua, Cuba, FMLN guerrillas in El Salvador, etc. These designations were made with the assistance of the Department of Defense's Defense Almanac, "International Security Relationships." The Almanac categorizes American security and defense relationships with other nations around the world.

It was also noted whether the initial story received additional or follow-up coverage. Follow-up was any article mentioning, even if only in passing, the specific violent event reported in an initial report. Taking approximately one year to complete, over one thousand days of New York Times coverage on microfilm was reviewed, often more than once, and photocopied in the search for follow-up coverage.

A simple "two day rule" was used to determine when the search for additional stories was to cease. If two consecutive days passed without any mention of the specific act of violence covered in the initial story, further searching was halted. If, however, the original violent act was mention, the search continued for at least two more days. This rule was necessary due to the sheer volume of coverage under investigation. What did all of this coding find?

Results

Follow-up coverage is, according to the results of the content analysis, related to two factors, both associated with official sources. First, the very presence of U.S. officials in a news story is associated with total coverage. Secondly, when designated as terrorism, identical acts of political violence tend to receive greater amounts of coverage. More interestingly, though, the terror designation itself tends to originate with government officials appearing in the story. In other words, terrorism designations in the news are often, though certainly not always cued by government officials. The New York Times confronted the ambiguity of terrorism by allowing government sources to do the defining of terrorism for it. In the process, the political landscape, who the good-guys and bad-guys are, which actors are legitimate and which are not, is defined. Let's next take a look at several specific findings.

Violence News Which Was Not Followed-up

The first and perhaps most striking finding is the relative silence of The New York Times beyond its initial report of some act of violence. Of 325 cases of initial violence stories found in two hundred days of Times coverage, only twenty-nine violent incidents (9 percent of all initial stories) received follow-up coverage.

It indicates, reports of battles or exchanges of gunfire were by far the least likely type of stories to receive follow-up coverage, with some 97 percent of such stories reported but once in The Times sample. Likewise, almost three of every four car bombings and seven of every ten hijackings failed to receive more than a single news story.

Very few incidents of violence, even those types most commonly associated with terrorism, such as car bombings and hijackings, receive more than one news article in one of the most thorough newspapers in the country. Follow-up coverage was infrequent.

Part of the answer is provided by a multiple regression analysis of the attribution variables "Number of friendly foreign officials and the number of United States officials" with total frequency of paragraphs of follow-up as the dependent variable.

TABLE 3.1 Percentage follow-up Versus No Follow-up for Different Violent Actions

Action	Percent Yes	Percent No	Totals
Bomb	12	88	(95)
Car Bomb	26	74	(23)
Shooting	5	95	(88)
Hijacking	33	67	(12)
Kidnapping	14	86	(07)
Other (gun battles, etc.)	3	97	(100)
Totals	(N=29)	(N=296)	

Thirty-three percent of the variance in the amount of additional coverage is attributable to the presence of U.S. officials in the story. While it is possible that some third variable is in a position of demanding both additional coverage and U.S. official response, what that third variable might be is not readily apparent.

What additional variables might explain the variance?

To address this question requires that we shift gears for a moment and examine the use of descriptive terminology found in the sample stories.

Use of "Terrorist" and "Terrorism" as Descriptive Labels

The evidence we are about to review indicates that "terrorism" stories those which use "terrorism" or "terrorist" as descriptive terms tend to receive more coverage than do any other violence story type. But we will soon see that a terrorism story is distinguished from a non-terrorism story by the presence of friendly government officials as news sources. No other variable, such as the type or location or victim of the violence so clearly differentiates the two. I turn next to describing this process.

Table 3.2 compares actor labels used to describe the perpetrator of violence in initial and follow-up stories.

TABLE 3.2 Comparison of Initial and Follow-up Stories for Actors

Label for Actors	Initial		Follow-up	
Rebel, Guerrilla	37%	(101)	11%	(18)
Security Forces	23	(63)	2	(3)
Gunman	12	(33)	1	(2)

(Contd.)

Interactive	12	(33)	0	(0)
Terrorist	11	(30)	48	(78)
Hijacker	2	(6)	5	(8)
Other	3	(8)	33	(53)
Total	N=(274)		N=(162)	

As this table indicates, whereas a modest 11 percent of the actors were described as "terrorists" in the initial stories (30 of 274 initial stories), 48 percent (78 of 162 follow-up stories) of the actor references in follow-up stories use the "terrorist(s)" actor designation. This suggests The New York Times tended to be more interested in "terrorism," just as one would expect given what is typically understood about the relationship between the news and terrorism. If it is a violent incident referred to as terrorism, The Times pays attention to it.

This leads us to the next question: Why is some violence reported in The Times understood to be about "terrorism" while violence of an exact or similar nature is treated differently? The nature of the violent act itself seems to have little to do with whether it is referred to as terrorism in any given article, as Table 3.3 indicates.

Note that in Table 3.3 even acts of violence most typically thought of as terrorism are generally not described by The Times as such. Of the shootings, 82 percent were not designated as terrorism. This reluctance to designate violence as terrorism even holds true for bombings and car bombings.

Reviewing a few examples taken from the sample might be helpful in gaining a clearer understanding of the phenomenon at hand. Among those car bombings not treated as terrorism, and given practically no coverage, were the following incidents: Two car bombs exploded in a Moslem low-income suburb in East Beirut killing at least ten. This occurred on February 27, 1982 and received three paragraphs of coverage.

On August 8, 1983 a car bomb blew up outside an open-air market in Baalbek, Lebanon. Thirty-three people were killed. Though this was a front-page story it was covered only once. No American sources were found commenting in any way in the story. A "psychopath" detonated a car bomb in front of a police station in Melbourne, Australia wounding twenty-three. Here an official was quoted as saying that this was specifically not a terrorist attack because the driver must have been a "psychopath, not a terrorist." It is interesting to note that one of the common explanations for terrorist motivations is psychopathology. Finally, on October 10, 1987 the American-backed Afghan rebels exploded a car bomb outside a mosque killing twenty-seven people.

TABLE 3.3 Action Type by Mention of Terrorism

Terrorism Mentioned

Action	No		Yes		Total
Other	94%	(94)	6%	(6)	(100)
Bomb	81%	(77)	19%	(18)	(95)
Shooting	82%	(72)	18%	(16)	(88)
Car Bomb	87%	(20)	13%	(3)	(23)
Hijacking	100%	(12)	0%	(0)	(12)
Kidnapping	100%	(7)	0%	(0)	(7)
Total	N=(282)		N=(43)		

These are but a handful of car bombings not treated as terrorism and not given more than one news story in The New York Times. On their own, Times reporters tend to avoid the use of the terrorism terminology. What, then, determines the use of "terrorism" or "terrorist" as a descriptive label in The New York Times?

We can begin to clarify this by noting the distribution of sources between initial and follow-up coverage. Recall the variable "source" is simply the person or agency specifically responsible for the actor or action designation coded for any given article. It is the "according to whom" portion of the central research question "Who did what to whom according to whom?"

Table 3.4 displays the distribution of sources (the source of the descriptive term used to describe some violent act) for both initial and follow-up stories. Descriptive terms of violent actor and actions which originate with the reporter overwhelm all other possibilities for initial stories at 84 percent. This statistic indicates that with breaking stories about violence, reporters tend to rely on their own descriptions of events. Reporters show a tendency to avoid the use of the ambiguous yet emotionally charged labels terrorism and terrorist in initial stories and instead use more neutral terms like guerrilla or rebel.

Yet, usage of the terms guerrilla and terrorist is essentially reversed as we go from initial to follow-up stories. At the same time, reporters writing follow-up stories tend to be less self-reliant in their characterizations, though they still comprise nearly half of the sources for actor or action designations. As we move from initial to follow-up stories other sources also become apparent. United States government officials or spokespersons constitute 18 percent of the sources in the follow-up coverage, up from zero in the initial stories.

TABLE 3.4 Sources Comparisons for Initial and Follow-up Stories

Source	Initial		Follow-up	
Reporter	84%	(244)	48%	(78)
Friendly Official	9%	(26)	20%	(33)
U.S. Officials	0%	(0)	18%	(30)
Hostile Officials	3%	(9)	4%	(7)
Police/Security Forces	1%	(4)	2%	(3)
Other	2%	(6)	7%	(12)
Total	(289)		(163)	

United States and friendly foreign sources together account for 38 percent of all actor and action designations in the follow-up stories. This is second only to reporter designations. This is in marked contrast to their total absence in initial stories and is probably explained by the fact that follow-up stories, unlike the breaking story, reflects the engagement of news routines which encourage reporter reliance on official sources. Though the origins and operations of these routines will be the subject of chapter five, a brief discussion of official-reporter interaction may be helpful at this point.

With the initial event the reporter is trying to meet the requirement of timeliness. Getting the story out first is most important. But with follow-up coverage the reporter is more likely to utilize "normal" news routines. The business imperatives of efficiency and predictability of supply encourages reporters working for newspapers like The New York Times to utilize news routines or "beats" which insure contact with legitimate, credible, reliable and typically official sources. Sources such as these offer something generally understood as "newsworthy" on a scheduled bases.

The bureaucracies of government are the most ready (and willing) source for reliable, scheduled flows of information, often in prepackaged formats. For instance, one recent study found that just under 64 percent of all citations regarding national security reporting in five leading U.S. newspapers originated with but four government sources. Likewise, Leon Sigal found news content in The New York Times and The Washington Post was comprised largely of "packaged" news. Some 70 to 90 percent of the news, depending on how the stories are categorized, result from such reporter-source interaction. Spontaneous events like those often found in the initial violence stories comprised only about 1 percent of the content analyzed by Sigal. The vast majority of what constituted news in The New York Times and The Washington Post were planned, controlled interactions between officials and reporters. This constitutes the normal or more typical operation of the news. It has considerable significance for this study of terrorism news coverage.

Table 3.5 is a two-by-two crosstabulation of "source" by "terror" as an actor or action designation. In other words, this table counts how many times "terrorism" or "terrorist" was used and compares it to who is using the terms in the news article. We see that references to "terror" come from U.S. sources about a third of the time. (Recall that references to terrorism comprises about half of the follow-up coverage). When a non-U.S. source appeared in the news about violence, they were usually talking about something other than terrorism. On the other hand, if a U.S. official talked about some violent event, he or she tended to refer to "terrorism" or "terrorists."

This tendency is even more pronounced when U.S. and friendly foreign sources are combined and compared to other source categories, as they have been in Table 3.6. Another third of the references to "terrorists" or "terrorism" come from friendly foreign officials. The remaining third is largely comprised of reporter references, "other" in this case.

Taken together, U.S. and friendly sources account for 67 percent of the references to terrorism in the follow-up coverage. "Terrorism" is violence much like the rest of the violence reported in The New York Times except for the presence of U.S. officials and their allies. As a consequence of their position as dominant news sources, officials are in a position of encouraging select renderings of terrorism stories. This replicates and reinforces the same sort of select renderings of terrorism found in official reports on terrorism produced by the State Department.

TABLE 3.5 All Follow-up Stories Only Mentions of Terrorism

Terrorism Mentioned

Source	Yes		No		Total	
U.S. Source	86%	(25)	14%	(4)	100%	(29)
Other	40%	(53)	60%	(78)	100%	(131)
Total	N=(78)		N=(82)			

Chi-Square = 18.101, p less than .001

TABLE 3.6 All Follow-up Stories Only Mentions of Terrorism

Terrorism Mentioned

Source	Yes		No	
US or Friendly	84%	(52)	16%	(10)
	100%	(62)		
Other	27%	(26)	73%	(72)
	100%	(98)		
Total	N=(78)		N=(82)	

Chi-Square = 47.705, p less than .001

If we turn the question around and ask whether hostile foreign sources (officials and offices of ideological and/or foreign policy adversaries of the United States) have the capacity to designate violence as terrorism, we find they do not. In fact, hostile sources are rarely heard, accounting for only 5 percent (four) of all terrorist references in the follow-up coverage. Ninety-five percent of the terrorist references originate with "non-hostile" sources.

The data also suggest that once violence is labeled as terrorism, it is more prominently displayed in the news. Follow-up stories about terrorism, for instance, tended to be longer than non-terrorism follow-up stories, with the former averaging 19.3 paragraphs as opposed to 12.5 paragraphs for non-terrorism follow-up stories. Measured in terms of total number of follow-up stories devoted to an act of violence, terrorism designated stories averaged eight articles whereas non-terrorism violence averaged over four articles. And when measuring attention by paragraphs, stories without the terrorism designation tended to be considerably shorter than those with the designation.

All in all, as politicians and counterterrorism officials often claim, "terrorism" stories do indeed tend to receive more prominent and extensive news attention. Yet, ironically, it would seem that it is these very officials who play a large role in designating some given act of violence as terrorism in the first place and, secondarily, encourage the extensive coverage.

This is not to say that officials interacting with reporters are solely responsible for the designation of violence as terrorism and the attention subsequently devoted to it in the news. This is obviously not the case. Well over half the designations came from reporters applying the terminology on their own. But even here it seems reasonable to consider the possibility that in some of these instances reporters are not entirely autonomous in their use of terminology. When reporters themselves are the sources of the terror designation it could be because the use of the terminology has already been sanctioned by official usage In this context, reporters feel free to use the terror designation without attribution, something they are normally quite reluctant to do. This does not, however, mean they are using it autonomously; they are already cued.

What the data presented above indicate are several things: First, we see a general reluctance on the part of The New York Times to devote resources to the coverage of most violent terrorist-like events beyond the initial story. This is contrary to the impression one would have from reading case studies of media coverage of "terrorism." Rather than extensive, even saturation coverage of politically motivated violence, it seems reasonable to conclude that most violent events, even kidnappings and hijackings, do not receive saturation coverage and that, indeed, such coverage is the exception rather than the rule.

Secondly, The Times also demonstrated something of a reluctance to apply the terms "terrorist" or "terrorism" independently from sources, usually friendly government officials. A good portion of the public dialog regarding "terrorism" was confined to the boundaries of official debate regarding political violence. As the previous chapter demonstrated, acts of terrorist-like violence, using the State Department's own definition, tended to be excluded from the public dialog regarding terrorism. Subsequent chapters will highlight the policy consequences of the particular and partial interpretation of terrorism.

Conclusion

What terrorism is, how it is best defined, remains the subject of intense debate. One of the common components of most definitions of terrorism, however, is the idea that terrorists attract an inordinate amount of media attention. Terrorists, it is usually explained, are very adept at using the news media to generate attention while the media tend to be particularly susceptible to being drawn into the terrorists designs.

The research findings described in this chapter add a new dimension to our understanding of the news media's role in political violence. First, while it is no doubt true that drama, particularly violence, attracts media attention, the quality and duration of media attention is influenced by another set of factors: Journalists follow news routines which encourage the use of legitimate government sources. Friendly government sources, not "terrorists," influence the extent of coverage which any given act of violence receives. These same sources influence the determination of who are and who are not treated as "terrorists" in the first place. Bassiouni and others adherents to the idea that the news media are used solely by terrorists focus all their attention on the relationship between reporters and violent political actors while ignoring the more well documented relationship between reporters and officials.

Secondly, the findings presented in this chapter also reveal an interesting irony. On the one hand, journalists are often accused by government officials of playing into the hands of terrorists. On the other hand, those same officials often cue journalists as to what is to be understood as terrorism in the first place. Yet, something more than irony may be present here. To evoke the alleged symbiotic relationship between terrorism and the news media is to subtly imply that the press works in an environment free from constraint and external pressure (some would say management). It reinforces the free press ideal while it clouds the operations of power on the press. As we will see in chapter five, the press is not free from multiple sources of constraint and pressure in their operation.

4

Functioning of Political Terrorism

Introduction

Terror is a superlative form of fear, and fear is a human emotion that pertains only to the living. The helpless victims who were massacred by the Abu Nidal group at the Vienna and Rome airports in December 1985 were not terrorized. They were simply murdered. Those who survived the massacre, either physically present at the airports or miles away learning of the atrocities through media depictions, were those who were perhaps terrorized.

Targets of Terrorism

While the above illustration is overly simplistic, one is well advised to approach the study of political terrorism by recognizing that the "victims" of political terrorist atrocities are not normally the "targets." Herein lies an important distinguishing feature that separates political terrorism from other forms of terror such as psychopathic.

The psychopath's victim is likely to be first terrorized and then killed, and is the principal object of the psychopath's atrocity. The terrorizing and elimination of the victim is both method and goal.

In contrast, the political terrorist's victim is symbolic. A victim is chosen who is representative of a target group that is strategically involved in the terrorist's political goals. When the Iranian-backed hijackers of TWA Flight 847 beat and killed U.S. serviceman Robert Stethem and threw his body on the tarmac at the Beirut airport, his death was not a direct objective of the terrorists. His demise was not their goal; rather, their goal was the elimination of U.S. influence in the Middle East in general and Lebanon in particular. Stethem was their victim, but not their target. Their target was the American public who observed the atrocity through the international media. The strategy for their target selection was based on the notion that the American public had the power to force a change in the Reagan administration's foreign policy for the Middle East and Lebanon.

Transmitting the Terror of the Atrocity to the Target

Obviously those present in the Vienna and Rome airport terminals during the Abu Nidal group's shooting and grenade explosions were more "terrorized" than those who later witnessed the atrocities through the international media. Further, of those learning of the atrocities through the media, it is likely that only those who were considering international travel, personally or by friends or associates, experienced some degree of fear. The association between the symbolic victim and the target audience is indeed a critical aspect of political terrorism effectiveness. However, regardless of the degree of association, a means of transmission must exist to make the target audience aware of what has happened before an atmosphere of fear can be created. Those who might not yet have heard of an atrocity are in no way terrorized by it. Given that one understands the basic rationale for the terrorist's tactical selection of a symbolic victim associated with the strategic target audience, the next item for consideration is how the terrorist transmits the terror of the violence perpetrated on the victim to the target group.

The focus of this analysis is necessarily the perpetration of political terrorism by groups and individuals not in power. However, it may be instructive to deviate briefly and consider how the transmission of terror as a superlative form of fear might be accomplished by a regime. For this examination, a regime is considered to be a government in power that has at its disposal all the forms of physical force normally associated with that position. It seems that the characteristics of the target population are a primary determinant in a regime's selection of the most efficient method of transmitting terror. For example, if the target population consists only of a few closely associated individuals say, the Charter 77 group in Czechoslovakia in the recent past—the persecution of one of them at the hands of the regime normally becomes immediately known to them all. Obviously, in such controlled circumstances, transmission of terror to the members of a small target population is not difficult to achieve and publicity is not a factor. In fact, regimes employing terrorism may choose to keep it a secret from the general population.

But if the target population is not closely associated for example, when it constitutes the entire population of a state a regime like Stalin's may choose to employ public processes of terror, such as trials and executions. Others, like some authoritarian regimes in Latin America, may choose to terrorize their political opposition through secret terrorist organizations. If such methods are employed, then publicity also becomes an important consideration to transmit the desired level of terror to the general target population.

However, the focus of this analysis is on political terrorists not in power, and the transmission of terror to a target population is then from a much different perspective. Normally the target populations are large and not especially closely associated. Through the perpetration of a violent atrocity on a symbolic victim, modern terrorists attempt to create an atmosphere of fear and then adroitly manipulate that atmosphere to influence the political behavior of the target population. If successful, such atrocities can bestow upon terrorists a capability to influence behavior that is extensively disproportionate to their actual political power.

To be effective in a political sense, the fear generated by the transmission of terror must, in turn, produce a level of intimidation in the target population sufficient to elicit the response desired by the terrorists. As noted by Sam Sarkesian, terrorism "is the creation of fear in a population in order to force the existing system to respond to the terrorists' demands and/or objectives."

Unique Characteristic of Terrorist Violence

To achieve effective distribution of terror to a target population, the violence used to create the atmosphere of fear must be perceived as a threat to each member of the population. Violence in general has a unique quality that provides for such a perception. As highlighted by Hannah Arendt, violence is unpredictable. Within a political environment, strength, force, and power can all be exerted with a certain measure of predictability of results, whereas the application of violence produces results that cannot be predetermined.

Louis Beres explains that the unpredictability of results from the application of violence creates an atmosphere dominated by fate. It "creates a devastating aura of uncertainty, one in which the hegemony of means over ends may paralyze the will of potential opponents." Within an aura of uncertainty dominated by fate and based upon violence, political terrorism, according to Beres, interestingly broadens its role as "an improvement upon war as the ultima ratio in world affairs, a strategy whereby the weak become effectual participants on the global stage." While state sponsorship and support of terrorism seem to weaken Beres's argument for what might also be termed a possible "tyranny of the minority in the world order through terrorism," his observation has strong merit. Terrorist atrocities, wherein the violence has been effectively transmitted to the target population and an aura of fear created, can yield disproportionate political power to the perpetrators and, in some instances, to their sponsors and supporters.

The purpose of violence for political terrorism is then as cited by the ancient Chinese proverb: "Kill one, frighten ten thousand." Or, as modified and updated by Jenkins, "The terrorist wants a lot of people watching rather than a lot of people dead."

Concept of Terrorist Violence, Political Power and the Media

Arendt's seminal work on political violence was oriented toward the employment of violence by totalitarian regimes. In that context, she made the observation: "Power and violence are opposites; where the one rules absolutely, the other is absent." There appears to be an interesting application of a somewhat parallel concept within contemporary political terrorism. One can postulate that the political power of terrorists is enhanced by the publicity they receive from the media. When that power is decreased by media disregard for their latest efforts, terrorists are prone to increase the level of violence, thereby increasing the media coverage with the hope of again increasing their political power. If this concept holds, then terrorist violence should also decrease as a terrorist group gains a level of political power that they perceive as sufficient. The precise phenomenon that demonstrates the accuracy of this hypothesis is, of course, the history of the Palestine Liberation Organization.

Transmission of Terror

In the modern world, international political terrorists have few problems and little difficulty in selecting a suitable symbolic and vulnerable victim and in committing an atrocity with a level of violence that can create fear in their target population, provided the violence of the atrocity is effectively transmitted. Therein lies the challenge for today's political terrorists. Terrorists do not have a self-contained capability to transmit the violent terror of an atrocity to their target population. Even with all the wonders of modern science available to them, contemporary political terrorists must rely on the powerful monopolistic resources of the media to transmit the terror of their violence. On some occasions terrorist groups have seized broadcast facilities. Terrorist demands often include publicity, and recently some terrorist groups have facilitated the transmitting of their violence through homemade videos, taped as their atrocity is being committed. However, it remains for the media to transmit effectively the terror of violence for terrorists. Only that worldwide network can sufficiently penetrate the very large audiences normally the targets of modern political terrorists. While acknowledging the diversity of the "motivations, ideologies, and allegiances" held by various terrorist organizations, hostage negotiations expert Abraham Miller has identified specific elements that are emphasized by all political terrorists. Among those common elements, Miller includes "exploitation of the media to publicize their cause." One can also observe that terrorist exploitation of the media reflects, in reality, a dependence upon the media for the transmission of terrorist violence to the target population. To once again oversimplify, if one does not know of a terrorist atrocity, one is in no way terrorized by it. Political terrorism as it is now practiced by international terrorists is above all dependent on the media for the transmission of terror. Without the media there is no terror, only murder and mayhem. Exceptions, of course, might be a few terrorized eyewitnesses who survive the atrocity.

Terrorism is not Dependent Upon the Media

Journalist Charles Krauthammer disagrees with the above observations. He cautions that not all terrorism is dependent on the media. He separates terrorist events into three categories, with differing needs for the media:

Assassination: the goal is to eliminate a politically important person, with publicity not desired by the assassin.

Attacks upon a specifically targeted group: the goal is to demoralize a group identified as the enemy, with the attacks independent of the media.

Random attacks to publicize political grievances: the target population is the world, and media coverage is a vital necessity.

If one holds to a rigorous definition of political terrorism, Krauthammer's assassination category with the objective of eliminating a specific political actor is not an act of terrorism. No one is terrorized; the victim is also the target, and with the killing the political goal is achieved. Certainly this is a category of political violence, but it is not the category of terrorism because terror is not involved. Krauthammer has made the debatable assumption, as have so many others, that assassination and terrorism are synonymous. Depending upon the rigor of one's definition of political terrorism, this assumption may not necessarily hold. Unfortunately overuse of the term assassination, as with overuse of the term terrorism, has led to an extreme vagueness about what is really involved. Members of the media frequently use the term assassination to describe any killing of an individual that has political overtones, and that usage is also unfortunately often employed by others.

Certainly assassination where, by definition, the goal is the elimination of a politically important personage is not terrorism in the pure sense of the word. As per the rigorous definition of terrorism offered in this analysis, terrorist victims have only symbolic value; as individuals they lack political importance.

Krauthammer's second argument that the terrorization of a certain group of persons with the intent to demoralize that particular group does not require media publicity is scenario-oriented and has limited applicability. Unless the target group is extremely small and in close contact, one must question how the murder or kidnapping of one of them could possibly terrorize the others unless the media publicize the event. The need for publicity for this category becomes identical with Krauthammer's third category, which he has so eloquently described: "This is where terrorists' utter dependence on the media begins." This general situation describes the overwhelming majority of international terrorist activities in the contemporary world.

As is recognized by literally everyone with access to independent radio, television, or printed matter, terrorists obviously have access to the media. Yonah Alexander and Seymour Maxwell Finger have noted, "as the world is shrinking through the revolution in communications, terrorists are assured extensive publicity for their wanton acts and enunciated causes. The immediacy and diffusion of acts of terror through the electronic media have consequently produced great psychological effects."

To proceed with the examination of the functions of political terrorism, one must consider if the transmission of terrorist violence by the media actually produces results for the terrorists, as indicated by Alexander and Finger's preceding statement. The next chapter investigates whether political power can actually be achieved through the employment of terror.

5

Development of the Mass Media

Introduction

The free dissemination of ideas and texts was promulgated most forcefully in the more ideologically homogeneous United States because under these conditions it was not as threatening to a dominant, established order; that order had never existed in the new world. The absence of sharp class prejudices and divisions in America made it easier to envisage a mass press. Further, in the nineteenth century, the rapid and ongoing democratization of American life, under the aegis of the liberal ideology which defined the nation, was partly responsible for the fact that journalism for the masses first developed in the United States, followed closely by England and other Western European countries. The United States pioneered the technology of the mass press, just as it was to lead the world in the development of the mass-produced automobile and of television. By 1910, some 24 million issues of daily newspapers were being published in this country, as against about two million in England.

The numbers, however, signify other qualitative differences. While Europe and America have both been homes to a free, i.e., freely competitive press, the American media (both newspapers and television) have always differed from the Western European and

English media for structural reasons that proceed from cultural, economic, and political variables as well as the sheer size of the United States.

First, the electronic media in the United States have been and still are primarily privately owned businesses, even though radio and television operate within the framework of public regulation of a sort. In most European countries, on the other hand, both radio and television have been primarily public enterprises. Even where private enterprise has recently come to play a more significant role, it is far less important than in this country.

Second, while newspapers in the United States and Europe are privately owned enterprises, the historical tradition in the United States has been quite different from that of Europe. On the European continent a great many newspapers and magazines began as the organs of political parties and remained closely affiliated with them. Others began as organs of the Catholic church, especially in countries such as Germany, where Catholics considered themselves an embattled minority, or France, where the church felt that it was crucial to protect its flock from the secularizing and anticlerical tendencies of much of the left's party press. As late as 1930, for example, about half the newspapers in Germany were essentially party newspapers. The Catholic church and the Catholic Center Party together published 312 newspapers, and the Socialist Party (SPD) 169. In England this was not true, although the British Labour Party did maintain a mass circulation newspaper of its own for many years.

Note that the continental pattern described above has changed considerably since World War II in both France and Germany. Today, fewer than 20 percent of the newspapers in Germany are formally affiliated with a political party. In terms of circulation the figure is only four or five percent, and the circulation of party-affiliated newspapers all over Europe continues to fall.

The American pattern was quite different. Some newspapers were party affiliated, and the Catholic church in this country (as well other religious groups) played a role in newspaper publishing. Since the middle of the nineteenth century, however, most publishers have considered themselves free of any attachments other than those of profit, the expression of personal views, and the desire to report the news. Even before the ideal of "objective" reporting began to take hold in the United States in about the mid-nineteenth century, editors and reporters were not intellectuals. They had little sense of the clash of ideological positions already so characteristic of European journals and newspapers.

The reasons for the differences between the European and the American press tell us a good deal about the nature of the American mass media. The United States was characterized by a broad ideological consensus during the nineteenth and early twentieth centuries. It was assumed that both liberalism (a democratic republic) and capitalism had a moral justification tied to a Calvinist ideology (even as that ideology was beginning to weaken). America did not develop a mass socialist party; nor did it develop a conservative party. For some of the same reasons, the country lacked explicitly ethnic or religious movements. To become an American meant to see oneself primarily as a free individual, not as the member of some corporate group. Immigrants could join, indeed were encouraged to join, various ethnic or religious groups, but they did not form political parties based upon such associations. To do so would be to violate the underlying American compact; in a "Lockean" individualistic society, only individuals were to be represented by political parties. The representation of group interests was considered illegitimate.

It is no accident that the whole notion of objective news reportage was first fully institutionalized in the United States at a time when most European newspapers still emphasized interpretive commentary. Living within the framework of a liberal consensus, American newsmen, like most other Americans, found it difficult to recognize that their view of the world might be shaped by a particular set of premises, a paradigm or Weltanschauun, which strongly influenced their views of social causation and, hence, their view of what the "facts" were. Under such circumstances the "facts" were merely the facts. As Michael Schudson notes:

Before the 1920s, journalists did not think much about the subjectivity of perception. They had relatively little incentive to doubt the firmness of the "reality" by which they lived. American society remained buoyant with hope and promise. Democracy was a value unquestioned in politics; free enterprise was still widely worshipped in economic life; the novels of Horatio Alger sold well. Few people doubted the inevitability of progress.

As awareness of the inevitable elements of subjectivity in news reporting began to grow in this country, the response was to place greater emphasis upon scientific understanding and training in order to approximate as closely as possible an "objective" reporting of the "facts."

On the other hand, the best European journalists, writing in societies rent by more or less severe ideological social-class conflicts and political parties based upon them, were far more aware that perceptions of social action were at least partly a function of the assumptions that were brought to them. These historical differences continue to influence the manner in which American and European newspapermen approach the news, though the Europeans are coming to resemble those in the United States more closely in some respects. Despite their greater sophistication today, American journalists, for the most part, still find it difficult to recognize that the facts are not merely given, but rather are, at least to some extent, determined by the "paradigm" (or world view or ideology) which one brings to them. In that sense, at least, some of the journalists who, during the 1960s, argued for an explicitly interpretive reporting did have a point, though they were often unaware of the underlying issues.

Of course, European countries cannot all be lumped together. In their relative freedom from censorship and belief in the possibility of objective reportage of the news, British journalists have more closely resembled their American counterparts than they did those of continental countries. On the other hand, the English media have always differed from the American in quite important ways, aside from those already mentioned.

Political reporting in England was, until quite recently, very much influenced by the fact that the relationship between journalists and politicians was sharply stratified. Politics in England was the preserve of "gentlemen" with "proper" educations from upperclass families, while most reporters came from lower middle-class backgrounds and had usually left school at age fifteen. Journalists working for the mass press, then, viewed political leaders with a mixture of deference and hostility, and politicians viewed most journalists with contempt. On the other hand, the editors of, and reporters for, a few leading journals were intellectuals who themselves came from "good" families and could mingle freely with leading statesmen. They were, however, exceptions.

In the United States, on the other hand, neither class nor educational differences between journalists and politicians were as pronounced. Thus, American newspapermen were never as deferential to bureaucrats or even politicians as their British counterparts tended to be. Indeed, Americans have always been more than willing to criticize, expose, and denounce "political malefactors," though less likely to develop fundamental criticisms of the political system, than were their European counterparts. All of this was noted by Alexis de Tocqueville in the 1830s:

The class spirit of the French journalists consists in a violent but frequently an eloquent and lofty manner of discussing the great interests of the state and the exceptions to this mode of writing are only occasional. The characteristics of the American journalist consist in an open and coarse appeal to the passions of his readers; he abandons principles to assail the characters of individuals, to track them into private life and disclose all their weaknesses and vices.

The American propensity for (and enjoyment of) exposing and denouncing political leaders stems from a powerful populist strain in American liberalism. Americans may have felt a strong attachment to their socio-political system, but they have always been wary of those to whom they delegated political power.

To the above must be added elements of our legal and political structure. In England, the cabinet, since the end of the nineteenth century, has consisted of a team in which the prime minister has been primus inter pares. Parliament, as well as the bureaucracy, has been dominated by the prime minister, the cabinet, and his or her party. Whatever disagreements might exist, say, within the Labour Party, it remained united on certain key issues. In the United States, on the other hand, the political fragmentation of Congress and its localism has tended to result in a variety of centrifugal pressures which encourage bureaucrats or congressmen to leak to the press information designed to counter policies desired by others in the government.

Further, even before Supreme Court decisions made it all but impossible for a public figure to sue a journalist successfully, libel laws were far less rigorous in this country than in England. In addition, unlike most European countries, we have no Official Secrets Act. In England, the publication of the Pentagon papers could have (and probably would have) led to very long jail sentences for the staff of any newspaper that had dared to publish them. Indeed, it is unlikely that the material would ever have appeared.

Finally, in England, until very recently, those elected to office were supposed to govern. They might be turned out eventually, but while governing they were given fairly wide latitude. This was far less true on the Continent, given the sharpness of ideological divisions, but even there the gap in status between newsmen and leading political figures was always considerable, except for intellectuals working for a few elite journals. In addition, the leeway permitted to government in preventing the publication of items "essential to the national security" was much greater. Though the pattern is changing quite rapidly, many European commentators still regard American political life as taking place in a fishbowl, as compared to their own countries.

The differences are partly cultural in origin. The European establishment has always considered the maintenance of order problematic. The view derives from a classical conservative world view. On the other hand, since the mid-nineteenth century, American liberals have generally assumed that order is relatively easy to maintain if the people are properly informed.

Development of a National Media Network

One additional unique quality of the American media deserves mention before we turn to the changes which have taken place during the past three decades. Unlike most Western European countries, America has historically lacked a national press. To quote Tocqueville:

In France the press combines a twofold centralization; almost all its power is centered in the same spot, and, so to speak, in the same hands, for its organs are far from numerous. The influence upon a skeptical nation of a public press thus constituted must be almost unbounded. It is an enemy with whom a government may sign an occasional truce, but which it is difficult to resist for any length of time.

Neither of these kinds of centralization exists in America. The United States has no metropolis; the intelligence and the power of the people are disseminated through all the parts of this vast country, and instead of radiating from a common point they cross each other in every direction; the Americans have nowhere established any central direction of opinion, any more than the conduct of affairs.

Magazines with national circulations gradually did develop as did newspaper chains. By the 1930s these included Time and Life. Even before World War II, a very few prestigious newspapers, such as the New York Times, boasted a national influence. Localism, however, was the dominant theme. The roaring 20s may have roared in some cosmopolitan centers like New York and (to a lesser extent) Chicago, but Babbitt dominated Main Street in most cities around the country, including the ethnic enclaves of metropolitan areas. in the short run, at least, most Americans remained relatively unaffected by the middle and upper-class culture of these cities. To be sure, most Frenchmen were unaware of the high culture of Paris, most. Englishmen were unaware of the high culture of London, and most Germans (during the Weimar Republic) did not pay much attention to Berlin. Middle-class "cultured" Frenchmen, Germans, and Englishmen, however, took their lead from newspapers and magazines published in the capital cities of these countries.

All these features of the American media predominated until the post-World War II period. Even in the midst of the Great Depression, most Americans were not especially conscious of the high culture of New York or Washington politics. Most also accepted the basic cultural and social parameters of their society as good and right and thought that those who wished to change them radically were either odd or evil. Such perspectives continued to be held by most Americans through World War II and were, perhaps, even reinforced by the war. As William O'Neill points out:

Good girls did not have sex before marriage. Good boys weren't supposed to but often fell on account of their animal nature which they could not help. Adult women knew their place was in the home. Racial minorities knew their place too, for the most part. White ethnics used to know their place, but had forgotten it. Luckily during the war it was discovered that they were God-fearing, family-loving and patriotic; so everything turned out all right.

The business of the country was still business. Government was supposed to balance its budget and not interfere with things, although, owing to the New Deal, this was less certain than before. Except for the physically or mentally disabled, poor people were looked down upon as shiftless and lazy. In the land of opportunity, there was no excuse for failure except being handicapped. By common consent, this was the greatest and freest country on earth.

This world view was reinforced by the images obtained from the newspapers, radio, and Hollywood. Newspaper publishers were relatively conservative, as were those who controlled the airwaves and motion pictures. Especially in the radio and movie industries, executives were primarily concerned with entertaining the public and making profits. They were not by any means all Republicans: many supported Franklin Delano Roosevelt and the New Deal. Their aim, however, was to reform and save capitalism, and their products by and large reinforced the American liberal Protestant consensus.

The working press was probably more liberal than were publishers, and some newsmen were even radicals. But the reins of authority were in the hands of the publishers, and reporters who wanted to keep their jobs stayed in line. Publishers and network officials also actively catered to the preferences of their advertisers. After all, many radio programs were directly controlled by the advertisers who sponsored them.

For the most part, however, the threat of economic pressure was not the major force behind the media's conservatism. News and entertainment took the hue they did largely because publishers and most reporters believed that was the way it was and should be. Key elites in American society accepted the broad framework of the American liberal consensus, and most did not even realize that there might be other ways to look at the world.

Walter Lippmann, criticizing the New York Times' hostile coverage of the Bolshevik regime in the 1920s, correctly pointed out that the issue was not the control of publishers or advertisers but rather:

> The news as a whole is dominated by the hopes of men who composed the news organization. In the large, news about Russia is a case of seeing not what was, but what men wished to see. The chief

censor and the chief propagandist were hope and fear in the minds of reporters and editors.

To be sure, in New York and a few other places, small groups of radicals were publishing journals, organizing workers, and with the onset of the New Deal, even entering government. For the most part, however, their influence on the broader social, cultural, and political underpinnings of society was minimal. Even when some of these people found themselves in positions in the culture where they might have an impact, a sense of limits (and fear) held them back.

In the meantime the nature of the American mass media was changing. As in so many areas, the changes were a function of both technology and affluence. Improvements in communication led to the development of journals with large national audiences, even as the development of the jet airplane, universal automobile ownership and a national highway system all contributed to the breakdown of regional differences and isolation.

Radio had developed national audiences, and by the 1930s newspaper chains were spreading and national magazines with large circulations were changing the consciousness of Americans. Time was, for a long period, the prime exemplar of the trend. Founded in 1923 by Henry Luce and Briton Hadden, its circulation had reached about half a million by 1936, prompting Luce to finally follow through with his plan to create a photo magazine. Within a short time Life far outstripped Time, made Luce one of the most powerful forces in American journalism, and prompted a series of imitators, even as did Time itself.

Thus, the United States was beginning to develop a national media network. That is, a relatively small group of media outlets was increasingly determining the manner in which the world was being presented to Americans. These outlets were centered in New York, (secondarily) Los Angeles, and for political news, Washington.

The trend did not really come to fruition until the late 1950s and early 1960s, coincident with the emergence of television as a major social force. By 1958 the number of television sets just about equaled the number of American homes, and the age of television really began, dominated immediately by the three major networks centered in New York.

The influence of television grew exponentially. Limited at one time by large-scale equipment needs, technological change increasingly permitted television to cover the whole world on the fly, and to transmit images almost instantaneously from and to all portions of the globe.

As the ubiquity of television increased, its credibility grew. No one could deny the power of its portrayals of reality when it was showing events "as they happened." In addition, television now could call upon experts to add to its credibility and, indeed, it created experts by defining them as such on television news and talk shows. It was used by various groups, including terrorist groups, to develop national and even worldwide attention and hence influence. Again and again, the news departments of the major networks set agendas by defining issues as important. Television even established the parameters within which issues would be discussed. Thus, for example, the drug issue of 1988 became a significant campaign issue because the media began to highlight it, and the framework within which solutions could be discussed was substantially determined by the information provided by journalists to the public. A similar pattern can be found in media coverage of such issues as nuclear energy and intelligence testing.

Anchormen on news programs became superstars, as wellknown as the president himself, and often more trusted. It is said, for example, that Lyndon Johnson became convinced that the war in Vietnam was lost when Walter Cronkite turned against it. On a February 27, 1968 special, Cronkite concluded that Vietnam was at best a stalemate. According to Ron Powers, Johnson turned to an aid after viewing the broadcast and told him that if he had lost Cronkite's support, he had lost the nation. The pattern has continued since Cronkite's time, though no one has quite achieved his credibility. Nevertheless, anchormen and women are very powerful people in America, and network executives are aware of it. Anchormen command huge salaries and are more or less their own masters. Within broad limits they can say what they want to.

Paradoxically, the growing influence of television increased the influence of a few eastern media outlets such as the New York Times, Time, Newsweek, and to a lesser extent, the Washington Post, and the Wall Street Journal. With the sources of political news increasingly centered in New York and Washington, and those responsible for producing, directing and reporting the news increasingly literate, key newspapers and magazines on the east coast took on new importance.

What television had done, of course, was to nationalize and standardize communication to an extent never before achieved in the United States. New York, Los Angeles and Washington styles and modes now became national styles and modes. And if the New York Times was read by the New York and the Washington elites, and those who produced the news for the television networks, it would also be read elsewhere. Even if it were not read, the issues which it considered important, and the approach it took to them, would become national currency.

For example, a 1972 American Institute of Political Communication study found that 96.9 percent of members of the Washington press corps read the New York Times and the Washington Post: 83 percent of a national sample of newspaper editors read the New York Times. The figure for a national sample of broadcast news executives was 56.3 percent. The proportion of those executives at the major networks who rely on the Times is even higher. In News from Nowhere Epstein argues that executives at NBC do not have the time to read anything else but the New York Times. It is, he notes, the New York Times which tells them what is important and why it is important.

Sampling congressmen and senators, Carol Weiss of the Bureau of Applied Social Research found that 67 percent read the New York Times and 82 percent read the Washington Post. The percentage of those reading the Times, especially, was equally high for other elites. In fact, the Times was read more widely than any other publication by various elite groups except for business elites and "owners of large wealth," who tended to rely somewhat more heavily on the Wall Street Journal. The same study found that Time and Newsweek received similar rankings among such groups.

The influence of the elite newspapers extends to foreign affairs. American diplomats increasingly obtain their information about the world from these media, supplemented by diplomatic or intelligence channels. As Leonard Sigal notes in his Reporters and Officials:

The news media, but especially the Times and the Post constitute one network in the central nervous system of the U.S. government. This network, unlike almost any other, transmits information throughout government, and often with greater speed than internal channels of communication. News organizations select the sights and sounds that Washingtonians will sense the next day. They thereby shape perceptions in their environment.

Most studies seem to agree, then, that the key national media consist of the three national television networks, the Cable News Network and PBS; the New York Times, the Washington Post, the Wall Street Journal, Time, Newsweek, and U.S. News and World Report. These media outlets are read and viewed by various leadership groups because they are perceived as influential and important, and they are influential and important because they are read by such groups.

It was expected that cable television, because it dramatically increased the number of broadcast channels available, would produce a return to localism as well as encourage special interest broadcasting. Certainly, the development of satellite and other technologies has encouraged local stations to act independently of the networks to some extent in news broadcasting. Other new technologies, including fiber optics, which permit an expansion of available telephone lines, may also encourage decentralization in information processing and distribution. So far, however, national patterns and influences continue to predominate. This is true, in part at least, because cable television has also tended to become concentrated in a few hands. It is also true, one suspects, because the nationalization of television communication has gone too far to be easily reversed.

By the mid- 1960s, most Americans owned television sets. Adults and children were watching television programs three or more hours a day. Television had become an integral part of American life, a genuine national news and image source. That continues to be true in the 1990s.

Television Business

Television is a major business in a competitive capitalist society. Whatever the social and political views of those who make decisions, the bottom line is capturing audience attention and increasing the size of audiences. This is what produces profits and insures solvency. By and large, therefore, commercial television entertainment will seek the lowest common denominator in order to capture mass audiences and the advertisements which accrue as a result. Within the limits set by societal control, this means emphasizing sexuality, comedy and violence of a sort. The emphasis of news programs is bound to center on the personal and the dramatic rather than upon the abstract and discursive.

It is hard to see how this emphasis can be escaped except in a society, such as the former Soviet Union, in which television was tightly controlled. Even in Russia, however, attempts have been made in recent years to follow just such a pattern in an effort to enlarge audiences even as censorship has been reduced. Given the expense of producing programs, including news programs and television specials, local network affiliates in America depend upon the networks for both entertainment and news programs. While some things have changed, the decisions about the news and entertainment which blanket America are made by relatively few persons in a few key cities.

The charge made by writers such as Edward Epstein, David Altheide, Robert Snow and others that television news necessarily emphasizes entertainment may not be warranted on the conscious level. Herbert Gans argues, for example, that newsmen do not let questions of audience appeal determine coverage. However, as Av Westin notes, such concerns are bound to play some role. Anchors, producers, and directors want audiences to tune in, not out. Ratings are closely monitored and they affect news judgment, as do time and financial constraints and availability of staff.

Of course, decisions as to what, in fact, will capture the attention of audiences are often based on the instinctive readings of audiences by those in charge of production and, thus, the values of such people come into play in a hit-or-miss pattern of decision making. Producers have and exercise more discretion than they (at least publicly) realize. Audiences are not turned off or on as quickly or easily as they assume. At one time, for example, it was thought that television reporters had to be male WASPS (white Anglo-Saxon Protestants) if they were to capture audiences. This has now changed as more and more Jews, women, blacks, Hispanics and Asians find themselves in front of the camera without apparent loss in audience attention. Nevertheless, audience and audience appeal are always in the minds of those making program decisions, even when it comes to choosing one anchor over another.

Television and the New Sensibility

It is difficult to separate the effects of television as an instrument of communication from the fact that it is a commercial enterprise, but one does not have to accept McCluhan's hyperbole to recognize television's profound effects on American life. By its very nature television adds new dimensions to the communication of information, and radically changes the rules of the game. The consequences for certain aspects of American life are clear. Far more than newspapers, radio, or movies, television provides its audience with a sense that what it sees is true and real. The audience sees events taking place in its living room. Stories, documentaries, even drama, take on a reality with which other media cannot compete. The written word and even the spoken word remain somewhat abstract to most readers and listeners, but moving pictures seen in the privacy of one's home are extremely compelling. Even if one knows that footage may have been spliced together and, conceivably, presents a somewhat distorted perspective (and few are aware of that fact), it is hard to escape the perception that one is viewing reality.

Television has broken down class and regional boundaries to a far greater extent than other media. Books and newspapers are segregated by area and readership. Only the well educated can read serious books, and the style of the New York Times only appeals to those with a certain level of education and affluence. Thus, to some extent, newspapers and books encourage the segregation of knowledge. Radio began to break down that segregation. Television goes much further. There are programs which cater to more elite audiences and are watched only by them, but insofar as television seeks the lowest common denominator and finds it, Americans as a group are introduced to the same themes in the same way. Roots and other "docudramas," as well as the six o'clock news, are watched by millions of Americans of all educational and social backgrounds, and they see the same pictures and receive the same information.

Television breaks down regional boundaries as well. The same voices, the same accents, and the same lifestyles reach rural areas in Arkansas as readily as the upper east side of New York, and insofar as those who live on New York's upper east side or in Los Angeles tend to have a more powerful say in what creates the reality which America sees, so they help change the expectations and views of all Americans.

At one point in time young people from rural backgrounds or small towns experienced genuine culture shock when they enrolled in an eastern elite college or even a major state university. They confronted new and different lifestyles for the first time. The cultural gap between rural America, the main streets of small town America and urban metropolitan areas has been considerably narrowed, and the effects of new metropolitan styles created in New York or Los Angeles spread far more rapidly than they once did.

The process begins early in childhood. As Meyrowitz points out, cultures in which knowledge is dependent on the ability to read require substantial preparation before one can penetrate many of the secrets of adult life. Television has broken that barrier. Children can and do watch television programs which tell them about the off-stage behavior of parents, and introduce them to themes which they would not have encountered until much later in life in the past. Young children are exposed to the news almost every day along with their parents. Most so-called family programs deal with concerns with which children would not have been familiar even twenty-five years ago, and millions of children are still awake at hours when more "mature" television programs are shown:

It is difficult for parents to control their children's viewing of television without limiting their own viewing as well. While a child has very limited access to the content of books and newspapers being read by adults in the same room, a television program being watched by adults is accessible to any child in the same space. Many children are exposed to adult news, for example, because their parents watch the news during dinner.

With book reading, a family can stay together in a single room and yet be divided into different households. In multiple-set television households, children and adults can be in different rooms and still be united into a single informational network.

Roots, MASH, Dallas, the Vietnam War and 1960s urban riots were seen by very large numbers of children under ten years old. All of this has played an important role in weakening traditional ties of church, ethnic group, and neighborhood. It has contributed to American social and geographic mobility as much as the revolution in transportation, in part because it has enabled Americans to feel almost equally at home in Oshkosh, New York, or Dallas. It has homogenized American culture and nationalized it.

It is impossible to understand the revolution which took place in American values and attitudes during the 1960s and 1970s without taking into account the influence of television on the fabric of American life, including its breaking down of old barriers and its weakening of old ties. For the first time, metropolitan America was becoming all of America. In the 1920s, the new therapeutic ethic of self-realization had only permeated a small section of America's metropolitan upper middle-class. By the 1970s, as the authors of Habits of the Heart point out, it had spread far more widely. Not surprisingly, few realize how rapid the pace of change has been. The events of the 1960s, including the rapid loss of faith in American institutions, and the legitimation of lifestyles once considered to be deviant, could not have occurred in a pre-television age.

America has become, as Richard Merelman points out in Making Something of Ourselves, a "loose bounded culture." Americans' primordial ties to family, locality, church, and what is considered appropriate behavior have eroded, and Americans have lost their sense of place. They are not alone in this, of course. Their experience is increasingly shared by Europeans, Japanese and, perhaps, even Russians. Certainly mass television is not the only factor at work. The revolution is real, however, and the epoch we live in is quite new."

As Merelman puts it:

The contemporary weakness of the Puritan, democratic and class visions of America has released large numbers of Americans from comprehensive group identifications and from firm social moorings. The liberated individual, not the social group must therefore become the basic cultural unit. Group membership becomes voluntary, contingent and fluid, not "given," fixed, and rigid.

Working-class parochials may continue to identify with those they know and with whom they work and live; but public reality is now such that we also know and develop ersatz intimate and intense relationships with public figures of all kinds, from anchormen to rock performers to politicians.

The impact of television on the substance of politics has been at least as great as it has been on our personal lives. Seeing political events, the expressions on faces, and the use of hands or eyes during an interview adds a concrete dimension to political figures, even as it may reduce the discursive elements in the message conveyed. Politicians who sweat on television (as Richard Nixon did in the 1960 presidential debates) lose points as compared to those who do not. The camera can make a political figure look as if he or she is evading a question or stammering and confused, and materials which might never appear in print, or at least would not have the same impact routinely appear on television.

Television has changed the very structure of political discourse. Political figures could once issue carefully written pronouncements to the newspapers. They now appear on television interviews with warts and stutters intact. Spoken communication, after all, is rarely as well structured as written discourse. We rely on all sorts of cues to get our message across, which work well in the lecture hall but not as part of a permanent television record.

Politicians, and others, are caught exhibiting behavior on stage which in other epochs would have occurred only off stage, thus breaking down the barrier between the two realms. In print, for example, politicians and others can set their thoughts down carefully. They conceal their doubts, their boredom, their prejudices when they present public statements. In the age of television, however, this is far more difficult, especially in time of crisis. As television becomes more and more ubiquitous, we all have increasing access to backstage behavior. The paradigm case is probably the Nixon tapes, though this owed little to television per se. But as Meyrowitz points out, Nixon and his colleagues were often engaging in just the kinds of obscenity and gratuitous insults that one finds in the backstage behavior of politicians or, for that matter, academics, doctors, or lawyers. We hardly realize it is present, because it rarely comes front stage. Most of us could not easily survive the monitoring of our conversations with close friends about other colleagues and groups; nor would we be terribly proud of our diction. In this sense, Big Brother is not watching you; Big Brother is you, watching. Indeed we are all watching each other and we are all aware that we are being watched, especially if we are in any way public figures.

Americans (and other peoples) long for great leaders. Yet, such is their ambivalence toward authority, that they also revel in their weaknesses. Television inevitably caters to that second wish. In so doing, however, it reduces our power to produce great leaders. Meyrowitz makes the point quite well:

The current drive toward intimacy with our leaders involves a fundamental paradox. In pursuing our desire to be "close" to great people we often destroy their ability to function as great people. "Greatness" manifests itself in the onstage performance and, by definition, in its isolation from backstage behaviors. In intimate spheres, people are often very much alike: they eat, they eliminate, they get tired, they sleep, they make love, they groom, they indulge in whims and self involvements.

When we see our leaders in varieties of situations and locations, when we observe them as they respond to spontaneous interviews or as they grow weary from a day of work or campaigning, we do not simply learn more about them. By searching behind the fronts of performers, we also change the roles that can be performed and perceived as well as the images that high status performers have of themselves.

The television revolution has affected newspapers and news magazines in a number of ways. It has forced them to turn to indepth reportage of the kind that television handles much less effectively. On the other hand, it has encouraged them partly for competitive reasons, and partly because television has created a new atmosphere to seek out the same dramatic off-stage exposure that television can achieve. Vietnam and Watergate certainly contributed to the development of an adversarial press, but the changing assumptions of media personnel as to what constitutes news and how one deals with political figures were more important in the long run. It was television reportage, too, which gave journalists the sense that they could make the news as well as report it, though many of them continue to deny that they do so.

Contemplating the end of Senator Joseph R. Biden's presidential aspirations in the wake of disclosures about his plagiarizing a speech by British Labour Party leader Neil Kinnock, the New York Times pointed out that television has fundamentally changed the structure of political campaigns in the past thirty years. In the 1950s indiscretions like those of Gary Hart would have probably been ignored by the media, taking their cue from party leaders. Now, however, matters are quite different. The media have taken over the job of judging candidates. Television tapes from vast libraries, actually showing Biden aping Kinnock in a New Hampshire living room, are powerful images indeed. ("The Big Eye is everywhere.") In addition, television comedians are now in a position to destroy political candidates. As the Times pointed out:

It could even be argued that once flaws are revealed they are distributed most efficiently, and decline is most rapidly accelerated, by the television comedians. In Joe Biden's week of agony, he was the favorite topic of Johnny Carson and David Letterman. Once be becomes the butt of a hundred jokes heard in a million bedrooms...it is hard for any politician to survive.

The Times is belatedly recognizing that a revolution has taken place in the nature and impact of the mass media in the United States (and in other advanced industrial societies) in the past thirty years or so. Television's impact continued through the 1988 primaries and election, as it did for the elections of 1990. Observers detected little evidence of "bias" in the horse race treatment of candidates in 1988, with one exception. Jesse Jackson was undoubtedly helped by the very favorable coverage he received in the national media during his presidential bid. In addition both he and the media were responsible for bringing the drug issue front and center, and persuading the public (justifiably or not) that Reagan's efforts in this area had failed. In 1990, the major media treated Democratic candidates with considerably more sympathy than they treated Republicans.

Those politicians whose style and personality fit in with the requirements of television have tremendous advantages over their colleagues, and can even outpoint their journalistic critics. Ronald Reagan's success as president until the Iran-Contra affair, clearly had something to do with his previous career. Given his earlier involvement in radio, motion pictures, and television, he was able to develop a style which enabled him almost always to provide newsmen with an onstage performance, which looked as if it were off-stage and thus seemed even more genuine. The ideal television performer, he foiled the attempts of media critics to diminish his popularity for his first six years as president.

Journalists sometimes claimed that they had been too easy on Reagan. As several systematic studies demonstrated, however, nothing can be further from the truth. From the beginning of his administration, and during election campaigns, they were quite critical. They simply could not touch him as long as he retained reasonable control of the circumstances under which he was interviewed, and made no obvious major policy mistakes. He could appear to be ordinary and yet a strong leader at one and the same time, no mean feat. And he could compete effectively with all the other celebrities (including anchors) who now appear regularly on television, an ability which the three presidents who preceded him lacked.

Martin Schramm offers a telling example of Reagan's skill. Leslie Stahl did a long piece on Reagan during the 1984 presidential election in which she described his brilliant use of television. In the course of her analysis she interspersed videos of Reagan with a biting commentary on his duplicity. According to Schramm, Stahl received a call from one of the president's men thanking her for the coverage. When she expressed some puzzlement at his reaction, he responded: "They don't hear what you are saying if the pictures are saying something different." Indeed they were. They showed a vibrant, strong, optimistic, serious president, with a down-to-earth sense of humor.

Of course, once the Iran-Contra affair broke, the media had a field day. For this and other reasons, Reagan was never able to reestablish his media dominance, although he regained some of his popularity just before leaving office.

George Bush's television presence has not been nearly as effective. Although he handles himself reasonably well, he lacks Reagan's acting abilities and is much more dependent upon the character of television and press treatment of him than was his predecessor.

Reagan is just one example. Even religious leaders with public concerns use the media as a mechanism for getting their message across. As one New YorkTimes reporter put it in describing the influence of Cardinal John O'Connor, Archbishop of the Catholic diocese of New York:

He has done this...by means of a forceful personality and a remarkable gift for engaging the media. Whether by intuition or by a shrewd understanding of contemporary political dynamics, the cardinal has used this gift to gain significant leverage in a world where the ability to capture the media's attention translates into political power.

Changing Profession

Even as the influence of the media (and television in particular) grew, the nature of the journalistic community was changing, as was the relationship of journalists to those who owned newspapers or mass news journals or television networks. In the 1920s and 1930s, the days of The Front Page, journalists, like most Americans, went to work after graduating from high school or even before. While some journalists and executives on leading papers were from upper middle-class backgrounds, journalism most often was a source of social mobility for working-class and lower middle-class youth. The generally Democratic sympathies of working reporters in the 1930s were partly a function of their class background.

After World War II the pattern changed. Increasingly, young men and women from upper middle-class backgrounds began to seek jobs in journalism and television as a way of partaking in an exciting and creative career and having an impact on society.

When Spiro Agnew viciously attacked the eastern media in the late 1960s and early 1970s as members of an elite establishment, he had a point, however bluntly he made it. Daniel Patrick Moynihan made the same point (in somewhat more reasonable and sophisticated terms) in 1971, only to be attacked in print by Richard Harwood, a Washington Post editor who attempted to maintain the old image of small-town and working-class reporter backgrounds.

It was clear even then, however, to those who looked at the evidence, that Moynihan was right. In a 1976 national survey of journalists, John W.C. Johnstone found that 88 percent were college graduates and 43 percent had completed some graduate work.

We found that journalists who work for the key national media today are far more likely than businessmen to have graduated from elite universities, and to come from relatively affluent backgrounds. Indeed, given the fact that most of them have married professionals and that the salaries of television reporters and anchors now reach astronomical figures, their incomes compare favorably with those of the business elite.

In short, major media journalists are a highly educated and fairly affluent group of individuals. They are clearly part of the middle and upper middle-class liberal cosmopolitan strata of the population. Journalism is no longer a source of social mobility for most -they arrived before they became journalists. Ironically, it is business today that is more often a means of climbing the social ladder. In our own study we found that a much larger proportion of business executives in major firms than journalists were from working-class backgrounds.

Journalists thus stand at the line of transformation of our loosely bounded culture. They are not, as Herbert Gans argues, merely traditional progressives interested in promoting responsible capitalism. Rather, they are liberal cosmopolitans, quite sympathetic to the cultural and social changes that have taken place in the last few decades. For example, according to Johnstone's et al. survey, fourteen percent of journalists working for elite media classified themselves as "far left," and 56 percent classified themselves as "a little to the left." In contrast, 37 percent of the nonelite portion of Johnstone's sample classified themselves as "left" or "far left." Among the general population at the time, the comparable figure was three percent.

Of course, one question proves very little. However, Alan Barton asked a much wider range of questions to a somewhat broader group of media leaders from thirty cities, with much the same results. The national media elite, as he defined it, was among the most liberal in the country, especially on cultural issues, but also on social reform and economic redistribution issues, despite its members' relatively high salaries. According to Barton's study the magazines leading journalists read include: the New Yorker

(56 percent); Harper's (51 percent); and the New YorkReview of Books (25 percent). By contrast, Commentary was read by fifteen percent of Barton's respondents, and the Reader's Digest by a mere eight percent.

A 1975 study conducted jointly by Harvard University and the WashingtonPost revealed much the same pattern among the Washington press corps, television executives, and editors of major regional newspapers. Sixty-one percent of the group voted for McGovern in 1972 while only 22 percent supported Nixon (among the population at large, Nixon received 61 percent of the vote to McGovern's 38 percent). Fifty-nine percent classify themselves as liberal or "radical."

The same results were obtained in a 1979 study of foreign correspondents by Research Forecasts. On the whole, foreign correspondents responded favorably to detente with the Soviet Union. A majority felt that we rely too heavily oil military force and that we should not ally ourselves with nondemocratic countries simply because they are anti-Soviet.

A wide-ranging study of newspaper journalists conducted by the Los AngelesTimes in 1985 also found them to be liberal and cosmopolitan in outlook. Nor are such attitudes merely a function of their backgrounds, for they are more liberal and cosmopolitan than members of the general population who share their demographic and educational characteristics. This study also concluded that journalists working for the New YorkTimes and the Washington Post are to the left of journalists working for the other newspaper outlets. The results of Fred Evans' 1983 survey were more or less the same as those of our in-depth study of the national media.

Why is the national media elite today liberal and or liberal/ left? A number of factors are involved. First, many of those who initially turn to journalism as a career do so because of a disenchantment with the dominant economic institutions of the society (witness Eric Sevareid's autobiography, Not So Wild a Dream). In America today those satisfied with the system tend to choose careers in business. Those who are more critical naturally gravitate to social service or intellectual occupations of various kinds, including university teaching and journalism. Such students concentrate their work in the social sciences and humanities, where they study under faculty members who are also often critical of aspects of the political order.

These early proclivities are further strengthened by the associations of journalists, especially if they succeed in the profession and obtain positions on major newspapers or on the major networks in New York, Washington, and other major metropolitan areas. For reasons discussed earlier, New York probably plays a more significant role than other cities, taking young men and women from around the country and transforming them into liberal and cosmopolitan New Yorkers. As Edward Epstein points out:

Producers (of television programs) who tend to read the same newspapers (particularly the New YorkTimes) and news magazines, commute to the same area of the city (New York), and discuss with friends the same agenda of problems can be expected to share a similar perspective on the critical themes of the day.

Obviously, many journalists and academics are conservatives or neo-conservatives, but the overall pattern is quite clear. Leading journalists by and large share the perspectives of the liberal cosmopolitan segments of the academic and New York intellectual communities. Journalists do not necessarily differ from others (including academics) in their inability to see beyond their own ideological commitments, despite their view of themselves as hardheaded, realistic, humane skeptics.

There is more to it than that. Journalism (like other professions) has always attracted men and women of a certain type. In his classic 1937 book on the Washington correspondents, Leo Rosten argued that journalists as a breed chose the profession out of a desire to startle and expose; to have the opportunity to project personal hostilities and feelings of injustice under the aegis of journalistic duty.

On the other hand, Joseph Kraft maintains that real changes have taken place in journalism in recent years:

Thirty years ago nobody would have been attracted [to journalism] by the thought of becoming rich, or important, or powerful. Fame was not the spur. It is now. The new entrants have their eye on the target and they are frankly ambitious those of us in the media have enjoyed an enormous surge in status and power in recent years. But while we have acquired confidence and self-assertiveness, there is no security. We are driven to keep moving forward, and in an adversary way. We are thus prone to that disease of the times narcissism. The narcissism of the journalist, of course, is not mere conceit. It consists in the belief that because we describe events, we make them happen.

Kraft's views are supported by a massive study of journalists conducted under the auspices of the Newspaper Readership Project and the American Society of Newspaper Editors in 1982. The authors' comments are worth quoting at some length:

In reviewing the totality of the survey and interview results, we have come to the conclusion that a fair number of journalists feel aloof from the public and have little regard for it. These attitudes manifested themselves in such findings as:

cynicism about the public's intelligence; isolation from community life and feedback; rejection of public input into newspapers; arrogance about the news person's role as gatekeeper; acknowledgment of feelings of being out of touch and holding different values.

While much of the data highlighted indicators of insularity and elitism among reporters, responsibility must be shared with management. Although managers have a better understanding of the newspaper's mission, some show as much disdain for the public as do staff members.

Of course many of the views of journalists are but shallowly held. They were educated at elite universities, but they are not scholars, and their careers discourage scholarly activity. They learn by reading newspapers and journals, and more importantly, by picking the brains of those they interview to develop a superficial sophistication about current affairs and topical issues. This is partly a matter of temperament and choice but it is also a function of their work. Operating under rigid schedules, and forced to deal with one breaking story after another, they do not have the time to investigate material in depth.

Reporters and editors can be among the sharpest critics of their colleagues when they are the subject of news stories. As David Shaw reports:

Many newspaper reporters are lazy, careless, cynical and inclined toward exaggeration, speculation and sensationalism.

Worse, they often decide what their stories should say before they even begin their research.

Who offers this scathing indictment of the nation's press? Gary Hart? Ed Meese? Nancy Reagan? Richard Nixon?

No, not this time. These criticisms were made by many of America's top newspaper editors and other prominent journalists. The basis of their criticism? Their own experience as the subjects of interviews and stories by other journalists.

Assuming these observations are correct, how does one explain the character of journalists? We hypothesize that journalists constitute a segment of those "metro-Americans" whose personalities differ sharply from the liberal bourgeois character type that emerged from Calvinism.

The traditional religious and cultural patterns of American society transformed aggressive drives from power needs into the need for achievement, and provided a rationale for self-restraint and community responsibility. The dissolution of that culture among metro-Americans is creating a new American personality type among members of the professional middle class. As the justification for achievement (i.e., competing with a standard of excellence set for oneself) declines, it is being replaced by a drive for power, the power to control or influence others. The need for power, as Rosten noted, is part and parcel of the attempt to maintain one's self-esteem, weakened not only by newer patterns of child rearing, but also by a loss of faith in a rational, ordered universe which provides a sense of ongoing meaning for one's life. For those to whom life now lacks such meaning, power is seen as promising immortality. Further, since everyone is viewed as seeking power, one must also seek power for oneself to avoid being dominated by others.

In a society which seems to lack both norms and boundaries, the emphasis is increasingly upon self-aggrandizement; a selfaggrandizement which inhibits the capacity for real intimacy. Indeed one can argue that the emphasis by metro-Americans on the need for intimacy and self-fulfillment is the desperate cry of those who can no longer achieve it because of changes in both the culture of American society and the national character of Americans.

Self-consciousness about such goals always emerges in a society when the natural capacity to achieve them has diminished. As we discovered in Roots of Radicalism, the ideological commitment of such persons to the welfare of the poor and downtrodden is often a rationalization for the desire to increase their own power and to bolster low self-esteem. In any event, it is no accident that such individuals have been increasingly drawn to the media in postwar America. For, in a postindustrial society in which a premium is placed on information, those who regulate the information have power. And the best way to regulate that information is not necessarily to control its source, but rather the mode and structure of its dissemination.

These are fairly strong statements, for they imply that the changes which have been taking place in the United States, especially among cosmopolitan elites, are not simply changes in understanding, but rather, have deeper roots. This means that they are less likely to be reversed in the short run, and constitute a broad cultural shift.

Our argument draws upon a tradition of political theory that places more stress on underlying character and beliefs than upon particular social and political attitudes. Theorists as different as Plato and Rousseau argued that, in the end, the character of a people was of greater significance for the health of a society than views about particular public issues. More precisely, they argued that the values and views required for a healthy social order could only take root if the character of a people supported such views and values.

As Rousseau put it in The Social Contract.

To these three types of laws is added a fourth, the most important of all; which is not engraved on marble or bronze, but in the hearts of the citizens; which is the true constitution of the State. I am speaking of mores, customs and especially of opinion on which the success of all others depends.

Personality, Ideology and The News

All of these questions have been asked by various media analysts who argue either that reporters' perspectives do not affect media output in the least, or that newspapers have a conservative tilt, whatever the views of journalists.

The argument that, whatever the perspectives of journalists, publishers, editors, and advertisers insure that the journalistic product is conservative is certainly the view of radicals as well as of media critics such as Ben Bagdikian, and even of the Columbia Journalism Review, still the most prestigious journal of media criticism. We can only touch on some of the issues here. However, the developing outlook of elite journalists during the 1950s was accompanied by a shift in the structure of power in the newsroom. Many publishers were still fairly conservative, especially in the provinces. Indeed, as Bagdikian notes, more newspapers in this country still endorse Republican than Democratic candidates. The power of publishers, however, is not what it was forty years ago. They are committed to hiring according to merit criteria, if only because they need good writers. The shift has been accentuated as family newspapers go public and issue stocks to raise cash. Under such circumstances bottom line financial considerations begin to outweigh personal social and political views. For these and other reasons they have lost a good deal of control over their staffs.

In the early 1960s, Rodney Stark described the changes on a metropolitan newspaper which he called the Express, and which was owned by a conservative publisher. No matter how hard he tried, the publisher was unable to hire the kind of staff he wanted. His best reporters (the educated, experienced "pros," as the author calls them) tended to be liberal. As a result, he lamented:

When I think of all the New Dealing, liberal propaganda that gets into this newspaper, I'm ashamed and angry. It's almost impossible to print the kind of newspaper America needs today, because of the kind of people we have to hire. I'd like to fire about half of them.

Nor is Stark alone in his observations. Halberstam, in The Powers That Be, chronicles the increased freedom of reporters to investigate and print the stories they wish to print, a development with which he is quite sympathetic. Stephen Hess, in his study of The WashingtonReporters, found the same pattern. Reporters rarely if ever complained of pressure being placed upon them to omit or tailor stories to the wishes of publishers. By contrast, Rosten, in 1937 found that a majority of reporters had a least some stories played down or killed for ideological reasons. Our findings are similar. Asked to rate their influence over stories in which they were interested on a scale from one (little influence) to seven (a great deal of influence), newspaper and television reporters clearly see themselves as quite influential in determining how they write and what they publish about events with which they are concerned. Their average self-rating was six; editors and producers gave a self-rating of five and executives rated themselves as between four and five.

At the same time, the influence of advertisers over the content of both newspapers and television has declined. Increasingly advertisers have come to feel that they could not and should not attempt to influence the content of news reporting. To sell their products, they have had to go to those publications which reach the audiences they wish to reach. Indeed, during the 1960s many even advertised in counterculture journals which were quite hostile to the business community. Advertisers also lost control over the content of television programming, including news programming. In the early days of television, advertising agencies and sponsors directly controlled much of the content of television programs and even produced them. By the end of the 1950s, however, control over programs had devolved to the networks themselves and: advertisers [had to] use television on whatever terms they [could] get it, for television is the most potent vehicle ever devised. As one agency man said once, "Bad television is better than no television."

Nor were publishers and advertisers the only ones at a loss. Even editors found that they could no longer fully control their staffs. The bright, young, well-educated reporters saw things in certain ways and insisted on reporting them as they saw them. And reporters were, by and large, likely to view events from a liberal, cosmopolitan perspective.

All this had been happening rather quietly during the 1950s, supposedly a time of reaction, but had been concealed by the Cold War consensus and the lack of sharp, polarizing domestic issues. The 1960s changed all that. The emergence of the civil rights issue and the Vietnam War revealed very quickly how weak the traditional establishment was. The new metro-Americans were not the conformist mass in split-level suburbs pictured in the 1950s. And the old elites, not outnumbered by them, but less and less sure of their own values, and often confronting offspring whose education was critical of those values, did not know how to react.

The result was the fragmentation of American political culture, and a distinct shift to the left by liberals who suddenly found themselves to be radical; and increased influence for a whole group of individuals who, it had been thought, were marginal to the culture. By the late 1960s, socialist communitarians, feminists and hippies had become an integral part of American cultural life in ways that they had never been before.

The national media were caught up and influenced by the events of that period, even as they contributed to the manner in which such events were viewed. Editors found it increasingly difficult to control reporters, and a whole series of reporters' journals, typified by More, were created to advocate reporters' rights, among other things. In many cases, newsrooms were brought to the brink of chaos as the result of clashes of ideology and authority. In Behind the Front Page, psychologist Chris Argyris described the situation at an anonymous newspaper which is clearly The New York Times. Argyris had been brought in as a consultant in an effort to reduce newsroom tensions. The pattern was indeed a chaotic one. The authority of the editor had been sharply curtailed and the ability of the staff to work together seriously impaired.

The sharpened adversarial stance of journalists vs. the government was partly a function of shifting attitudes toward public authority, a shift shared with many other young professionals. It was also, however, the result of an awareness of the fame and influence such an approach could bring, heightened by the events surrounding Watergate, and supported by new technologies. In addition, the Supreme Court's Sullivan decision, and a number of cases following it, all but immunized journalists against successful libel suits by public figures. This served to heighten the sense of power of many journalists.

By the late 1970s, the authority of editors was being restored to some extent on some newspapers, and the more radical journalism periodicals, like the underground press, had all but disappeared. But it was not restored completely, and publishers, by and large, have not even tried to reclaim all the ground they lost. Furthermore, regardless of whatever authority publishers regained, they are now operating under an entirely new set of guidelines. Editors and publishers have themselves changed even as they have (along with reporters) contributed to a changing world. Many have come to accept new paradigms for understanding reality which like the old understandings operate unconsciously. Tom Wicker touches on this when he points out that all reporters must rely on an instinct for truth as they attempt to make sense out of the world about them. Unfortunately, one person's instinct for truth is another's bias. Many journalists have grown somewhat more skeptical of easy solutions to social problems in the wake of disillusionment following the breakup of the New Left and the Great Society. Yet they have not become reattached to traditional values and institutions, and their instinct for truth continues to mirror a (somewhat chastened) liberal and cosmopolitan world view. Since these views are mostly held unselfconsciously, reporters and editors find it difficult to see them for what they are. As Jeremy Tunstall puts the matter from a radical perspective:

Along with the more blatant censorship by others goes the more important "self-censorship" of the journalist as he systematically attempts to fit events into a particular world view whose basic premises he sees as embodying a faithful portrayal of society. So-called "objectivity" becomes a matter of interpreting and analyzing the event dispassionately in the light of the accepted paradigm of "how things happen" and "what the social universe looks like." That the paradigm itself may be false is a question which occurs on very rare occasions.

Summary

The shifting role of the media as one factor contributing to the social changes which are taking place in the United States. Some of the factors which have produced changes in the influence of the media and in the kind of messages it transmits have resulted from a rapidly changing technology. The emergence of television certainly contributed to the growth of a national media elite as well as to what kind of messages are now communicated by the media, to whom and with what effect. These changes have had a profound impact upon American society in ways that are just beginning to become clear.

In many ways, this has all been to the good. Our society is more humane today and, in a number of areas, more sophisticated than it was forty years ago. On the other hand, the contemporary liberal and cosmopolitan lifestyle of middle-class professionals depends on the orderly routine bourgeois behavior of millions of ordinary people. If they come to share the lifestyle of those who rely on their support (and they are beginning to), there is some question as to whether the foundations of the society will enable it to function in ways which permit the style to remain viable. Paradoxically, as Rousseau suggested about the impact of the philosophers of the French Enlightenment: those responsible for the creation and distribution of mass culture know enough to be skeptical, but not enough to seriously examine the possibility that skepticism can contribute to the decay of those very values and structures which enable them to live the lifestyle they so much enjoy.

We see at every side huge institutions, where our youth are educated at great expense and instructed in everything but their duty magnanimity, equity, temperance, humanity and courage will be the words of which they know not the meaning. The dear name of country will never strike their ears.

6

Managing the News

Introduction

When terrorist violence, particularly violence at the hands of enemy regimes or sub-national groups, served to encourage desired policy goals, the administrations' spokespersons were quite vocal in their denunciations. While it might be argued that it made political sense for the Reagan and Bush administrations to ignore the terrorism of strategic allies such as Iraq, UNITA in Angola, and the Afghan Mujahideen, it is strikingly less clear why the news media would do so as well. Why, for instance, were some acts of politically motivated violence extensively covered and understood as terrorism while others were generally ignored?

The difference, I have argued, was largely a function of political power understood as issue management. This argument presupposes considerable control over the content of information carried over channels of mass communication. The purpose of this chapter is to describe how the Reagan and Bush administrations managed news content, including news regarding political violence. The chapter begins with what is by now a rather familiar description of the corporate operating environment of the contemporary news media. Ben Bagdikian and James D. Squires, among others, have described the injurious consequences of the new business ethic in contemporary news media, one which undermines the importance of independent journalism.

The bulk of the chapter is devoted to a description of the Reagan administration's efforts to take advantage of these developments in the news business. An elaborate institutional structure was established in the administration to manage news and issue content to the administration's benefit.

Corporate Milieu: Money, Media, and News Management

Todd Gitlin has noted the sometimes confusing array of explanations of news content. While some explanations are "journalist-centered," regarding news as the product of professional news judgments, others regard the news as the product of organizational factors. Closely related to these are explanations of the news that focus on the pressures journalists bring to bear on one another, often referred to as "pack journalism." Another variant on the organizational explanation is Tuchman's "phenomenological" approach. In this view the news is a "social construct" which both reflects and recreates power relations in society.

Herbert Gans has sought to synthesize these various approaches. For Gans, news is information which is transmitted from sources to audiences, with journalists who are both employees of bureaucratic commercial organizations and members of a profession summarizing, refining and altering what becomes available to them from sources in order to make the information suitable for their audiences. Because news has consequences, however, journalists are susceptible to pressure from groups and individuals (including sources and audiences) with power to hurt them, their organizations, and their firms. Sources, journalists, and audience coexist in a system, although it is closer to being a tug of war than a functionally interrelated organism.

Gitlin argues these "tugs of war" are resolved through the operation of political power, a power understood as the management of audience perceptions of reality. Philip Schlesinger has similarly stated that news is "the exercise of power over the interpretation of reality."

Though these expressions are similar to the descriptions of power offered in chapter one, we need to take the analysis of power and news to another level and ask how power manifests itself in the day-to-day operation of news organizations and in the working lives of journalists.

Concentration of Media Ownership

Central to nearly all explanations of news content is consideration of the concentration of mass media ownership. When Ben Bagdikian first published his superb book, The Media Monopoly in 1983, fifty corporations controlled nearly all of the major media. By the time The Media Monopoly went to a second printing in 1987 the number had been reduced to twenty-nine. By 1989, with the takeover of Warner Communications by Time, Incorporated, the number of major media owners was reduced to twenty-five. At the 1980s rate of media mergers, Bagdikian estimated that by the turn of the century most media in the United States will be owned by five to ten corporations.

These were not just communication corporations buying other communication corporations. Their reach extended to nearly every corner of American life. The same people who brought you the movies, Columbia Pictures, also sold Coca Cola. The defense industry giant General Electric (light bulbs, refrigerators, nuclear warheads, jet engines) also owned RCA and the National Broadcasting Corporation (NBC).

The concentration of ownership in the media is quite apparent. What is not so apparent is how political power is exercised through the corporate media. What are the links between corporate ownership of the media and the actual content of the news? There have been several responses to this question, each differing more in emphasis than in substance. While some have argued that there is a "chain of command" running from the owners to the reporter on the beat, others have put forward the argument that the imperatives of the business world alone are sufficient cause for banal, "safe" news.

According to the "chain of command" argument, reporters and editors must produce news that is in compliance with the ideological disposition of the owner or board of directors. In this view the news is not what happened, or even what reporters say happened, but rather what the owners and news executives decided to print or broadcast. News, in short, must pass a political test. Critics of this view have argued that it is often too reductionist, lacking the flexibility needed to accommodate the complexity of politics, particularly political violence. It forces us to look for "smoking guns," evidence of directives given by owners to editors and reporters as to what is politically acceptable. Evidence of this sort is often difficult to find.

While not necessarily discounting the chain of command thesis, others speculate that corporate ownership of the news media asserts itself in more subtle ways. This might be called the "market forces" argument. Doug Underwood, for instance, has noted that the concentration of media ownership has produced subtle but important changes in the way stories are written, even what stories are written. The test of news worthiness employed by editors, in Underwood's estimation, is not a political test but rather an economic one. Editors consult marketing spreadsheets, not the publishers politics. David Burgin, editor of the Dallas Times Herald, has noted that "The new power in the industry is the marketing director. I want to see more swashbuckling editors, like Ben Bradlee or Jim Bellows. But those days are dead. Now it's marketing and target marketing and more marketing." James D. Squires, former editor at the Chicago Tribune, expressed the same idea this way: "Today, with few exceptions, the final responsibility for newspaper content rest with the business executive in charge of the company, not the editor."

There are important political consequences to this development. When profit is the driving force behind the corporate news business, like any other business, news as a commodity above all other considerations will lack the consistent critical edge of news content produced by a truly adversarial press. In exchange for predictable news gathering routines and profitability, the press gives up a certain degree of independence. This is largely the result of the relationship between commercialism and "objectivity" as conventionally applied to the press.

Objectivity

The fact that the owners and managers of news organizations seek a return on investment is not a new development. But the degree to which this is solely the case, according to former editors such as Bagdikian and Squires, is new. This new focus, along with the greater concentration of media ownership, reinforces tendencies long a part of the commercial press.

News as a commodity must be treated like any other mass production item. Production costs, for instance, must be kept to a minimum to encourage profitability. The resulting marketing practices have generally been referred to as "objectivity."

Objectivity emerged in the wake of the formation of the Associated Press in 1848. Selling stories to the widest possible audience required standardized stories stripped of all obvious political markings. The use of standardized formats simply presenting the who, what, when, where, and a credible source's version of why and how meant that the widest possible market share would be attracted to, or at least not offended by, the story content. A politically bland, standardized newspaper wrapped in market-tested stylishness sold to the widest possible mass market.

Because the reporter could not speak for him or her self and still remain "objective," nearly everything said in the story had to be attributable to some, often official, source. The more official, legitimate, and credible the source, the more efficient and marketable the story. It simply made better economic sense to take information from sources regarded as credible (noncontroversial and/or official). To do otherwise invited the additional expense of conducting special investigations to document the claims made by alternative sources (read nonofficial) who were likely to invite attack by politically powerful actors. In this way officials essentially subsidized news gathering by reducing the cost of information acquisition. The point made by Bagdikian, Squires, and other critics of the contemporary corporate press is that the dynamic put into place with the formation of the Associated Press has gotten out of hand, and in the process has undermined cherished free press ideals.

The result of news commercialism has been a strong press predisposition to report what officials wanted reported, as they wanted it reported, and when they wanted it reported, particularly in foreign affairs. Objectivity forced the reporter to appear less intelligent than he or she actually was. Former New York Time's reporter David Halberstram put it this way:

Despite all the fine talk of objectivity, the only thing that mildly approaches objectivity was the form in which the reporter wrote the news, a technical style which required the journalist to appear much dumber and more innocent than in fact he was. So he wrote in a bland, uncritical way which gave greater credence to the utterances of public officials, no matter how mindless these utterances. Thus the press voluntarily surrendered a vast amount of real independence; it treated the words and actions of the government of the United States with a credence that those words and actions did not necessarily merit.

Every step of the journalistic process involves a value-laden decision. What of the infinite possibilities is to be covered and what is to be ignored? Which of the infinite observations confronting the reporter will be noted and which goes unnoticed? If noted, which will be prominently displayed on page one and which will be buried under a back-page fold? The point Squires, Bagdikian, and other critics have made in recent years is that these sort of questions are increasingly answered according to marketing decisions, and not according to some older tradition of civic responsibility. Underwood put it this way: "What worries us (veteran reporters) is whether the true value of the business—the craft of writing, the vigor of investigating, the sense of fairness and equity, the gut-level impulse to want to right wrongs will survive in the new MBA-run, market-driven newsroom.

There is some danger here of romanticizing "the good old days of journalism." The relatively wide distribution of news media ownership during the early years of the Vietnam war did not lend itself to more critical reporting. Likewise, during World War II, as Paul Fussell has shown, the news sanitized and distorted the brutalities of war. What is clear is that contemporary conditions undermine whatever critical independence previously existed in the press. Here are a few of the consequences of corporate journalism.

First, costly investigative journalism gives way to "fluff" pieces, what some drolly refer to as "News Lite." After studies in the 1970s indicated a declining readership and, even worse, that younger people were watching television news instead of reading newspapers, newspapers sought ways to reverse these trends. The American Society of Newspaper Editors hired marketing expert Ruth Clark to devise a strategy. She concluded newspapers should use more graphics, features, briefs, and "help-me-cope" pieces. In the ensuing years, many newspapers followed this advice, with Gannett USA Today the most notable example.

In this environment hard news suffers. With finite resources, newspapers which brim with food, weather, sports and how-to sections, do not devote the resources needed for independent investigative journalism. Besides, appearing too aggressive may be bad for business. Stories can backfire. It is much safer—and market tested—to run more features or rewrite government press releases. Controversial issues are simply too dangerous from a marketing perspective.

In the fiscally conservative milieu of the corporate media, the journalists discover the limits of controversy through a long socialization process. Veteran New York Times correspondent R. W. Apple described it this way:

The way to the top really communicates its views to the rest of the paper is through the subordinate editors, and even more important than that through longtime discussions with and shaping of people who are going to be senior correspondents. You can't do a lot as an editor in New York to set the tone of a Moscow correspondent's dispatches; it's just too far away. So you send somebody to Moscow who is in tune with what you want the newspaper to be. You use your system of promotion and personnel assignment to see that that happens.

Middle of the road to conservative journalism, tied to the official line is the result.

Secondly, besides the tendency to produce non-controversial "fluff" pieces, the very availability of news is affected by the worldwide distribution of correspondents and news bureaus which, in turn, reflects the economics of news gathering. Critics of the current system of international news gathering note the typically sporadic coverage of the Third World. Natural disasters or political instability and violence may temporarily draw media attention, only to find it quickly fade. We saw this pattern in the data presented in the last chapter. Mort Rosenblum calls this the "coup and earthquake syndrome." It is also sometimes referred to as "parachute" journalism and international "pack" journalism.

The problem with pack or parachute journalism is that it focuses on dramatic political events rather often more staid processes. As a result, wars, famine, and other social and political upheavals seem to spring out of nowhere in places previously unheard in the news.

Even during the pack's crisis reporting, historical circumstances and processes are often missing from the news. Instead, events are put into context for the newly arrived journalist by the embassy and local elite. The consequences are the same: Official sources dominate the news.

The heavy reliance on official sources and the costs incurred for doing otherwise point to the ultimate consequence of the commercial news media: The news media are left susceptible to being "managed" by dominant sources. Managing the public's issue agenda by managing the news has become a major preoccupation of government officials. Though this seems no less true of the Clinton administration than of the Reagan and Bush administrations, I am particularly interested in developing a more complete understanding of the Reagan administration's news media management apparatus. The Reagan administration created a sophisticated media management apparatus to take advantage of and reinforce the news gathering tendencies of the corporate media. The purpose of this apparatus was to set the issue agenda of the press, and by extension, the American public. This apparatus and how it functioned is described next.

White House and News Management

Mark Hertsgaard On Bended Knee: The Press and the Reagan Presidency and John Anthony Maltese Spin Control: The White House Office of Communication and the Management of Presidential News present detailed descriptions of the news management apparatus put into place in the White House in the 1980s and 1990s. Both authors interviewed scores of former officials of the Reagan and Bush White House, as well as reporters, editors, producers, and other network executives.

James Baker, David Gergen, and Michael Deaver were most directly responsible for media management during Ronald Reagan's first term. All agreed on one thing; controlling news content was essential to governing, to making policy and implementing it. Former White House communications director, David Gergen, put it this way: "To govern successfully, the government has to set the agenda; it cannot let the press set the agenda for it." Lou Gerig, former head of the Office of Media Liaison remarked that "We really tried to define the agenda every day." President Reagan's last director of communication, Thomas C. Griscom told Maltese something quite similar: His job was "to help set, influence, determine public opinion." To that end, he told Maltese, the administration had to control and manage the agenda.

This meant managing news content as much as possible. Leslie Janka, former deputy press secretary for the administration remarked that "The whole thing was PR. This was a PR outfit that became President and took over the country. Their first, last and overreaching activity was public relations." To set the terms of debate about issues it wanted discussed, the admipistration established a sophisticated media management apparatus run out of the White House by Reagan's top aides. There were several components to this apparatus. The purpose of these meetings was to establish long-term media strategy. Those usually in attendance were David Gergen, Michael Deaver, Richard Wirthlin, Richard Darman and Frank Ursomarso. Ursomarso told Maltese that Gergen was constantly pushing long-term planning. "'Frank, you've gotta be focused on the future. You've gotta be out there.' And I'd say, 'Well, I'm out there thirty days.' And he'd say, 'That's not enough.' You've got to be out there six months.'"

The Blair House meetings were, however, only the first layer of the Reagan White House issue management apparatus. The second layer consisted of the daily media management coordinating meetings. A meeting of the White House communications group took place every weekday morning at 8:30. This was where the specifics of publicity campaigns were determined and designed. Whereas the Blair House meetings "may see the smoke beginning, or the opportunity available down the road, at the communications meeting we talk about how we will sell our story." "What do we want the press to cover today, and how?," was how one former participant described the daily objective of the communications group meeting. Deaver explained how the group operated:

We would take a theme, which we usually worked on for six weeks say, the economy. The President would say the same thing, but we had a different visual for every one of those stops. They see the President out at the auto plant because imports are down and American cars are up. They see the President at a high-tech plant in Boston because high-tech means jobs. Pretty soon it begins to soak in, pretty soon the people begin to believe the economy is getting better.

Repetition of the desired message was key. In order for the White House version of reality to overwhelm all competing messages, the President and his surrogates had to say the same thing over and over again. "It used to drive the President crazy," said Deaver, "because the repetition was so important. He'd get on that airplane and look at that speech and say, 'Mike, I'm not going to give this same speech on education again, am I?' said, 'Yeah, trust me, it's going to work.' And it did."

Prior to the communications group meeting was the "line of the day" meeting held at 8:15 and chaired by James Baker. Among those typically in attendance was Larry Speakes, deputy press spokesman, Richard Darman, the man who sat in the powerful position of managing the document flow into the Oval Office, and media advisors Michael Deaver and David Gergen. As Deaver described the purpose of the meeting, it was to "make sure we're all saying the same thing."

By coordinating their responses, Reagan administration officials attempted to shape news content. Events and issues the administration wanted played up received a barrage of official statements employing nearly identical language, while questions regarding events and issues the administration wanted to remain obscure were met with stony silence. This calls to mind the study results described in chapters three and four. The predilection of the press to rely on official sources, and the extraordinary efforts of the administration to take advantage of this predilection, produced selective "publicity campaigns," to use Herman's term for describing the media and official denunciation of select (enemy) political violence. These publicity campaigns were highly orchestrated by the administration.

Once agreed upon, the line of the day was immediately made available to other senior administration officials through computer electronic mail messages. By simply calling it up on one's computer screen, an administration official could be sure to be abreast of the coordinated response to certain questions that might be asked during encounters with the press that day. Others in the bureaucracy were apprised of the day's planned responses with conference calls. The use of conference calls for foreign policy coordination was in place from the very start of the Reagan administration. Each morning, Ursomarso and Lyndon "Mort" Allin of the Press Office staff, held conference calls on secure lines with public affairs officers in the State Department, Defense Department, Central Intelligence Agency, and the National Security Council. During these calls the officials attempted to anticipate the questions that might come up that day and coordinate their responses. According to one participant, the calls went something like this:

It was like, 'Okay, what do we say about Lebanon today? We'd go through the paper and see a story about South Africa, say, and figure out how we wanted to handle that. 'Well, no-comment it,' we'd decide, or 'That's a Pentagon story, we will shut up. State, you've got the lead on George Shultz's press conference in Brazil.' Now the White House may say, 'Look, the President's got a statement tomorrow, so shut up today, goddamnit, just shut up, don't pre-empt the President, (we'll) cut your nuts off if you leak anything out on this one,' that kind of guidance. Other times we would say, 'Here's what we're going to say, everybody just say it at once. I don't care if you're asked the question or not, everybody in the administration today praises Gemayel's leadership,' or Mubarak's leadership, or whatever it is."

Howard Teicher of the NSC remarked that when he was at the National Security Council, each day began with a 7:30 A.M. staff meeting dealing with the press. "The first thing we did," Teicher explained, "was deal with the press, and often times we never got beyond that; just contingency talking points for whatever was in the media that day." Shaping that day's news was a top priority of the administration.

The communication group and line of the day meetings were only the start. Throughout the day the White House would continue in its efforts to control the news. Gergen, for instance, acknowledged that he frequently called reporters working on a story.

I tried to call them back late in the afternoon, after they had their information and wanted to put in some kind of context. That's what everybody referred to as 'spin control,' but I thought it was important, if they were way off base, to draw them back, or if they had something to make sure they had some sense of what the White House view on it was.

Gergen routinely called all three of the major television networks just prior to the airing of the nightly news to find out what they were going with that night. The calls were often followed, said Gergen, by a "flurry around here trying to influence what they were doing." Michael Deaver, who effectively took over as communications director after Gergen was reassigned, said the practice of calling reporters and network executives was "absolutely necessary."

The Reagan White House efforts to manage the news did not even end there. Weekly seminars for the spokespersons from various federal agencies were another component of the administration news management apparatus. At these seminars, one in the morning given by Donald Regan on economic matters and the other on foreign policy given in the afternoon by Robert McFarland, spokespersons were coached on the issues they were to promote. Again, the idea was to coordinate language, to encourage those who spoke for the administration to speak with one voice.

Another component of the Reagan administration's agenda setting apparatus were the public opinion surveys conducted by Richard Wirthlin. Shaping and directing the content of the public issue agenda required extensive monitoring of public opinion. Wirthlin conducted over five hundred surveys in Reagan's eight years in office, all funded by the Republican National Committee. These monthly surveys "probed just about every aspect of public affairs on a scale unmatched in U.S. history." According to Advertising Age, Wirthlin's polls were also unmatched in detail.

Richard Beale of the White Communications Office worked with Wirthlin to determine issue priorities and content strategies for the administration. Frank Ursomarso explain the system this way: The Office of Communications "determined what issue would be top priority, second priority what the visibilities would be for the various themes." Ursomarso used the example of an issue concerning the Justice Department. "Then I would have to get together with the fellow at Justice and say, 'Look, this is the priority that we're going to be working on, and this is what we're trying to do. Now, how can you help and what can we do together and what do you know?' "

The idea was to "somehow move that issue and keep the visibility up."

To keep track of the success of their campaigns, Ursomarso's office "would generate graphs from his computerized system showing the number of minutes devoted to various stories. We would use those graphs to determine, in part, how well we were doing." Setting the tone and content of issue dialog in the news was the name of the game.

One example of how all this came together to structure the news occurred in 1982. Wirthlin's polls detected rising public resentment of Reagan administration policies that favored the wealthy while hurting the poor. The perception of Reagan as a friend of the rich was fueled by Nancy Reagan's expensive tastes. As Michael Deaver put it, "We had all those negative stories on Nancy Reagan at that time. You take the budget cut stories and pair them with the stories about the new (White House) china and the refurbishing of the dresses and all that, and it was beginning to hurt. We could see it in our polls." The White House public relations apparatus began devoting its energies to planning media events designed to counter the emerging grassroots issue of administration coddling of the rich and powerful. It effectively had to be made a "non-issue."

The White House media experts hit upon the idea of an antidrug abuse campaign. Mrs. Reagan was soon making the tour of drug abuse centers and schools warning about the evils of drugs. Though certainly not a complete success, the strategy seemed to help her image problem. Lee Lescaze of The Washington Post remarked, "It suddenly became clear to us that we were not to take swipes at Nancy Reagan." The press simply did not have it in them to attack her on such a mission of mercy, even if it was understood by nearly everyone within the Washington press corp to be a cynical public relations ploy.

Deaver and company's handling of the administration image problem regarding education policy offers another example. In 1983 Wirthlin's surveys detected a two-to-one disapproval rating of Reagan's education policies, largely due to cutbacks in funding. It was decided by the Blair House group that this had to be countered. The themes of the campaign were merit pay for teachers and better discipline. Among other media events, the White House invited the "teacher of the year" to the White House. It also made a tough talking, baseball bat and megaphone wielding New Jersey principal something of a national hero as a part of the campaign. Reagan himself made twenty-five speeches during the campaign. More accurately stated, Reagan gave the same speech twenty-five times. As Saul Freedman, a Knight-Ridder correspondent, said, "They understood that to shift the fulcrum of the debate, you have to do it with repetition, which the President is very good at." By the end of the campaign, without Reagan administration education policies changing the least, Wirthlin's surveys detected a two-to-one margin in support of Reagan administration education policies.

Staging the news even included staging deadly international armed conflict. The Reagan administration felt shackled by the apparent reluctance of most Americans to allow the U.S. to become involved in Third World conflicts. This reluctance is generally referred to as the "Vietnam syndrome." It will be discussed more in chapter seven. On August 19, 1981, the administration took its first crack at reversing the Vietnam syndrome when United States Navy jets encountered jets from Libya over the Gulf of Sidra. In the ensuing air battle, U.S fighter planes downed two Libyan jets.

The White House media crew had, as always, planned this encounter to the last detail. The confrontation was originally scheduled for July but was postponed by chief of staff Baker. He feared that it would draw too much media attention away from the administration's legislative victories. A sense of timing was crucial to good news management. Once underway, though, the White House was ready. That morning Reagan was taken to the USS Constellation off the Virginia coast in time for a photo opportunity. On the news that night the Commander-inchief was on the bridge, in naval garb and binoculars in hand. It was surely one of Reagan's finest roles. (Kaddafi tried a similar media event with his own navy and was roundly ridiculed by the American press.) The pictures on the news that evening subliminally conveyed the impression that Reagan was there in the heat of battle in the Gulf of Sidra, and not as he actually was at the time of the encounter in bed sound asleep and undisturbed by his staff.

This episode is telling the administration's policies regarding terrorism, including its media tactics, were not meant to end terrorism, at least not all terrorism. After all, the United States was a major supplier of weapons and training to various regimes and guerrilla groups which routinely utilized terror tactics. Rather, like the encounter in the Gulf of Sidra, the administration was in search of a means by which it could overcome the Vietnam Syndrome, among other objectives.

Bringing in the CIA

The White House evidently came to the conclusion that it needed help in its news media and issue management efforts. According to Robert Parry and Peter Kornbluh, the White House brought on board senior covert operations specialists from the Central Intelligence Agency (CIA). They were assigned to the White House to create and manage a propaganda operation directed at members of Congress, the press, and the American public. The principal players in this operation were CIA Director William Casey and Walter Raymond, Jr., described by Parry and Kornbluh as the CIA's leading propaganda expert.

Once assigned to the Department of State, and "retired" from the CIA (it would have been illegal for the CIA to be directly involved in such domestic propaganda activities), Raymond created the Office of Public Diplomacy for Latin America and the Caribbean (S/LPD). Though housed in the State Department, S/LPD was not directed by it. Rather, it was under the guidance of "RIG," the "Restricted Interagency group" comprised of National Security Council staffers Oliver North, CIA Central America Task Force chief Alan Fiers, and Assistant Secretary of State for Inter-American Affairs Elliot Abrams. One source quoted by Parry and Kornbluh acknowledged that S/LPD was closely modeled after CIA overseas propaganda operations. "They were trying to manipulate (U.S.) public opinion using the tools of Walt Raymond's trade craft which he learned from his career in the CIA covert operations shop." Another source reported by the Miami Herald described S/LPD's efforts as a "vast psychological warfare operation."

The specific purpose of the operation was to put pressure on Congress and the news media to support the administration's war effort in Central America. As Raymond himself described it in a July, 1986 memorandum, "In the specific case of Nica(ragua), concentrate on gluing black hats on the Sandinistas and White hats on UNO (the contras)." This meant encouraging Sandinista atrocity stories while the more numerous Contra transgressions had to be ignored. This, of course, was the same technique apparently applied to "terrorism" reporting.

It also meant looking for new angles for selling desired policies to a reluctant Congress and American public. When, for instance, Wirthlin's opinion surveys in 1983 discovered that Americans were beginning to be alarmed by the influx of Latin American refugees, Reagan tapped this concern by suggesting that this "tidal wave" could be stopped only by crushing the leftist movements in Central America. In a June 1983 speech, Reagan warned that unless a tough stand was taken, these "feetpeople" would be "swarming into our country."

Raymond's operation also turned into something of an American Ministry of Information. In its first year alone, S/LPD arranged 1,500 speaking engagements (these included radio and television, and editorial board interviews), distributed material to 1,600 college and university libraries, 520 political science faculty, 122 editorial writers, and 107 religious organizations. It also published three booklets on Nicaragua. Furthermore, according to a February 8, 1985 S/LPD activities report to the NSC.

Correspondents participating in programs such as the 'McLaughlin Group,' ' Agronsky and Company,' and 'This Week with David Brinkley' receive special materials such as the report on Nicaragua's Military Buildup expeditiously and have open invitations for personal briefings."

At every available point of leverage the administration attempted to direct media toward those issues and issue interpretations it wanted covered, as it wanted them covered. At the same time, it sought to turn media attention away from those issues and events it wanted left untouched. The administration was capable of managing the news as it did in part due to the corporate induced docility of commercial journalism. As the data in previous chapters indicate, with regard to such activities as guerrilla wars in Angola and Afghanistan, Iraq's continued support of terrorism, and politically motivated violence more generally, the administration was often stunningly successful in this effort.

The press, though, is not monolithic, and neither are the politically powerful who tend to dominate the debate. There are real policy differences between liberals and conservatives, Democrats and Republicans, though the differences are often marginal. There are also instances of inadequate socialization of reporters in the field. At times, journalists do report highly critical stories. We shall see an example of this in chapter six. In short, despite the economic and political pressures described to this point, enforcement mechanisms are necessary to keep the mainstream press, such as The New York Times, in line. "In line" means reporting those prepackaged events without too much deviation. We next turn to a review of several enforcement mechanisms used to encourage a particular news content.

There are at least two major enforcement mechanisms intended to keep the news in check: Co-optation of key journalists referred to here as fawning, and attacks by government officials and other powerful political actors against journalists who stray too far outside the bounds of acceptable controversy referred to here as flak.

Co-opting the Press

Successful news management required more than just the docile inclinations of the corporate news media. By cultivating friendly but controlled relations with journalists, and severely punishing or threatening to punish those who did not cooperate, Reagan administration officials were able to enhance their media management capability.

Many of the components of the news management apparatus outlined above were not new. David Gergen, a former Nixon administration aide, had taken many of the techniques described above straight out of the Nixon White House. The line of the day meetings and the conference calls, for example, were features of the Nixon White House. But unlike the Nixon administration, the Reagan administration, at least on the surface, also attempted to foster good relations with the press corp.

Charming the press often meant simply paying attention to the creature comforts of journalists. An attempt was made to provide the White House press corp with everything they could possibly need-except uncontrolled information. Deputy assistant to the President Joanna Bistany explained the White House philosophy this way:

If you give somebody a comfortable place to work, good facilities, provide food because you know they can't take time to go to a restaurant ten miles away to eat, and in general provide the creature comforts, how then can someone turn around and bite the hand that feeds him? I had reporters (at the 1983 Western economic summit meeting) in Williamsburg tell me, 'Jesus Christ, how can I write a nasty story? Every time I need something, somebody is there to provide it for me. I've got two phones right in front of me, food over there, it's really hard to write a nasty story'."

Reporters also had what was essentially unlimited prepackaged information from throughout the Executive branch, a strategy which has been referred to as "manipulation by inundation." This was the same technique used by the Committee on Public Information (CPI), established during World War I to coordinate propaganda. The CPI "discovered in 1917-18 that one of the best means of controlling news was flooding news channels, with 'facts,' or what amounted to official information." Leslie Janka, a press officer in both the Nixon and Reagan administrations described the strategy this way:

As opposed to Kissinger and Haldeman and that crowd, whose view was that you control the media by giving them bits and pieces (of information), the Reagan White House came to the totally opposite conclusion that the media will take what we feed them. They've got to write their story every day. You give them their story, they'll go away. As long as you come in there every day, hand them a well-packaged, premasticated story in the format they want, they'll go away. The phrase is 'manipulation by inundation.' You give them the line of the day, you give them the press briefings, you give them facts, access to the people who will speak on the record. And you do that long enough, they're going to stop bringing their own stories, and stop being investigative reporters of any kind, even modestly so.

Despite all of these enticements to simply go along, not all journalists passively rewrote administration press releases. This was particularly true of journalists who operated outside the White House and Executive branch beat system. In order for "manipulation by inundation" to be successful, the costs of going outside the daily authorized press feeds had to be raised to unacceptable levels. Herman and Chomsky have referred to these measures as "flak" the sanctions politically powerful actors impose on individual journalists and even entire news organizations should either begin to take adversarial journalism too seriously. They outline how powerful actors, such as advertisers and conservative media watchdog groups, exert pressure on the press to conform. What is offered below is an elaboration on Herman and Chomsky's basic argument. We will begin with a review of the methods of "official flak."

The most effective method of handling a recalcitrant reporter was to freeze him or her out of insider reporting opportunities. Operating in the highly competitive Washington, D.C. press environment, where much of the terrorism spectacle was created, meant journalist were always vulnerable to being locked out. For instance, New York Times national security affairs correspondent Leslie Gelb was barred for a time from future press briefings by the State Department's Politico-Military Affairs office. Gelb had written an article on U.S. contingency plans to deploy nuclear depth charges in the territorial waters of eight allied countries, none of which had been told of the plan. Even though Gelb based his article on information already published in the foreign press, the State Department did not like the article and barred him from press briefings.

Journalists are also careful of what they say or write, remarked Howard Teicher of the NSC, because "they don't want to burn their bridges. We don't shoot-off knees in Washington, but if someone wrote that Richard Haas (formerly of the National Security Council) or anybody else was duplicitous, they're not going to return his phone calls." Teicher continued: "The ultimate parasitic relationship in this town, particularly in foreign policy, is the symbiotic, parasitic relationship between policy makers and I'm not talking about desk officers here (between) mid-to-senior level policy makers and the press."

With so few credible and "legitimate" sources from which to choose, especially on the White House beat, journalists simply could not afford to be too adversarial for fear of retaliation. Beyond being barred outright, retaliation for overzealous reporting might also come in the form of favoring one's competitor with the next hot inside tip.

"Its hard to avoid the analogy of the White House press corp as a bunch of caged hamsters thoroughly dependent on their masters for their daily feeding," remarked former Boston Globe White House correspondent Walter Robinson. This was particularly true of The New York Times, said Robinson. It was "shameless."

It's so important for The Times to be first that they throw their standards out the window. There's general resentment among other print reporters of The Times and The Post because of their access. It's so much easier for (second term chief of staff) Don Regan to drop something in there as a trial balloon, and then everybody else will pick it up.

This later point is worth emphasizing. Controlling The New York Times, as well as The Washington Post, was crucial for the administration. If The New York Times ran a story, sometimes because an administration official wanted it printed, the rest of the news media would usually follow suit. If, on the other hand, the administration could hinder the reporting of The New York Times, other papers faced difficulties filling the breech. Controlling Times' reporters created a de facto control over much of the national news agenda. What happened to former Times correspondent Ray Bonner illustrates this.

Following the March, 1982 Constituent Assembly election in El Salvador, New York Times Central America correspondent Ray Bonner was pulled from El Salvador by Times editors and reassigned to the financial desk in New York. Unlike much of the reporting coming out of El Salvador following the election, Bonner had continued to write of the atrocities committed by the Salvadoran army, the suspension of the modest land reform program, and of the massive frauds that had occurred in the election itself.

In January 1982 Bonner and photojournalist Susan Meiselas were the first to investigate the massacre of nearly eight hundred people at El Mozote, El Salvador. Washington Post correspondent Alma Guillermoprieto was soon to follow with her own account. In his story, Bonner described "the charred skulls and bones of dozens of bodies burned under burned-out roofs, beams, and shattered tiles." The story came at a particularly bad time for the Reagan administration as it attempted to "certify," as required by Congress, that El Salvador was making progress in its human rights conduct.

Bonner was attacked almost immediately by the State Department, conservative media watchdog groups, and even by other news organizations (Time magazine and The Wall Street Journal accused Bonner of political bias). Thomas Enders, then assistant secretary of state for interAmerican affairs, claimed before a congressional committee that "no evidence could be found to confirm that government forces systematically massacred civilians." And the commander of the U.S. military advisors in El Salvador, Colonel John Waghelstein, was reported to have told one U.S. reporter, "I'd like to get (Washington Post reporter John) Dinges and Bonner up in a plane." This was an apparent reference to a torture technique used by the U.S. military in Vietnam.

Though he did not face Colonel Waghelstein in an airplane, Bonner was pulled from El Salvador. "That story," said Bonner, "was the beginning of the end of my career at The New York Times."

Was Bonner pulled for political reasons? Michael Massing has argued that he was. Bonner also believes this to be the case, something then New York Times executive editor, Abe Rosenthal, vehemently denied: "That's bullshit. There's no other way to put it. It's plain, old-fashion bullshit." Bonner, instead, was reassigned, said Rosenthal, because he had proven himself and the Times had decided to bring him home to "train" him.

Whatever the reason behind Bonner's reassignment, the results were the same. Correspondents believed they had to be "more careful," that is, less critical of the Salvadoran government, security forces, and the Reagan administration policies in El Salvador. As Massing quoted one reporter, "(Bonner's transfer) left us all aware that the embassy is quite capable of playing hardball. If they can kick out the Times correspondent, you've got to be careful." Bonner also raised the same point: "I've had other Central America reporters tell me that after I left they found it harder to get their stuff in." While "the New York Times reported this much," spreading his arms wide, "there was that much space," narrowing his arms, "for others to file similar stories. Several reporters told me that after I left, it left them with that much less space, since their stories weren't being legitimized by (their editors) seeing the same angle being reported in the New York Times."

And what of the reported massacre at Mozote? In October, 1992, a team of forensic archaeologists finally offered gruesome confirmation of Bonner's and Guillermoprieto story. The New York Times article described it this way:

Nearly 11 years after American-trained soldiers were said to have torn through El Mozote and surrounding hamlets on a rampage in which at least 794 people were killed, the bones have emerged as stark evidence that the claims of peasant survivors and the reports of a couple American journalists were true.

The former Post correspondent, Alma Guillermoprieto responded this way to the stories eleven years after the fact:

Two journalist from leading newspapers, traveling independently of each other, provided the same evidence. There were photographic documents, credible sources."

"It was very, very hard to fight the Reagan administration; it's very hard to fight any administration. What we see is that administrations with the press about "national security' concerns. Encouraged by administration hard-liners, Reagan had originally planned to eliminate all background and off-the-record interviews. His more astute media advisors, however, successfully argued against such a move. They realized these were important devices for manipulating the press when controlled properly, and it was up to Gergen to achieve that control. This simply meant that no one outside of Gergen's press office could take a call from the press unless approved. The proposed ban and the possibility of future polygraph tests was intimidation enough. As we will see in a moment, there were further attempts to seal-off uncontrolled access to officials.

Beside limiting reporter's uncontrolled access to officials, issues were also managed by placing tighter restrictions on documents. In 1982 Reagan signed Executive Order 12356, giving administration officials broader authority to withhold information for reasons of "national security." The stricter classification of material not only restricted the press from gaining access to hitherto public documents, it also excluded Congress, government contractors, researchers, and scientists.

Furthermore, documents classified under the presidential order were made exempt from disclosure under the Freedom of Information Act. It even contained a provision allowing for the reclassification of previously declassified documents. In hearings before the House Committee on Government Operations, féderal officials who had been called to testify even refused to rule out the possible use of physical force or illegal entry to regain control of previously declassified material.

The executive order also changed the basic classification period from six years to an indefinite period of time, stating only that information shall remain classified "as long as required by national security considerations." Executive Order 12356 attempted to placed the documentary record of federal employees outside the reach of the public, but it was only a beginning.

In 1982 the administration also began a campaign of intimidation against both officials and reporters who strayed outside of the media script. In 1982 Secretary of Defense Weinberger forced more than a score of Defense Department employees to take polygraph tests in an effort to find the source of a leak regarding future American military needs. Then in March, 1983 Reagan issued National Security Directive 84. It permitted the government to review, prior to publication, all written works by former employees. The directive required over 128,000 government employees to sign secrecy agreements which would have, had the directive been successful, subjected them to lifetime censorship.

The directive was, however, met by considerable protest. By December only a handful of federal employees had signed the secrecy agreements. Of those who had, none were top-level officials. Congress eventually placed a moratorium on its use effective November 22, 1983 to April 16, 1984. By February 1984, Reagan officials were forced to suspend the key provisions of the secrecy agreements and polygraph tests. Though the administration had failed to implement the secrecy agreements, this was only a temporary setback for Reagan officials.

The administration's zeal for secrecy was back in the news by the end of the year when it announced that a space shuttle mission scheduled for launch on January 23, 1985 would be "secret." This latter episode prompted New York Times correspondent Hedrick Smith to write "The Reagan administration's efforts to impose tight security on the next mission of the space shuttle reflects both an urge to protect the national security and what some intelligence specialists see as a broader, longterm drive to curb the flow of information on such issues to the public." The extent of the administration's determination was about to be revealed.

After the failure of the national security directive, the administration developed a new strategy. Two months before the directive was scrapped, Under Secretary of Defense Fred Ikle told reporters that the administration was likely to seek tougher penalties against those who leak information to reporters. "The laws are not adequate. We have decided to fight it on all fronts."

The Justice Department opened the attack with the criminal prosecution of a Navy intelligence analyst named Samuel Morison. Morison had sold satellite photographs of a Soviet aircraft carrier under construction to Jane's Fighting Ships, a highly respected British publication specializing in military matters. All three of the photographs in question had been previously published. Morison's intention in providing the British publication with the photographs, or so he claimed, was to raise public consciousness of what he perceived to be a greater Soviet threat then had been generally acknowledged.

The Justice department pursued Morison's conviction by pushing for new interpretations of various espionage laws, including the 1917 Espionage Act, the Espionage Act of 1947, and the Communications Intelligence Act of 1950. Simply stated, the Reagan Justice Department wanted to prosecute as "spies" officials, starting with Morison, who made unauthorized disclosures to the press.

The interpretation of the espionage laws sought by the administration was provided by Federal District Judge Joseph H. Young. In ruling against a pretrial defense motion for dismissal of the charges against Morison, Judge Young asserted that even though the case did not fit the mold of a "classic spy scenario," it made little difference: "The danger to the United States is just as great when this information is released to the press as when it is released to an agent of a foreign government." Morison was eventually convicted and sentenced to two years in prison.

The Supreme Court contributed to the government's expanding capacity to control information when on October 17, 1988 it failed to set aside Morison's criminal conviction.

What are the consequences of the Morison case? A legal brief filed by most of the major news organizations, including The New York Times, stated that adoption of the prosecution's interpretation of the espionage laws would "affect, and perhaps dramatically alter, the way in which government officials deal with the press, the way in which the press gathers and reports the news, and the way in which the public learns about its government." Morton H. Halperin, then with the American Civil Liberties Union, and a former member of the National Security Council under Henry Kissinger's stewardship, concluded that the Morison conviction constituted the creation of an official secrets act.

Any government employee who gives any classified information to any newspaper will have broken the law and any newspaper that publishes it will also have broken the law. The statute as interpreted would prevent much of current public debate on national security issues.

The use or threatened use of espionage laws was probably rather exceptional. The more immediate objective was to intimidate the news media and the uncontrolled sources upon whom they relied in investigative reporting. Threatening government workers with espionage laws was merely on the far end of a continuum of threats employed to halt uncontrolled news contact.

A less extreme practice was to simply fire violators of the veil of official secrecy. In 1986, the Reagan administration fired Assistant Undersecretary of Defense Michael Pillsbury for, as it was alleged, disclosing to reporters the administration's plans to give advanced Stinger missiles to the American-backed rebels in Angola and Afghanistan. These are the missiles later used to shoot down, among other aircraft, civilian airliners.

In other instances even more "passive" violations of secrecy led to dismissal. Following the war with Iraq, the Bush administration and Pentagon persistently suppressed discussion of total Iraqi war-related deaths, "directing analysts and military officers not to provide estimates or professional judgments." In 1992 a Census Bureau demographer was fired for including widely published estimates of Iraqi war-related deaths in her official calculation of the total population of Iraq (158,000 dead, including 118,000 civilian war-related deaths). The population estimate were calculated for the Census Bureau's "World Population 1992" handbook, an unclassified document generally available to the public. She had provided these population estimates, including the Iraqi death toll estimates, to an inquiring reporter. Soon afterward, two of her supervisors removed her copy of the report, rewrote it, and claimed the total Iraqi civilian casualties actually stood at five thousand. A former intelligence officer was quoted by The Post as saying "I think Beth (the Census Bureau demographer) is collateral damage in the government campaign to avoid discussing the question of Iraqi casualties."

Government officials outside the media management loop were not the only targets of official wrath. The Reagan and Bush administrations also took aim at the journalists who received the information. Initially this came in the form of verbal attacks on the patriotism of the press, as we discussed earlier in the Bonner case.

Secretary of State George Shultz, for instance, said in 1983, "it seems as though the reporters are always against us and so they're always seeking to report something that's going to screw things up." In 1985 Secretary of Defense Casper Weinberger asserted that by publishing details of the secret space shuttle mission, The Washington Post had given "aid and comfort to the enemy," language suggesting treason. Reagan's science advisor, George Keyworth, 2nd said in February of 1985 that "the press is trying to tear down America" and "seems to be drawn from a relatively narrow fringe element on the far left in our society." But the campaign to silence uncontrolled press coverage soon took on an even more ominous tone.

The administration convinced The Washington Post to pull on article it was preparing on the secrets of underwater eavesdropping. Robert Pelton, a former employee of the National Security Agency, had been convicted of selling this information to the Russians. Since the Russians already had the information contained in the article, and probably more, The Post did not believe national security would be put at risk. The Post even submitted several versions of the article to government officials. None were approved. Though The Post eventually relented and suppressed the main substance of the story, the episode did not die.

William J. Casey, director of the Central Intelligence Agency, began making threatening telephone calls to news agencies, and even met with Washington Post executive editor Ben Bradlee to warn him of possible prosecution under the espionage laws regarding the underwater eavesdropping matter. He also met with Deputy Attorney

General D. Lowell Jensen, the man in charge of the Morison case. Casey wanted the Post, The Washington Times, The New York Times, Time, and Newsweek prosecuted under the espionage statutes for having printed details of intelligence gathering operations. A few days later, on May 19, 1983, Casey asked the Justice Department to consider prosecution of the National Broadcasting Corporation (NBC) for having broadcast a report based on the same information The Post had obtained.

On all fronts, the administration seemed to be turning up the heat in the effort to intimidate the news media. As one respected journalist told Mark Hertsgaard, the administration was "moving to expand the bridgehead that it won by successfully squelching a Washington Post article" Casey and the rest of the top administration officials were trying to create a sense of menace when it came to reporting on anything remotely connected with "national security."

Soon there was a new twist on the threats. Casey told the Washington Journalism Review that "we need to get better control over that whole process" by enacting legislation that would explicitly ban the "misuse of classified information." That is exactly what came next. In 1986 the administration submitted legislation to Congress which expanded the definition of a spy to include journalists who receive unauthorized leaks. The administration's proposed legislation increased the penalty for such activity to "death by firing squad" for those convicted.

The legislation would have also permitted the government to decide after the fact whether documents that have already been released to the media could lead to "grave risk of substantial danger to the national security." Under these provisions a reporter who writes about nearly any national defense or foreign policy issue based upon such documentation could theoretically face rather severe penalties.

Though the legislation was unsuccessful, the legislative campaign against leaks continued into the Bush administration. In August, 1989, some fifteen bills were under consideration in the House and Senate regarding the transmission of secrets to any third party, foreign agent or news reporter. The Bush administration even favored legislation which would have made it a crime to disclose nonsecret information. Even in the form of proposed legislation, these measure were sure to have a chilling effect. And that was the intent. Such draconian measures by the Reagan and Bush administrations most likely caused more than one re porter or news organization to think twice about pushing too hard on leaked stories. In light of these measures, it really is little wonder that a foreign journal broke the arms to Iran for hostages story.

Freedom of Information Act

The United States government estimated it created just under seven million official secrets in 1990, though no one could say for sure due to government secrecy. The Information Security Oversight Office reported that this figure actually represented a significant reduction from the zenith of government secrecy in 1985 when the Reagan administration produced fifteen million secrets. According to James Bamford, the National Security Agency alone produces from 50 to 100 million classified documents a year. The exact figure is difficult to establish. Another estimate puts the total amount at forty tons of material per day.

One of the principle means of chipping away at this mountain of classified material is the Freedom of information Act. The 1966 Freedom of Information Act (FOIA) was intended to provide the public with greater access to information concerning what their government was doing and why it was being done. This intention was seriously undermined by an amendment passed in 1986. The expressed purpose of the amendment was to aid academic and journalistic research by exempting it from costly search, review and copying fees. It went into effect in April 1987. The rationale was that the changes would allow for greater public access to government controlled information. The result, however, has been quite the reverse.

The amendment gave agency bureaucrats editorial discretion over the material under its contrgl when assigning fee waivers. Anyone who is a "representative of the news media" is, indeed, qualified for the fee waiver. But a requester must also meet a second standard: Discloser of the requested information must be "likely to contribute significantly to public understanding of the operations or activities of the government and is not primarily in the commercial interest of the requester." Furthermore, the guidelines state that the

"Bare assertions by requesters that they are 'researchers' or 'have plans to author a book' are insufficient evidence that a contribution to understanding by the general public will ultimately result from a disclosure." This language placed agency and department officials in the position of determining scholarly potential or newsworthiness of all requests. A few examples indicate that agency officials were not reluctant to exercising that discretion.

The managing editor of the Addison County, Vermont, Independent was denied a fee waiver by the Central Intelligence Agency when he requested information regarding CIA recruiting activities on the campus of Middlebury College, one of Addison County's biggest employers. The Independent, a small paper published twice weekly, had at the time about 7,500 paid subscribers. The CIA responded as follows:

Although you are an editor of the Addison Press (sic), the information you seek does not meet the regulatory requirement of current event interest to the general public. Therefore, you will be responsible for search, review and reproduction fees.

Due to the Independent's small size and meager operating budget, the search was canceled.

Researchers have fared no better under the new guidelines. For instance, a University of California, Irvine, professor found it impossible to obtain information held by the FBI and CIA regarding ex-Beatle John Lennon. Lennon had been the subject of FBI and CIA scrutiny since the late 1960s. The agencies in question would say only that to release such information would jeopardize national security. In court, the FBI went so far as to argue that even explaining why releasing then 14-year-old documents on a dead rock star would jeopardize national security would itself jeopardize national security.

This is the real crux of the problem regarding the FOIA. Discretion of what can and cannot be released is almost entirely in the hands of officials who represent agencies with an interest in disclosing as little as possible. Unless one has the financial resources to use the court system when a FOIA request is denied, discretion is in the hands of those agencies. Even if requesting organizations have the financial backing to pay for searches and possible court costs, searches may take months, even years, with no guarantee that any information will make it past the hurdle of national security.

There is even evidence that documents which have been released may not be authentic or free from tampering. In 1992, congressional investigators of the SP-100 nuclear space reactor found a two-page set of instructions issued by NASA on how to handle FOIA requests. According to Congressman Howard Wolpe (D-Mich.), the NASA document instructed its employees to rewrite or destroy documents so as to, quoting from the instructions, "minimize adverse impact" and to mix up documents and camouflage handwriting so as to make the significance of such documents "less meaningful." Finally, the document instructed employees to take steps to "enhance the utility" of various FOIA exemptions.

The effectiveness of the Freedom of Information Act was reduced even further when Ronald Reagan signed an executive order just two days prior to the end of his presidency which gave him the power to deny access to any Reagan administration era document that he feels "might impair" national security, law enforcement or the "deliberate processes of the executive branch." Whether it is the result of this executive order or changes to the Freedom of Information Act, it is usually the case that only a minuscule portion of the documentation is ever released.

Attacks on journalists and their sources who stray outside of the controlled environment established by Gergen, Deaver, Baker, and others, in combination with the weakening of the Freedom of Information Act, made critical reporting exceedingly difficult for news organizations, even those of The New York Times' stature. Conservative fiscal organizations like the Times, operating in a hostile political environment, were better off playing it safe. Simply take the line of the day, find a Democrat, if possible, willing to comment on it and call it a day. If the restraints of commercialism and the efforts of the administration were not enough to convince an editor that this was the wisest course of action, administration allies in some of the very countries most likely to see gross violations of human rights and terrorism also had an interest in placing restraints on the issue content in the news. In places like El Salvador, reporters who did not toe-theline were threatened with death, not prison sentences. Many were actually killed. This is the final form of flak.

Deadly Flak

While not a factor in reporting in the United States itself, violence or the threat of violence is an ever-present reality for reporters in some parts of the world. This must be taken into account when trying to understand the relative weight given to political violence stories.

In 1987 the Committee to Protect Journalists documented nearly six hundred incidents of press abuse taking place in seventy-five countries around the world. Twenty-six journalist were killed. The year before the Committee recorded fifteen killings, fifty-six assaults, and 190 arrests or kidnappings And in 1992 there were fifty journalists killed, ninety in jail and a total of nearly two thousand attacks directed at journalists.

At times the killings seemed to be without motive, such as the killing of ABC correspondent Bill Stewart by a Somoza National Guardsman in 1979. But all too often the killings were deliberate. For example, in El Salvador, during the 1982 Constituency Assembly elections, four Dutch journalists were shot to death at close range by the Salvadoran Treasury police. According to the 1993 United Nations Truth Commission report on El Salvador, after police officials interrogated the journalists, they killed them in an ambush. This had been ordered by a senior Salvadoran military officer in Chalatenango province.

At first Salvadoran authorities claimed the newsmen had been caught in a cross fire, a story that soon lost all credibility. The bodies of the journalists were put on display at the morgue while much of the international press corp, in town that week for the elections, were marched through to view the bodies. The display was shocking. The Dutch had not just been shot. Their partially-clothed bodies revealed horribly mutilated genitals and other signs of torture. In the words of one American reporter interviewed in the film documentary "In the Name of Democracy,""Everyone left there (the morgue) as white as a sheet. And those who had made contact with the guerrillas, canceled them and got on the next plane out of town."

Salvadoran presidential elections, three journalists were once again killed in separate incidents, all by the Salvadoran military. Reuters photographer Roberto Navas was shot in the back as the motorcycle he was a passenger on was waved through a military checkpoint. Mauricio Pineda, a soundman for a Salvadoran television station, was killed after the van in which he was riding was raked by soldier's automatic weapons fire. The van was clearly marked "PRENSA."

The third victim was once again a Dutch cameraman, Cornel Lagrouw. He and several other journalists were caught in a cross fire after Salvadoran troops moved in to retake a village held by guerrillas. After Lagrouw was hit, his friends, including two American journalists, tried to take him to the nearest hospital. While driving back toward San Salvador, a Salvadoran army helicopter began firing its machine guns at the car, once again clearly marked as a press vehicle. They were forced to take cover in the home of a Salvadoran peasant family while Lagrouw bled to death in the car.

Conclusion

The intent of this chapter has been to specify the mechanisms used in the exercise of political power. The news, including news of political violence, is the product of economic and political forces. institutions. These implications are certainly mixed, though in my view more negative than positive.

A final word should be added. To a larger extent than hitherto, issues that intersect science and public policy are becoming more central to the political process. Whether we are concerned with the "greenhouse" effect, energy sources, acid rain, IQ testing, nuclear power, or the use of therapeutic drugs, a range of issues has emerged which journalists generally are ill equipped to handle, for most journalists are quite ignorant of scientific issues and find it very difficult to deal with them accurately. This only increases the tendency for ideology to play a role in determining how the public comes to view these problems. Insofar as decisions require that the public be adequately informed, the mass media have not and are not making as positive a contribution as they might.

7

Destruction of International Terrorism

Introduction

It also used the terrorism spectacle as a rationale for the conduct of otherwise problematic policy options here at home; specifically, domestic intelligence investigations of political opposition groups. In the previous chapter, New York Times reporter Charles Mohr indicated the administration's intentions in revising terrorism statistics were clear. The new numbers could be used to justify increased surreptitious surveillance of political dissidents at home as well as military intervention abroad.

A campaign against terrorists in the wake of the 1979-80 Iran hostage crisis was an almost sure-fire way to offset the setbacks experienced by the intelligence community in the 1970s.

Reining in the FBI

The 1970s were difficult years for the American intelligence community. Public and congressional confidence was shaken by one revelation of misconduct after another. A complete review of the decades of intelligent community abuses at home would require far more space than is available here. It is worth noting, however, that every intelligence agency the Central Intelligence Agency, the Federal Bureau of Investigation, the super-secret National Security Agency, and Military Intelligence had at least one known domestic surveillance program in the 1950s, 60s, and early 70s. Even the Internal Revenue Service became involved in the search for and harassment of political enemies. On the basis of what had been made public by 1976, one critic charged that the intelligence agencies wielded a "frightening degree of secret, sometimes illegal, and often uncontrollable power." They were, in short, a "corrupt force in American society."

A review of the code names of the numerous operations, all directed at domestic political groups and individuals, reveals the scope of the invasion of privacy: The CIA ran operations CHAOS, SETTER, MERRIMAC, and RESISTANCE; beginning in the 1950s the FBI conducted operations COINTELLPRO, VIDEM, and STUDEN; Military Intelligence ran CABLE SPLICER and GARDEN PLOT; the National Security Agency conducted MINARET and SHAMROCK; while the Internal Revenue Service ran LEPRECHAUN and the Special Services Staff.

The scope of these various inquiries was substantial. At the time of Senate hearings chaired by Senator Frank Church (1975-76), it was revealed the FBI office in Washington, D.C. alone had more than 500,000 domestic intelligence files on groups and individuals. Among those now known to have been included in the FBI files were Supreme Court Justices Felix Frankfurter and William O. Douglas, Dr. Martin Luther King, Dr. Benjamin Spock, Garry Wills, Bertolt Brecht, and John Lennon. Novelist John Steinbeck was watched for thirty years. The Bureau even dispatched agents to the hearings of the Senate Foreign Relations Committee to monitor statements made by Senator Wayne Morse and other Senate critics of the Vietnam war to compare them to the "Communist Party line."

The Bureau conducted electronic surveillance and, when that failed, did black-bag jobs burglarized offices and homes. Harassment of dissident political groups and the civil rights movement was common. Prior to his assassination, for example, the FBI attempted to force Martin Luther King to commit suicide by threatening to make public an alleged extra-marital affair.

The Bureau also monitored the mails. One target was a fifteen-yearold high school student who had attempted to write to the Socialist Labor Party for information needed to complete her project for a high school civics class. The Bureau, smelling danger, conducted a "subversive activities" investigation. The local credit bureau and the chief of police were questioned by agents about the student and her parents. Agents even visited her school and told the principal that the student had been placed under investigation due to her contact with the Socialist Worker's Party.

The CIA was also interested in the U.S. mails. In a twenty-year period ending in 1973, the CIA had opened and photographed nearly 250,000 letters, producing a computerized index of 1.5 million names. The IRS also created files. It collected information on more than eleven thousand people and groups. The military kept files on approximately 100,000 civilians.

For decades, the intelligence community had conducted a freewheeling campaign against tens of thousands of Americans associated with dissident political movements, the civil rights movement and its leaders, and even U.S. Senators and Supreme Court justices. The Church committee concluded that:

Too many people have been spied upon by too many government agencies and too much information has been collected. The government has often undertaken the secret surveillance of citizens on the basis of their political beliefs, even when those beliefs posed no threat of violence or illegal acts on behalf of a hostile foreign power. Groups and individuals have been harassed and disrupted because of their political views and lifestyles.

In short, speaking out was considered treasonous by the intelligence community. Revelations of intelligence community abuses, both foreign and domestic, led to demands for strict new regulations of the intelligence community. But the Reagan administration would reverse these restrictions with its focus on terrorism at the beginning of the 1980s.

The Backlash

In the wake of the Church committee hearings in the Senate and the Pike committee hearings in the House of Representatives, the American intelligence community was placed under tighter controls after 1975. Several government entities, particularly those associated with domestic intelligence gathering, were either reorganized or eliminated altogether. The Subversive Activities

Control Board (SACB) within the executive branch was eliminated. It was one of the agencies that had been charged with ferreting out Communist affiliations of organizations and groups. The Internal Security Division of the Department of Justice was reorganized, becoming a subdivision of the Justice Department's Criminal Division. It had been in charge of prosecution of violations of federal law pertaining to internal security. Many of the government files maintained on private citizens were eliminated. The Attorney General's List of Subversive Organizations, for instance, was eliminated. And the Privacy Act of 1974 forced the U.S. Civil Service Commission to cease using its Security Research Files and Index. It had been in use since 1942 to cross-index information on potentially subversive groups. Prospective federal government employees were no longer interrogated regarding their political loyalties on the standard employment application form.

Changes in Congress were equally sweeping. The House Internal Security Committee (HISC) and the Subcommittee on Internal Security of the Senate Judiciary Committee (SISS) were eliminated. (Describing the history of these two congressional committees, including the witch hunts of the McCarthy years, the Heritage Foundation report laments their elimination, remarking that both had "for many years performed invaluable services in investigating internal security threats.")

Most important, and most vexing to conservatives, were the changes in the authorization given the FBI to conduct domestic intelligence investigations. President Ford's reactions to the criticisms of the intelligence agencies were carefully calculated. He attempted to appease the critics while retaining as much latitude as possible for the intelligence community. There would be, for instance, no new sweeping restrictions. In effect, President Ford indicated that:

value judgments about intelligence activity were relevant to the regulatory effort only insofar as they had been made visible in the law. This was, even in the initial concept, an essentially conservative response to growing public, legislative, and judicial concern about the intelligence agencies.

The most direct expression of this balancing act was Executive Order 11905, United States Foreign Intelligence Activities, issued on February 18, 1976. Pursuant to Executive Order 11905, the "Levi

Guidelines," as they came to be known, were formulated by Attorney General Edward H. Levi in the spring of 1976. Two separate sets of guidelines were actually created, one for domestic security operations and another for foreign counterintelligence activities. Of most interest to us are the guidelines for domestic operations.

Of special interest to the Congress and the Attorney General was the level of justification needed before an intrusive domestic intelligence investigation could be initiated. Such investigations include active surveillance such as wiretaps. Specifically, it was questioned whether the new guidelines would employ a strict criminal standard or a looser national security standard.

Under the guidelines eventually adopted, surveillance of domestic groups and individuals could only be done where there was likelihood such groups or individuals were about to use force in violation of the law. This was, in short, much closer to the criminal standard. Authorization for intrusive surveillance was also limited to ninety days, though with the possibility of renewal upon expiration.

The Attorney General told the Church committee at the time that these limitations approached as close as was possible the criminal activities standard desired by the critics of the intelligence community. Many critics, however, felt that Ford's Executive Order and the Attorney General's Guidelines did not go far enough. With a new Democratic administration coming into office, more changes were about to be made.

Subsequent changes made by the Carter administration reinforced and in some instances extended the restrictions placed on the intelligence community. The Foreign Intelligence Surveillance Act was passed in 1978. It required an elaborate review process of all proposed electronic surveillance. If an American citizen was subject to surveillance, a high-level executive official had to certify the information was needed for the national defense. Full approval also required approval of an interagency panel chaired by the Director of the Central Intelligence Agency. If approved there, the proposal had to be sent to the Attorney General. In addition, once approved by the Attorney General, special designated federal district court judges had to approve the proposed electronic surveillance operation. The judge could issue a special oneyear warrant when foreign powers were targeted and a ninety-day warrant when U.S. citizens were involved.

Executive Order 12036, issued on January 24, 1978, also enhanced the control and management of the intelligence community. Ford's Executive Order 11905 had allowed the infiltration of domestic organizations within the United States if such organizations were composed primarily of non-U.S. persons and it was reasonably believed to be working on behalf of a foreign power. Carter's Executive Order imposed more restrictive formal regulation and review processes. Covert surveillance at home had, in short, become very difficult.

Conservative Response

Critics of Carter's Executive Order believed that the restrictions placed on the counterintelligence divisions of the FBI and CIA severely hampered their ability to ferret out suspected terrorists and Soviet and Cuban spies. Samuel Francis, an analyst for the conservative Heritage Foundation, gave expression to this view in 1980 when he stated that the internal security threat is greater (in 1981) than at any time since World War II. Since 1974 there has been a domestic cutback. The House Internal Security Committee has been abolished, the Attorney General's list of subversive organizations is no longer extant, and a great many files on subversives have literally been destroyed. Whenever you have that kind of collapse of internal security operations you are going to have subversive types popping up. You have these people prepared to use violence and conspiratorial methods against the United States.

Francis was the editor of the intelligence portion of the 1981 Heritage Foundation report Mandate for Leadership: Policy Management in a Conservative Administration. Written by several anonymous individuals from within the intelligence community and in close collaboration with the Reagan administration, the report laid the intellectual groundwork for future administration policy.

The report reflected the same deep suspicion of nearly all political opposition groups that was evident in the intelligence community prior to the restrictions of the 1970s. Terrorists seemed to be of particular concern to the authors of the report. Because terrorists often emerged as the impatient brethren of otherwise peaceful opposition groups, authorities must keep extremist movements under at least moderate surveillance, become familiar with their public positions and members as well as their unstated goals, adherents, and fringe elements, and be prepared to escalate surveillance of whatever groups seem likely to engage in more extreme activities.

To monitor such a broad scope of potential enemies, internal security files should not, the report stated, be "restricted to actual or imminent threats." In other words, the more strict criminal standard should be dropped in favor of the looser national security standard. Who, exactly, might be excluded from surveillance was not clear. Monitoring could at first utilize public records. In other instances, the more serious surveillance "can be carried out by the use of such intelligence techniques as wiretapping, mail covers, informants and, at least occasionally, surreptitious entries."

Measures such as these were necessary, said the report, because terrorists and other types of subversives are difficult to detect: Clergymen, students, businessmen, entertainers, labor officials, journalists and government workers may engage in subversive activities without being fully aware of the extent, purpose or control of their activities. Surveillance should also include "radical and new left" groups and "antidefense and anti-nuclear groups."

The Heritage Foundation report, not surprisingly, also recommended that Attorney General Edward Levi's 1976 guidelines for the Federal Bureau of Investigation (FBI) be amended to provide law enforcement officials greater latitude in domestic political surveillance. It would have appeared to anyone carefully reading this report in 1981 that the Heritage Foundation's authors were declaring war on any and all dissent from official policy. Things amorphously referred to as national security and counterterrorism were placed at the top of the list of priorities. As the Heritage report concluded, "It is axiomatic that individual liberties are secondary to the requirements of internal security and internal civil order." As we will see below, the Reagan administration set priorities along these exact lines.

Rolling Back the Restrictions

To accomplish the unleashing of the intelligence community required a "significant reorientation of public attitudes about intelligence in order to make clear the agencies' important contributions which had been obscured and, indeed, greatly jeopardized in the era of reform." The revision in terrorism statistics was most certainly a part of the effort to reorient public attitudes. Counterterrorism was the hook upon which the argument for a revitalized intelligence community could be hung. Several columnists and other commentators also came through with a flurry of press reports and columns initiated by conservative critics of, as one of them put it, "the recent orgy of revelations and restraints."

Reagan's proposed revision to Carter's Executive Order 12036 was circulated within the administration in early 1981. When leaked to the press it immediately raised considerable concern for it appeared to be a significant departure from the Carter order. Besides offering a more positive language than was found in Carter's order ("Restrictions on Intelligence Activities," for instance, would become "Conduct of Intelligence Activities"), the oversight role of the Attorney General was downgraded, the requirement to collect information by the least intrusive means was eliminated, restrictions on domestic group infiltration was relaxed, the definition of "United States person" was narrowed, the President's role in approving the most intrusive surveillance techniques was eliminated, and the CIA would in some circumstances be allowed to engage in electronic surveillance within the United States.

Disclosure of these proposed changes put the new administration on the defensive. Presidential counselor Edwin Meese attempted to assuage public concern by indicating that the final version of the order would not substantially change the role and function of the CIA. But at the same time he reiterated that the purpose of the policy review was to improve the nation's ability to fight terrorism. John Shattuck of the American Civil Liberties Union noted that Meese's remarks provided little comfort to those who feared that "a new talisman, 'terrorism,' may come to center stage in Washington," one which offered justification for the unleashing of the intelligence community.

On December 4, 1981, President Reagan issued Executive Order 12333. For our purposes, the central feature of Executive Order 12333 was the deemphasis on the protection of constitutional liberties. This constituted a significant departure from Carter's 1978 order.

Specifically, though intelligence agencies were to give full consideration of spheres of individual rights that might be infringed upon by intelligence activities, there was no requirement to preserve these rights.

There would, for instance, no longer be the presumption of the preeminence of individual rights when in conflict with intelligence gathering needs in combating terrorism, as tenuous as that presumption may have been before. Whereas the Carter administration had declared the primacy of established constitutional principles confining governmental powers, the Reagan administration sought once again to balance constitutional liberties with intelligence needs almost entirely predicated upon counterterrorism.

Attorney General's New Guidelines

Attorney General William French Smith released two sets of guidelines for domestic investigations. First, The Attorney General's Guidelines on General Crimes, Racketeering Enterprise and Domestic Security/Terrorism Investigations (henceforth referred to as Domestic Security Guidelines) provide guidance for all investigations by the FBI of crimes and crime-related activities. All investigations under the Domestic Security Guidelines had to meet a strict criminal standard based on a "factual threshold" an indication of criminal wrongdoing. The employed factual standard was whether one was "engaging in a political enterprise for the purpose of furthering political or social goals (using) force or violence and a violation of the criminal laws of the United States." Though broad, the guideline required the FBI to establish a criminal connection to the persons or person under investigation.

The second set of guidelines were even more ambiguous. Entitled "The Attorney General Guidelines for FBI Foreign Intelligence Collection and Foreign Counterintelligence Investigations" (henceforth referred to as the FCI Guidelines), they covered "all foreign intelligence, foreign counterintelligence, foreign intelligence support activities, and intelligence investigations of international terrorism conducted by the FBI pursuant to Executive Order 12333."

The FCI Guidelines remain partially classified. What is known about them is that they are "national security" investigations with some type of foreign connection. No criminal standard applies, unlike the rather loose criminal standard used with the Domestic Security Guidelines. There are, in short, no provisions for the protection of constitutional rights. In fact, the FCI Guidelines even give conditional authorization to infiltrate groups "that will influence rights protected by the First Amendment," for example through assuming a leadership role in an organization.

Furthermore, in the absence of the "enterprise" standard found in the Domestic Security Guidelines, FCI Guidelines allow the FBI to investigate entire political organizations, even if most of its members are not suspected of being involved in international terrorism. The FCI Guidelines define a terrorist as "an individual or group that knowingly engages in international terrorism or activities in preparation thereof, or knowingly aids or abets any person engaged in such activities."

In short, without the slightest solid indication of criminal wrongdoing, the FCI Guidelines allow the FBI to conduct wholesale investigations of entire organizations. As Gary Stern concluded, the "problem with having separate and lower standards for international terrorism investigations under the FCI Guidelines is that it allows the FBI to target United States persons who may be engaged only in First Amendment activities."

"Supporting foreign terrorists," is a rather ambiguous standard, to say the least. In light of the construction of terrorism in the news and in public consciousness it is no standard at all. All that is required is the designation of an adversary as a terrorist in public documentation and the line-of-the-day meetings. Anyone who questions U.S. policy in connection with that adversary could be culpable of supporting foreign terrorists. Domestic opposition groups are placed in the position of being mere fronts for international terrorists. This is exactly what occurred.

Search for Enemies

Rumors of surveillance by government agents had been floating around the Central America activists community since at least 1981, though the FBI had always denied involvement. This remained true until January, 1988 when the Bureau was forced to release about a third of its headquarters files on one particular activist group in response to a Freedom of Information Act lawsuit brought by the Center for Constitutional Rights. Though riddled with deletions, these documents and subsequent investigations indicate that once again the FBI was involved in politically motivated surveillance of First Amendment activity, this time in the name of counterterrorism.

The Committee in Solidarity with the People of El Salvador (CISPES) expressed its support for the "opposition movement in El Salvador (the Democratic Revolutionary Front [FDR] and the Farabundo Marti Front for National Liberation [FMLN] and attempts to educate the U.S. public regarding the situation in El Salvador" This statement placed CISPES, along with hundreds of other organizations throughout the United States, in direct opposition to the policies of the Reagan administration.

On March 30, 1983 the FBI began a counterterrorism investigation of CISPES under the provisions of the FCI Guidelines. The Washington, D.C. office of the FBI directed eleven field offices to begin investigating the involvement of individuals and the CISPES organization in international terrorism as it affects the El Salvadoran government, and (authorizes) the collection of foreign intelligence and counterintelligence information as it relates to the international terrorism aspects of this investigation.

This, however, was not the first investigation of CISPES by the FBI. In September, 1981 the FBI opened a criminal investigation of CISPES to determine whether it was in violation of the Foreign Agents Registration Act (FARA). By February 23, 1982, the FBI concluded "there was no specific evidence indicating CISPES was acting on behalf of, or at the direction of a foreign power or group." Thirteen months later, the FBI began its second investigation, but this time under looser and classified FCI standards which require no indication of criminal behavior.

The preliminary basis for opening the FCI investigation of CISPES rested upon two points: First, a statement in one of CISPES's own publications that it "provides international support for the opposition movement in El Salvador." and, second, the terrorist designation of the FMLN/ FDR by the FBI.

Besides relying on the unsubstantiated terrorism charge against the FDR/ FMLN and the statement of support for those organizations found in CISPES publications, the FBI relied on another source: Frank Varelli.

A Salvadoran nationalist and the son of a former Salvadoran interior minister and national police chief, Varelli was a paid informant for the FBI. According to an Interim Report produced by the FBI's Criminal Investigative Division, Counterterrorism Section, Varelli told the FBI that CISPES was supplying the FMLN with military aid, "forwarded through Mexico for ultimate use by the guerrilla forces in El Salvador." Varelli had infiltrated CISPES's Dallas office in early 1983. The Interim Report further stated that the investigation of CISPES was predicated primarily upon information furnished by Mr. Varelli that the activities of CISPES were being directed by the FDR and the FMLN, giving reason to believe that certain members of CISPES were or may have been engaged in international terrorism, or knowingly aiding or abetting those engaged in terrorist activities, specifically the FMLN.

Once the CISPES investigation became public the FBI and Varelli parted company. The Bureau claimed Varelli had lied to them; Varelli said the FBI urged him to fabricate information which would support the U.S. government claim that CISPES was supporting terrorism.

It is clear from documents obtained by the Center for Constitutional Rights that the FBI's probe of the domestic opposition movement to Reagan administration policies in Central America actually went well beyond the infiltration of a single "terrorist" organization. Like political surveillance of the past, the FBI conducted a broad sweep against ideological opponents. It is known, for instance, that the FBI kept files on at least 2,375 individuals and 1,330 groups. The investigation involved all fifty-nine FBI field offices and created 178 spin-off investigations. One document listed 138 suspect groups somehow connected to CISPES. Included on the list were Oxfam America Inc., the American Civil Liberties Union, the American Federation of Teachers, Amnesty International, the Southern Christian Leadership Conference, the Catholic Maryknoll Sisters of America, and at least one chapter of the United Auto Workers Union. Furthermore, the techniques used were anything but restrained.

In Houston, agents recorded car license plate numbers of all vehicles near an anti-war demonstration. The list was distributed to five field offices. Most field offices took photographs of demonstrators and circulated them to other federal agencies. The Detroit office was particularly prolific in this regard. Agents in Mobile, Alabama even monitored radio talk programs. And a document from the Denver field office indicated the FBI either secured the address book of an opponent to U.S. Central America policy or had somehow copied addresses and telephone numbers from it. In at least one instance the Bureau wiretapped an A Salvadoran nationalist and the son of a former Salvadoran interior minister and national police chief, Varelli was a paid informant for the FBI. According to an Interim Report produced by the FBI's Criminal Investigative Division, Counterterrorism Section, Varelli told the FBI that CISPES was supplying the FMLN with military aid, "forwarded through Mexico for ultimate use by the guerrilla forces in El Salvador." Varelli had infiltrated CISPES's Dallas office in early 1983. The Interim Report further stated that the investigation of CISPES was predicated primarily upon information furnished by Mr. Varelli that the activities of CISPES were being directed by the FDR and the FMLN, giving reason to believe that certain members of CISPES were or may have been engaged in international terrorism, or knowingly aiding or abetting those engaged in terrorist activities, specifically the FMLN.

Once the CISPES investigation became public the FBI and Varelli parted company. The Bureau claimed Varelli had lied to them; Varelli said the FBI urged him to fabricate information which would support the U.S. government claim that CISPES was supporting terrorism.

It is clear from documents obtained by the Center for Constitutional Rights that the FBI's probe of the domestic opposition movement to Reagan administration policies in Central America actually went well beyond the infiltration of a single "terrorist" organization. Like political surveillance of the past, the FBI conducted a broad sweep against ideological opponents. It is known, for instance, that the FBI kept files on at least 2,375 individuals and 1,330 groups. The investigation involved all fifty-nine FBI field offices and created 178 spin-off investigations. One document listed 138 suspect groups somehow connected to CISPES. Included on the list were Oxfam America Inc., the American Civil Liberties Union, the American Federation of Teachers, Amnesty International, the

Southern Christian Leadership Conference, the Catholic Maryknoll Sisters of America, and at least one chapter of the United Auto Workers Union. Furthermore, the techniques used were anything but restrained.

In Houston, agents recorded car license plate numbers of all vehicles near an anti-war demonstration. The list was distributed to five field offices. Most field offices took photographs of demonstrators and circulated them to other federal agencies. The Detroit office was particularly prolific in this regard. Agents in Mobile, Alabama even monitored radio talk programs. And a document from the Denver field office indicated the FBI either secured the address book of an opponent to U.S. Central America policy or had somehow copied addresses and telephone numbers from it. In at least one instance the Bureau wiretapped an opponent of administration policy. On April 8, 1983, just nine days after the start of the FCI investigation, the San Juan field office was so eager to do a good job it suggested to Washington that it be allowed to index or otherwise observe all people of El Salvadoran extraction in Puerto Rico and the U.S. Virgin Islands.

Conservative political organizations were also utilized by the FBI in their investigation of the opponents of U.S. foreign policy objectives in Central America. For instance, the Executive Director of the Virginia Based "Young Americans Foundation," obtained CISPES documents by attending a CISPES chapter meeting. He then sent copies of these documents to Edward J. O'Malley, assistant director of intelligence for the FBI. O'Malley then sent them, classified "Secret," to at least thirtytwo listed FBI offices around the country.. This was the pattern of FBI conduct. Don Edwards, (D-Calif.) has remarked that "not one criminal act was expressly charged to CISPES, yet through innuendo and guilt by association, CISPES was prosecuted, tried, and found guilty of subversion.

The CISPES investigation was a politically motivated search justified by, as the ACLU spokesperson described potential investigations of this sort back in 1981, the "talisman of terrorism." Nor was it in all instances simply a matter of dispassionately collecting information. The New Orleans field office, for instance, sent a Teletype to FBI headquarters in Washington, D.C. which stated:

It is imperative at this time to formulate some plan of attack against CISPES and specifically, against individuals, (deletion) who defiantly display their contempt for the U.S. government by making speeches and propagandizing their cause while asking for political asylum. New Orleans is of the opinion that Departments of Justice and State should be consulted to explore the possibility of deporting these individuals or at best denying their re-entry after they leave.

References to "un-American activities" such as this are dispersed throughout the heavily edited documents. Another memo, this time from the Chicago office to Director Webster, rather disdainfully refers to CISPES members as "60's activist types" who "surround themselves in more than one activity or organization which has the look of legitimacy." The subject of another secret memorandum merely discusses an article taken from The Cincinnati Inquirer. The article refers to persons and organizations who are "involved in activities contrary to the foreign policy of the United States" This, too, is telling. Merely being on the wrong side of U.S. foreign policy was at the heart of the CISPES "counterterrorism" investigation.

News Repair

The director of the FBI at the time of the CISPES investigation, sent a secret memo to the Bureau's Jacksonville, Florida office. In the memo Webster praised that office's "aggressiveness in approaching this investigation." It is, said Webster, "appreciated by FBIHQ." He concluded by giving the Jacksonville office "Authority to conduct physical surveillance on the Florida State University campus for the purpose of identifying leaders of CISPES and their activities."

Despite the existence of this memo, Oliver B. Revell, executive assistant director of the FBI and the man directly in charge of the CISPES investigation in Washington, claimed in testimony before the United States Senate that Webster was "removed" from the CISPES investigation. Though Webster knew of its existence, said Revell, he "did not authorize any of its activities." Revell further claimed that "The case never rose to the level that it require the Director's approval or review."

The incident was telling and revealed something of a news repair process similar to the one described in chapter six. Once again, journalists from the mainstream news media seemed eager to employ selective memory and deletion of fact (beyond the FBI's deletions of another sort with the FOIA request).

Retrieving History

Webster told the House Judiciary Subcommittee on Civil and Constitutional Rights, chaired by Don Edwards (D-Calif.), that CISPES and other opponents of Reagan's policies in Central America were not under investigation and that claims to the contrary were "unfounded." When asked by Rep. John Conyers whether "anybody who is a member of CISPES is automatically suspect," Webster responded as follows: "I think the most important question is whether anybody who is a member of CISPES is subject to being interviewed and the answer is no. We are not keeping track of the membership of CISPES as such." Note that Webster changed Conyers' question. Conyers asked whether CISPES members automatically become a "suspect." Webster changed it to "being interviewed." Webster also added "as such" at the end of the last sentence. Webster's testimony was given less than a year after he had sent the memo to Jacksonville authorizing FBI surveillance on the campus of a major state university and praising that office for its aggressive manner. Revell's claim that Webster and the rest of the FBI hierarchy was unaware of the details of the CISPES investigation may be correct, but serious questions remain.

Edward's committee held hearings to investigate the possibility that the FBI might in some way have been connected with the break-ins of Central American refugee sanctuary churches and Reagan administration Central America foreign policy opposition group offices. The Center for Constitutional Rights (CCR) and the National Lawyers Guild reported ninety-three break-ins and harassment of opposition members and sanctuary churches by May, 1987. In its testimony before the committee, the CCR and the Fund for Open Information and Accountability testified they had learned of the existence of over thirty volumes of CISPES related materials in the Washington Headquarters and Dallas offices alone.

The CCR had first filed a Freedom of Information Request with the FBI in 1986. When the Bureau did not comply, CCR filed an administrative appeal on the grounds of impermissible delay. That was filed in June, 1987 and was denied. The CCR then filed another appeal, this time with federal district court in Dallas. Before a hearing could be scheduled the FBI contacted CCR to negotiate a release date. Though an agreement was reached, only about a third of the material was ever released. The Bureau eventually released more than two thousand pages of classified material to the House Subcommittee on Constitutional and Civil Rights.

There were at least two different FBI response strategies to these developments. First, once the CCR analysis of the released files began to receive coverage in the national press, the FBI claimed the investigation was motivated solely because of suspected criminal activity on the part of CISPES. The Bureau issued a statement in January, 1988 which stated:

The predication for and focus of these investigations is alleged criminal activity rather than the motives and beliefs of those being investigated. The FBI is sensitive to the constitutional rights of the American public and the Bureau has no interest in interfering with the exercise of these rights.

On January 23, 1988 a Justice Department spokesperson, Patrick Korten, told The Atlanta Constitution the investigation had a proper criminal predicate. He repeated that assertion on the McNeil/ Lehrer News Hour.

After Webster was selected to replace William Casey as director of the CIA, the new FBI chief, William Sessions, also denied the existence of a political motive behind the investigation. "The political motivation, I find none of that in there. The fact that there may be a perception that there is a thrust to the investigation, I would deny that categorically."

The Bureau next pursued a two-track damage control strategy: First, while continuing to insist that the investigation was proper in its inception, Oliver B. Revell claimed it was eventually pulled in improper directions by the deceptions of its chief source, Frank Varelli. On February 24, 1988, Revell, the man in charge of the investigation of CISPES in Washington, told the Senate Intelligence Committee that Varelli had misled investigators and that much of his information was later found to be "blatantly false" or "concocted."

The second track was to portray the investigation as relatively lowkey and unimportant, done largely at the initiative of lower-level managers at field office level. It was at this point that Revell claimed Webster had only partial knowledge of the investigation. To bolster the claim that the investigation was motivated by a determination to discover whether CISPES was a terrorist organization, Revell read a statement at the February 24 hearing which implicated the group as such. This was strongly criticized by Rep. Edwards. According to Edwards, Revell claimed that CISPES was "believed to have been established with assistance of" the U.S. Communist Party and the Salvadoran Communist Party. He fails to point out, as Edwards noted, that had such assistance been given, it would not have been illegal. "Instead," said Edwards, "he (Revell) left the impression that it was something sinister."

Revell also pursued a similar tactic in remarking that the FMLN conducted terrorist activities in El Salvador, CISPES supported the FMLN, ergo, "CISPES was somehow connected with these activities." Similarly, it was claimed that the FMLN was "a principal component of the DRU," a Cuban based group. "Thus," said Edwards, "the FBI tied CISPES to Fidel Castro, based on CISPES' support for a group that was affiliated (with) another group that was set up with the involvement of Castro."

Finally, "Guilt by ideological association was stretched to the breaking point," said Edwards, when the Bureau suggested a link between CISPES and bombings that had taken place in Washington, D.C., to quote the Bureau, at "about the same time" a CISPES rally was being held in Washington.

It is interesting to note that even though Congressman Edwards found Revell's assertions outrageous, at least one wire service treated them as news. The lead for the Associated Press dispatch reporting this last assertion reads: "When the FBI infiltrated a group of opponents of President Reagan's Central America policies, it suspected they were behind the still-unsolved November 1983 bombing of the U.S. Capital." The dispatch never mentions the grounds upon which the FBI based its suspicions or Edwards response.

What concerned Edwards the most was the FBI's behavior in its attempt to deflect criticism of its CISPES investigation. Said Edwards, My concern is that the FBI's response to the widespread criticism of its CISPES investigation was an unprecedented release of defamatory file information, suggesting links to Communists, or terrorist groups. This release of unsupported allegations, few of which involve possible criminal conduct, is a major violation of the key rule for police investigatory files -that none of the information can be published except according to established rules and safeguards.

No press source, as far as can be determined, reported Edward's comments. The Associated Press, of course, did report the bombing assertion. The New York Times coverage of Revell's testimony was also interesting. Philip Shenon, The New York Times reporter covering Revell's testimony in the Senate, referred to the "unusual public hearings of the Senate Intelligence Committee," calling "a rare public session for the usually secretive intelligence Committee." One was left to draw the inference that Shenon was informing the reader that Revell's testimony was a dog and pony show, meant more to deflect public criticism than anything else.

Nevertheless, the imperatives of "objectivity" led Shenon to treat what Revell said in an uncritical fashion. This was most evident in the language used by Shenon. Revell "acknowledged," not claimed, the FBI was mislead by Varelli. Revell "disclosed," again, not claimed—that Webster was uninformed, contrary to documentation available at the time. The reporter was passive as the bureau conducted its campaign to re-establish legitimacy. The stakes for the FBI were high. As Sen. Bill Bradley (D.-N.J.) remarked at Revell's testimony, "The FBI's reputation was on the line."

Symbolic Solutions

After Revell's testimony the Bureau promised an internal investigation. In June, 1988 an anonymous official(s) told Shenon of The New York Times that the internal report "recommended disciplinary action against a number of bureau officials." In September, Sessions gave public testimony before the Senate Select Committee on Intelligence. He admitted three points: (1) The investigation should have never been opened in the first place. (2) The spin-off investigations of other organizations opened between 1983 and 1987 should not have occurred. (3) There had been "irregularities" in the investigative techniques used by field agents. He was warmly praised by committee members for his forthrightness.

He also claimed that the major problem in the investigation came in October, 1983. That was when FBI headquarters in Washington expanded what had been to that point a fairly limited inquiry by "alerting bureau offices throughout the country to gather information on Cispes." When Sessions told Congress that six mid-level officials of the Bureau were to be disciplined, someone (Shenon doesn't say who) asked why more senior officials had not been disciplined. Sessions responded that "his review showed that others at the bureau, including Mr. Webster and Oliver B. Revell, had no reasonable way to know of problems with the Cispes investigation." As with alleged CIA involvement with Salvadoran terrorists, the CISPES investigation was reduced to aberrational conduct of field officers.

New York Times reporter Shenon did not point out that it was Revell who had approved transmission of the teletype in the first place. The teletype went to all field offices instructing them to "locate all local CISPES chapters, leaders, members and associates." Why did Shenon fail to point out the discrepancy between Sessions' testimony and the public record? The CCR had given The New York Times copies of released documents, including the October directive from Revell to all field offices. Why the Times did not pursue the contradictions was difficult to understand.

One possibility was the Times reporter simply did not read the released FBI documents and the public testimony given by Webster (and had not been alerted to it by any of the members of Congress). Or perhaps the Times reporter succumbed to the imperatives of objective journalism. The testimony given by both Revell and Sessions were dramatic and extraordinary. Giving such testimony in open session indicated an agreement to do so between committee members and the FBI. Why? One can only speculate. What was clear was that given the openness of the meeting and the aura of good feeling between committee members and an FBI director "coming clean," The New York Times was not about to indicate that the emperor, or in this case the director, had no clothes.

The leading newspaper in the United States seemed impressed or indifferent. The New York Times editorial board had nothing to say of Sessions confessions. The Washington Post declared in an editorial on the 20th of September that Sessions' testimony and the

FBI investigation of itself was "thorough, credible and generally well received." As far as can be determined, no press source raised the fact that sufficient evidence existed to suggest that Webster and Revell were far more aware and involved in the CISPES investigation than their testimony claimed. With the leadership absolved of responsibility in the public ritual of contrition before Congress, the CISPES episode could be treated as a mere aberration. As was the case with the investigation of U.S. government involvement in Salvadóran death squads, it is inferred field officers merely run operations far more vigorously than their bosses in Washington intended or realized.

The press followed suit by forgetting the CISPES investigations ever occurred. (Of course, referring to it as the "CISPES investigation" subtly limits the apparent gravity of the broad scope of targets engaged by FBI agents.) By the end of 1988, William Sessions would be found on the cover of the national newspaper supplement Parade. The cover title is: "The Man Who Would Restore the FBI." The only mention of the CISPES investigation noted that it was concluded to have been overly broad. The whole affair is put aside in this way: He (Sessions) told me (the reporter, Peter Maas) following his CISPES testimony that the Bureau has to work within the constitutional limits. 'It happened,' he said. "It was a failure of standards. New guidelines are being drawn up. I am confident it won't happen again.

By the summer of 1989, The New York Times seemed eager to complete the restoration of the FBI and William Sessions, its new director. In one of those generally flattering profile pieces The Times does on federal officials, Sessions is portrayed as a skilled administrator. The only mention of the CISPES investigation comes in two brief paragraphs, out of nineteen total:

Mr. Sessions seemed to tighten his grasp on the leadership of the agency last fall by his skillful handling of the political damage from the Bureau's inquiry into a group that opposed the Reagan administration's policy in Central America. Lawmakers praised Mr. Sessions for his candor and willingness to censure six FBI employees for mishandling the investigation.

Parade Magazine and The New York Times offered assurance that all was once again well with the FBI. At the same time, the investigation of CISPES and scores of associated organizations and hundreds of individuals was well on its way to being forgotten.

Unfortunately, by the fall of 1989 the FBI was back in the business of investigating the Central America peace movement. In Los Angeles, an FBI agent named Caldwell threatened a Salvadoran refugee with deportation if he did not act as an undercover agent for the Bureau in its surveillance of a Los Angeles church providing medical care for El Salvador. Congressman Edwards was said to be demanding a full explanation from Director Sessions.

For anyone with the slightest awareness of the history of political surveillance in this country, reassurances such as those offered by Director Sessions have a hollow ring to them. World War I saw the General Intelligence Division of the Bureau of Intelligence (the precursor to the FBI) supply information that led to the arrest of 6,300 resident aliens and the long-term detention of two thousand without due process of the law. The Slacker Raids of 1918 saw fifty thousand men arrested "without warrants or sufficient probable cause for arrest." When Congress enacted the Espionage Act punishing "disloyal utterances, two thousand persons were prosecuted under the act based largely on information supplied by the Bureau of Investigation. In 1920, agents arrested ten thousand persons believed to be members of various factions of the Communist Party. Just prior to the outbreak of the World War II, domestic political activity of the FBI (constituted as a part of Attorney General Harlan Fiske Stone's efforts to reform the Bureau) once again emerged. It is not much of an overstatement to say that to one degree or another the FBI has been involved in domestic political surveillance since its inception as the Bureau of Investigation. To treat the CISPES investigation as an aberration from the FBI's normal conduct was to fail to recognize history and what it can tell us about today and tomorrow.

Conclusion

The FBI used their classified counterterrorism FCI Guidelines to conduct investigations of those in opposition to the Reagan administration's policies in Central America. They did so pursuant to Executive Orders issued by President Reagan and guidelines crafted by his attorney general, guidelines that allowed the very sort of surveillance activity once made impossible by 1970s era restrictions. Terrorism became the talisman needed to pursue desired solutions which once again violated the constitutional rights of American citizens.

8

Media and Public Opinion of Terrorism

Introduction

Modern technology has provided small terrorist groups with a powerful instrument the mass media which willingly or unwillingly serves their needs. As Laqueur put it: "The media are the terrorist's best friend. The terrorist's act by itself is nothing, publicity is all". Several terrorist organizations realized the potentials of media-oriented terror, in terms of effectively reaching huge audiences. A study of all incidents of international terrorism during 1968-1980 revealed a significant increase in terrorist acts that victimize Western nations (though the perpetrators are nonWestern) and are directed to attract the attention of the Western media. No wonder that J.B. Bell argued: "It has become more alluring for the frantic few to appear on the world stage of television than remain obscure guerrillas of the bush". Terrorist theory was gradually realizing the potency of the mass media. Acts of terrorism were more and more perceived as means of persuasion, when the victim is "the skin on a drum beaten to achieve a calculated impact on a wider audience".

One of the most influential theorists of modern terrorism was the Brazilian Carlos Marighela, whose "Minimanual of the Urban Guerrilla" became a sourcebook for many terrorist movements all over the world. In his publications, Marighela outlined the various uses that can be made of the media: "To kidnap figures known for their artistic, sporting, or other activities who have not expressed any political views may possibly provide a form of propaganda favorable to the revolutionaries. Modern mass media, simply by announcing what the revolutionaries are doing, are important instruments of the propaganda. The war of nerves, or the psychological war, is a fighting technique based on the direct or indirect use of the mass media." The coordination of urban guerrilla action, including each armed action, is the principal way of making propaganda. These actions, carried out with specific and determined objectives, inevitably become propaganda material for the mass communication system. Bank assaults, ambushes, desertion and diverting of arms, the rescue of prisoners, executions, kidnapping, sabotage, terrorism, and the war of nerves, are all cases in point. Airplanes diverted in flight, ships and trains assaulted and seized by guerrillas, can also be solely for propaganda effects.". These views are present in various forms in other terrorist literature and publications. This led several scholars of terrorism to reconceptualize the phenomenon of terrorism in the framework of symbolic communication theory. Thus, for example, Karber suggested a new model of analysis: "As a symbolic act, terrorism can be analyzed much like other media of communication, consisting of four basic components: transmitter (the terrorist), intended recipient (target), message of violence necessitates a victim, whether personal or institutional, but the target or intended recipient of the communication may not be the victim". Dowling suggested applying the concept of "rhetoric genre" to modern terrorism, arguing that "terrorists engage in recurrent rhetorical forms that force the media to provide the access without which terrorism could not fulfill its objectives". Some terrorist events become what Bell has called "terrorist spectaculars" that can be best analyzed by the "media event" conceptualization.

Several studies revealed the impressive success of terrorists in gaining media coverage. The explanation for this success is provided by Bell: "These new transactional gunmen are, in fact, television producers constructing a package so spectacular, so violent, so compelling that the networks, acting as executives, supplying the cameraman and the audience, cannot refuse the offer". Terrorist events are often so newsworthy that the media cannot ignore them. In their analysis of newsworthiness, Galtung and Ruge list twelve indicators claiming that the higher the total score of an event on these predictors, the higher the probability that it would become news. Their list included factors such as: intensity, unexpectedness, unambiguity, scarcity, reference to elite nations and/or elite people, personification, and events of negative nature. It is quite clear that many terrorist events meet, or are preplanned to meet, these conditions. However, most of the studies focused on amount of coverage as a measure of terrorism's success and not on the effects of this coverage on public opinion.

Terrorism and Media Effects

The lack of studies on the effects of mass-mediated terrorism may be partly explained by the theoretical and methodological complexity of conceptualizing and measuring media effects. Traditional scholarship on this subject has been divided between the "powerful media" paradigm, arguing major media effects, and the "weak media" paradigm which holds that media effects are minimal. Early empirical research on the effectiveness of the media was dominated by the image of an omnipotent media and a mass society. Society was believed to consist of atomized individuals, unconnected to each other and vulnerable to the suggestions, if not dictates, of the media. As Katz observed, "The assumption was that the media would operate totally (on every eye and ear), directly (without interference), and immediately (evoking collective reaction, as if from one person)". However, subsequent empirical evidence suggests that the media are less effective than was previously assumed. The flow of communication is less direct than was once thought: mass media ordinarily do not serve as a sufficient and necessary cause of opinion change but rather function among and through a nexus of mediating factors. As Berelson put it, "Some kinds of communication on some kinds of issues, brought to the attention of some kinds of people under some kinds of conditions, have some kinds of effects". Two factors were found to limit media influence: audience selectivity (in exposure, perception and retention) and interpersonal influence. No longer viewed as strictly atomistic and passive, audiences of the mass media were increasingly understood to have the autonomy to avoid, resist and twist messages that challenge their preconceptions and attitudes. This selectivity and interpersonal processing of media messages have been found to act as filters of mass mediated influence, contributing to reinforcement rather than change of audience opinions.

Leading scholars of media effects to focus on more specific effects and especially on those which do not trigger defense mechanisms such as selectivity. Concepts such as *climate of opinion, status conferral, cultivation and reconstruction of reality, knowledge gap,* or *agenda-setting* may serve as examples of these specific effects that caused, to some extent, "a return to the concept of powerful mass media". It appears that when the media are the sole source of information, and when no predispositions exist (or, at least, when they are not antagonized), the media increases effectiveness in shaping images, attitudes and perceptions. As Noelle-Neumann argues: "Consonance eliminates selective perception and increases the effects of mass media. The thesis that mass media do not change attitudes but only reinforce them cannot be upheld under conditions of consonance and accumulation". Moreover, in many cases of terrorism, the public is informed only by the media and does not have any established attitudes toward the conflict involved. Under these conditions, the Dependency Model suggests that the media may have a strong impact on the public agenda, images and attitudes. The present study set out to examine this hypothesis, when related to massmediated terrorism.

Effects on Public Opinion

In order to establish the causal relationship between media coverage of terrorist events and its impact on public opinion, one has to control other factors and to maintain the sequence of coverageexposure-change. Experimental research designs are often the preferred solution for the identification and measurement of causality since they provide the ability to control or eliminate the influence of external factors and to activate the desired sequence of stimuli. An experimental design was used in the first study of the effects of press coverage of terrorist events. In this experiment, the attitudes of subjects exposed to press reports of two separate terrorist incidents were assessed before and after exposure. The experimental group was compared to a matched control group that was not exposed to the press reports. This experiment was limited to press coverage only and the dependent variables were only evaluative attitudes.

The present study employs the same experimental design but media coverage was enriched to include both press and television coverage (separately, to enable inter-media comparison), and the impact was measured on more dimensions than merely evaluative attitudes. Specifically, the dependent variables related to media effects in terms of status conferral, agenda setting, level of information, and affective attitudes.

A random sample of two hundred Israelis, all adult Jews living in urban areas, completed seven Likert-scaled items constituting a general scale of attitude toward terrorism. The questions explored the conditions under which terrorism might be regarded as justifiable. Scale scores, along with socio-demographic characteristics (age, education) were used to pair subjects so that they could be randomly assigned to one of the experimental or the control groups. This matching procedure was repeated four times in order to yield four experimental groups, each with 25 subjects, and four matched control groups, each also with 25 subjects. Every experimental group was then exposed to one medium (press reports or television news) with its coverage of one or two specific terrorist events. These terrorist incidents were:

South Mollucan Train Seizure

A group of South Mollucans seized a train near Beilen, the Netherlands, in pursuance of its goal of wresting an independent republic from Indonesia. The event involved the killing of three people and the subsequent triggering of an attack by sympathizers who stormed the Indonesian Consulate in Amsterdam. The terrorists were captured and given heavy prison sentences.

Croatian Hijacking

A group of Croatians seized control of a TWA jet enroute from New York to Canada, redirecting it to Europe. The aircraft made "bombing runs" over London and Paris, dropping leaflets that called for the establishment of an independent Croatian state. Prior to departure, they had placed a bomb in New York, which later exploded, killing a police officer. The media event came to an end in Paris, where the terrorists surrendered to the authorities.

These particular events were selected so that they would be remote in time, location and political setting from the subjects in question. These events are not representative of the full range and character of international terrorism. They were selected because of their suitability for testing the impact of the media on the public in situations where the public has little prior knowledge or established attitudes.

Following the design for the experiment, each of the four experimental groups was exposed to coverage of one of the two incidents by one of the two media studied. Thus, one experimental group was asked to read the newspaper *Yediot* (Israel's leading daily) from that period, with all its reports on the South Mollucan case, while another experimental group was exposed to the press coverage of the Croatian case. The two corresponding control groups were presented with issues of the same newspaper but with no reports on terrorist incidents. Similar procedure was applied to television coverage: two experimental groups were asked to watch videotaped television news programs ("*Mabat,*" the Israeli television news program) that included reports on the South Mollucan case, for one group, and the Croatian case for the other experimental group. Again, the corresponding control groups were exposed to television news programs containing no reference to terrorism in any form.

C. E. Osgood's semantic differential scales were used to measure attitudes. Particular use was made of Osgood's evaluative dimension, notably scales which possess high loadings on his first rotated factor, the evaluative factor. Subjects were provided with a list of evaluative adjectives on a seven-point scale, including such pairs as "kind-cruel," "just-unjust," "brave-cowardly," and others. The postexposure questionnaire also included questions about the importance of the problem at issue, the need to solve it, the need to report it in the media, self-reported changes in interest and knowledge, and other aspects of awareness and information (wording of scales and statements included in the questionnaire are presented in the tables).

If hypothetically the control groups and their corresponding experimental groups experienced the same changes in attitudes, then the change could not be attributed to media exposure but to other factors. However, if the experimental groups underwent attitudinal changes but their corresponding control groups did not, the changes should be attributed to the exposure. Before-after comparisons were undertaken separately for each of the experimental groups because each involved a different medium and terrorist event. The principle of statistical normality could not be assumed. The computation involved controlling the variable of general predisposition toward terrorism. A t-test for matched pairs was used to assess the difference between the "before" and "after" differences, calculated for each pair and for each scale. Average scores are computed from seven-point scales, where 1 represents the negative extreme of the semantic differential (e.g., bad, cruel, unfair, etc.), and 7 is the positive extreme (e.g., fair, brave, honest, etc.). Table 8.1 presents groups' means before and after exposure to press reports.

The comparison of the scores before and after press exposure reveals that exposure does tend to affect certain aspects of the terrorists' image. While the evaluations made by the control groups changed little, most of the experimental groups' scores changed significantly and in some instances substantially. The experimental groups' evaluations remained largely negative, but they moved in the direction of an improvement of the terrorists' image on most evaluative scales. The predominant image remained one of disapproval but this disapproval decreased after exposure. This imageimproving effect is more salient for certain evaluative dimensions, namely: brave-cowardly, just-unjust, good-bad, fair-unfair, and honest-dishonest, but not on the other scales (i.e., kind-cruel or valuable-worthless). This impact of press coverage was similar for both events even if the two events involved rather different actions, motives, and outcome. The magnitude of image improvement was almost identical for the two cases.

Table 8.1. Changes in evaluative attitudes toward two terrorist groups after exposure to press coverage

	South Mollucan case			Croatian case		
Scale	Averages before	Averages after	Matched t test	Averages before	Averages after	Matched t test
Good-Bad						
Experimental	2.03	3.14	2.21	2.17	3.09	2.09
Control	2.12	2.21		2.23	2.19	
Just-Unjust						
Experimental	2.19	3.32	2.99	2.74	3.48	2.78
Control	2.22	2.17		2.76	2.80	
Kind-Cruel						
Experimental	1.85	1.87	n.s.	1.78	1.83	n.s.
Control	1.87	1.79		1.82	1.85	
Fair-Unfair						
Experimental	1.87	2.88	2.83	1.96	2.73	2.16
Control	1.83	1.94		2.02	1.98	
Honest-Dishonest						
Experimental	1.57	2.07	2.08	1.76	2.32	2.10
Control	1.65	1.70		1.72	1.59	
Brave-Cowardly						
Experimental	2.02	4.43	3.76	2.43	3.97	3.51
Control	2.16	2.28		2.35	2.24	

Table 8.2. Impact of press coverage on the public's perceptions

	Percent "agreeing" with statement			
	South Mollucan case		Croatian case	
	experimental	control	experimental	control
"the problem which caused the event is important"	48	16	44	21
"the problem should have been reported by the media"	53	21	47	26
"the problem should be solved by international institutions"	43	26	46	24**
"people should know about this event and its causes"	47	25	48	23
"I know and understand the background of this event"	32	16	47	29
"I would like to know more about this subject"	51	32	53	28
"this is a topic I might discuss with my friends"	38	29 n.s.	34	32 n.s.

Note: the statistical significance of the difference between the groups' proportions is tested under the null hypothesis of no difference.

The next step was to study the impact of press exposure in terms of agenda-setting, status conferral and self-reported level of information and interest. Table 8.2 presents the responses of both experimental and control groups to a series of questions related to these aspects.

Since each of the experimental groups was matched with a control group, the differences in response rates presented in Table 8.2 should be related to press exposure. The observed differences between the groups provide abundant evidence to the agenda-setting and status conferral functions of media coverage. Thus, subjects who were exposed to press reports of terrorist incidents tended to see the issue as more important, to believe that international solution is desirable, and to hold that media coverage and public attention were merited. Press exposure created both awareness and interest: the experimental subjects were more likely to report an interest in and knowledge of the issue in question. However, exposure did not encourage interpersonal communication. It appears that press coverage of these specific cases would not yield public discussion or debate but rather inform and shape images on the individual's level.

Television coverage yielded a somewhat different impact. Again, the impact was mainly in the direction of improving the evaluations on certain dimensions (justunjust, honest-dishonest, and brave-cowardly) for both cases. Terrorists continued to be regarded as unfavorable but these disapproving images became less so after exposure. However, unlike the results of the press exposure, television's impact differed for the two events. Television coverage of the Croatian incident produced more change on more scales than did coverage of the South Mollucan event. There is a good reason to believe that this difference is explained by the nature of the specific television reports on the two events. TV coverage of the South Mollucan case focused on the hijacked train and included dramatic footage of murdered hostages, masked gunmen, tense negotiations, and the terrorists' eventual arrest. Given the macabre character of some of the footage, it is perhaps not surprising that the experimental group did not change its views of the terrorists' cruelty and unfairness. By contrast, coverage of the Croatian hijackers was essentially nonviolent in theme. It focused mainly on the hijacked TWA aircraft, the leaflet drop, and the eventual landing and surrender in Paris. The Croatians' only victim, a New York police officer, was only briefly mentioned. The centrality of violence in television coverage of the South Mollucan case may be the reason for the different impact of the two incidents. Press reports on the two events were more similar and lacked the dramatic visual presentation of the victims, thus yielding similar effects in terms of image change.

While television coverage produced somewhat different patterns of attitudinal change for each incident, the broadcasts did not produce substantially differing results in terms of agenda-setting or status conferral. Table 8.3 presents the comparison of the perceptions held before and after exposure to television reports.

Table 8.3. The impact of television coverage on the public's perceptions

"the problem which caused the event is important"	52	17	49	22
the problem should have been reported by the media"	57	24	56	27
"the problem should be solved by international institutions"	51	23	48	27
"people should know about this event and its causes"	44	21	50	24
"I know and understand the background of this event"	27	18	31	24 n.s.
"I would like to know more about this subject"	46	30	42	24
"this is a topic I might discuss with my friends"	42	26	38	27

Television reports were found to confer status on the problem, the participants, and the coverage itself. In both cases, subjects exposed to television coverage were more convinced that the problem is important, that it should be reported by the media, and that it should be solved by international institutions. TV coverage heightened subjects' interest in the event and its causes, increased the likelihood of personal discussion of the issue, and strengthened the subjects' assessment of the need to inform the public about the case. All of these effects are]statistically significant when compared to the matched control groups.

The present study revealed the impact of mass-mediated terrorism on the public, mainly in terms of image formation or redefinition. Boulding has suggested three ways in which messages might engender redefinition of an image: through "addition" (when receivers interpret information about a subject they have not previously organized), through "reorganization" (when a part of the image is changed by creating new meanings or new relationships in the image), and through "clarification" (when receivers reduce their uncertainty by giving some aspects of the image higher definition). The findings of the present study regarding the media's impact on the terrorists' image may be related to all three types of image redefinition. In the specific cases involved, the media served as the sole source of information and interpretation. Thus, the media can form or redefine images. In many terrorist events reported from abroad, the public is dependent on the media for information and interpretation. The public lacks any established attitudes or perceptions. These conditions are considered by the "dependency model" as optimal for the media to achieve significant effects: "The potential for mass media messages to achieve a broad range of cognitive, effective and behavioral effects will be increased when media systems serve many unique and central information functions. When people become heavily dependent upon the mass media for the information they need to resolve ambiguity, the defining or structuring effect of mass-mediated information is considerable". The dependence on the media for clarifying terrorist events and the lack of preexisting attitudes or other sources of information can account for the image change caused by exposure to media presentations of terrorist events.

The comparison of impact across media reveals interesting similarities and differences: both press and television led to image changes and heightened the importance attributed to the issue. Press reports were found to be somewhat more effective in forming attitudes and perceptions than television, while exposure to television coverage was more effective in encouraging interpersonal communication. These differences may be explained by the different functions of each medium, the audience's needs directed to each medium, and the different format and content of presentation in each medium. When considering these attributes, the effectiveness of the press is highlighted. Press reports are more detailed, provide more information and analysis, and appeal better to the public's cognitive needs. Television presentation is more condensed and focuses on the visual, and often dramatic, features of the event. Thus, television is more effective on the emotional rather than the cognitive dimension. Television indeed might be more inherently effective at encouraging interpersonal communication than the press. Exposure to television is more of a group experience while the consumption of newspaper reports tends to be a more isolated experience (a finding revealed by many "uses and gratifications" studies, highlighting the integrative function of television).

What is surprising in this study's findings is the image-improving effect. Before turning to various explanations of this specific "redefinition of image" caused by the media, it must be reiterated that the findings are delimited by the measure of short-term effects, the use of particular terrorist events that may misrepresent the full domain of such events, and the choice of politically "remote" incidents. However, within these limits, the impact of the "theater of terror" can be emphasized as long as the "show" does not trigger defense mechanisms by creating cognitive dissonance. What is it about media coverage of terrorism that may contribute to its image-improving effect? Several aspects are suggestive.

Rationalization of Terrorism

Media coverage of terrorist events must explain the motive for the cruel and brutal aggression, directed mainly to innocent victims. By looking for a motive, and by presenting the political or social background media reports often rationalize terrorism. Keeping in mind that terrorists are often motivated by a true political, social, or cultural grievance, this reasoning done by reporters, media analysts and, as it often happens, the terrorists themselves when being interviewed, may lead to sympathy and identification.

Labeling of Terrorism

Terrorists are dubbed with a rich variety of labels, ranging from murderers to freedom fighters. Some of these labels are loaded with positive values (e.g., liberation movement, popular front, freedom fighters) that may affect the image and attitudes held by a public unacquainted with the issue.

Terrorists as "Underdogs"

Coverage of terrorist events often highlight the unequal ratio of the small group of terrorists up against many security forces, counterterrorist units, snipers and police, heavily armed with sophisticated weaponry. The fact that most terrorists are ready to sacrifice their lives (and in fact most terrorist attacks leave the terrorist injured or killed), may further enhance the image of the desperate "underdogs."

"Stockholm Syndrome" of the Media

Victims of terrorist attacks, especially in cases of kidnapping, were sometimes found to associate themselves with the terrorists and their motives and even to help them (for a collection of studies on this syndrome). This phenomenon, named after a case in Stockholm, Sweden, was partially explained by the victim's surprise to find unexpected humanity in the terrorist. The mass media, which tend to focus on these unexpected terrorist behaviors (human gestures like release of a pregnant woman, stroking the head of a crying child, or giving a helping hand to a frightened elderly hostage), may be themselves subjects of this Stockholm Syndrome, carrying it to their huge audiences.

9

Media's Influence on Terrorism

Introduction

The problem of distortion normally abounds in the processing and dissemination of any information. This major problem and others are passed from the communicator to the consumer of information. In the case of the media's coverage of political terrorists, the end result could be the formation of erroneous perceptions by the public.

It should be recognized that the modern media, while seemingly a giant impersonal apparatus, is indeed composed of individual persons, each seeking to achieve personal aims, and each susceptible to human failings. The transfer of information by the media to their audience is, in its basic essence, the communicating of information from one human being to another. All the frailties and failings of humanity are involved in this process. As a simplistic example, the recipient is subjected to the interpretation of the information by the communicator, which may or may not be factual, and at best reflects the values and biases of the communicator.

The numerous difficulties involved in the accurate transmission of information have plagued literally every profession, and studies in this area are voluminous. A review of the literature allows one to more directly focus on those communications issues of importance in the media's coverage of terrorism. Prominent among processing and dissemination issues is the media's portrayal of terrorists and their atrocities.

Importance of the Media's Portrayal of Terrorism

In democratic societies with political systems based on plurality, the public's perception of events may determine which policy alternatives are available to the government. To the extent that the images of political terrorism, as portrayed by the media, affect the public's perception, those images are of significant concern to the society as a whole. The importance of this issue has been illuminated by the Task Force on Disorders and Terrorism of the U.S. National Advisory Committee on Criminal Justice Standards and Goals: "Depictions of incidents of extraordinary violence in the mass media are significant influence on public fears and expectations."

In discussing the importance of the public's perception of terrorists and their atrocities, Miller has centered on the proposition that sensational terrorist acts publicized by the media can make the public so amazed at the terrorists' description of reality that it will question its own assumptions of morality and the political system. For Miller, such a redefinition of values holds the seeds of revolution. If one accepts the hypothesis that the public's perceptions of events can influence policy alternatives, then it follows that disseminating factual, nondistorted information on important domestic and international events is vital to the stability of a society.

Influencing Perceptions through Labeling and Terminology

When reviewing the literature on terrorism, one becomes quickly impressed with the semantic problems of labeling and terminology that apply directly to the media's influence on the public's perceptions. Biased images and false perceptions can be created as simply as with a choice of words. Referring to a group involved in political violence as "guerrilla" imparts an image far different than referring to it as "terrorist." Guerrilla is the term for irregular armed forces involved in political violence through the conduct of combat operations against military targets, whereas terrorists do not attack the military strength of their political opposition but rather hit symbolic targets that are most often innocents. Similarly, referring to the killing of a person during an act of political violence as an execution imparts a far different image than if it is referred to as a murder. If the news media choose terminology provided by the terrorists, they may inadvertently transmit terrorist arguments sympathetically to the public.

A review of media broadcasts and publications, as well as scholarly texts on the subject of terrorism, shows a remarkably casual interchanging of the terms atrocity, incident, act, event, and attack. It is perhaps worth noting that the media and scholars writing in England, Italy, West Germany, and Israel countries where the realities of terrorist violence may have more personal meaning tend to describe terrorist violence more as atrocities rather than simply as events or acts. British journalist Nicholas Ashford has also observed that the British press normally refer to the IRA as terrorists and the PLO as guerrillas: "But the IRA affects us directly and the PLO does not."

David Williamson has objected to the media's labeling of practically all violent political events perpetrated by individuals or groups as terrorism. He regards this overuse of the term as dangerous:

There may be value to a disciplined avoidance of the term "terrorism" when the events involved are better defined by older terms: extortion, assault, murder, blackmail, maiming. These are concepts of criminal behavior well understood within a reasonably coherent construct of what is and is not acceptable.

Examples of possible media influence on public perception through labeling and terminology can readily be found in the Middle East. In the mass media of the 1970s, the word Palestinian seemed to connote terrorism. The dangers connected with such labeling, and the possible resultant perceptions imparted to the public, became clear during the later Israeli invasion of Lebanon. As noted by Thomas Friedman, the New York Times bureau chief in Jerusalem, after the massacre of Palestinians at the Shatila and Sabra refugee camps:

The Christian Phalangist militia, and, to a certain extent, some Israelis, had so dehumanized the Palestinians, labeling everything they touched as "terrorist"-terrorist tanks, but also terrorist hospitals, terrorist doctors, and terrorist nurses that they could no longer distinguish between true terrorists, guerrilla fighters and innocent women and children.

Friedman noted a similar labeling phenomenon in Israel after the arrests of twenty-seven Jewish men who had committed atrocities against Palestinians in the Occupied Territories:

Some Israeli newspapers describe them as "Jewish terrorists," implying condemnation of the crimes they are accused of. But the defendants' supporters refer to them as the "Jewish underground," a term that evokes images of the underground that fought for Israel's independence in the 1930's and 1940's. The state-run Israeli radio has also come to refer to the 27 men as members of "the underground."

In spite of the heinous nature of the violence perpetrated by the twenty-seven terrorists against innocent civilians, favorable descriptive labeling by the Israeli media likely contributed to the Israeli public's perception that, when polled by the newspaper Ha'aretz, showed 31.8 percent regarding the terrorist atrocities as justified.

Legitimization of Political Terrorists and Terrorism

In their study of the functions of the mass media in contemporary society, Paul Lazarsfeld and Robert Merton have observed that publicity from the mass media in and of itself confers status. Through coverage of terrorists and their atrocities, the news media can also bestow status. The result, and clear danger, of that phenomenon is that terrorists committing such heinous crimes as kidnapping and murder can be transformed from common criminals into political figures. Live televised interviews with terrorists can give them the same status as the media accords to respectable politicians. The elevation of terrorists to the platform of legitimate politicians obviously serves to confuse the public about the true means and goals of the terrorists.

British journalist John O'Sullivan has described television as "a leveling and homogenizing medium." He readily admits it is "very difficult to interview terrorists without presenting them not as a species of criminal but as a species of politician." Brian Crozier, former director of the London-based Institute for the Study of Conflict, has also noted that the television media may specifically contribute to the legitimization of terrorism: "It is in the nature of television as a medium that it tends to favor the revolutionary side."

While Crozier's reflection on the nature of television may be generally agreed, it still remains for the human element of the news media to choose what information is disseminated and how it is portrayed. The aggressive trend toward sensationalism in newscasting, which accelerated in the 1960s, has apparently continued unabated. It is possible that while providing an intense spotlight for the high drama of terrorism, the news media tend to ignore the basic facts. This could justify William Perdue's critique of their "inadequate coverage of the sources of political violence, with bias favoring coverage of the high drama that gives twisted expression to those grievances."

In sum, the public's perception of terrorism can likely be influenced by the media's use of terms and labels, with a significant result being the possible acceptance as legitimate politicians of terrorists guilty of heinous crimes. News media selection of legitimizing terms and labels and the presentation of the high drama of terrorism, especially on television, tends to glorify terrorists in roles of legitimate revolutionaries rather than as kidnappers and murderers.

Dissemination of Terrorist Propaganda

The public's perception of terrorism can be influenced not only by the content of news coverage but also by the context in which it is presented. Analysis and comment have become increasingly prominent in the news media. It is a skillful exercise for which, especially in the United States, network news stars are paid high salaries. Such handling of the news should be expected in societies with free-enterprise economic systems, where journalism is a competitive business and profits must be realized in order to continue operations. Basically, news events normally offer an equal opportunity for presentation to all the networks and other segments of the news media. It is through the flair of presentation that the competing media hope to influence the public's selection of which news program to view or which publication to purchase. Using television as an example, increases or decreases in ratings derive from the public's selection of a certain news program, and with those ratings come profits or losses.

According to H.H.A. Cooper, within the presentation lies the "true power" of the media: "the ability to convey not news, but the true sense of our life and times." The potential for contemporary news analysts and commentators to influence the public's perception of events indeed appears significant: "It is no exaggeration to aver that he who controls the media is most powerfully equipped in the struggle to win the hearts and minds of the people."

An example offered by a Turkish journalist, discussing the murder of Turkish diplomats by Armenian terrorists, serves to illustrate that propaganda victories could be awarded to terrorists through media analysis of news and history: "News that a Turkish Ambassador has been killed is generally coupled with commentary on how the Armenians were murdered by those Turks seventy years ago. Suddenly the murderers become freedom fighters."

Formal Models of Propaganda

When attempting to evaluate the exploitation of the media by terrorists one is well advised to prepare for the task through familiarization with the arts of semantics and propaganda. Assuredly, by simply employing the basic concepts of business management an analyst could attempt to measure the efficacy of a terrorist campaign. However, with the success of contemporary political terrorism likely hinging upon effective exploitation of the media, one should also be familiar with semantics and propaganda, semantics being simply "the relationship between words and what those words represent" and propaganda being "a systematic attempt by an individual or a group to control the attitudes of others."

The preceding paragraphs have attempted to illuminate and emphasize the importance of a segment of semantics the choice of terms and labels by the media—in influencing the public's perception of terrorism. The literature also shows that the media may, inadvertently or intentionally, become involved in disseminating propaganda during their coverage of terrorism. The following are some of the more basic works in the field of propaganda that enable an analyst to more readily identify situations in which the media may be influencing public perceptions of terrorism through dissemination of propaganda. Inherent within any terrorist propaganda analysis model are four basic elements: (1) the target of the deception (a population), (2) the medium for delivering the message (the atrocity), (3) the purpose (the influencing of political behavior), and (4) the truth (the facts that are to be distorted). Among the better known of the propaganda analysis models is that developed by Lasswell to demonstrate the analysis of communications. He has most simply demonstrated it in two dimensions:

Communications Question	Field of Research
Who	Control analysis
Says what	Content analysis
In what channel	Media analysis
To whom	Audience analysis
With what effect	Effect analysis

Elizabeth and Alfred Lee, of the Institute for Propaganda Analysis, have developed "Tricks of the Trade," which is a listing of seven methods used in contemporary propaganda:

1. "Bandwagon": conveying to members of the public that everyone else is accepting a concept, therefore they should join the crowd.
2. "Name calling": affixing a derogatory label to a concept, thereby encouraging its rejection.
3. "Glittering generality": affixing a virtuous label to a concept to encourage its acceptance (opposite of name calling).
4. "Testimonial": connecting a popular or a disliked personality to a concept to encourage its acceptance or rejection.
5. "Card stacking": selectively accumulating fact or fiction to support or discredit a concept.
6. "Transfer": relating a concept to an existing generally accepted or rejected program.
7. "Plain folks": portraying the promoters of a concept as ordinary people, therefore their concept is acceptable.

The Lees' list of propagandist tricks provides a connection between semantics and propaganda models. Modern linguists have progressed beyond the earlier assumption that language was a neutral medium for thought expression. Some now advocate that "what we perceive and how we think are restricted by the language we speak."

Samuel Hayakawa's "ladder of abstraction" is also a valuable tool in considering the effect that the media's vocabulary has upon the public's perception of a reported terrorist event. The pen has been alleged to be more powerful than the sword; likewise, Hayakawa postulates that some words are more powerful than others. As one moves up Hayakawa's ladder, concrete words factual words upon whose meaning people usually agree are replaced by less specific words with more abstract meanings. This movement away from a shared semantic understanding creates an environment favoring misinterpretations. The phenomenon is clearly demonstrated when terrorist kidnappings and murders are referred to as incidents or events.

In sum, the analysis of a terrorist propaganda campaign includes examination of both the content and the context of media coverage. Through semantics and conscious or unconscious propagandizing during the processing and dissemination of information, the modern news media can help shape public perceptions of terrorists and their violence that may vary in both objectivity and veracity.

Newsworthiness of Terrorism

While performing the basic communication function of gathering information, it is within the general category of disinformation, or omission, that the power of the free press in a democratic society can be most clearly demonstrated. Using the label "newsworthy," media executives can exercise ultimate authority, with no appeal, on what information will be broadcast or published for public consumption and what information will be ignored.

The literature generally agrees that the media's determination of what is newsworthy in terms of terrorism coverage is governed by: (1) the media's evaluation of the relative importance and significance of a specific event as compared to other current events, (2) the specific event's sensational appeal, and (3) the particular media's policy toward covering such events.

Technological advances in communications have also proved to be a powerful force in determining what information is newsworthy. The format of "news" has progressed rapidly in the last half-century from printed word and radio broadcasts, to anchormen reading summaries of the day's events on television, to video coverage of news events as they occur. The term newsworthy seems to have been broadened to the extent that video coverage has become a requirement.

As early as 1963, Reuven Frank, NBC's producer of the "HuntleyBrinkley Report," noted that the "highest power of television journalism is not in the transmission of information, but in transmission of experience . . . joy, sorrow, shock, fear. This was the stuff of news." Perhaps as recognized by Robert Friedlander, terrorists actually design their atrocities for television: "Terrorism is quintessentially a coup de théâtre, which requires an impressionable audience for its dramatic impact."

The omnipotence and omnipresence of television has brought calls for the need to assume more responsibility for its use. As related by television newscaster Daniel Schorr: "Television has come to replace government as an authority figure. It confers prestige and identity. It must learn the responsibility that goes with its influence. That means not encouraging terrorists by giving them the rewards of massive notoriety."

The literature on political terrorism illuminates what might be termed a state of naivete in terms of the power of television to exacerbate violence in general. As stated by television critic Harry Waters, "A better question is whether commercial television after 25 years of scientific data linking video violence with antisocial behavior will ever accept the fact that it can be a deadly potent carrier."

In sum, through semantic labeling, the casual employment of terms, and involvement with propagandizing for various ends, the media can create public perceptions of terrorists and their atrocities that vary in both objectivity and veracity. Further, a democratic society's free press possesses absolute power in determining what is sufficiently newsworthy to be disseminated to the public. The medium of television is apparently ideally suited for exploitation by political terrorists. By nature, television news seeks sensational drama, with its related influence on the public's perception of an event. The news media's television coverage of terrorism is especially vulnerable to legitimatizing terrorists as politicians, whereas in reality they are kidnappers and murderers.

Terrorist Strategies for Achieving Publicity

As a weaker form of political violence than total or limited war, terrorism normally involves a relatively longer period of struggle for the achievement of objectives. Strategies for a prolonged campaign of terrorism focus on psychological warfare and its vital element of publicity. In his Manual for the Urban Guerrilla, Brazilian Carlos Marighella delineated terrorist strategies for utilizing the media: "Inevitably all armed actions strive as propaganda vehicles that are fed into the mass communications system kidnappings, sabotage, terrorism, and the war of nerves, are cases in point."

History has shown that terrorist strategies and tactics have been modified over time as the benefits offered by technological advances in the media have been recognized and exploited. An early leader of the Algerian resistance, Abane Ramdane, while advocating the urbanization of the FLN campaign of violence, observed that "killing ten French people in the desert went unnoticed while the killing of one French person on a busy street in Algiers would receive coverage in the international media."

After the Israeli defeat of the Arab armies in 1967, PFLP leader George Habash urged the Palestinians to adopt terrorism as a more effective weapon. He noted, "to kill a Jew far from the battleground has more effect than killing 100 of them in battle; it attracts more attention. And when we set fire to a store in London, those few flames are worth the burning down of two kibbutzim. Because we force people to ask what is going on."

There are several instances where political opposition movements, which were relatively unknown but had been in existence for several years, gained international recognition with the commission of a single act of violence with sufficient severity to attract the Western media. The cause of the Croatian separatists, little known to the American public, received extensive coverage by the U.S. media with their September 1976 hijacking of a TWA flight. They carried no real weapons and had no chance of being given sanctuary; their only goals and demands were for the media's attention.

In 1977, three days of continuous media coverage of three simultaneous barricade and hostage atrocities achieved worldwide recognition for previously unknown Hanafi Muslim terrorists. Their leader, Hamass Abdul Khaali, surrendered to Washington, D.C., police with the admission that he never anticipated his demands would be met by the authorities. His obvious primary aim was publicity.

Terrorist Tactics for Exploiting the Media

The challenge for terrorists in planning a campaign is to design their atrocities to maximize publicity benefits toward achievement of their specific political objectives. Four factors are identified in the communications literature as "media-selection criteria" that terrorists have apparently often considered while planning atrocities: (1) timing attacks as responses to political developments or to coincide with historically significant dates, (2) choosing physical targets with ready access for the news media, (3) affecting a large enough population and inflicting a sufficient number of casualties to ensure coverage, and (4) victimizing elite persons or targeting elite governments.

Examples of precise planning by terrorists for the exploitation of the media are readily available. European terrorist groups have seemingly perfected the tactic. A West German television editor described the coverage of the 2nd June Movement's kidnapping of West Berlin mayoral candidate Peter Lorenz:

For 72 hours we just lost control of the medium. It was theirs, not ours. We shifted shows in order to meet their time-table. Our cameras had to be in position to record each of the released prisoners as they boarded the plane to freedom, and our news coverage had to include prepared statements at their dictate. It must be the first recorded case of how to hijack a national T.V. network.

During his Christmas 1975 kidnapping of the OPEC oil ministers in Vienna, Carlos waited in the OPEC headquarters building with his hostages until the television cameras arrived to record their exit. As per the well-known quip: "Don't shoot, we aren't on prime time yet!"

Terrorists operating in differing scenarios assuredly have varying publicity objectives. However, from a review of recorded atrocities one can distinguish common publicity goals for the majority of terrorist groups, especially those with longer histories of operation. Alexander has summarized that, "relying on immediate and extensive coverage of television, radio, and the press for the maximum amount of propagandizing and publicizing, terrorists enhance the effectiveness of their violence by creating an emotional state of extreme fear in target groups."

O'Sullivan has also identified the benefits terrorists can expect to derive from their exploitation of the media. The media "help the terrorist spread an atmosphere of fear and anxiety provide him with an opportunity to argue his case to the wider public bestow an undeserved legitimacy on him."

There is nothing unique about organized political terrorists' exploitation of the media. Even the most demented perpetrators of violence demonstrate an understanding of the phenomenon. In Indianapolis in 1977, a disgruntled customer affixed a gun to the throat of a mortgage firm manager and forced him in front of the television cameras shouting, "Get those goddamn cameras on! I'm a goddamn national hero!" When the U.S. Secret Service began its interrogation of John Hinckley after he shot President Reagan, he immediately asked, "Is it on TV?" Hinckley later told psychiatrists that he had planned the assassination before news cameras to gain maximum media attention.

As per Schlagheck's listing, the media fulfill the terrorist's desires for many things including: (1) the attention of large audiences to publicize grievances and demands, with the opportunity to recruit members from that audience while increasing popular support, and (2) the opportunity to show the inability of the government to protect its citizens, since it appears weak if it negotiates with terrorists and repressive if it chooses harsh measures.

Concern about terrorist exploitation of the Western media is not confined to government or academic circles. A 1986 Gallup poll in the United States showed that 51 percent of the respondents felt the press gave terrorists too much coverage, 60 percent felt that press coverage increased the chances of future terrorist acts, and 52 percent agreed that terrorist manipulation of the press is a major factor in unsatisfactory press coverage of terrorist events.

Media Responsibility

The terrorists' ability to exploit the media, there are frequent calls for the free press to demonstrate more responsibility. However, there seems to be little agreement as to what constitutes media responsibility. Some call for restraints on the media's coverage of terrorism. Others call for what they term media responsibility during the reporting of terrorism, but few offer a precise description of what that responsibility involves or how it should be exercised.

There are apparently at least two boundaries that attach to media responsibility: (1) refraining from assisting terrorists and (2) informing the public. Between those two boundaries are lively discussions of what the media should and should not do in covering terrorists and their atrocities. For example, Cooper has related the issue of responsibility to the media's depiction of terrorism: "The media certainly does not create the terrorist, but like a skillful make-up artist, can assuredly make of him either a Saint or a Frankenstein's monster. If the media indeed contributes to the terrorist problem, it is not too much to hope that it can also contribute to its solution."

The issue of media responsibility in the coverage of political terrorism can be viewed from three functional categories: (1) refraining from inspiring terrorists, (2) avoiding participation in terrorist atrocities, and (3) avoiding tactical errors while covering atrocities.

The phenomenon of contagion, which is often referenced in the literature, falls within the first category of inspiring terrorists. There are many views of how contagion functions, but the primary thrust is that terrorists, or potential terrorists, are influenced by the media's coverage of other terrorists and they attempt to imitate or emulate them. Those who would doubt the contagion phenomenon should consider journalist Daniel Schorr's notation concerning the attempted assassination of President Reagan by John Hinckley: "As television again and again, remorselessly, hypnotically, played the videotape of the shooting, the Secret Service recorded an astonishing number of further threats against the President."

The actual participation of the media in terrorist activities can take various forms depending upon the motivation of the particular journalist. Edward Epstein has identified one motivational aspect that can lead to what has been labeled "source dependency": "The problem of journalism in America proceeds from a simple but inescapable bind: journalists are rarely, if ever, in a position to establish the truth about an issue for themselves, and they are therefore almost entirely dependent on self-interested 'sources' for the version of reality that they report."

For example, in 1969 the Black Panthers alleged that the FBI and the police were involved in a genocide campaign against their organization. The media accepted that allegation without challenge, and published the Black Panthers' claim that twenty-eight of their members had been killed by law enforcement officials. The extent to which this unverified, and later proven false, claim was accepted by the public was later demonstrated by respected black leader, Dr. Ralph Abernathy, when he also accused the United States of genocide. In reality, the number of Black Panthers killed by police was only two, far less than the ten policemen that had been killed by the Panthers. While that true fact was known to reporters who worked closely with the Black Panthers, none of them rejected the Panthers' allegation as false, likely for fear of losing their special access to information on Panther activities.

The above form of participation could perhaps be termed "willful ignorance." The U.S. news media are not unfamiliar with the employment of this tactic to gain special access to materials. During the Vietnam conflict, members of the press recorded and broadcast for the North Vietnamese staged Christmas celebrations for U.S. prisoners of war. To gain access to those "events," members of the news media had to ignore the North Vietnamese preparation of the U.S. prisoners, which included beatings and other more severe forms of physical and mental torture, to ensure that the POWs would "perform" properly at the ceremonies. This same style of willful ignorance was demonstrated by the media when they covered the visits of Jane Fonda and Ramsey Clark to North Vietnam, in preparation for which at least one POW was severely injured.

The phenomenon of source dependency, and the resultant exploitation of journalists by terrorists, is worldwide. A reporter and photographer for a leading West German magazine once accompanied BaaderMeinhof terrorists during the actual perpetration of an atrocity in Hamburg. In England, the public-subsidized BBC, along with Independent Television (ITV), broadcast a televised interview with a leader of the IRA in which he announced the intensification of an IRA bombing campaign. A week later the IRA bombed two pubs in Birmingham, causing the deaths of twentyone persons. Cooper likened that involvement by BBC and ITV to the World War II broadcasts by "Lord Haw Haw," William Joyce, who announced the departures of the German bombers for their attacks against British cities. Perhaps not too dissimilar from the BBC's involvement was the publication by the New York Times of a lengthy article on the Vietnam conflict by Bernardine Dohrn of the Weathermen while she was on the FBI's most-wanted list.

The third category of media responsibility involves the commission of tactical errors by members of the media during ongoing terrorist atrocities. For example, during a 1974 hostage-barricade situation in Washington, D.C., police were able to monitor the terrorists and their hostages through a two-way mirror. This gave the police the distinct advantages of complete knowledge of what was going on and the capability of employing snipers to protect the hostages if necessary. Unfortunately, members of the media became aware of that situation and broadcast it on the radio. The terrorists heard the broadcast and immediately covered the mirror.

As another example, during the 1977 Hanafi hostage-barricade situation in Washington, D.C., a reporter standing by the side of the building observed a basket being lowered from the fifth floor of the eight-story building. It had previously been reported that all hostages were being held on the eighth floor. The reporter deduced that someone must yet be free and hiding from the terrorists. He immediately broadcast that information on radio. Fortunately, the Hanafis missed the report. Hanafi hostage and Washington Post columnist Charles Fenyvesi cites this example as illustrating that "terrorism is a war situation a reporter must take sides and must determine whether he is interested in preserving life and helping hostages, or whether he is interested in getting the scoop."

Later during the Hanafi hostage-barricade situation, members of the media observed the police moving containers into the building. The media broadcast that the police were preparing for an assault. The terrorists heard the broadcast and the lives of the hostages hung in the balance before negotiators could finally convince the Hanafis that the containers were only the food they had demanded.

The category of media tactical errors can be divided into two segments, depending on whether the errors are made at the scene of a terrorist atrocity or in a noncontact situation. The noncontact aspect includes situations wherein the media's dissemination of sensitive information serves the terrorists and possibly endangers the lives of others, whether hostages, potential victims, or law enforcement personnel.

As an example, in a 12 May 1985 story, the Washington Post reported that President Reagan had approved a covert program designed to prevent terrorism by preempting terrorist strikes on U.S. targets in the Middle East through the training and supporting of counterterror groups in the area. One such counterterror group consisting mostly of Lebanese, without U.S. authorization, attempted to kill the Hizballah leader Mohammed Hussein Fadlallah with a car bomb. Fadlallah escaped injury but more than 80 bystanders were killed and 200 injured in the Beirut suburb. While the unauthorized actions of that group were clearly regrettable, it is also clear that the story by the Washington Post concerning covert U.S. programs to deal with terrorism in Lebanon put the lives of several U.S. hostages and operatives in grave danger, and could have provided the motivation for other terrorist atrocities that closely followed the attempt on Fadlallah. The vilification of U.S. covert efforts, and the inevitable result, was later deplored by columnist Joseph Kraft: "The intelligence community comes back into the headlines, and into the public pillory. American agents abroad do become subject to retaliation. A major asset of foreign policy is thus weakened, if not rendered inoperative. The loss incurred almost always dwarfs the wrong that was to be righted."

While reviewing the results of the Washington Post's revelations of Reagan's covert initiative, Livingstone and Arnold observed that, "If one examines the popular media, it is easy to get the impression that the real threat comes from the governments grappling with the complex threat posed by terrorism rather than from the terrorists."

In sum, the question of media responsibility involves inspiring terrorists to commit atrocities and encouraging violence-prone individuals to become terrorists. It also involves media association with terrorists as sources of information. Further, tactical errors by the media can endanger the lives of hostages, potential victims, and others. To more fully comprehend how such situations can develop, consider Miller's description of the media's motivation in the coverage of terrorism.

Terrorist episodes, especially hostage situations, are made of the stuff that sells copy. They are dramatic and violent, and life hangs in the balance. The pendulum of decision making swings back and forth: demand, counterdemand, give and take. There is the human interest element, the anxiety-ridden relatives waiting for fate to make its move. Whose loved ones will survive and whose will perish? In such situations there is pressure for a scoop, for some new angle, for an exclusive interview with the perpetrators. The journalistic rewards are great, and these sometimes take precedence over common sense and concern for the life and welfare of the victims.

Myth of a Symbiotic Relationship

The media's performance during such crises as the November 1979 seizure of the American embassy in Tehran or the June 1985 hijacking of TWA Flight 847 has prompted numerous academicians, journalists, and government officials to declare that a state of symbiosis exists between the media and terrorists. There are numerous descriptions of this reportedly mutually beneficial relationship. As observed by Miller: "Terrorism is dependent on publicity. Terrorists need public attention, newspeople need news."

For a state of symbiosis to exist between dissimilar organisms both must derive advantages. This mutually advantageous association distinguishes symbiosis from parasitism. To evaluate the relationship between the media and terrorists, their environments and organic functions must be considered.

A free press operating in the marketplace of a liberal democratic society must make a profit to survive. This profitability factor applies on an individual basis to the numerous firms comprising the media of a democracy and is of overriding importance to each of them in the short term. Terrorist atrocities, an attractive source of sensational coverage, sell the news and provide these crucial short-term profits. However, the long-term principal concern of the media as a whole is the survival of their host society. Without the personal freedoms guaranteed by liberal democratic laws, none of the individual firms could operate and the free press would cease to exist.

Political terrorists targeting the governments and citizens of liberal democratic societies seek the destruction of those societies. As explained in previous chapters, media coverage can be a powerful force in creating the environment of fear critical to terrorist achievement of that goal. Individual firms of a free press gain the advantage of profitability and economic survival by sensationalizing terrorist atrocities, and their coverage also contributes to terrorist success. Unfortunately, continued terrorist success, enhanced by media coverage, leads to the ultimate goal of the political terrorist the destruction of the target society. In the short term, both the terrorists and individual media firms gain advantages, but in the long run, when the terrorists gain their ultimate political goal, the free press, as part of the host society, is destroyed as well. The short-term symbiotic relationship has run its course and the true longterm parasitic nature is revealed.

Almost without exception, the literature's numerous illustrations of the alleged symbiotic relationship are limited to the near term. None extend their investigation into the long term. Such an investigation of the demise of democracy in Uruguay demonstrates that, when nurtured by the media, a terrorist campaign can indeed result in the destruction of the host democratic society and its free press along with it. The originators of the Uruguayan Tupamaros terrorist campaign were intellectuals with a demonstrated appreciation for the value of publicity. They skillfully exploited the Uruguayan and international media. The press initially viewed the Tupamaros sympathetically and contributed to an environment within which the Tupamaros could expand their operations while becoming more effective. As the Tupamaros intensified their violent opposition to the duly-elected government, media coverage of their atrocities contributed to the creation of an atmosphere of fear. Government authorities responded with counterterror policies that increasingly repressed individual rights. Loss of individual freedoms brought a loss of popular support for the government and, in the chaos of fear and repression, a military coup succeeded. The formerly democratic government was ousted by an authoritarian military regime under which democracy and the free press both disappeared. The Tupamaros had achieved an ultimate terrorist goal of destroying the target society. Unfortunately for the Tupamaros, the military regime later demonstrated that political terrorists opposed to a powerful authoritarian government will not long survive.

Miller has also warned of the eventual demise of a democratic society's media when intensive coverage of atrocities provides continued support to terrorists. Choices must be made "between the media's right to disseminate information and a society's right to exist." The often-declared symbiotic relationship between the media and terrorists, when viewed in its entirety, is a myth. The correct label for that relationship is parasitic, not symbiotic.

10

Media Coverage of Osama Ben Laden

Introduction

Osama ben Laden has become a global cult figure, status symbol, and fashion icon. During a field trip to the Southern Thai province of Satun in late 2002, we chanced upon a Thai-Muslim T-shirt and poster vendor who was selling T-shirts with the image of Osama printed on them. Next to the Osama T-shirts hung another one that carried the image of the equally gruff and macho-looking Che Guevara. We asked the vendor who he thought Guevara was. His reply (and it may well have been an honest one) was: 'Osama's brother of course'. Globalization has created a global village and the village market is a riot of floating signifiers and symbols.

That we now live in a globalized world is a fact that no society can deny or reject. Globalization has made its presence felt in even the remotest corners of the world and today it can no longer be said that there exist any localities that are truly insular. The boundaries of time and space have collapsed and the parochial is now a thing of the past. The multiple geographies and epistemologies of the world are now in close proximity (if not overlapping) with each other. The global has become localized, as the local has become globalized.

This chapter sets out to examine the complex developments that took place in Malaysia in the wake of the September 11 terrorist attacks on New York and the Pentagon in the United States. In particular it aims to study the ways and means through which the events in the United States were seen, understood, and recontextualized in the local Malaysian context by the two main Malay-Muslim parties in the country, the ruling United Malays Nationalist Organization (UMNO) Party and the main Malay-Muslim opposition Pan-Malaysian Islamist party (PAS).

We intend to assess the impact of globalization on local political and cultural spheres, and how events in one part of the world can have long-term cons equences for others if and when they are recontextualized and adapted to local needs according to the idiom of the locally specific. Our thesis is that the events of September 11 - occurring as they did in a country that is a superpower and whose hegemonic grip on the rest of the globe is undeniable - had an indirect impact on other localities far away. The locality in question here is the discursive and political terrain of Malaysia, and the events of September 11 were interpreted and used by both UMNO and PAS as a trigger for further political mobilization on the local level. The success of these parties' tactics depended, however, on their reading of the event itself and how it was going to be interpreted by the local Malaysian public - which happens to be a highly complex and heterodox constituency divided along cleavages of race, ethnicity, religion, and class.

11 September and after: how an event thousands of miles away impacted on the political terrain of Malaysia

On September 11, 2001, an event that took place on the other side of the world became the latest unforeseen variable to shape the political terrain of Malaysia. In the early hours of that September morning, the twin towers of the World Trade Center (WTC) in New York were rammed by two airliners hijacked by unknown individuals. Minutes later, both towers collapsed to the ground, killing thousands who were still trapped in them. Reports then came of a third airliner that had crashed into the Pentagon building, and a fourth that was intercepted and shot down before it could reach its intended target - the White House. To bring home the reality of the events that took place thousands of miles away, the Kuala Lumpur

Commercial Centre (KLCC) twin towers were evacuated the following day, after a bomb scare that came just as Malaysians were coming to terms with the loss of Malaysian workers who were missing or killed in the New York attacks.

As the events following the aftermath of the attack were broadcast all over the world by American media channels like CNN, emotions ran high. A shocked and bewildered American public soon became angry, frustrated, and vengeful. Adding fuel to the fire were the American media that immediately pointed a finger of accusation to Islamist militant movements and, according to their critics, the Muslim world at large. The editorials of American newspapers were quick to condemn what they regarded as the 'international menace' of Islamic fundamentalism and scores of experts were roused from their academic slumber to comment on the danger posed by the new 'Islamist international' that was poised to take over the free world.

The paranoia and xenophobia stoked by the media was soon echoed by the establishment itself. The US government responded with calls for revenge and retribution, and in the days that followed the President of the United States, George W. Bush, vowed that those responsible for the attacks would be made to pay and that the United States will lead the new global 'Crusade' against terrorism - an unfortunate choice of words that only added to the confusion and anxiety of the time.

Coming as it did at a time when practically every single government in the Muslim world was faced with institutional crises, economic collapse, and/or a credibility deficit, the event of September 11 forced the political elite of the Muslim world to take sides. This fact was driven home by the President of the United States himself, who bluntly stated that 'you are either with us or with the terrorists'. Overnight, the monochromatic oppositional dialectics of the Huntingtonian thesis had been turned into a reality, and the Muslim world was forced to live with the consequences.

By the third day after the attacks, a clearer picture had begun to emerge: Both the CIA and FBI laid the blame for the attacks on the Saudi dissident-turned-fugitive Osama ben Laden and his al-Qaeda group that was based in Afghanistan. The fact that Osama was based in Afghanistan also meant that the Taliban regime there was brought into the picture. By drawing a link between the attacks and Osama and the Taliban, the US authorities had given the impression that the problem they were facing was one of global proportions. The FBI and CIA claimed that Osama ben Laden's al-Qaeda network stretched from the United States to Southeast Asia.

The US establishment was clearly trying to give the impression that this was a global problem that was not confined to the United States alone. Numerous experts in public relations were drafted to the cause and given the task of helping the Bush Administration get its message across to a wider audience. But the declaration of a 'global crusade' against 'Islamic terrorism' had only succeeded in antagonizing vast sections of the global Muslim community when it was the last thing the United States needed to do. The inept handling of the complex and sensitive matter of cooperation with Muslim governments also helped to ignite local tensions that had been simmering under the surface in many of the Muslim countries. The first to suffer were the governments of countries like Pakistan, Bangladesh, India, Indonesia, and the Philippines, all of which were facing growing unrest thanks to the activities of local Islamist opposition movements within their own borders.

Pakistan's government under General-turned-President Pervez Musharraf was brought into the US-led coalition as its most problematic and reluctant partner with the use of a somewhat oversized carrot and an overly endowed stick. Promises of economic aid and a cancellation of outstanding loans were coupled with threats of even more comprehensive sanctions and international isolation should the Pakistani government fail to comply with the demands of Washington. In time, Islamabad agreed, but not without paying a heavy price in the form of massive demonstrations and violent protests in all the major cities of the country, courtesy of Islamist parties like Jama'at-e Islami (JI) and Jamiat'ul Ulama-e Islam (JUI). To compound matters further, Pakistan's entry into the US-led coalition, reluctant though it was, infuriated many senior leaders of the armed forces and intelligence services who had been working with the Taliban and the numerous Jihadi and mujahideen groupings in the country all along.

In neighboring Indonesia, groups like the Front Pembela Islam and Lashkar Jihad were immediately mobilized and took to the streets as soon as the United States announced its unilateral move to confront its foes abroad. But like Pakistan, Indonesia was also caught in dire straits of its own. The country's President Megawati Sukarnoputri flew to Washington to discuss the implications of Indonesia's involvement in the international campaign against Osama ben Laden and the Taliban, though it was soon clear that the sensitive matter of Indonesia's spiraling debt problem was also put on the agenda. Realpolitik considerations aside, the Islamist parties and movements in Indonesia were less pragmatic in their approach to the problem. The Indonesian president was warned by the country's Islamist groups (and members of her own government) that any attempt to appease the Americans would lead to a backlash at home with heavy political costs.

The Philippines was likewise forced to deal with a backlash from Islamist groups and movements in the troubled island province of Mindanao in the south. Soon after the American response was made known to the international community, the Abu Sayyaf group renewed its attacks on Filipino government installations and outposts all over the province, and a new wave of hostage taking was soon on the way. (As the crisis developed, hysteria and paranoia quickly overcame the redoubt of reason and common sense. There were even suggestions that Osama, like some Saudi Pimpernel, had somehow managed to escape from his lair in Afghanistan and was now in hiding with the Abu Sayyaf in the lush tropical undergrowth of Mindanao.)

The September 11 attacks thus had many long-term and far-flung consequences for Muslim and non-Muslim relations. For the countries in Asia with sizeable Muslim minorities, it opened up old wounds after decades of internal civil conflict, and served as a justification for clamping down on local Muslim resistance movements. Worse still, the fear of Islamic militancy was exploited by some as a convenient way to whip up anti-Muslim sentiment, disguised as part of the now-global 'War on Terror'. In Southeast Asia the worst affected countries were the Philippines - where fears of renewed militancy on the part of Islamist movements in the south were intensified - and Indonesia, which experienced its own national tragedy with the bombing of tourist spots in Bali that only contributed to the weakening of its tattered economy. Like its neighbors Indonesia and the Philippines, Malaysia was likewise drawn into the fray at the least opportune moment.

Jihad comes home: the Pan-Malaysian Islamic Party's reaction to the US-led campaign against Osama ben Laden and the Taliban

Any number of people can use (Islam) for their own objectives. The main thing for them is to gain power. We are going to be faced with this problem for a long time. We know that we in Malaysia are vulnerable to such forms of extremism, like every other country in the world. Every one of us is vulnerable.

The attacks on New York that took place on September 11 caught the Malaysian government by surprise. For the government of Dr. Mahathir, it would be yet another unsolicited external variable that would have to be dealt with in the same way like the Iranian Revolution, the Soviet invasion of Afghanistan, the Salman Rushdie *Satanic Verses* controversy, the Gulf War, the Bosnian conflict, and the war in Chechnya. Then, as now, external variables such as these had only forced the stakes in the Islamization contest between the state and the Islamist opposition, and widened the gulf between UMNO and PAS.

The Afghan conflict of the 1980s, for instance, compelled the UMNO-led Malaysian government to commit itself to a pro-Islamic stand thanks to pressure from the Islamist opposition parties and movements at home. It was during this time that we begin to get the first reports of Malaysians going to Pakistan to join the ranks of the Afghan mujahideen. Most of them traveled from Malaysia to Islamabad or Karachi and then to Peshawar, then on to recruitment and training camps in the tribal areas along the North West Frontier Province (NWFP) before entering Afghanistan. It was well known that a number of young PAS members and supporters had become involved in militant activities outside the country by then. Some of the more committed members of the party (like C. N. Al-Afghani and Fauzi Ismail) had actually left the country in order to train as mujahideen in places like Peshawar in Pakistan. The deaths of young men like Fauzi Ismail and Abdul Aziz Samad in battlefields far away added to PAS's image as a party that was committed to the struggle of Islam and the jihad against its enemies. UMNO could only fight a rearguard action against the encroachment of the Islamists on their primary constituency, the Malay-Muslims.

But the Islamization race between UMNO and PAS that was being accelerated thanks to external variable factors such as these only contributed to the inflation of Islamist discourse in the country and the raising of the level of public expectations. During the Bosnian conflict the Malaysian government played a leading role in voicing the concerns of the Muslim community worldwide. But by the time of the Chechnyan conflict, the government's vigorous defense of Muslims abroad was comparatively dampened thanks to the growing influence of Islamic radicalism in its own backyard.

Even before the attacks on September 11, 2001, the Malaysian government was already taking the threat of growing Islamist militancy in Malaysia seriously. Political leaders, senior members of government, and heads of the state's security services were openly discussing the problem of growing militancy among some sections of Malaysian society, particularly the younger generation of Malay-Muslims, returning students from abroad, and the local Islamist parties and movements.

Since the days of intense UMNO-PAS rivalry and conflict in the 1980s terms like jihad had begun to penetrate deeper into the terrain of popular political discourse and these were seen as indicators of a significant shift closer to a more radical form of Islamist politics. By 1999-2000, the Malaysian political scene was abuzz with stories about Jihadi and mujahideen cells operating all over the country.

In June 2000 the Malaysian public was stunned by the sudden revelation that a major arms heist had taken place in the town of Gerik in Perak. The heist was carried out by a group of fifteen men who were dressed in army uniforms driving in Pajero jeeps painted green to look like Malaysian Army vehicles. After infiltrating the two army camps, they managed to get away with more than a hundred pieces of military hardware including hand-held rocket launchers, machine guns, and automatic rifles. The group was finally tracked down to its hideout in Sauk, where it was encircled by government security forces and the army. After a brief siege and shoot-out, the members of the group were forced to surrender, but not before they had killed two of their (non-Muslim) hostages.

In the trial and investigation that followed, it was revealed that those responsible for the arms heist were members of a local Malay *silat* (martial arts) group called al-Maunahled by an ex-army corporal named Mohammad Amin Razali. They were accused of trying to topple the Malaysian government and to overthrow the king in order to bring about an Islamic state by force of arms. The al-Maunah group was put under surveillance and ten of its leaders were sentenced to ten years' imprisonment each. The Islamic party PAS claimed that the entire episode was a government-orchestrated 'sandiwara' (play-acting) that was meant to tarnish the name of Islam and Islamist movements in general. The government accused PAS of having sympathy with such movements, but to its embarrassment it was soon revealed that some of the al-Maunah members also belonged to the ruling UMNO Party.

In the same month that the al-Maunah group was arrested and put on trial, a second 'Islamist militant' group was identified in the country. This was the socalled 'Jihad gang' that was alleged to be responsible for a number of bank robberies, kidnappings, and murders in the country. The group was also accused of several attacks on non-Muslim places of worship, attacks on business premises they regarded as haram (unlawful) in Islam, and the murder of an Indian Member of Parliament. (MP Joe Fernandez of the Malaysian Indian Congress Party). After a failed robbery attempt on a bank, two members of the gang were wounded and taken into custody. Once under police custody the wounded members of the gang were made to confess and during their interrogation they revealed the identities of themselves and their fellow gang members. The group was finally rounded up by June 7. The Malaysian authorities then revealed that most of the members of the gang had participated in numerous jihad campaigns in Afghanistan and Ambon, Indonesia. Many of them were also graduates from foreign Islamic universities and madrasahs in Pakistan, Egypt, and the Arab states.

In the following year the government had detained ten Islamist activists - many of whom were members of PAS - on the grounds that they belonged to an underground militant group called the Kumpulan Mujahidin Malaysia (KMM, Malaysian Mujahideen Movement). The leader of the group was said to be Ustaz Nik Adli Nik Aziz Nik Mat, the 34-year-old son of the Murshid'ul Am (Spiritual Leader) of PAS, Tuan Guru Nik Aziz Nik Mat. Though Nik Adli was only a teacher at a religious school in the state of Kelantan (of which has father was the Chief Minister), the authorities claimed that he had studied in the madarashs of Pakistan and that he had spent time training and working with the mujahideen in Afghanistan. Several of the other men arrested had also traveled to Pakistan for religious education and military training with the mujahideen operating along the Pakistani-Afghan border.

On September 25, Nik Adli was placed in detention for two years under the ISA. The son of the Murshid'ul Am of PAS was accused of plotting a campaign to establish Islamic rule across the region. 'Your actions were aimed at toppling the government through an armed struggle and replacing it with a pure Islamic state comprising Indonesia, Mindanao and Malaysia' read the detention order. Nik Adli was also alleged to have been planning to overthrow the Malaysian government, plotting assassinations, and sending Muslim fighters to fight Christians in Indonesia's Maluku Islands. His period of alleged military training in Afghanistan in the early 1990s was also listed in the list of accusations, but there was no overt allegation of direct links to the Taliban or the al-Qaeda network of Osama ben Laden.

PAS's official media organ *Harakah* described the arrests of the KMM members as part of the Mahathir Administration's attempt 'to woo the Americans'. The paper also claimed that PAS would intensify its efforts to show how UMNO was anti-Islam. For the leaders of PAS, the arrest of veteran mujahideen fighters in Malaysia was something totally incomprehensible. PAS regarded its ex-mujahideen members as role models for the rank and file of the party, and their commitment to the Islamist struggle was seen as exemplary forms of conduct to be emulated, not criminalized. The leader of the Kelantan Youth Wing of the party, Takiyuddin Hassan, claimed that such commitment and willingness to sacrifice their lives 'could only come from those who were committed to the Islamist struggle', and that PAS was 'proud of the fact that its members were willing and able to make such sacrifices in the name of their religion'.

In the same month that PAS members were being rounded up, Malaysia's Foreign Minister Syed Hamid Albar stated that clandestine 'Islamist militant' networks were operating in the cross-border regions between Malaysia, Indonesia, Thailand, and the Philippines. The kidnapping of Western tourists off the coast of the

East Malaysian state of Sabah by Abu Sayyaf guerrillas operating from their base in Basilan was cited as a prime example of the new sort of asymmetrical security threat faced by the governments in the region.

In an effort to seize the initiative on the issue, Kuala Lumpur had played host to the leaders of Indonesia, Thailand, and the Philippines - Presidents Megawati Sukarnoputri, Thaksin Shinawatra, and Gloria Arroyo - who had visited the country to discuss matters of bilateral concern, one of which was the problem of Islamist militant networks operating in the region. Soon after, the governments of Malaysia, Indonesia, and the Philippines issued a series of statements to the effect that they would henceforth be increasing the level of cooperation among their intelligence and security services to deal with the problem of religious militancy in Southeast Asia. The gravity of the situation was made more apparent when the 26-year-old Malaysian youth Taufik Abdul Halim was blown up in a shopping mall in Jakarta by an explosive device that he was carrying himself. His intention was to detonate the device in the shopping center at a time when it would be full of customers.

While the political temperature in Malaysia was rising yet again, the country witnessed a number of financial and political scandals that could not have come at a worse time for the Mahathir Administration. One particular scandal which helped to give the Islamist opposition the added leverage that they sought was the financial crisis within the Lembaga Tabung Haji (Hajj Pilgrims Management Fund) which reported a loss of several hundred million ringgit, allegedly due to financial wrong-doings by a number of administrators in the body as well as other major financial losses due to poor investments made elsewhere.

As if that was not enough, the Malaysian government was soon forced to issue a series of public denials in response to reports by foreign press agencies that the country had become a hub for transnational Islamist networks and terrorist organizations. The Prime Minister's Department and the Ministry of Finance categorically denied that terrorist funds had been deposited in Malaysian bank accounts and financial houses.

Thus matters had already come to a head in Malaysia and the other countries of the ASEAN region long before the two hijacked jetliners crashed into the twin towers of the WTC. The attacks on New York and the global media campaign that followed in their wake merely accelerated the deterioration of relations between the government of Malaysia and the Islamic opposition in the country. Here was a case of a global event having a multiplier effect on what was a local and domestic political struggle.

The tide turns yet again: PAS's response to the American bombing of Afghanistan and after

Kewajiban berjihad ini menjadi tanggungjawab mereka yang berada di negeri yang diserang dan negeri yang bersempadan dengannya, sementara umat Islam yang berada jauh dari tempat kejadian wajib memberi perhatian dan sumbangan.

On 7 October, after nearly four weeks of tension and nervous anticipation, the United States finally struck.

In a series of late-night sorties, American cruise missiles rained down upon a number of military targets in Afghanistan, including Taliban training camps near Kabul, Kunduz, Mazar-e Sharif, and Kandahar. American and British jets soon broke down the defenses of the country, leaving ordinary Afghan civilians at the mercy of their newfound enemies. The response from the Islamist movements worldwide came as fast as the news of the attacks was spread via the Internet.

The following day, Malaysia's Prime Minister Dr. Mahathir openly stated his dissatisfaction with the US-led attack. In a press conference held in Parliament, the Prime Minister said 'war against these countries will not be effective in fighting terrorism'. Although he was also careful to state that the attack on Afghanistan should not be regarded by anyone as an attack on Islam and the Muslim world, Dr. Mahathir did question the wisdom behind the action and pointed out the negative consequences that were sure to follow. Domestic political concerns were also not far from the mind of the Prime Minister. In a thinly veiled warning to the Malaysian Islamist parties and groups that might think of extending their support to Osama or the Taliban, he pointed out that 'we will not tolerate anyone who supports violence and will act against these irresponsible people or anyone who backs terrorism'.

On the same day (October 8) the leaders of PAS came out with their strongest statement yet against the Americans. For the

Murshid'ul Am of PAS, Tuan Guru Nik Aziz Nik Mat, the attack on Afghanistan was clearly an attack on Islam and Muslims in general. Speaking out in defense of the Taliban government, he claimed that:

The US hates the *Taliban* because the latter is firmly committed to upholding Islamic values. Osama bin Laden is just an excuse for the US, which has time and again shown its hostility towards Islam, to wage war against the religion.

PAS's President Ustaz Fadzil Noor also stated not only that the attacks were against Afghanistan's Taliban regime but that they constituted a direct assault on Muslims the world over. Speaking to local and foreign journalists in a press conference of his own, Fadzil Noor said that 'America has attacked a small and defenceless country like Afghanistan without showing the world strong reason or proof, (and) they are war criminals'. He then added: 'If the Americans are really waging a war against terrorism, why don't they attack Israel, who are terrorists against the Palestinians?' The President of the Islamist Party ended the interview with a clarion call to arms when he stated that: 'all Muslims must oppose these criminals - this time, there is no denying a call for *Jihad*'.

PAS based its critique of the US-led international effort on several premises. The first was the claim that there was no direct proof and evidence that Osama ben Laden and/or the Taliban were directly involved in the attacks on New York and the Pentagon. Secondly, the leaders of PAS argued that the terrorist attacks themselves were fundamentally a reaction against US foreign policy and the fact that US conduct in the Arab world was seen to have a pro-Zionist, pro-Israel slant to it. For them it was the United States, and not Osama or the Taliban, that was the real terrorist state in the world. Thirdly, PAS also claimed that the entire operation was linked to a broader American-Zionist agenda to demonize Islam and to weaken any Muslim state that was prepared to challenge the hegemonic might of the United States anywhere in the world.

The logic of PAS's critique was couched in terms of oppositional dialectics that pit the West against the Muslim world. Having drawn a chain of equivalences between the United States, Western Europe, Israel, and the so-called 'Zionist conspiracy' to overthrow and dominate the Muslim world, PAS also drew a second chain of equivalences which linked together Islam, the Taliban, Osama ben

Laden, and themselves as the defenders of Islam and the Muslim *Ummah*. What eventually emerged was a zero-sum logic of confrontation which - like George Bush's now-infamous 'you are with us or against us' statement - left no middle ground for waverers and neutral parties.

Things finally came to a climax on October 10 when PAS declared a jihad against the United States and its coalition partners and gave the go-ahead for its members to openly join and support the Taliban. The party's Secretary-General Nashruddin Mat Isa stated that: 'If there are any PAS members who would like to go for *jihad*, we cannot stop them because *jihad* is a religious duty. They don't need to seek party approval if they wish to take up the fight in Afghanistan.'

Soon after PAS leaders like Fadzil Noor, Mohamad Sabu, and Mahfuz Omar were calling for a total boycott of all American goods and services, and even for the Malaysian government to send troops to Afghanistan to help resist the US-led attacks.

The Malaysian government wasted no time before it reacted to this latest turn of events. On October 11, six alleged 'militants' were arrested and detained under the Internal Security Act (ISA) on the grounds that they were part of a clandestine underground network that was plotting to overthrow the country by using terrorist tactics. Five of the men concerned were religious teachers based in various madrasahs all over the country and they were all said to be part of the KMM led by the son of the Murshid'ul Am of PAS himself, Ustaz Nik Adli Nik Mat.

These arrests had little effect on the resolve of the Islamist opposition, though. Immediately after Friday *Juma'ah* prayers on October 12, PAS leaders called for a massive gathering outside the US embassy in the diplomatic quarter of Ampang, Kuala Lumpur. The gathering was meant to serve as a show of support for PAS leaders who intended to deliver a memorandum to the US ambassador (who had just been posted to the capital) and to demonstrate PAS's endorsement of Osama ben Laden and the Taliban. Though the event was meant to be a peaceful gathering, the mood had been set by the leaders of PAS themselves who had been vocally condemning the United States over the past few weeks.

By 2.00 p.m. about 3500 PAS supporters showed up to demonstrate in front of the embassy. Most of them had come directly from the mosques located at the KLCC and Tabung Haji complex nearby, and many more came from the mosques in Kampung Baru and Kampung Datuk Keramat. This was certainly the biggest demonstration that had been organized in Kuala Lumpur after the reformasidemonstrations of 1998. But this time round, the mood and tenor of the gathering had an altogether different edge to it. Many of the younger members of the party were wearing T-shirts, banners, and armbands with slogans like Allahuakbar,Lailla ha illallah, and Jihad on them. Placards and banners were hoisted with slogans like 'Stop the War', 'We love Jihad', 'Crush America', 'Taliban/ Afghans are our brothers' written on them.

Some of the major leaders of PAS who were present, like Fadzil Noor, Mustafa Ali, and Nashruddin Mat Isa, were finally allowed to enter the embassy to deliver their memorandum. Others like Mohamad Sabu were there to fire up the crowd with speeches. (At least one PAS leader - Hatta Ramli - was on hand to calm down the demonstrators, but to no avail.) The mood turned ugly when the police ordered the crowd to disperse. Just as the PAS supporters began to line up to perform their prayers (solat hajat) in fron of the entrance of the embassy, the armored police truck let loose a blast from its water cannon and doused the crowd with chemical-laced water. PAS's noisy and emotional demonstration had shown just how far the party was prepared to go to get its point across. But what the leaders of the party did not account for was the reaction that was to follow.

Back in the dock: the reversal of PAS's fortunes in the wake of the Afghan bombing crisis

The reaction to PAS's demonstration of force came from two important quarters. Firstly, the non-Malay and non-Muslim communities in the country - already shocked by PAS's declaration of jihad and show of support for the Taliban - were appalled by the rhetoric and tenor of the Friday demonstration. The local non-Malay press gave significant coverage to the event, with photos of PAS supporters marching in the streets and quotes from the PAS leaders themselves. PAS's call for a jihad against the 'enemies of Islam' clearly had a negative impact on the perception of PAS by the non-Muslims in the country. Overnight, fears of renewed religious militancy were rekindled thanks to the fiery rhetoric of the PAS leaders and followers themselves. These fears were intensified even further as a number of churches were attacked and burnt in different parts of the country. The Christian Federation of Malaysia later issued a statement claiming that those responsible for the arson attacks were motivated by anti-Christian sentiments aroused in the wake of September 11, though they did not single out PAS as the main culprit.

Soon after the non-Malay parties in the Barisan Nasional began to lend their weight as well. The Women's Wing of the MCA (Wanita MCA) organized a number of public forums to discuss the problem of religious militancy and the controversial issue of the Islamic state in Malaysia. The Vice-President of the Gerakan Party, Dr. S. Vijayaratnam, argued that the governments of the West (and the United States in particular) should 'review whatever positive perceptions' they may have had of PAS in the light of recent developments within the party itself and the stand that it chose to take over the Afghan issue.

The other constituency to be affected by PAS's sudden reversion to radical politics was the international diplomatic and business community. Already worried about the political instability in the region as a whole, the latest developments in Malaysia did not go down well with foreign investors who were already worried about the safety of their investments in the country.

Unaware (or oblivious to) the negative image that it would create for itself at home and abroad, PAS's decision to support the Taliban and declare a jihad against the West was the biggest own-goal scored by the party against itself over the past few years. By publicly voicing its stand in favor of Osama and the Taliban the party had alienated itself from vast sections of the local and international community, and pushed itself back to the margins of the local political scene. For many local and foreign observers, it was as if the veil had finally fallen, and PAS had revealed its true self at last. Despite the fact that the more urbane and polished technocrats within the party had been speaking the language of democracy and human rights for the past few years, it was now clear where the sympathies and loyalties of the Ulama leadership really lay. The image of the young PAS supporter with clenched fist in the air, wearing an Osama ben Laden

T-shirt and shouting 'destroy the American *kafirs* and Jews', dealt a major blow to the image of the Islamist party in the same way that the image of the ex-DPM Anwar Ibrahim with a black eye had dealt a major blow to the credibility of the state's security and judicial institutions three years earlier.

The situation was exploited to the full by the Mahathir Administration, which saw it as the best justification for its own policies vis-a-vis the local Islamist opposition. Henceforth, the Malaysian government's crackdown on Islamist cells and networks - both real and imagined - would receive less criticism from foreign and local observers. By presenting itself as the face of 'moderate' and 'progressive' Islam at work, the Mahathir government had managed to outflank the Islamist opposition and reposition itself successfully.

This fact was made all the more clear when the US Trade Representative Robert B. Zoellick (who was on a visit to Malaysia and the other countries in the region) publicly stated that President Bush 'was pleased with the support given by Malaysia'. The United States then extended its thanks to the Mahathir Administration for the support it had shown to the United States despite the difficulties it had to face from the local opposition (meaning PAS). By then it was clear that an entente cordiale had been struck: neither Malaysia nor the United States was prepared to let political differences get in the way of economic necessity. Trade between the two countries amounted to US$38 billion a year and the United States was, after all, Malaysia's biggest trading partner abroad. (Under such circumstances, it was difficult to comprehend the rationale behind PAS's calls for a trade boycott against the United States, which made little sense to the Malaysian business community in particular.)

The US Trade Representative was also careful to mention all the key words that were necessary for the upward shift in bilateral relations to register: Zoellick stated that Washington viewed Malaysia as an Islamic country which could 'serve the others as a role model for leadership and economic development' not only for the region but for the rest of the Muslim world as well. As an *Islamic* country Malaysia was described as 'modern', 'progressive', 'liberal', and 'tolerant' - precisely the terms that were required to form a positive chain of equivalences that the Mahathir Administration was looking for.

The newly improved relationship between Kuala Lumpur and Washington was also reflected in the new understanding between the two governments. The US Trade Representative spoke not only about economic matters but also raised a number of concerns related to security issues. In his meeting with the Malaysian Minister for Foreign Affairs, Syed Hamid Albar, the two men discussed the various strategies and tactics that could be used to combat the phenomenon of international 'Islamic terrorism'. Later the US Pacific Fleet Commander-in-Chief, Admiral Dennis Cutler Blair (who was on a tour of ASEAN), praised the Malaysian government for its help in the global campaign against international terrorism and vowed that Malaysian and US armed forces and security services would cooperate even more in the future against the threat of terrorist networks and militant cells posing a security threat to both countries.

This new understanding would later be cemented when the leaders of Malaysia and the United States finally met for the first time (on October 20) at the APEC conference held in Shanghai a few weeks later. After the meeting between Dr. Mahathir and George Bush, both men agreed to seek ways and means to combat the threat of international terrorism and to increase the level of cooperation in both trade and security matters.

Back on the home front the Mahathir Administration added the final touches to a package of political and economic policies that was designed to maintain public order and get the economy back on the road to recovery. On September 29, 2001, Dr. Mahathir suddenly announced that there was no need for PAS to push its demands for further Islamization as Malaysia was already 'an Islamic country' and that the whole Muslim world regarded Malaysia as a model Islamic state. The new budget that was revealed on October 19 was aimed at jump-starting the economy and to help medium-scale local entrepreneurs and civil servants in particular.

More good news for the Mahathir Administration was soon to follow: On November 14 the Parti Bersatu Sabah (PBS) which had left the UMNO-led Barisan Nasional (BN) ruling coalition on the eve of the 1990 general elections and which had been the sole opposition party in the East Malaysian state of Sabah finally declared that it would rejoin the BN. Less than a week later, the President of the Malaysian Islamic Youth Movement (ABIM), Ahmad Azzam Abdul Rahman, publicly stated that ABIM felt that Dr. Mahathir was indeed a 'model Muslim leader' and that Malaysia was a 'model Islamic society' for the rest of the Muslim world to follow. The apparent U-turn by one of the biggest Islamist movements in the country provided the UMNO-led BN government with more room to maneuver and it meant that PAS's desire to mobilize Malay-Muslim support behind its calls for jihad had failed. With DAP out of the Barisan Alternatif (BA) opposition front and Keadilan in tatters, PAS was well and truly isolated and marginalized.

Having lost on the home front, PAS turned its attention to the outside world instead. On November 16, the ASEAN Muslim Secretariat (AMSEC) which was under the auspices of PAS and based in Kota Bharu, Kelantan, organized a regional conference on global terrorism. The conference was attended by representatives from Muslim organizations from all over the ASEAN region, including countries like Malaysia, Brunei, Indonesia, Singapore, Thailand, the Philippines, Myanmar, Laos, Cambodia, and Vietnam. At the end of the conference, the Secretary-General of AMSEC, Mahfuz Omar (who was also Head of the PAS Youth Wing), read out a joint statement where the delegates at the conference condemned the United States as the biggest terrorist state and described George Bush and Ariel Sharon as the two most wanted terrorists in the world.

But even then PAS was no longer able to muster the support that it needed in its campaign at home. A host of internal and external factors ranging from PAS's tactical blunder in supporting the Taliban's call for jihad, the growing concern over the threat of international terror, the renewed violence in some parts of the ASEAN region like the southern Philippines and Indonesia, and the mood swing of the populace had ensured that PAS's advances had been checked for a while at least.

It appeared as if PAS's gains over the past three years had been all but squandered, and that the party would once again have to begin at the grassroots level. (A fact borne out by the local university council elections that took place in the same week and which saw PAS and UMNO once again fighting out their proxy wars on the grounds of the local campuses.) Thus it could be said that the event of September 11 did have long-lasting and far-reaching consequences indeed. As a result of that fateful attack on the WTC in New York, the face of Malaysian politics had been changed once more.

After Osama, enter Saddam Hussein

Barely a year after the US-led invasion of Afghanistan came whispers of another conflict against a Muslim country: Iraq.

By the middle of 2002 the political leadership in Washington was already intimating that it would set its sights on Saddam Hussein and the Ba'ath regime settled in Baghdad. In a matter of weeks Osama ben Laden slipped out of the picture and the void was filled by Saddam Hussein - erstwhile ally of the United States and the Arab dictator who was once celebrated by UNESCO as an exemplary Arab leader who paved the way for the modernization of his country and his people. The US government first tried to justify the invasion of Iraq by trying to establish a link between the Iraqi regime and other terrorist organizations like Osama's al-Qaeda movement. The argument then shifted to the claim that Iraq was in possession of weapons of mass destruction (WMD), and finally rested on the claim that a 'regime change' had to be effected in order to 'save' and 'liberate' the people of Iraq from their own government. The US-led initative failed, however, to gain external support and the United States could only count on its long-term ally Britain - under the leadership of Prime Minister Tony Blair and a Labour government - to fill the ranks of the thinly spaced 'coalition of the willing'.

The reaction from the Muslim world was of open and unreserved hostility, and from Morocco to Indonesia Islamist leaders and movements condemned the unilateral action of the United States as an open declaration of war against Islam and the Muslim world. Islamist opposition movements called on Muslims to boycott American goods such as fast foods and entertainment products, while Muslim retailers reported soaring sales of 'politically correct' Islamic products like Mecca Cola that had recently been launched in France. This reaction was echoed by other non-Muslim leaders as well, and the Pope issued a number of stern warnings and condemnations against both the American and British governments for their action. The newly appointed Archbishop of Canterbury went so far as bluntly stating that Tony Blair's support for US military aggression was wholly un-Christian, and that the British Prime Minister had no right to base his actions on any religious grounds. In the meantime Saddam Hussein replaced Osama ben Laden as the most visible and widely circulated image of radical Islam in the global media.

Saddam Hussein had made headlines in the early 1990s as a result of the first Gulf War and the image of Saddam as popular anti-American icon was already in circulation all over Malaysia and Indonesia by the 1990s. This time round Saddam would make a second appearance in Malaysian Islamist circles as the embodiment of radical Islamism and anti-Americanism, though the nature of the conflict - which was both uneven and lacked the legal sanction of the United Nations - meant that popular sympathy for Saddam Hussein and the people of Iraq was greater and wider than was the case for the Taliban regime in Afghanistan.

PAS was not the only Islamist movement that bitterly opposed the US-led war against Iraq: popular opposition against the US action came from all quarters of Malaysian society, from the Malaysian Council of Churches (which, following the example shown by the Pope and the Vatican, held a nation-wide Sunday mass for the sake of the Iraqi civilians) to secular Malaysian human rights NGOs like ALIRAN, JUST, SUARAM, and HAKAM.

PAS, for its part, had learnt the lesson from the Afghan conflict of 2001-2002: This time round the leaders of the Islamist party were less inclined to issue blanket condemnations against the West *in toto*, and the rhetoric of jihad and holy war was visibly restrained. Though the Islamist party did organize huge demonstrations and prayer sessions in the two states under its control - Kelantan and Trengganu in the north - it was careful not to heighten the level of tension that was already high in the country.

UMNO, on the other hand, tried its best to turn the situation to its advantage by tapping into popular anti-Americanism that was evident across all sections of Malaysian society. The Youth Wing (Pemuda UMNO) of the UMNO Party, along with the youth wings of the other component parties of the ruling National Front (BN) organized a mass-based nation-wide anti-war movement called Aman Malaysia (Peace Malaysia) that was aimed to bring together the various components of Malaysian society against the war (led by the ruling UMNO Party, of course). PAS expressed little interest in working with this movement, though Aman Malaysia did received the support of the Malaysian Islamic Youth Movement (ABIM), the biggest Islamist NGO in the country.

The leaders of PAS expressed their skepticism for UMNO's Aman Malaysia venture and pointed out that despite the anti-war rhetoric of the Mahathir Administration, the Malaysian government was still a close military and strategic ally of the United States and that the Malaysian government had agreed to set up a regional anti-terror center in Malaysia that would serve the entire ASEAN region, with the help of US intelligence personnel from the CIA and FBI. This in itself proved that the Mahathir Administration was still working hand-in-glove with the Americans, and that the anti-war rhetoric of the Malaysian government was a mere surface phenomenon. PAS leaders also argued that the Malaysian government was in no position to condemn the actions of the United States, or accuse the latter of human rights abuses, considering the fact that more than seventy alleged 'Islamist militants' had been arrested and detained under the Internal Security Act (ISA) and were not given the right to a free and open trial before a court of law.

In the event, the Second Gulf War began in mid-February 2003 and ended a month later with the fall of the Saddam Hussein government and the mysterious disappearance of its leader. By then the Mahathir Administration was secure in its seat of power, while PAS was once against back where it started: marginalized on the stage of national politics. Despite its attempts to salvage its public image, PAS's appearance as a militant and radical Islamist party that was generated during the first Afghan conflict had stuck. In the country survey on Malaysia published by The Economist magazine on 5 May 2003, PAS was described as a conservative, reactionary, and radical party with the 'fundamentalists (in it) having the upper hand'. The report also noted the Islamist party leadership's desire to impose Sharia law and Hudud punishments all over the country and their 'enthusiasm for cutting off hands'.

Conclusion: lessons from September 11 and the Second Gulf War of 2003 - the impact of external variable factors on the domestic politics of Malaysia

The September 11 tragedy and its aftermath are a classic example of how a localized event can take on global proportions and have a long-term effect on other localities in other parts of the world. Temporal and spatial orders have collapsed altogether in this rapidly shrinking world whose political and cultural geography has been reduced and narrowed thanks to globalization itself. The local has become the global, and vice versa.

Malaysia, as a developing country that is very much exposed to external cultural, economic, and political influences, is particularly vulnerable to such external variable factors. As the events of the past few months have shown, the impact of such external variables is never predictable and in the Malaysian case the consequences of September 11 have been exploited by all parties concerned for their own immediate political objectives. In the end, it was the government of Dr. Mahathir that managed to reap the most benefits from the event itself (thanks in part to the blunders by the Islamist opposition), and in the wake of the Afghan campaign has been able to successfully reposition itself in terms of not only the local political audience, but the international one as well.

The success of the Mahathir Administration was due partly to its correct reading of the reaction to the September 11 event. The UMNO-led BN government correctly estimated the sense of shock, horror, and apprehension that was bound to emerge in specific sections of the Malaysian community - the urban middle classes, the non-Malay, and non-Muslim minorities and the foreign business/diplomatic community. Sensing the growing sense of alarm among those who felt that Malaysia was in danger of being drawn into the web of international 'Islamic Terror', heads of state and leaders of UMNO in particular were quick to address the issue and to placate the fears of the general public. Nothing was spared in the effort to ensure the Malaysian (and international) community that the Malaysian state would remain on its secular, moderate, and capitalist course (even if the Islamic state debate had not died down in some quarters). UMNO leaders were careful to insist, time and again, that theirs was a brand of 'modern', 'progressive', 'liberal', and 'tolerant' Islam that would not allow itself to be hijacked by 'militant' and 'extremist' elements. Here was a case of a local political elite correctly interpreting the mood swings and shifts in perception that were bound to be brought about by the events that took place thousands of miles away in New York.

PAS, on the other hand, was held captive by its own local constituency. Failing to recognize the swing in public opinion, the leaders of PAS mistaken brought the party to the brink of ruin by declaring that they would support the jihad called for by Osama ben Laden and the Taliban. Seemingly unaware of the catastrophic results that were bound to follow (a strange and unexplainable factor indeed, considering PAS's long experience in the field of Malaysian politics), the PAS leadership pressed on regardless down a path that would only lead to its marginalization and isolation in the country. Here was an example of a political party that totally failed to understand the magnitude and depth of the mood-swing in Malaysia, among both the Malays and non-Malays. While it is true that PAS managed to score points among their own natural followers, the Malay-Muslims, their losses concerning the general Malaysian public (and international opinion) were considerable.

As the events of September 11 have clearly shown, Malaysian politics is clearly plugged into the global current and is no longer isolated from external influences. As the country gravitates ever closer to the center of globalization's orbit, events such as the September 11 tragedy are bound to play an even bigger role in the domestic politics of Malaysia. The boundaries between 'inside' and 'outside' are no longer there. The frontiers of the imaginary homeland go as far as the cameras of CNN or the Al-Jazeera network will take you. Malaysia has entered the global stage, and the world has come knocking on its door bringing with it unprecedented challenges that can never be ignored.

11

Role of Media in September 11 Events

Introduction

What made the September 11 events so distinctive was precisely the extent to which the loyalty of immigrants in the West suddenly became a key issue. Writing from the Netherlands, Ed Klute, director of the broadcasting research institute, Stoa, reported that 'In the Netherlands all satellite dishes were sold out within several days of the World Trade Centre attacks. Islamic communities have asked cable companies to relay Al Jazeera, like CNN, on the local cable networks'. 'British Muslims must answer some uncomfortable questions' roared Hugo Young in his Guardian column. What September 11 threw up for Britain most profoundly, said Young, was the question of whether 'all citizens of migrant stock, particularly Muslims, actually want to be full members of the society in which they live?' (And, as if in answer to this, two months after the September 11 events, one of Britain's Asian newspapers, Eastern Eye, felt the need to declare that the 3 million British Asians were loyal to that country; the results of a survey amongst British Asians were regarded as 'a slap in the face to all those who have been muttering in the rightwing press that the loyalty of Britain's most dynamic community lies elsewhere - whether it be India or Islam'. Everywhere, it seemed, President Bush's rhetorical question, 'are you for us or against us?', was thrown at immigrant citizens, and particularly at those with Islamic backgrounds and beliefs.

And this was in the light of the sense that they might well feel that they were 'against us'. There was an awareness that many immigrants who had come from undeveloped and poor zones of the world to the 'West' might well have good grounds (both economic and cultural) for being resentful towards their countries of adoption. It was not so difficult, actually, to imagine immigrant groups as being anti-American in their responses to the events. One commentator in the Guardian newspaper did not hesitate to argue that Osama bin Laden's 'constituency is the immigrant and dispossessed, the internally displaced, second generation migrants, refugees and rural communities which have fled from war and famine to unhappy and overcrowded metropolitan areas'. With their almost unconscious anti-Americanism and their divided loyalties, it was inferred, migrants could not be trusted to share the same concerns and sensibilities as us, their 'host' nations. And in a context where migrant communities were perceived to be turning to transnational television stations for news and information, was there any basis for thinking positively in terms of their loyalty to us? More likely, if they were watching Al-Jazeera or channels from their 'homelands' (in foreign languages) they would be thinking differently.

In this chapter, I will be looking at one particular immigrant population in Britain, that of Turkish-speaking migrants, and I will be focusing on the implications of their engagement with transnational Turkish media for the way they interpreted and reacted to the events surrounding September 11. Did Turkish migrant viewers, who were watching television from Turkey, think differently about the September 11 events? Were these Turkish migrant viewers exposed to a different kind of public debate, which then contributed to them being isolated from the discussions taking place in Britain at the time? And would members of the 'host' society - as represented by Hugo Young, for example - have grounds for feeling nervous, suspicious, vulnerable, or threatened? Was there a challenge to 'the values and norms that constitute the obligations that are central to being British'?

The 'problem' of transnational media in the light of the September 11 events

Until quite recently, a decade or so ago, migrant populations arriving in Britain only had access to English language television stations, the staple diet of the four national terrestrial channels and satellite-based channels like Sky (they had to program their video recorders for the (very) occasional movie aired in their own language, in the late night slots on the more specialist channels). As far as mass communications were concerned, then, immigrants were basically dependent on the media output of the host nation. And this restriction of access turned out to be a consoling reality for the 'host' society. In the 'majority' culture, there was always the hope and expectation that, through exposure to host-nation media, immigrants would find their way into the symbolic 'home' of the national community in which they had come to be based. This resonates with the sense, expressed by thinkers in the field of media studies, such as Paddy Scannell and (more critically) David Morley, that national broadcasting has played a pivotal role in bringing into being 'a culture in common' to whole populations and 'a shared life'. Historically, national media systems have aimed at 'articulating the dispersed members of the nation to the centres of symbolic power'; and they have done this through 'the production of a shared sense of reality, which is materially inscribed in the dailiness of the newspaper or media broadcasts'. Thus, it has been argued, for immigrants, if they want to be part of the imagined community that they have moved into, it is crucial that they come to participate in the shared public sphere of its national media culture. And, by the same token, from this perspective of the socializing function of broadcasting, anyone who is unable or unwilling to be part of the ordinary life of the daily diet of television would be seen to fall outside the 'shared life' of the nation.

This was the cultural logic of the era of national broadcasting systems. And it was a logic that came to be challenged from the early 1990s with the advent of new global and transnational television channels - channels such as Zee TV, Asianet or Sony Asia, MBC or Al-Jazeera, Phoenix or the Chinese Channel. These were all channels targeting linguistic/ethnic communities across national boundaries, making it possible for migrant communities to have access for the first time to 'alternative' mass media channels in their own languages. In the particular context of the case study community being considered in this chapter, it is now the case that, all across the European space, Turkish-speaking populations are now able to tune in to the numerous satellite channels broadcasting programmes from Ankara and Istanbul. It is possible for Turks in Europe to watch the official state station TRT-INT, as well as a plethora of commercial stations, such as Kanal D, Show TV, ATV, CNN Turk, NTV, Star. In addition, there is also the Kurdish language Medya TV, targeting Kurdish populations across Europe, Turkey, and the Middle East. These developments in transnational media have had very significant implications for how Turkish and Kurdish migrants experience their lives in Europe, and for how they think and feel about their experiences for a detailed account of this). We may say that the emergence of transnational broadcasting has put the sense of belonging to the national family of the 'host' culture into question. This has been the 'problem' created by the new transnational broadcasting systems.

In the period before the September 11 events occurred, however, the nature and extent of this 'problem' had not really become apparent. Responses to the transnationalization of broadcasting had been somewhat varied. At one end of the spectrum, there were actually those who viewed the availability of television 'from home' as a confidence-building mechanism for recent immigrants. According to this view, watching transnational television channels does not lead to disconnection or ghettoization of immigrants, but helps, rather, in the building up of their confidence with respect to who they are. This line of thinking echoes a strand of multiculturalist thinking, which argues that, in the multi-ethnic societies of today, the way forward is through the recognition of the immigrants' 'right to difference'. The argument has been that cultural identities should be treated with equal dignity in the common public space, and that minority populations should be 'given a voice'. Within the British context, which is the particular focus of my concerns in this chapter, we should note that there has been relatively little attention being paid to the implications of immigrant communities watching their own television stations. I think we should take this as an indication of a predominantly multiculturalist outlook in the British approach to minority cultures (in Britain, it might be noted, in an area as sensitive as education, state-run single-faith schools from primary level onwards have been allowed for some time now). The prevailing attitude has been one of tolerance towards the different kinds of practices of immigrant and minority communities with television consumption never seeming to be at all significant as one of these practices.

At the other end of the spectrum, however, the response to the new phenomenon of immigrants switching over to channels from home and away has been in terms of fears about the development of (minority) parallel societies and the undermining of integrationist policies and approaches. In the German context, for example, where Turkish immigrants occupy the central stage as the largest population of immigrants, we can find very critical statements focusing on the implications of transnational television for the imagined community of Germans. The most extreme version of this argument has been elaborated in the alarmist writings of Wilhelm Heitmeyer, in a discourse centred around anxieties concerning cultural ghettoization, the dangers of 'Islamic fundamentalism', and the marking out of new 'lines of ethno-cultural confrontation and conflict'. This kind of thinking has even been articulated among some members of the minority Turkish community in Germany. Thus Cem Ozdemir, a Turkish-origin MP in the German Parliament, and well known for his integrationist approach, is quoted as saying

I wish that the satellite dishes hadn't been invented. The number of Turkish families watching German television has decreased. In lots of families only

Turkish channels are being watched. In these channels very little information is to be found about the German society. We know this for a fact that watching or listening to channels which are not German leads to the deterioration of the language of the foreigners living here. It is not enough to say 'don't watch Turkish television.' It is a natural right to be able to keep and use one's own language. But, by allowing this we are also transporting trouble to this country.

In Ozdemir's view, transnational Turkish channels negatively affect language acquisition; they create fissures in terms of immigrants' loyalty; and they import homeland politics into the host nation by linking migrants in an instantaneous fashion to the country they left behind. Transnational television in this outlook, then, is seen as a dangerous development with negative impact on the integration process.

The September 11 events put a whole new spin on thinking about the implications of transnational broadcasting. We may say that they massively reinforced the second of these two perspectives on the significance of transnational viewing, confirming already existing worries about the divisive effects of transnational channels. More and more voices started to lend support to the view that too much toleration of immigrant cultural practices was proving to be detrimental. The September 11 events served to crystallize fears and anxieties around issues of the integration of minorities. In Britain, for example, there was at the time already increasing alarm following the so-called race riots in the summer of 2001 in the northern cities of Bradford, Burnley, and Oldham, where mainly white and Asian youths had staged days of running street battles. Reports from the inquiry into these disturbances - they were published after the September 11 events - pointed the finger at the segregation of ethnic communities. 'Whilst the physical segregation of housing estates and inner-city areas came as no surprise,' said one of the reports, 'the team was particularly struck by the depth of polarisation of our towns and cities, and the extent to which these physical divisions were compounded by so many other aspects of our daily lives'. The issue, then, was to do with the extent to which ethnic communities segregated themselves culturally: on the basis of 'separate education, language, work, places of worship, and social and cultural networks'. One could see how the attraction of transnational television stations among immigrant populations could be read as being 'problematical' in this light. In Britain, too, transnational media could be associated with the dynamics of cultural fragmentation and the erosion of the national 'culture in common'.

The overall conclusion of the committee producing the report was that 'many communities [now] operate on the basis of a series of parallel lives. They do not seem to touch at any point, let alone overlap and promote any meaningful interchange'. In the post-September 11 environment of paranoia around Islamic extremists and around loyalty to the nation, what was earlier tolerated as unexceptional cultural practices of minorities was turned around as an accusation of isolationism. 'Some Muslims,' said Britain's Europe Minister, Peter

Hain, 'are cutting themselves off and feeding both rightwing politics and their own extremists'. Whereas before September 11 the liberal persuasion could feel comfortable in allowing the so-called 'Muslim community' its difference, the aftermath of that critical event produced a complete reversal, with liberals coming to feel that their core beliefs were being undermined, and that the limits of multiculturalism had been reached.

In the light of the September 11 events, then, it is quite clear why there has been an increased concern about the uptake of transnational television. The availability of channels from elsewhere has been perceived as a fundamental challenge to the project of national unity, coherence, and integration - it does not seem to fit, that is to say, with the project of addressing immigrant differences within the terms - and boundaries - of the host-nation state. Transnational channels now increasingly seem to be opening up a new kind of cultural space that escapes the control of the host political community. They afford immigrant communities access to other media cultures, and consequently to alternative discourses, agendas, and perspectives. The fear, then, is that immigrants will use this new opportunity to reinforce their sense of belonging to their homelands, or to consolidate their belonging to their communities of belief and faith. This was the fear that was at large following the September 11 events.

The new world of 'us' and 'them'

What was crucial about the attacks on the Twin Towers and the Pentagon on September 11 was that, on that and the following days, television viewers from all over the world were abruptly turned into global witnesses of a historic and momentous event. In the face of what the world's television screens were showing, there was a global collective sense of shock and awe.

In that brief period of time, all television stations from around the world were creating the same sense of a singular and seemingly inexplicable event taking place in the United States. In the first days of the coverage of the September 11 events, the world's media were united in just relaying the same horrifying pictures, with minimum commentary, as if to simply bring home the epic, the horrific, and the historic nature of what was taking place in front of our shocked eyes. September 11 was a critical event, in the sense intended by Das; it was the kind of event through which people's lives might be propelled in new directions, and new kinds of feeling and thinking jolted into being. It was a critical event, also, in the sense that there were no ready-made answers to what had unfolded. The available frames of reference seemed inadequate for explaining the meaning of it all. Clearly, there was a need to engage in an arduous thinking process before any understanding of the events could take place.

But what came into play, instead of thinking and understanding, was an entirely unthinking mode of response. It was a reaction born out of anxiety and fear of the unknown. Very quickly, the events began to be framed within the predictable defensive rhetoric of 'us' against 'them', where 'us' stood for 'civilization', and 'them' for everything that was 'primitive' and 'uncivilized'. The events began to be made sense of in terms of the now familiar polarization between the West, synonymous with 'freedom and democracy', and its 'Other', associated with every possible form of 'evil'. And when it came to be known that the enemy was Osama bin Laden and al-Qaeda, then, of course, it was easy to mobilize the familiar tropes that opposed the West to the world of Islam. At this particular historical moment, of course, the 'clash of civilizations' mentality was 'in the (Western) air' - these events could seem to be a vindication of Samuel Huntington's epic prognostications.

Everything began to seem to make sense now that it could be 'explained' in terms of the imagined affinity between Islam and violence. And so, instead of reflecting and trying to understand the meaning of what appeared meaningless, public opinion in the United States and Europe became engulfed in a cloud of unknowing. Or, we might say, 'the West versus Islam' became the rigid template for ignorant thinking. This was clearly the template that was drawn upon in much of the British media. Here, in the tabloid press, you could see such headlines as 'Praise to Allah - dancing with joy the warrior race of fanatics born to detest the West', 'This fanaticism that we in the West can never understand', 'In the heart of London demands for a Holy War'. Popular newspapers could only think in terms of such polarization (which means, of course, not really thinking at all). On British television, what we saw were repeated images of the heavily bearded Osama bin Laden, the heart of the heart of the 'axis of evil'. And when we saw images of Palestinian children apparently cheering at the carnage in New York and Washington, this could only reinforce the sense of a contest with absolute evil. And, as the coverage progressed, the locus of evil was no longer in Afghanistan or Palestine, but seemed to be closer and closer to 'home'. Writing on the rise of Islamophobia in the British media, Allen remarks on the way in which the British media juxtaposed images of Muslim men burning American flags whilst brandishing rifles with angry young men shouting outside a north London mosque. Afghan women covered from head to toe in the burqha followed by women wearing the hijab protesting against military action outside the Pakistan embassy in London.

Now there was no longer any distance between us and them. Fear, anxiety, and resentment were beginning to be provoked by the 'Muslims within'.

So, this was how 'we' were thinking about 'them'. But what also have to be taken into account are the ways in which coverage of September 11 also encouraged us to think about 'us'. Who were 'we', and what did we stand for? This means taking note of the emotions that we invested in our sense of 'we' - which may be regarded as an issue concerning the nature of the West's narcissistic investments. And we should also reflect on how 'we' came to be configured - or reconfigured - in opposition to the enemy. The United States of course, but clearly 'we' was more than just that. Who or what, then, after September 11 could count - count themselves, that is to say - as part of that peculiar Western category of 'us'?

At the most fundamental level, 'us' stood for the American society. And it was emotionally linked to the idea of the United Sates as 'blameless victim', and to the powerful sense of wounded pride among the American people. This was the greatest American tragedy since Pearl Harbor, and, like that earlier disaster, there was a sense of both humiliation and indignation that such an event could happen on 'sacred' American soil. The discursive order that emerged out of this chaos was built around patriotic ideals and fervour. Americans were quickly learning again what it really means to be an American. Even a leftist and critical thinker like Todd Gitlin seems to have experienced the resurgence of American pride and national reassertiveness. 'The American people were stirred by patriotism after the eleventh, and I with them,' he declared. 'They inverted the wound of the WTC into protestation, pride, and the flag as a badge of belonging'. This was a time for bonding and belonging - and for asserting the superior and exclusive nature of the American bond. The flag spoke for the United States - it became a ritualistic focus for restoring a sense of American community. What was being mobilized was reinvigorated national patriotism enhanced with religious sensibility. Janet Abu-Lughod has described very well how national religiosity became a key reference point in the endeavour of restoring the American social fabric in the aftermath of the attacks: 'Ground Zero' was also called 'sacred ground', spontaneous and televised ceremonies took on a religious tone, icons and 'totemic' symbols (flags, lapel pins) became ubiquitous, hymns were sung. 'This is sufficient,' she concludes, 'to suggest the religious character of the response - a response intended to galvanise the society for unity'.

But it was not just a question of the symbolic and ceremonial tropes that helped to make sense of the events for the imagined community of Americans. It was also crucial to buy the rest of the world - the rest of the world that could be included in the category of 'us', that is to say - into the crusade against 'evil'. The United States needed to build the other key Western nations into its symbolic agenda. Abu-Lughod draws our attention to the discursive strategies that were crucial and necessary for gaining broader support for the American cause. What was emphasized in this rhetorical development was that it was not just Americans who were killed in the attack on the World Trade Center, but citizens from across the world. The catastrophe of September 11 was referred to as 'a crime against humanity' - all people of the 'civilized' world were its victims. And all these 'good' people were consequently encouraged to join the crusade of retribution (the so-called Operation Enduring Freedom) against the forces of evil. As Abu-Lughod puts it, the punishment was to be executed by '"our kinds of people" - in the manichean spirit of "you are either with us or against us"'. And so, in the name of civilizational values, the citizens of the 'free world' were invited to become virtual Americans. Shawcross took up and propagated this rhetorical trope in the pages of the Guardian newspaper. 'The attack on America is an attack on us all,' he declared. 'We are all in this together. We are all Americans now.' 'America remains,' he continued, 'as it has always been, a beacon of hope for the world's poor and dispossessed and for all those who believe in freedom of thought and deed.'

And so the strategy of global containment after the events of September 11 mobilized the symbolic language of American patriotism and 'American values', driven (ironically, for the sceptical among us) by religious fervour and the rhetoric of crusade. The discourse of 'good versus evil' was unleashed on the world, instituting an absolute imaginative polarization between those who are 'for us' and those who are 'against us'. And those who belonged to this latter camp were imagined, moreover, as absolutely and eternally against - against reason and enlightenment. 'The enmity runs too deep' warned a writer in the New York Times Magazine, commenting on Al-Jazeera television: 'The truth is that a foreign power can't easily win a "war of ideas" in the Muslim world'. This is the rhetoric and mythology of civilizational clash. On the basis of this rhetoric and mythology, it became possible to institute a regime of US-style jihad, in which 'deviants or persons who might be LIKE the perpetrators of the crime are also to be punished. Arabs, Sikhs, and others with swarthy complexions'. Hence, the unrelenting Western aggression since September 11, from the bombing of Afghanistan, to the widespread persecution of migrants, refugees, and asylum seekers who are not of 'our kind'. And to the point, surely, that the 'beacon of hope' mythology would become extinguished.

It is in this context that I turn to consider the position of those who have found themselves positioned as the enemies within - ethnic minorities, especially the Islamic ones, living in the West. These are people who now find themselves classified as fundamentalists, or potential fundamentalists; and criticized for behaving, or thinking, or even just looking fundamentalist. In one focus group discussion that I conducted, one of the participants remarked with dismay on how his neighbours, who had previously said hello to him every morning, had now stopped doing so. 'Everybody started calling us bin Laden,' he said.

You started to feel guilty. Your neighbour says, 'Well he's a Muslim, too, he's from Turkey.' You start feeling guilty, as if you've done something wrong. It's because they blamed it on us, because it was the Muslims who had done it.

What he is sensitive to is a certain paranoia - a normalized paranoia - about those who come from an 'alien culture', who keep themselves to themselves, and who watch television coming from the 'other' side. In the new world order of 'us' and 'them', migrants living in Western countries - like the Turks and Kurds in Britain - found themselves in a particularly difficult and invidious position.

Turkish migrants, transnational television, and September 11

Migrants were figured as an anomalous category - they might live in the Western heartland, but they were not 'of it'. They were de facto positioned as being anti-American, even when they might have no strong identification with the world of Islam. It became dangerous for them to pose the necessary questions about the September events: Why did this attack target the United States? Why would these terrorist-believers have killed so many innocent and defenceless people (including themselves)? How could one think beyond revenge and retribution? And how could one think through the question of fundamentalisms and fundamentalists? If they seemed to voice any criticism of US foreign policy, migrants/minorities were immediately condemned as disloyal, and potentially treacherous - not 'with us', and therefore 'against us'. Being 'with us' had to mean wholesale acceptance of the 'American' truth. Complex or balanced or ambivalent thinking was simply off the agenda. There was no apparent way between the Manichean positions of 'us' and 'them' - you had to have one identity, one loyalty, or the other.

What I want to do now is to explore the responses of Turkish-speaking people in Britain (London) to the events of September 11, considering particularly their experiences of finding themselves 'between camps', and their attempts to negotiate their situation of what we might call double displacement and estrangement. The focus will be upon their relation to the media in the period after September 11, and on their reflections on watching this particular media event. How did the Turkish migrants relate to the media coverage of the September 11 attacks, then? Did watching Turkish news make any difference in terms of how the Turkish migrants made sense of and interpreted the events? What did they think of the attacks? There is a view that says that Turks watched Turkish television as an expression - a reflex - of their 'belonging' to that culture. This seems to be the view put forward by Ed Klute, for example, when he seeks to explain the attraction of transnational channels during the post-September 11 period. 'Islamic audiences as well as other ethnic minority groups turned to satellite stations like Al-Jazeera based in Qatar, Turkish satellites and the Internet,' says Klute, because 'these media offer them news and information based on cultural values with which they are able to identify'. I want to suggest, in contrast to this view, that what was going on was far more complex than this. This means moving beyond the reductionist association of television consumption with the assertion of identity. In my account, migrants used the media, not in terms of identity gestures, but - like other categories of (non-migrant) television viewers - to think about the events of September 11. I maintain that they watched Turkish television in a thinking mode, moving between different language channels, and with an awareness that there was, in fact, no news source, and no 'cultural values', that they could straightforwardly 'identify with'. In the eyes of their 'host' country, their position seemed clear - they were the Muslims within - but their own self-image was, actually, a great deal more complex and contradictory.

What is apparent from the research I have undertaken is the peculiarity of the Turkish position with respect to the September 11 events - a peculiarity of perspective that comes from the complicated and distinctive relationship of Turkey with respect to both the Western world and the Islamic world. The point is that, through a long and complex historical process, Turks have become in one sense a part of both of these worlds, and yet at the same time outsiders of both. What is significant is their complex inside-outside stance with respect to both possibilities of 'belonging'. I would say that the Turkish perspective is characterized by a significant - and interesting - sense of cultural dislocation, involving considerable cultural ambivalence towards both the Western and the Muslim cultural orders. And, in the context of the September 11 developments, it was this cultural ambivalence that came into play. Positioned alongside the other 'Muslims within', the Turks felt at some distance from the wider Islamic protests (many Turks have a strong secular identity;

and religious Turks differentiate themselves from Middle Eastern (Arab) Islamic culture). Coming from a secular, EU-orientated, NATO-member country, Turks may feel that they have Western credentials, but there is a distrust of the West (and many Turks in Britain come from leftist, internationalist, Third World - and consequently anti-American - backgrounds). The Turkish experience was one of double alienation, we might say. The taking of sides was never, therefore, a straightforward possibility for the Turkish migrants I spoke to in London.

Let me now try to put across something of the nature of the Turkish responses to my questions concerning television spectatorship and intellectual-imaginative response to the events of and following September 11. I can do this under three headings, each drawing out something of the ambivalence of attitude and thought in the people that I interviewed, and showing how, as a consequence of this predicament, Turkish migrants were forced into a position of independent reflection. My aim here will be to consider how much 'identity' or 'belonging' informed Turkish people's thinking about the September 11 events, and also the extent to which their position of structural ambivalence (with respect to both Western and Islamic cultures) could be used to complicate and reframe the processes of responding to and thinking about those events. We may say that there was a certain kind of tension between 'belonging' and thinking, in both cultural and political senses - often ending up in impasse and dogmatic closure, but from time to time leading to productive insights and questions.

Identity and Ambivalence

In order to understand the responses of Turkish migrants to the events of September 11, we have to take account of their particular and distinctive position in British society, and of their wider sense of cultural location. I have referred to it in terms of a double displacement. Turks come from an Islamic country, but very many of them do not feel that being a Muslim is central to their self-image (and those who are religious generally distinguish their religious culture from that of the Middle East). They have strongly identified with Western values, but are generally not acknowledged as being Western, and often themselves have a certain anti-imperialist animosity towards the West. We might characterize their position as one of double dislocation. The Turks that I spoke with live in Britain, often having British passports, but they do not strongly identify with it and with its culture and values. They live away from Turkey, and can be very critical indeed of the country they left behind - Sunni Muslims, Alevis, Kurds, Turkish Cypriots, and leftists, most have problems with what Turkey stands for. What is apparent is detachment and critical distance with respect to both potential poles of identification. What is particular to very many of the Turks living in London is a perspective of cultural ambivalence.

This condition of ambivalence did not seem to cause anyone to suffer unduly. I would say that Turkish migrants were generally able to accommodate the different elements in their cultural experience. And in the context of Britain, where their 'minority' presence was relatively invisible, Turks did not feel the need to become engaged in identity politics - unlike South Asian and Afro-Caribbean migrants, say, particularly, whose presence was more numerous and symbolic. For many Turks, then, the complexities of identity were not a live and pressing issue. We might even say that they could appreciate the virtues of ambivalence. But the events of September 11 changed all that. Suddenly, in the context of the rekindled discourse of Islam and the West, the identity of Turkish migrants could no longer be left as a sleeping dog. The 'problem' was that they came from an Islamic country. They were compelled to reflect on their complicated relation to Muslim identity. And also to confront the complex nature of their engagement with Western culture. Turks found themselves in a particularly position in the imaginary polarization between 'us' and 'them'. Which world did they belong to? Where was their real allegiance? Their cultural ambivalence might now be interpreted in some quarters in terms of contradiction.

Following September 11, Turks found themselves aggregated into the categorical domain of 'Islam'. Their religious identity was pushed to the fore, and they were consequently incorporated into the alien world of 'them'. This was a development that produced quite conflictual feelings. On the one hand, there was resentment: many Turks know very little about Islamic religion and culture, they do not regard Islam as central to their sense of self, and they certainly do not have any interest in jihad politics. They emphasize their secular identity, and have endeavoured to distance themselves from Muslim concerns and values. But, on the other hand, Turks also found themselves paradoxically identifying with the Muslim position in the post-September 11 period. They could identify with Muslims as underdogs (as the enemies of the United States), and they identified with them on political grounds when Muslim minorities in Britain began to be subjected to racist vilification and attacks. Thus, in a discussion with a family with a strong left-wing, Alevi background, the father expressed the extreme discomfort of his response when he found out that the attacks on New York and Washington had been carried out by Muslim extremists. 'I was very concerned about this,' he declared.

There are thousands of Muslims living in European countries. OK, I don't dress like them. Unless they interfere with me, I don't interfere with them. But I thought that racist attacks on them might increase. I too come from a Muslim country. I can't go out in the street and scream that I'm an atheist. Me, my children, my family, could easily become a target for such racist attacks.

More significant than his distance from Muslim politics, at this moment, is his concern about the threat that Muslims in Britain were experiencing - and his awareness that, in the perception of many British people, he and his family were counted in the same category.

Many of the men in another group explained how they had suffered as a result of increasing xenophobic and anti-Muslim sentiments in Britain. We were discussing what people felt when they heard about the September 11 attacks. What was the nature of their reactions? 'I felt panic,' said one of the participants.

Because I live in England, among the English, I said to myself, that's it. Because Muslims are being blamed, I said to myself 'This is the end of us' My first reaction, at that moment, was to be very glad, but afterwards, because this event was linked to Islam, everybody was afraid. I said to myself, there are only a few Muslims here [he lives in a town outside London], and they're going to finish us off.

Turks in London got to know what it is like to be classified and vilified as Muslims, then. But, at the same time, they also came to be aware of, and to share, the anxious and fearful feelings that British people were experiencing. This point was brought home when we moved on to discuss the different experiences and perceptions of Turks in Turkey and Turks in London. 'The relationship between Britain and the United States is very strong,' remarked one of the participants.

Because you are here [in London], you are in danger. And that's why people here are so fearful and so confused. But people in Turkey, they don't imagine they will be attacked - Turkey is a Muslim country. For someone living in London, it's different. My aunt [who lives in London] kept worrying that London would be bombed.

Many of the women participants in focus groups reported feelings of anxiety and fear that there might be attacks on London. They talked about the stories and scenarios that their children were bringing back from school, and of the widespread fear that certain buildings in London, such as Canary Wharf, could become targets for further terrorist strikes. 'If there is a second target, I thought, it will be England,' said one woman. There was the perception among Turkish migrants, then, of threats coming from two different directions, the sense of being in double jeopardy.

As I have already indicated, most of the Turkish migrants that I spoke with were of a secular orientation. Their beliefs and values were very much in line with the modern Turkish commitment to Western 'civilization' and 'modernity'. They have been successfully socialized into the ideology of 'West is best', and are anxious to distinguish themselves, as progressives, from the 'regressive' mentality of religious people, and particularly from Taliban-style 'fundamentalism'. Like Western viewers, they too regarded al-Qaeda and the Taliban as radically 'other'. In this particular context, they were generally inclined to identify with the cause of the Western 'us'. 'It's good that the U.S. intervened in Afghanistan, and that the backward regime there collapsed,' remarked one informant. 'I see this as a positive thing, that America has been getting rid of the monster it created,' another added. They were opposed to what Osama bin Laden stood for. But, at the same time, they were also inclined to express suspicions about what the United States stood for. There was a profound distrust of the United States. In one group, composed of Turkish Cypriots, one young participant said that she was 'glad that the women of Afghanistan would be liberated'. But, at the same time, she was also expressing severe misgivings about the rationale for American intervention, thinking that the attacks on New York and Washington 'could be part of America's own game plan, to open the way to attack Afghanistan. America was looking for a pretext.' Another woman in the group gave support to this suspicious speculation. 'Those who set up the Kennedy scenarios could have set this one up easily,' she remarked. 'America has a tradition of intervening in other countries. They divided the world into two: those who like America, and those who don't. For those countries they decide to intervene in, they look for a reason to do so.' If there was a sense of distance, then, from the Islamic cause, this combined with a deep unease and scepticism about the motivations of the United States.

In all the focus group discussions that I conducted, this kind of anti-American sentiment was constantly present. Participants expressed their genuine sorrow for the innocent victims of the attacks; and many had their own experiences and stories of suffering in Turkey, and could therefore go some way, at least, towards understanding what ordinary people in New York must have gone through. But they expressed bitter contempt for the seats of power in the United States, for the Pentagon and the White House. Anti-American sentiments cohered around an image of the American state as a powerful, arrogant, and destructive force. There was a great deal of discussion among group participants about the conflict and devastation that the United States has wrought upon the world - references were made to Hiroshima, Palestine, Vietnam, and Chile, as well as to Kurdistan, and Turkey. People complained about how, despite the massive loss of lives in these places as a direct result of American intervention, these massacres had all been conveniently forgotten. The invasion of Afghanistan was seen as simply the next incident in a serial history of US military assertion and expansion. As the young daughter in a family I interviewed put it:

It was clear [following September 11] that America had a definite response. It was clear that it would go to war. It was like that in Vietnam, too. People opposed it so much. What America want is clear and obvious, it wants to be the most powerful country in the world.

Many of the Turks living in London are from leftist backgrounds, with a strong anti-imperialist and Third World orientation, and they had consequently harboured animosities towards the American state. Over time, and in the context of living as migrants in Britain, these hostile feelings had become dormant - part of their formation, but no longer functioning in an active mode. What the events on and after September 11 did was to stir up memories, resentments, and political reflexes concerning the United States. For the first time in many years, Turkish migrants (including their children) were reminded of how the United States had figured in their lives, and were impelled to think about its significance again (this is a point that I shall pick up on again a little later in my argument).

What I want to emphasize at this point is the extent to which the cultural reference points of Turkish migrants were disturbed by the events from September 11 to the invasion of Afghanistan. Until this time, it seems that the complexities of the migrants' internal cultural geographies were not problematical. They came from an Islamic country, but they had clearly distanced themselves from religious points of reference. They had been aligned with the left and the cause of anti-imperialism, but that was in the past, and they had subsequently adapted to life in the First World. What occurred in the aftermath of September 11 was that the by now peaceful coexistence of the different parts of their biographies and beliefs was disturbed. Their relationship to Islam was suddenly rendered more complex. And their complicated feelings about the hegemony of the West, and particularly the American superpower, were once again being reactivated. We may say that the events of September 11 confronted Turkish migrants with new experiences of ambivalence in identity and identification.

Media and scepticism

The next observation to be made is that, whilst Turkish migrants do indeed like to watch Turkish television, and did so with particular engagement during the period following September 11, this should not be interpreted in terms of them being or becoming a captive audience of their 'homeland' media.

The Turkish cultural domain should not be conceived or imagined as some kind of 'imprisoning cocoon', to use Baumann's turn of phrase. Watching September 11 on Turkish television by no means entailed confidence or trust in Turkish broadcasting sources, or the suspension of critical reflection and thought. And it did not in any way preclude access to other cultural and informational spaces. On the contrary, I would say that frustrations about the nature and quality of Turkish news actually encouraged viewers to turn to alternative sources of information - and when they turned to these other sources, then it was with an equally sceptical and critical stance.

In many of the group discussions that I undertook in London, participants would talk about how they routinely ranged across both Turkish and British channels, as they tried to find out more about the September 11 events. In one particular discussion, involving a group of Kurdish men, participants compared notes on the coverage of the catastrophe by both Turkish and British channels. The objection lodged against Turkish channels was that they did not provide sufficient analysis of what was happening. 'On the whole, they showed pictures of the atrocities,' complained one of the participants, 'but they didn't do very much in the way of interpretation'. ''They were hypocritical and opportunistic,' another member of the group objected, 'they didn't report objectively.' He noted the way in which the Turkish state and media had sought to co-opt the terrorism issue for their own ends, 'creat[ing] the impression, look we were right, we too have been suffering from terrorism, this is what terrorism is like'. A third participant in this group brought up the question of British coverage of the September 11 attack, observing that, in his view, it had been overly emotive, especially at the beginning, when 'they were talking about the last phone calls from the planes, and as you listened your eyes filled with tears'. A further critical observation on the British media related to how the British (and American) channels were drawing on the imagery of the crusades. As one of the participants put it, 'British television started putting the blame on Muslims, interpreting the events as a war between Muslims and Christians. There was no logic in this, only an aggressive attitude, a sensationalist attitude.' The participants in this group ranged across channels, then, and they did so with no illusions about the authority or objectivity of broadcast news (Turkish or British), and no criticism spared.

The Turkish migrant viewers that I interviewed were extremely sceptical about the quality and reliability of Turkish media, then.

But clearly they were not, as a consequence, inclined to be sympathetic towards British media as a more reliable source of information. Scepticism in one direction provoked scepticism in the other. In one group discussion, one of the participants remarked, with some bitterness, that even if you had started out with some sense of loyalty to, or trust in, a particular channel, after September 11 this trust was sorely tested. He pointed out how British television had suggested that the terrorists were Afghans, when in fact they were Saudis. 'This was such propaganda,' he objected, 'and yet nobody reflected on that. And that's a big contradiction'. 'I kept my eyes and ears open,' he went on, 'but nothing critical got through, you didn't hear any different voices. I wasn't able to get much of a critical perspective.' In another discussion, a young Turkish (Alevi) man said that he found British channels subservient to the government's pro-American policies: 'They don't want to wake people up. I think the Americans knew about the attack beforehand. They're misleading people'. What was apparent, then, in all the focus groups I conducted was a generalized scepticism (in the case of the Kurdish group referred to above, even when they occasionally made comments on coverage by the Kurdish channel, Medya TV, they were unimpressed - Medya TV's news was second-hand, taken from the BBC or CNN - or it simply relayed official positions, declarations, and rhetoric).

What I would argue, then, is that the response of Turkish migrants to September 11 was not a consequence of watching Turkish television, and of what they were being told by the Turkish media. More significant for understanding their responses were, I think, their capacity and their readiness to range across channels in search of information about September 11. As one informant expressed, with particular clarity:

When there's a news item about a world event, we always look at British television as well. We compare them both [British and Turkish]. If our satellite dish was working, we would have done the same. We would have watched the news on both, to see who says what; a bit of curiosity, a desire to catch a bit more detail about something. We think that they all report in a biased way. Maybe we're mistaken, maybe what they're reporting is correct, but we're not satisfied. That's why we change channels, move across different channels, to have more knowledge, to be reassured, to be better informed. As long as I'm not satisfied, I look at other channels, to see what this one is saying, what that one is saying. It's a kind of a small-scale research on our part.

The thinking of Turkish migrants was in fact shaped much more by this 'small-scale research' on their part, by the continual comparisons they were making between channels and programmes, and by the critical distance that this consequently gave them from the ideologies and biases of both Turkish and British broadcasting cultures. I would also argue that this condition of cultural mobility gave rise to a generalized scepticism about the coverage of September 11. It was a scepticism that was in line with the general ambivalence that Turks felt about the events that had polarized Western and Islamic worlds - a scepticism that in fact accommodated their reluctance to align themselves with one or other of these opposed camps.

Thinking and its Vicissitudes

Turkish migrants in Britain, with respect to both Turkish/ Islamic and Western connections. These Turks felt themselves at the same time within and without both the 'us' and the 'them' cultural spaces. And I have then gone on to consider the significance of media consumption for their thinking about September 11, suggesting that their mobility across both Turkish and British media sustained a generally reflexive, and consequently ambivalent and sceptical, stance towards the events. What I now want to argue is, first, that it was this in-between position that they found themselves in that forced Turkish migrants to think; and, second, that it also informed the logic of their thinking processes. This is to go against the idea that Turks responded as they did as a consequence of their Turkish identity, or on the basis of what Turkish television was telling them (against the idea that, in the weeks following September 11, they became drawn into the Turkish public sphere). My point is that, with no sense of a singular authoritative resource to draw on - as a consequence from their sense of distance from all sources of informational authority - Turks had to do a lot of thinking for themselves. As well as thinking about the immediate circumstances of September 11, there were suddenly issues to be thought about concerning their own perspective. They were compelled to think in order to try to address the implications and consequences of their own ambivalent positioning.

The key issue must then concern the nature of the thinking process. Following Cohen, I want to draw attention to the way in which people mobilize all kinds of more or less productive forms to think with. What came out in my focus groups was how people might draw on aspects of their own backgrounds and lived experiences to make sense of what they were seeing. As leftists or as Kurds, for example, they have been confronted with massacres before, and they know what it is like to be persecuted. But at the same time, as Cohen notes, people may also use dogmas, names, or 'facts' to think with - which may mean not thinking very well at all. What was apparent in my discussions was the ease with which 'known' truths and realities could be invoked. I was interested in the tropes and rhetoric of these Turkish migrants, and in the degree to which the available dogmas and explanatory frames of reference might be put under challenge by the new context of cultural complexity and ambivalence.

The first thing to note here is the extent to which thinking in the focus group sessions centred on what might be called the American question - and, with this, we are back to the issue of anti-Americanism. I was struck by the incessant questions being posed about the US role in the chain of September 11 events. Was it really conceivable that Osama bin Laden could have undertaken such a massive strike alone? How was it possible for the United States not to have known about the attacks in advance? Might the CIA have had some hand in these events? Maybe the US economy was in need of an attack of this kind? What was the connection between bin Laden and the United States? How many people actually died? Didn't they say that the number of people working in the World Trade Center was between 25,000 and 50,000? Was it really possible to empty those huge buildings so quickly? Did the US government conceal the real figures? Why was the United States declaring war on Afghanistan? What was the nature of US interests in the Afghan region? Was the real agenda to do with the natural resources? And so on. Of course, these were not questions being posed only by these Turkish migrants, but they were questions that were posed with particular scepticism, incredulity, and indignation by them.

What was significant, then, was how the attention of discussants became so focused on the United States, and, to be even more precise, on US foreign policy. Participants in the groups were highly critical of the US government's interventionist policies in the Middle East, as well as in other parts of the world. They were concerned about the relation between US foreign policy and the predatory interests of American companies operating in the global economy. And they were particularly attentive to the strategic and military manoeuvring of the US government in regions with significant oil, petroleum, and natural gas resources. (And they deplored the apparent insensitivity of the American people with respect to what their own government was doing across the world in their name.) What was clear was that the United States was not regarded as an innocent party, but as being highly implicated in the events that had unfolded - even as implicated in some way in the attacks of September 11. In the minds of these Turkish migrants, it was as if the United States was on trial, and they were taking the stance and perspective of the prosecution. The United States was in the dock, and it had better be ready to defend itself against a world that was now ready to impeach it.

The United States was on trial, and the general assumption among those that I spoke with was that it was guilty; the onus was on the United States to demonstrate its innocence. There were two different logics at work in the prosecution and condemnation of the United States. The first was an argument out of historical precedent - and, at the same time, out of the political biographies and experience of these accusers. Thus, as I have already suggested, the invasion of Afghanistan seemed to make sense in the context of the past history of US military intervention and aggression. There was indeed a kind of plausibility in this kind of explanation of what was going on, particularly from those who had a Third World political formation. It did not seem fanciful to link September 11 to Vietnam and to Palestine, and even to make a connection back to Hiroshima (perhaps by way of Pearl Harbor). The second kind of logic was more questionable. This was grounded in a certain perverse interpretation of the American state's motivations; in an imagination of the United

States as a perverse force in world politics. According to this line of reasoning, it was the United States itself that was behind the September 11 attacks. There was speculation about how it might actually have used al-Qaeda to deliver the attacks, and then debate as to why it would have undertaken such a perverse operation. One Kurdish informant told me that when he learned about the defence technologies in operation around the Pentagon, his conclusion was that only the United States could have launched the attack. 'I think that this is an internal U.S. matter,' he said, 'an act by the deep state, that America hit itself.' Another man in the same group concurred: 'I think it was the CIA, the CIA's own men, not bin Laden. Anyway, bin Laden was working for the CIA' (focus group, London, 1 March 2002). The underlying suspicion was that the United States had initiated the attacks on September 11 in order to create a pretext for its subsequent invasion of Afghanistan. On quite a few occasions the name of Mossad was thrown into the equation, to suggest that there was an Israeli connection to the September 11 events. 'The day when the attacks happened, was it twelve hundred or so Jews, that didn't go to work that day?' asked one man (focus group, London, 1 March 2002). At this point, thinking seems to have got caught up in the imaginative dimension of conspiracy theory and urban myth. Of course, this kind of rhetoric was again not specific to these Turkish people, but we may say that such tropes did resonate more fully with their own painful experiences, and their accumulated dogmas, too.

What we have to consider here, I think, are the real difficulties in thinking through the issues of September 11. There are, of course, the manifest difficulties caused by lack of information and knowledge about what happened on September 11, or about the activities of Western forces in Afghanistan. The secrecy and censorship that characterized the post-September 11 period made it very difficult for anyone to come up with a reasoned and substantiated response, whatever media sources they might have access to. But, in the context of the present argument, I want to consider another difficulty that Turkish migrants experienced when they tried to think about the events of September 11, one that derived from the complex nature of their relation to those events. The problem is that their thinking, which is shaped by both experiences of persecution and dogmas about persecution, can easily become frozen - resorting to a rigid template that subordinates all realities to a defensive scheme. When this happens, the potentially creative possibilities that might emerge from their position of cultural ambivalence are closed down. In their place, we may find the rhetoric of dogmatic (pseudo-) resolution. The issue, then, is whether and how it might be possible to move beyond this kind of intellectual and imaginative foreclosure. Earlier, I characterized this issue in terms of the struggle between thinking and identity/belonging. Here I will consider it in terms of the struggle between complex thinking and dogmatic thinking.

I want to refer to a discussion that occurred in one of my focus group discussions, among young Kurdish migrants. And I want to make a contrast between the perspectives of some of the participants. What I will suggest is that, in the interchange between these people, it is possible to discern something of the struggle between different thought styles, between contrasting modalities of thinking. Early in the discussion, one of the young women in the group, I will call her Ay°e, talked about her shock at the way her parents had responded to the events of September 11 - her shock at the extent of their hostility towards the United States:

Personally, [she says] I don't have anti-American feelings. But when I came home that day, when I looked at my parents - and there were lots of neighbours in our house. My parents were saying 'it's not right that people should die [in the World Trade Center], but something like this was necessary for them [the United States], they needed to experience this pain '. But this was very different from what I felt. How could you think anything like this? My mother's reaction was ... she said, 'thousands of Kurdish people have died in the Middle East, and this was as a result of America's politics, or British politics'. OK, there are these politics, people are being massacred. But quite honestly it seemed very wrong to me to be glad about the people massacred in the United States.

But Ayse is then accused, by another woman in the group, of adopting an 'emotional approach' to the events of September 11. When asked what she means by this, this second woman replies, 'She comes home and says to her parents, "how ruthless you are, people are dying and how could you think like this?".' She finds Ay°e too sensitive, and suggests that she has been overly influenced by what she has seen on television ('The death of these people, the collapse of the buildings, blood, people crying, blood being spilt. Of course, this affects you. That's why we have this emotional response.') A third woman in the group also reacts against what she, too, considers to be Ay°e's overly emotional stance. 'We are not affected by this emotionally,' she says, 'because, what we are saying is, lots of children are dying. We're more used to these things. We've either heard it from our relatives, or from people who have been tortured.' What we are seeing here is a confrontation between a mode of thinking that privileges immediate and spontaneous response to the September 11 events, and one that privileges invested collective experiences and commitments. In the first case, what is being valued is the honesty of emotional response to the events of September 11, while, in the second, the premium is put upon emotional detachment and lucidity, which is regarded as the only way to get at the truth of the events.

At a later point in the discussion, there is some debate about whether Osama bin Laden could be blamed for the attacks, or whether the United States in some way planned them. One young man, whom I will call Ali, makes the case for the plausibility of this latter scenario. He speculates on the available evidence:

Five thousand Jews hadn't gone to work that day. You think, and Israel enters into the equation. Then you say to yourself that something is going on. It's either bin Laden who did it, or Mossad, or Israel, or America. If we look at it objectively, let's start off saying that it wasn't America. You look at the information you've got, you evaluate America's power, how they use people, and you think about how this event could be beneficial for the American economy. On the other hand, what kind of proof did they give that bin Laden did it? Nothing. They just came and said it's bin Laden. Who is bin Laden? They started picking up on him after the event. Who is Israel most connected to? America. It again links there, it links to America. The logical links are to America.

Ali's 'case' is detached and dispassionate, but it is trapped in a dogmatic mode. His 'evidence' works according to a kind of deductive and pseudo-rationalistic logic, based on what he already 'knows' about Americans, Jews, and Muslims. The world is made to conform to the rigid template that orders his mental space. In contrast with Ali's schema, Ay°e has a more nuanced perspective, a more qualified approach to September 11. She is more prepared to take in the 'facts', and more prepared to accept the complexity of the evidence. Ay°e takes into account the debates that were conducted in the British media, and acknowledges the different tenor of those debates. 'The British press didn't directly accuse bin Laden,' she observes. 'People debated this in the newspapers. Most of the people in England don't care about it. They don't have any desire for revenge. They don't say, "let's attack the Middle East".' Of course, she is influenced by her Kurdish background, and she is ready to acknowledge some of the points that Ali is making. But her position is generally one of greater ambivalence, recognizing the difficulties and uncertainties in the available evidence. 'I'm not saying that it is bin Laden who staged the attacks,' she says, 'But, in my mind, I can't accept that something like this could have been planned by America.' Ay°e is prepared to contemplate certain paths of thought that are not all conceivable within Ali's more defensive and two-dimensional worldview.

What we see in this group discussion, then, is a tension between two different modes of thought. One kind of thinking was more informed by a sense of 'belonging' to a collective project and experience, and carried with it the danger of being closed to new possibilities; the other was more in touch with the ambivalences in the position of Turkish migrants in the period following September 11, and more open to complexity, qualification, and reformulation. In the discussions taking place within this group, we can see an encounter between flexible thinking and dogmatic thinking: thinking in which 'individuals use tropes to think their way through problematic situations', and thinking in which individuals 'employ cultural tropes to secure themselves', to adopt Cohen's distinction. I have said that the identity question, with respect to the West versus Islam agenda, was for a long time a sleeping dog. What the events of September 11 did was to bring it back to consciousness. The dialogue and debate in this group brought out precisely what is at issue in this question, showing how different selves might mobilize different forms to quite different intellectual and imaginative ends.

Summary

The whole interpretative frame in the West surrounding the September 11 events has been one of a binary polarization, between the West and Islam: the West associated with civilizational values and Islam with violence against it. Turks and Kurds, however, do not immediately fall into one of the polar positions. We might say that what characterizes the Turkish mental space is the way in which relations to the West and Islam are negotiated positions; and that there are many nuances and varieties of the negotiated positions (and these positions are not fixed and stable). However, the binary reading of the September 11 events imposed a rigid frame, expecting a wholesale rejection of one camp and the embrace of the other. This mode of being is clearly very much against the idea of entertaining negotiated positions where the central feature is interaction between and mobility across different registers. Turks, following the tragic events of September 11, were pushed to abandoning their seemingly fuzzy, contradictory, and compromising positions, and to embrace en masse one or the other. This, they were very reluctant (and perhaps, luckily, unable) to do.

Another point we have to understand about the Turkish-speaking population in London is that many of them are from leftist backgrounds (of different kinds) with strong anti-imperialist and Third World orientations, consequently harbouring anti-American sentiments. These sentiments, which were dormant, were woken up after the September 11 events. I would hasten to add that an important contributory factor here was the employment of the polarized thinking that marginalized and criminalized migrants, especially from Islamic backgrounds. Many in the focus groups complained about how they began to feel guilty because of the way in which Muslims were blamed for the attacks. 'I wish it was Karlos (Cakal) [who'd done it]' said one of them bitterly. People felt cornered and they felt justified in unleashing their anti-American sentiments as a way of explaining the events.

We could say that what they heard on the media in general (this includes the Turkish transnational media and the British media) did not help them in any way to revise their deeply felt anti-Americanism. It was either only those with sophisticated thoughtfulness, or those with the least anti-American feelings in them, who were able to hear the nuances and pick up the different tones across the different media. We have discussed elsewhere how the care structures of the Turkish media do not quite work for the Turkish migrants living their lives outside of the routines in Turkey. Turkish migrants relate to Turkish television from a critical distance. They do not watch the Turkish channels from the inside, so to speak, but actually operate in and across many cultural spaces at once and there is a constant comparison going on. When Turkish people in London were watching the coverage of the September 11 events, they were already coming from a position of dislocated viewing, already having in their mental spaces past reflections on how Turkish channels had covered (in biased ways) important events, like the Galatasaray-Leeds football match incidents. There was already a critical sensibility as to how Turkish channels covered the news in particular. This sensibility, we find, was much sharpened during September 11. Their critical distance made them aware of the ideologies and biases of the Turkish channels during this period. This is a point that goes against the idea that Turkish migrants would think differently because of their different cultural and national identity, that they automatically become publics of another discourse about the September 11 events.

There was not much coming from the Turkish stations that would help the Turks to modify their anti-American drift. Nor was there much coming from the British channels. On the contrary, British channels were seen as the propagators of the crusader mentality. With no singular authoritative resource to draw on, Turkish people in London had to do a lot of thinking for themselves. We find from talking to Turks and Kurds that this thinking process was rather a difficult one. On the one hand, they were in a doubly estranged position. They were identifying neither fully with the West nor with Islam, yet it was also very difficult to articulate what the new negotiated position would be between these now polarized positions. This required creative and reflective thinking. Of course, the clash of civilizations mentality around was not helping in this endeavour; when the emphasis tilted towards clash, it was very difficult to think about interaction and negotiation. On the other hand, their experiential and dogmatic learning told them about the persecution and destruction caused by the US (and British) politics in the world.

There was a danger of beginning to see the United States as evil number one.

This is certainly not the creative and complex thinking that was required following the critical events of September 11. In our discussions, we did, however, see a tension between two different modes of thought - one informed by a sense of 'belonging' to a collective project and experience and hence a reaffirming one, and the other more open to complexity, and therefore more risky. The first modality carried the danger of rigidity and foreclosure, and the second the danger of being blinded by spontaneity and confusion.

I would like to end with an important observation, coming out of the last group discussion that I quoted from. In this group Ay°e and Ali represent these different modalities of thinking, but what has been crucial for the discussion in this group to carry on was that these different modalities were in a dialogical relationship with one another. In other words, Ay°e and Ali were prepared to talk to one another and learn from one another. It was this dialogue which enhanced the thinking in this group. Ay°e needed to hear Ali's rational, detached, historically informed views on the suffering caused by the US politics in the Middle East, and, by the same token, Ali needed to be sensitized to the nuances in the American and British positions with respect to the September 11 events. Rather than defending their corner to the exclusion of the other position, they were prepared to allow themselves to move in and out of these different modalities of thinking. This kind of dialogical mode, surely, is a first step in creative thinking, that kind of thinking that we still lack in the aftermath of September 11.

Postscript

The assumption has been that the national public sphere is moved and shaped by a singular national structure of feeling. September 11 provided a challenge to this basic assumption. The reality is that societies have become more complex and that the idea of a unitary public culture has become more problematical. This is what September 11 brought to the fore. What became apparent was a fracturing of public opinion. What became clear were the potential consequences of the new social reality in which societies are made up of people with multiple allegiances, transnational connections, and transcultural references.

A further assumption has been that the national and international have been separate spaces. It has been imagined that the national space could in some way be detached from the wider world of 'international affairs', and in some way insulated from its repercussions. September 11 showed that this was also a problematical basic assumption of the national mentality. What we have seen is the difficulty in keeping the events in Palestine and Iraq out of the public space of Britain. It has become increasingly difficult to keep them at a distance, to confine them to the world of other people's problems.

These challenges have become ever more apparent; even more so with the bombing of Afghanistan and the war on Iraq. But what we find is that the media are still operating within the logic of the 'national'. The gulf between what national media systems say and report and what the public wants to hear is getting deeper and wider by the day. This became evident during the bombing campaign of Afghanistan and then during the war on Iraq when the British media came increasingly under attack for being biased. There was all the more reason to seek out alternative sources of information. Perhaps more than ever before, the media with their fixation on the 'national' were not in tune with the increasingly transnational and diverse sensibility of the audiences. This is of major concern, especially in the context of our desire for creative thinking in times of crises.

12

Impact of Terrorism on September 11 Events

Introduction

The frontlines of what was feared to be 'America's war against Islam' were drawn in what then seemed an unlikely political geography. In Iran in the late 1970s, 'suddenly out of nowhere' came this massive revolutionary movement in the name of Islam. It ousted the Shah (the staunchest and most loyal ally the United States would ever have in the Muslim Middle East) only to prepare the stage for the face-to-face confrontation of Islam with the 'Great Satan' (or rather, the United States with the 'Axis of Evil'). And the frontlines of a future war were drawn when Ayatollah Ruhollah Khomeini announced (after his triumphant return to Iran from exile in 1979 as the leader of the first Islamic revolution of the postcolonial age) that the United States was out to get Islam and that all other conflicts in the world were mere distractions, only to cover up the US's ultimate goal: the destruction of 'true Islam' by all means (military, political, cultural, communicational, etc.), even by creating an 'American Islam'.

Despite his belonging to Shi'ism (a minority religion within the larger Sunni Islamic world), Ayatollah Khomeini was addressing the Islamic umma (a transnational, transcultural, truly global entity).

He was, perhaps, the first among Muslim scholastic ulama worldwide (including the Sunni ulama) to anticipate the imminence of a phenomenon, which then seemed still unlikely. He envisaged that Islam (replacing communism) would soon emerge as the US's foremost ideological and political rival in the context of the high-tech transnational and transcultural milieu that was to be a feature of the global age.

This new milieu (although it was designed and driven primarily by US media institutions, and largely in line with US 'national interests') certainly suited a new generation of Islamists that was emerging as a major political and ideological protagonist of the future (in ethnic, national, and transnational representations). In this milieu, religious rhetoric would dominate political language, and modern religious ideologies would inspire modern religious wars.

The war that was declared by George W. Bush in revenge for the September 11 attacks came to many Muslims in Iran (and elsewhere in the Muslim world) as only a confirmation of Ayatollah Khomeini's prophecy. Ironically, though, President Bush seemed the least likely candidate to make such a declaration. His dubious winning of the presidential race in 2000 had made him a seemingly weak president. But the exigencies of time soon made him the first president that would take the United States to its religious origins through new religious wars: 'war on terror', 'war for the liberation of the oppressed'; and it seems more wars are yet to come. He was frank enough to promise no definitive end to the wars that the United States must fight against 'Evil'. In a sense, Bush's rise from a humble origin to prominence resembled the rise of Ayatollah Khomeini from a junior religious rank in a minority Islamic sect to the leadership of an Islamic revolution with transnational appeal, and a religious state with claims to a new global order.

That the Islamic revolution of Iran (despite its origination among the minority Shi'ite Muslims) had inspired a 'fundamentalist' politico-religious thesis of militant 'Islamic resistance' against the United States (as the nemesis of Islam) within the larger Muslim world (and particularly in the madrasa system) had always been feared. The Hizbullah, the Islamic Jihad, and Hamas were only a few examples of the protagonists of the militancy inspired by the 'Islamic revolution'. Nevertheless, the government and the media in the United States seemed to be shocked by and unprepared for what came on September 11, 2001.

So all seemed so unexpected, and yet how expectedly they came. The proliferating number of Islamist revivalist movements worldwide since the late 1970s (most sharing in their expression of hate for 'American hegemony') should have taught the United States something about the imminent threat of radical Islam; but it had not. The 'Attack on America' had to remain unexpected, the conspiracy theorists would say, in order to provoke in the US public a rage of revenge necessary to support the wars the United States was to wage.

Conspiracy theories aside, the Americans were pretty quick in discovering the culprits of the September 11 attacks in a group (Al-Qaeda) whose members had been trained and inculcated in the Islamist ideological schools, fashioned after the Shi'ite revolutionary madrasas in Iran, which had popularized the idea of shahadat (martyrdom). Ironically, the militancy inspired by Ayatollah Khomeini's revolutionary reading of Islam in the name of shahadat was actualized in the Sunni madrasas that had now mushroomed all over the Muslim lands through the efforts of the Arab Al-Qaeda.

It is true, as some reform-minded Iranian Islamists have been trying to assert, that two seemingly different kinds of political Islam have emerged in the Islamic world since the 1980s: a Shi'ite type in the 1980s and a Sunni type in the 1990s. But it would be naive to ignore the historical and intellectual, not to mention structural, interconnections between the two types of political Islam. The Shi'ite type of political Islam was clearly connected with the victory of the Islamic revolution in Iran influencing Shi'ite movements in Lebanon, Iraq, Saudi Arabia, Bahrain, and Kuwait in the 1980s. And the Sunni type was connected with Osama Bin Laden, Al-Qaeda, the Taliban, and the Wahhabi circles in Saudi Arabia, Kuwait, and other Gulf states, Daghistan, and Chechnya, as well as with the Islamic madrasas in Pakistan and Afghanistan. But the Shi'ite connection was no barrier against the adoption by the Sunni Islamists of the doctrinal-ideological contributions of the Shi'ite Islamists to political Islam.

The revolutionary Islamists in Iran had pursued the official policy of 'the export of the revolution' for more than a decade, well into the 1990s, to ensure the propagation of the revolutionary reading of Islam, as well as to enlist activists and sympathizers in the Muslim world. This would be achieved in various ways, even by way of inciting revolutionary insurgency against secular states ruling the Muslim nations (e.g., Iraq, Egypt, and Jordan).

The cornerstone of this revolutionary reading of Islam was the mystical idea of shahadat, which would deliver the soul of the shahid (martyr) from the sinful world, and the limbo of purgatory, into the highest levels of God's heaven. This immediate delivery of the soul would also mean the immediate cancellation of all the sins that the shahid might have committed before his shahadat. It referred to the traditional mystical idea of leqa-Allah (union with God), which promoted virtual annihilation of the mystic's body to set the soul free for ascendance to heavens.

Yet this new militant mysticism is distinct from traditional mysticism, based on passivity with regard to material interests (including politics), and purification of the soul through meditation, peace of mind, and love for others. In an inverse manner, it offers a fervent promotion of revolutionary politics involving the takeover of state power through the use of force, and the violent elimination of the hated other in a crave for self-annihilation. Real blood, instead of metaphoric wine, is the symbol of this new militant mysticism. And in it, the war with infidel others known as the 'lesser jihad' (jihad-e asghar) would take priority over the 'greater jihad' (jihad-e akbar), the war against the desire of the self (nafs) for earthly pleasure, power, and wealth. Here too, the inversion of priorities with respect to traditional mysticism has been evident.

That the Sunni type of political Islam had no apparent organizational, and little geographical, connection with the Iranian Islamic revolutionaries of Shi'ite persuasion, though, did not prevent it from adopting, very soon, a main aspect of the revolutionary reading of Islam offered by the Shi'ites: shahadat. The development of the most effective and most destructive Muslim weapon yet (i.e., the suicide bomber) out of the religious concept of martyrdom was certainly the contribution of the Islamic revolution to Islam's firepower in what is believed to be 'resistance at all costs against domination and occupation'.

The body of the martyr, accumulated as it is with historical feelings of repression, humiliation, victimization, frustration, and hate, has developed into potent warfare, which has proved almost impossible to counteract at a mere technical level. Of late, and perhaps all too late, even such secular states as Iraq under Saddam Hussein took a turn for the adoption of the militant Islam inspired by martyrdom as a means to mobilize Muslim sentiments in its confrontation with the United States.

Although the reform-minded Iranian Islamists consider the Shi'ite type of political Islam a modernist movement and the Sunni type a reactionary and backward movement, it is not too difficult to see deep-seated intellectual, if not organizational, connections between the two. Certain revolutionary ideologues in Iran had virtually revived and promoted what later found a more clear-cut representation in Afghanistan under the Taliban. In its promotion of violent struggles against the 'enemies of Islam', and its strict enforcement of moral codes repressing human desire for pleasure, the revolutionary reading of Islam offered by the hard-line Iranian Islamists was not all that distant from what Al-Qaeda and the Taliban advocated. The religious hard-liners in Iran might even have been the forerunner of the so-called 'Arab Afghans'.

Yet the violence that the Islamic revolution promoted was certainly considered legitimate in that it pursued a 'good end', namely the liberation of the 'oppressed Muslim believers' from the 'oppressive Western colonizers' and the 'criminal Zionist regime'. It thus provided spiritual, if not material, support for all radical anti-Western and anti-Zionist forces, and particularly for the Islamic liberation movements, in the countries ruled by the 'puppet regimes'.

Legitimate violence notwithstanding, even within Iran the waning of the radical militancy of the revolution since the mid-1990s had made the people unprepared for the September 11 attacks. Such a strong blow against the United States on its own soil by a force that acted in the name of Islam was hardly conceivable even in the imagination of the Iranian Islamists, who were now experimenting with the so-called 'project of reform' popularized since 1997 by the reformist President Mohammad Khatami. This was the case, even though the force attacking the United States was using the familiar rhetoric of the scholastic Islamic revolutionism originated in Iran.

What the revolutionary reading of Islam brought to the Muslim world - and (thanks to the 'globalization' of the transcultural and transnational messages of Islam) to the rest of the world - was, however, much larger than the image of Osama Bin Laden, or that of Saddam Hussein for that matter. Surely, these images, constructed as they have been by the insatiable zeal of the global media networks (both Western and Islamic), seem to make it easy to define enemies worth going to war with. Yet the image of Osama and other representations of Islamic militancy represent an inescapable duality which is inherent to political Islam.

Osama, in particular, could be considered a clever student of the Islamic revolution in its high radicalism. He even seems to be representing the militant side of Islam, particularly in confrontation with the United States, even more fully than the direct inheritors of the legacy of the Islamic revolution. But his Islam, to which even secular Saddam appealed belatedly, could also be the representation of what Ayatollah Khomeini had called the 'American Islam', one created by the United States in order to give it reason and justification to destroy the 'true Islam'. After all, was there ever any lack of evidence that Al-Qaeda and the Taliban, as well as Saddam's Ba'athist regime in Iraq, had flourished on US aid?

If 'true Islam' (as even radical Islamists would agree) holds the sword in one hand, and the book in the other, then Al-Qaeda and the Taliban (not to mention secular-turned-Islamist Saddam) have certainly carried the globalization of the Islamic zeal for militancy to its limit. The fact is, though, that Islam cannot thrive on the soil they have burnt, whether they represent the true or fake Islam. After all, the firepower of the suicide bomber is of little help in building a modern nation-state (which is the only form of modern collective existence that can be imagined). It could remain a potential arsenal for a life and death struggle for survival; but if the war is ever going to end, Islam will need to come to the scene with more constructive capacities.

To be sure, what has secured the thriving of Islam in the modern world is owed much more to the fast increasing number of its believers worldwide (through high rates of reproduction, migration, exile, and conversion) than to the spectacular actions of the would-be martyrs. In their representation as nation, community, and ethnic or social group, these growing Muslim populations, whether in Muslim-majority states or in Diaspora, are developing into modern Muslim publics, thanks largely to the emergence of a globally mediated public sphere. And it is the emergence of these growing Muslim publics that has been pushing an increasing number of the ulama and lay intellectuals in the Muslim lands, and in Diaspora, to endorse a different kind of Islam, one that does not hesitate to openly advocate peace, dialogue, and pluralism.

The emergence in Iran since the late 1990s of a trend away from the revolutionary ideology and religious militancy in the interest of 'religious democracy' is an example of the influence of this different reading of Islam. It is this new re volutionary-turned-reformist trend that now considers radical political Islam of the Sunni type a threat to Iran because of its geographic proxomity to Iranian borders. In post-revolutionary Iran, Islam has certainly developed into a political and public force, which seems capable not only of involving politics, but also of playing the part of a civil institution checking the perennial phenomenon of unaccountable power, which has been so prevalent in the postcolonial Muslim-majority states.

The entry of political Islam into the public domain in Iran has certainly involved both a new militant posturing and calls for freedom, justice, and peace. While its militant spirit is articulated in terms of a radical critique of Western modernity (as a reminder of Western imperial domination), its emancipatory and egalitarian messages have inspired a public awakening with regard to the opportunities posed by the same modernity.

This dual representation of Islam has attracted attention on a global scale since September 11, 2001, but it has been around for much longer. At any rate, it should not have come as a surprise. After all, the dual representation of Islam is, in essence, not much different to that of the West. The colonial West, not to mention the US-led Western alliance since World War II, has also displayed its jaundiced face time and time again, as a crusader for freedom and justice, and as a military power ready to repress non-conformance to Western (now mainly American) values with brutality.

This dual representation was in clear display in the reactions of the Islamic State of Iran to the September 11 attacks on New York and Washington. The initial reaction to the attack on the United States (by a force that was readily branded 'Islamic extremism') was one of discord and disorientation - to the extent that most Islamists here had to officially dissociate themselves from this attack, calling it a 'non-Islamic' act. But soon enough, the militant posturing raised its irrepressible head reminding everybody of the fact that the rhetoric should not lead them to lose sight of the fact that this militant posturing is part and parcel of the lived experience of Muslims. And that Iranian Muslims are no exception to this rule.

In this chapter, I wish to demonstrate how the September 11 attacks and the subsequent events are being absorbed by a state dealing with a crisis of legitimacy, and a nation driven by an internal dynamic to decide its future course of development. What makes this process peculiarly interesting in Iran is that it is taking place in the context of the concurrent emergence of a domestic and globally mediated public sphere. My premise is that the emergence of a religious public sphere in Iran is essentially a process marked by the simultaneous nationalization and globalization of Islam.

Public resurgence of Islam in Iran: the emergence of a religious public sphere

It took almost two decades before the religious revivals (flaring since the late 1970s) practically forced the secular intellectuals and even politicians (in both the West and non-West) to finally concede the political force of religion in terms of something other than 'backwardness' and 'irrationality'. Yet this recognition was often in the Huntingtonian term of 'civilizational difference', or more accurately, in terms of 'complete' versus 'incomplete' modernization; and alternatively and yet narrowly in terms of 'fundamentalism' and 'terrorism'.

Meanwhile, new generations of Muslim intellectuals have produced new religious discourses that tend to suggest new approaches to the problem of the West with Islam, which reflect the voices of the margin not merely as an outgrowth of modern history, but as claims to alternative or parallel histories. The Iranian 'religious intellectuals' surely belong to this category. Whether, and to what extent, they will succeed in their endeavor is another matter, certainly out of the scope of the present discussion.

The renewed attention in the West to saving 'the free world' from a 'terrorist threat', or from 'the threat of weapons of mass destruction' - and the US-declared mission of bringing 'freedom to the oppressed' surely needs an ideological justification; particularly so as these ends are to be achieved through wars that seem to have no objective frontiers, but a blatantly religious language. This ideological justification is more likely than not to be sought in 'intellectual', let alone 'rhetorical', attempts (currently underway) at saving what is salvageable of the grand narrative of 'secularism' (even if this requires the abandonment of some of its principle premises). Had old secularism not supplied the ideological justification of the civilizing mission of Europe in its colonial conquests in the nineteenth century? Why should the new secularists shrug off the proud responsibility of giving an intellectual bent to the civilizing mission of the West in the postcolonial age, which is now to suit the process of globalization? The outcome of the project of revising the grand narrative of secularism to fit the requirements of the global age will surely prove crucial to how the problem of the West with Islam is reformulated and handled this time around. And this is sure to be also crucial to a new breed of Muslims worldwide.

Certainly, the attempt at re-evaluation of the secularization thesis is not a new venture. What is perhaps new here is the entry of this new breed of Muslims on the scene of this revision process, which is fundamental to the ongoing process of secularization. Not surprisingly, the entry on the scene of new players from the Islamic societies has added to the complexity of the task of revising secularism. New indigenous political and intellectual trends represented by native political activists and charismatic figures (in what has been established as the presumably 'traditional Islamic world') have brought in a new ambiguity to the ongoing process of secularization, both in their own societies and in the global domain. This ambiguity, by nature, is likely to both strengthen and weaken the secularization process. Notwithstanding the ambiguity, though, the new Muslim intellectuals are set to contribute, ironically, to resolving certain enduring paradoxes of modern thought (e.g., public-private, tradition-modernity, etc.). But these contributions (while often incorporating some notion of secularization) have posed a serious challenge to the ideology of secularism, and its defenders in Western academic, journalistic, and political circles.

Nonetheless, the public resurgence of Islam since the late 1970s has remained understudied. In Iran, at least, this is certainly the case. Here, more than twenty years after the victory of the Islamic revolution, there has emerged, almost in seclusion, a lively and highly contested public sphere, which cannot be but a significant consequence (intended or not) of the victory of the Islamic revolution of 1979. The scant attention to the development of a public sphere in Iran may be precisely due to its religious origin, which makes it an oddity given the assumption that the modern public sphere is a product of the modern processes of secularization. The emergence of Islam as a 'public religion' of political force is by no means limited to Iran; nevertheless, the Iranian case seems to be a novel example of how traditional religions 'continue playing important public roles in the ongoing construction of the modern world'.

Yet Islam's contribution to the modern world may prove vastly different to what some liberal advocates of 'public religions' expect; surely, it is not a contribution made by a religion accepting 'the normative principles of a liberal public sphere'. The lack of attention to the reality of a non-secular, non-liberal, and blatantly religious public sphere is still fueling ignorant speculations about Islam and its political nature.

This ignorance was put on full display in the US strategy to declare war on what President Bush called the 'Axis of Evil' (including a large Muslim population) in late January 2002, while the supposedly 'militant', and presumably 'evil', (Iranian) Islamists were calling for peaceful dialogue and debate. Particularly so, since the latter's effort in reaction to the US 'war on terror' was ostensibly directed at developing a 'rational' and 'universal' approach to the problem of terrorism (of which Iran claims to be a primary victim). No matter how sincere or hypocritical the Islamist call for dialogue and reason, it has won large degrees of public sympathy - and (thanks to the Europeans) not only of the Muslims - as against the untenable US strategy of 'going to war for peace'.

Notwithstanding the militant spirit inspired by Islam as a discourse of power, one cannot fail to appreciate that Islam in Iran has developed into a public religion whereby the modern concepts of 'subjective rights', 'human dignity', and 'social justice' have been taken for granted. What is more, it has offered to tackle the 'social and moral ills' of modern societies. New political trends and social movements here testify to the emergence of new Muslim publics that are increasingly aware of the essentially modern and global context of the Islamic revival. Moreover, these new publics are prepared to engage with problems of modernity as active protagonists at both national and global levels, even if such an engagement should require political, doctrinal, and cultural adaptation. The process of the rise of political Islam in Iran thus involves a concurrent nationalization and globalization of the religion. While the politicization of the religion is a product of previous movements for national liberation and cultural defense, it also serves as a motivational source for new political and religious movements with global claims giving modern dimensions to Islam as a traditional religion and culture.

The revolutionary revival of Islam in Iran, the establishment of an Islamic state here, and the relentless post-revolutionary attempts to shape Shi'ite Islam into a politically driven public culture have in many ways contributed to the actualization of the public and political potentials of Islam in the modern world. But, as already noted, these contributions are not exactly in line with what some new liberal theories of 'public religions' anticipated. Yet, indeed, the resurgence of Islam in Iran provides ample evidence in support of the rejection of the socalled 'secular' assumptions about the declining political power and public significance of religion, and its increasing privatization.

Talal Asad has been right in exposing the partiality of 'enlightened' intellectual attempts at saving the secularization thesis by simply conceding the continued importance of religion in the modern world. Such concessions may not suffice in addressing the anxiety and fear of the religious believers in Islamic societies (like Iran) with the continued threat of the secularist ideology, now backed by outrageous military threats, to their religious and cultural traditions - though it may go a long way in addressing the moral conscience of the liberal proponents of the thesis.

In all clarity, the religious language adopted in the US war rhetoric is testimony to how the new battle-lines are being drawn in the context of already existing skirmishes. What makes many Muslims (from Africa, to the Middle East, to East Asia) read 'America's war against terror' as an 'American war against Islam' is that this war had been too well prepared to be a contingency plan adopted only after what happened on September 11. That the only choice made to deal with the problem with the Muslims was for war can tell even more about why some US politicians are so undisturbed, and even seem gloating at the prospect of what they could gain from such a war. For most Islamists, the war in Iraq is further testimony to the far-reaching diabolical plans of the United States in the Muslim Middle East involving a 'reshaping of the political geography of the region' in the interest of Israel.

Viewed from this perspective, the United States does not seem to be an innocent victim of a vicious attack by Islamic extremists; it may even have (knowingly or not) produced Frankenstein's monster. Was not the military zeal for conquest in Iraq encouraged, and even boosted, in the early 1980s by the United States (in the hope of containing what seemed to it at that time to be 'the greater threat of the Islamic revolution')? Even the Americans themselves have acknowledged that the eight-year war between Iran and Iraq was only to contain the Islamic revolution in Iran. But when Iraq became the major threat, then the United States developed the new policy of 'dual containment'. After September 11 this grew into a war against whoever is not with the United States. It should be obvious why the United States has been inclined to employ a religious rhetoric (most articulately voiced in the terminology of 'axis of evil'); the enemy is a religious force, if not a religion.

The continued political and public influence of Shi'ism (and its living representatives), on the one hand, and the failure of the modern secular state to advance valid claims to representation of the nation, on the other, were significant in hindering the emergence of a secular public sphere in Iran. Surely, the secular state of the Shah prior to the 1979 religious revolution, with its comunicative resources (e.g., national radio and television) and its censor of the alternative media (and what was considered subversive voices), was able to claim virtual control of a reluctant public. But the scholastic Shi'ite ulama, with their spiritual, social, and financial connections with the community of believers, and with their control of the medium of the mosque, were able to pose real claims to representation of a consenting public at the grassroots level.

The challenge of the Islamists in Iran to the secularist ideology of the monarchic state has had serious implications for the development of political modernity here. It has certainly given voice to a thus far repressed history, namely the history of Shi'ism (i.e., the narrative of Ahl-e-beyt transmitted by the hadith), with potential to both challenge the universal history of modernity and to find a place in it. By reviving this repressed history and a curious appeal to Western intellectual tradition, Iranian Muslim intellectuals (including some Islamists) are trying to discern what made Iran a marginal outgrowth of a powerful and prosperous center of modern civilization. A significant aspect of such a project is the impetus to incorporate some of the most fundamental concepts of modernity (e.g., civil society and democracy) in light of an alternative (religious) history.

The new political and public efforts in Islamic Iran at redefining the Shi'ite faith is increasingly shifting toward making religion compatible with the requirements of modernity without questioning the ultimate domination of the public domain by religious values and principles. Here, the religious politicians and ideologues, having established control on the boundaries of the public domain through a popular revolution, are making gradual concessions to liberal and secular views.

The boundaries of the predominantly religious public sphere, one could develop a better understanding of the new developments in Shi'ite Islam (as both a public religion and a political culture) in the context of a modern nation-state. The role of mediated representation in shaping this public religion into the main element of 'nation-building' cannot be overemphasized. It has come to bear significant consequences for the relationship of religion, state, and nation, and for the redefinition of the boundaries between 'public' and 'private', 'openness' and 'secrecy', and 'individual' and 'collective'.

It is increasingly evident that the Shi'ite religious tradition is undergoing certain major transformations (as we speak) in terms of its public representation. But this process is difficult to discern unless Shi'ism is placed in the proper perspective of the construction of a religious public sphere, distinct from what is known as the modern Western (bourgeois) public sphere; and yet a public sphere that bears the indelible mark of its Western counterpart. There is no bourgeoisie (in its European sense) in the Iranian Islamic context, for example, and hence no liberal bourgeois public sphere; but the question of open and free public debate as the centerpiece of public sphere is as valid in Iran as anywhere else.

The construction of a Shi'ite Islamic national identity in Iran may thus be viewed as part and parcel of the process of redefining the boundaries of the public sphere. And yet this process has, in turn, implicated the search for national imaginary in ventures that have taken the Muslim clergy and lay intellectuals to totally new domains, which require new interpretations of the faith involving the production of new religious forms and even new contents. And it is perhaps the neglect of the meaning of these innovations that has made the Iranian case, in the words of two Washington Post journalists, a 'quandary' for the United States.

Revolutionary Resistance to Secularism

The revolutionary resurgence of Islam in Iran in defense of religious traditions, and its push to forge a uniform religious (Shi'ite) identity, have ironically contributed to the emergence of a differentiated public sphere, which is at one and the same time modern and traditional. In order to discern this process, one has to first understand how the politicization (and popularization) of religion is shifting the boundaries between public and private, on the one hand, and state and society, on the other. Here, one immediately finds oneself dealing, in particular, with the shifts in the religiously inspired political discourse of the revolution in the context of a mediated public experience of religion and politics. And this inevitably implicates the contributions of this experience to the emergence of a democratic turn in how religion is understood and how power is exercised in tackling the problems of a modern nation-state in a global environment.

The political and public force of Islam in Iran is rooted, more than anything else, in the symbolic, or cultural power, of religion in post-revolutionary Iran and the process of what may be termed 'symbolic exchange', which is best captured in the development of a religiously dominated mass communication. The symbolically based political power and public influence of religion in Iran is arguably connected at a fundamental level with the means of this symbolic exchange, namely the communication media (from the humble pulpit to high-tech technologies).

The main outcome of the Islamic revolution was a constitution, which made the state responsible, among other things, for creating a cultural environment where the religious believers (i.e., the Shi'ite believers) could practice their faith free from the intrusions of immoral ideas and acts. This was evidently a reaction to the modernizing, and yet authoritarian, efforts of the Pahlavi monarchy that had allowed the presentations of irreligious symbolism to flood the public culture.

The revolutionary takeover of the national radio and television, the revival of the tradition of Friday prayer congregations, the introduction of Islamic punishments qesas (retribution), the veiling of the women in public places, were part of the program of standardizing a strict version of Shi'ite public morality. To this may be added the strict adherence (particularly since the victory of the Islamic revolution) to commemorating the cyclic events on the Shi'ite calendar (including the organization of mass ceremonies, publication of books and posters, production of films and television programs, etc., in the memory of the Ahl-e-beyt). On top of these, there have been a fundamental overhaul of history books in the interest of religious history and the introduction of a special program of religious education as part of the mass education curricula, not to mention the closure of all bars, liquor stores, brothels, etc.

All this was organized and funded by the newly established Islamic state; but in doing this, the state relied on a pre-existing socio-cultural receptivity at the public level. The intent was to Islamize both the form and the content of the public culture. The public elements (already existing at a grassroots level) facilitated this systematic process of desecularization of the public sphere. The annual ceremony of Ashura (the commemoration of the martyrdom of Imam Hossein) was the most popular along with the annual celebration of the birthday of Mahdi, the monji. But there were numerous other occasions on the Shi'ite calendar as well. In time, the takeover of the symbolic structure of the public culture was supplemented by a systematic institutionalization of the religious codes. The war with Iraq, which began in 1980, helped a great deal in creating an opportunity for the mobilization of media resources not only to the service of the popularization of the Shi'ite narrative, but also to the institutionalization of a militant reading of the faith.

The religious state organized and funded various institutions, events, ceremonies, research programs, exhibitions, community occasions, rituals, congregations, etc., to reintroduce the tradition of Ahl-e-beyt to the Islamic nation. For example, Imam Ali and Imam Hossein, the legendary figures of Shi'ite history, were introduced not only as the sources of spiritual emulation, but also as political and public figures with extraordinary human qualities, to serve as role models to the younger generation. These personalities were presented as practical models for the living of how to combine such qualities as free thinking, fairness, humility, and compassion, with decisiveness, sticking to principles, and even powers of coercion. Their sayings and tradition inspired not only stories, poems, films, and other cultural products, but also new battle cries for the Revolutionary Guards Corps and the militia (Basij) forces in war against 'external enemies and their domestic agents' on both military and cultural fronts.

With the wiping out of the bars, discos, and other 'hedonistic' public places, the mosques, with their loudspeakers broadcasting adhan and other payers, became the sole places for public activity in the neighborhoods. For example, during the war with Iraq, the mosques became both sites for recruiting local volunteers (Basijis) for war mobilization, and neighborhood centers for distribution of basic goods from foodstuffs to home appliances at cheap prices. To be sure, the mosque remained, as always, a place of worship, but also increasingly an invaluable medium for the clerical ideologues and preachers of the official reading of religion to establish face-to-face contact with the community of believers on various religious occasions (occurring in cycles on the Shi'ite calendar). The television camera on these occasions would bring the religious propaganda and political agitation to the wider public. This became possible as the local production rapidly increased the numbers of TV sets in households after the revolution, and as the religious authority rendered watching television halal (permitted) in a reversal of fatvas (religious edicts) that had considered it haram (sinful) under the monarchic regime.

National radio and television (renamed 'the Voice and Face of the Islamic Republic') were undeniably the most effective and far-reaching media, whose significance was recognized when they were granted independence from all ministries. The ultimate control of the Supreme Leadership, and the supervision by the representatives of the three branches of power, were an indication of an early recognition of the special qualities of the magic box. The television became, perhaps, the most influential means of giving new forms and even new contents to the articles of the faith. But this process has been an arduous, painful, and complex one, which requires separate attention.

It was also charged with the new mission of spreading Islamic culture at the public level. Before it became a major promoter of freedom of expression since the late 1990s, this Ministry was in charge of the censorship of printed publications (from the press to poetry), films, and all other literary or artistic productions. Beside the Ministry for Culture, various new government and non-government institutions took the responsibility for spreading both traditional ceremonies and a certain ideological interpretation of the Shi'ite ethical and moral codes, at the public level. These included the Islamic Propaganda Organization, the new bureaus for ideological inculcation in almost all government ministries and institutions, and an increasing number of community religious organizations.

To this must be added the educational institutions, and particularly the universities. Their significance was also recognized from very early on. It may suffice to mention that the whole enterprise of the so-called 'cultural revolution', beginning in 1980 and going on for many years after, was originated in the campaign to bring the universities, as a bastion of secularism, under religious control. The motto 'the unity of seminary and university' was initially meant to turn universities into something of a seminary, although this project was modified in time in new terms: 'the universities would incorporate the religious element', and 'the religious seminaries would be more receptive to modern science'. The printed publications, though, kept their traditional appeal to the intellectuals. A new generation of religious intellectuals, trained in both seminary and university education, began to emerge in the early to mid-1990s, who would add a new element to the public sphere, transforming its unitary form and opening up its restrictive boundaries.

The new intellectual interpretations of the Islamic tradition in Iran have been fundamental in allowing for cultural, social, and political critique within a public sphere defined by Islam. Yet one has to understand that the capacities of Islamic tradition for reinterpretation and innovation contributing to social and political critique are limited by constraints that the same tradition places on public debate and criticism. The role of a new intellectual movement, which has become vocal since the presidential elections of May 1997, is significant in expanding the domain of the public sphere by encouraging a public practice of negotiating the Islamic symbolism under the rubric of reform. But, naturally, this is faced with resistance by the defenders of the entrenched official interpretation of this symbolism, who fear the 'unholy' implications of this movement of reform for the security of the established politico-religious order.

Notwithstanding its limited gains in institutional power since the May 1997 presidential elections, the so-called 'movement for reform' has created an intensifying public desire for 'civil society', as a site of political expression of the really existing social and cultural pluralities. The rise of public challenges to entrenched authorities via alternative interpretations of religion is certainly owed to this 'movement of reform'. The achievements of the reform movement in the public sphere aside, one must also note the sum contribution of the reforms to the consolidation of a new sense of religiously inspired nationhood. This clearly involves a gradual shift in the Islamic political-cultural discourse from 'the boundary-minded forms it assumed after the advent of European imperial expansion into Muslim lands to a more confident and differentiated internal and external dialogue'.

It is in the midst of the new challenges to the political power of the Shi'ite scholastic establishment that the challenge of the Western secularist ideology, backed by the threats of a US military attack on behalf of a Western alliance, has again raised its irrepressible head. The challenge here is once again the challenge of modernity. Hence, the increasing recognition, even within the religious establishment, that the Shi'ite faith and symbolism cannot remain in the top political position, confident of the control of the public domain, in the isolation that would immunize it to the intrusions of political modernity.

This is, at least partly, a consequence of the fact that the secularization enterprise, which had served as the intellectual core of Western democracy in the nineteenth century, was constructed in the process of the complex relationship of Western colonial powers and the inhabitants of the non-Western (including Islamic) societies. Evidence points to the fact that the whole expanse of empire, including both the West and the non-West, was the scene on which the secularization drama was played. The works of the secularist Iranian intellectuals of the late nineteenth and early twentieth centuries are clear evidence of the intense desire on the part of these intellectuals to fit Iran into the history of Western modernity. This was the case despite some serious theoretical and practical challenges that were posed to the intelli-gentsia by the defenders of the religious history of Iran. If this project was forcefully pursued in the constitutional revolution and its aftermath, the rise of the Islamic revolution marked its apparent reversal.

The renewed intellectual attention to the question of 'secularization' began in the mid-1990s after the publication of an article by the lay intellectual Abdolkarim Soroush, which was in fact a critique of 'Western secularism' if not 'the process of secularization'. Ever since, it was gradually recognized in the religious intellectual literature, and increasingly in open public debates, how central the secularization thesis was, not only to the self-understanding of modernity, but also to the search of traditional (religious) communities for a 'dignified identity' and 'national sovereignty'. Here one should also note the increasing influence of modern disciplines of social sciences on the new religious intellectuals. In fact, many of the new religious intellectuals tended to study sociology and political science in Iranian and Western universities, unlike the previous decades when engineering faculties were the breeding ground of the older generation of religious intellectuals.

In light of this new knowledge of the Western modernity a revision of the revolutionary movement of the late 1970s has already been underway since the late 1990s through public debate at multiple levels in an atmosphere where foreign intervention, except through willing and selective adoption of ideas, was absent. By references to the Western experience, a generation of new 'religious intellectuals' has been keen to develop a deeper understanding of the revolutionary experience than that offered by the clerical ideologues. President Khatami's writings, preceded and followed by numerous books, essays, articles, dissertations, etc., by other religious intellectuals dealing with similar themes, were a clear indication of this new trend. By taking a comparative perspective on the rise of new, religiously motivated, social and political movements in both the West and the non-West, Iran's new religious intellectuals have been trying to make the religious challenge to secularism a force to reckon with, not in militant terms, but in intellectual terms.

Impact of September 11

The September 11 attacks on New York and Washington and the subsequent American threats against Iran came at a time of heated debate and serious political competition between the two main factions, namely 'reformists' and 'conservatives', which were now deployed along institutional lines. The 'reformists' had taken the elected institutions such as the Parliament (Majlis-e Showra-ye Islami) and the presidency as their stronghold; whereas the 'conservatives' had kept control of the Council of Guardians (Showra-ye Negahban), which checked the parliamentary legislation, and the judiciary, with its power to prosecute and punish the reformists. The consequences for 'the project of reform' of what is increasingly seen as 'America's war on Islam' could be significant. It has provided both the 'conservatives' and 'reformists' with opportunities to advance their countervailing causes.

But one thing is clear: the warmongering strategy of President Bush has created an indispensable opportunity for the further development of political and public capacities of Islam. Such a development is set to contribute to further popularization and hence democratization of political Islam. But it does not seem to serve the cause of what the United States promotes as democracy. For Iran, the rise of a Muslim public is increasingly an impetus to frequent references to democracy and human rights in Iran's foreign policy vis-à-vis the aggressive posturing in the US war rhetoric. (If successful in convincing the religious public of the democratic merits of Islam, the Iranian Islamists believe that Muslims could then even find more effective means of resisting and even foiling US designs against them.) But for the United States to cope with the rise of the new Muslim publics worldwide, it will demand increasing rates of sophisticated policy making, perhaps a fundamental overhaul of how Islam has been understood and treated so far (what has so far been unfortunately lacking).

In order to clarify how the September 11 attacks and their repercussions have been received in Iran, one needs primarily to contextualize these in the mediated environment of public debate and opinion making that has come about in Iran in recent years. The efforts by the Iranian Islamists subsequent to the September 11 attacks are a clear indication of how the project of building an Islamic nation-state in Iran has to come to terms with global incidents of enormous proportions. The bellicose rhetoric of President Bush in his State of the Union address on January 29, 2002 (placing Iran on the 'Axis of Evil'), which led to the wars in Afghanistan and Iraq in a matter of one year, has made the task ever more difficult.

As already noted, Iran had to deal with the September 11 attacks on New York and Washington and their repercussions while engaged in heated debates over a plethora of political, cultural, social, and economic issues. The issue of 'security' was one example of the sort of topics debated just before the attacks. It followed from increasing reformist pressure on the political establishment for democratization, pressures that were deemed by the conservative faction threatening to national security. The judiciary and the Council of Guardians were the primary target of the reformist critique, as they were sending the reformist journalists and activists to jail, as well as blocking legislation that would lead to more political openness (and hence to a decline in conservative power).

Calls for respect for civil liberties, legal protection for freedom of expression, creation of new job opportunities, and a fairer distribution of wealth notwithstanding, worrying statistics about crime, prostitution, and other 'illegal and immoral acts' were also deemed threatening to national security. The conservative media took the usual line of attributing the political and moral crises to the American cultural invasion, and the judiciary, the police force, and the hard-line vigilantes were urged to combat 'the domestic agents of the enemy' who were accused of trying to corrupt the society. A new crackdown on the reformist journalists and activists was about to begin on charges of 'disturbing the mind of the public', 'posing a threat to national security', and 'insulting religious sanctities'.

Naturally, 'the agents of moral and cultural decay' would not be immune to this crackdown.

The conservative judiciary launched a campaign against violations of Islamic laws bent on reviving the practice of 'implementing Islamic punishments in the public'. The argument was that such an approach to punishment would intimidate those who might harbor designs for law-breaking and immoral acts. By contrast, the supporters of the opposing so-called 'reformist' faction argued that the Islamic punishments 'were not meant for revenge, nor for the destruction of the culprit', and that 'the main objective was prevention of social corruption'.

The conservative propaganda peaked when less than two weeks before the September 11 attacks (on August 30) a clerical advocate of the so-called 'conservative' faction (a former Minister of Intelligence), Hojjatoleslam Dorri Najafabadi, enraged the reformists after he had admired the Taliban for 'providing security for their people'. As a critic of the reformist agenda of President Khatami, he used his speech in a Friday prayer congregation in Tehran to question Khatami's government for its so-called policy of tasamoh (tolerance). He criticized the laxity of the government with regard to 'subversive' and 'permissive' elements that were 'poisoning' the cultural atmosphere and 'destabilizing' the political system.

President Khatami had bragged about his efforts to legitimize (despite all ambiguities) what he called 'tolerance of the critics' since his victory in the 1997 elections. The relatively open political atmosphere since 1997 was surely used (and even abused) by the conservative critics of Khatami as much as (if not more than) his supporters. But the president was adamant that tasamoh and tasahol (non-violence) were at the heart of the social and political teachings of Islam, and that 'violent and reactionary views had no bearing on the truth of Islam'. He thus insisted that his critics would be tolerated, hoping that this would serve as a model to conservative hard-liners urging them to also tolerate their critics. Responding to conservatives calling for Taliban-type domestic security, Khatami only said in a press conference on September 1:

We want neither a Taliban type security, nor a Taliban type Islam. We have tried to offer a fine image of Islam based on spirituality and democracy, which could serve as a role model for the Muslim world. It would be too dangerous now to take the Taliban's Islam as our own model.

And according to a reformist cleric, Nasser Qavami (also a Member of Parliament), those who sought a Taliban-type security wished to bring a Taliban-type government to power in Iran, otherwise, 'the Taliban had brought no security to Afghanistan'.

Ten days after this episode, New York and Washington were attacked, striking almost everybody with shock and awe. As already noted, the initial reaction of Iranians to the attacks on the United States, was one of discord and disorientation to the extent that most Islamists here had to officially dissociate themselves from these attacks, calling them 'non-Islamic' acts. Iran's initial sympathy with Americans as 'victims of terror' came despite the fact that the earlier US support for the Taliban and Al-Qaeda in Afghanistan, and for the Saddam regime during its war with Iran in the 1980s, was common knowledge in Iran. The national television and the printed publications gave wide coverage to the official condolence message sent by President Khatami to 'the American people', although the Iranian president carefully omitted the US government as the recipient of his message.

Even the Supreme Leader, Ayatollah Ali Khamenei, known for his staunch anti-American stance, came out (after a silence that lasted for a few days) in 'condemnation of terrorism in any form'. Although he was critical of the US strategy to go to war against 'terrorism' without either defining what the term meant and consisted of, or producing any evidence of the guilt of the targets of attack. In the Friday prayer congregations all over the country, the orators followed the Supreme Leader in giving sermons whereby the United States was cautioned and invited to 'self-reflection'. On September 25, 210 Members of the Iranian Parliament expressed sympathy with 'the victims of terrorist attacks on America'.

Meanwhile, the Supreme Leader called on the United Nations General Assembly (and not the Security Council) to take the lead in the campaign against terror. He was particularly keen to call on the Organization of Islamic Conference to take an active part in the anti-terrorist campaign. Insisting that Iran was itself a victim of terrorism, for which it had had to pay a high price, he invited first and foremost a clear definition of terrorism. Yet he announced that Iran would not take part in any anti-terrorist coalition that was led by the United States, and called on the 'Muslim nation of Iran' and 'Muslims all over the world' to close ranks in anticipation of future threats from the 'enemies of Islam'. Later developments attracted an increasing number of statesmen of the Muslim countries to somewhat side with Iran distancing themselves from an American 'war on terror'.

The effort at fomenting a united front of Muslims (on both domestic and international scenes) in reaction to the American 'war on terror' was certainly an indication that the Iranian Islamists were sensitive to the perils of this war. For them, this war signified nothing short of an American push to launch 'a new political and communicational crusade against Islam'. This fear became even more intense when the United States waged war in Afghanistan. The war in Iraq was an additional cause for concern as it held the prospect of the application of the idea of 'regime change' to other countries of the 'Axis of Evil'. The careful politicking of the Iranian leaders with regard to the threats of the United States certainly signifies concerns about global threats to Islam. But surely, the concerns with global threats to Islam are also tied with concerns about what is seen as threats to 'national interests'.

Ironically, references to 'national interests' in Iran had, for some time, had a dampening effect on trends of support for global Islamist militancy bent on hatred of the United States. Since the 1997 presidential elections, to be precise, which brought the reform-minded junior cleric Mohammad Khatami to popularity and prominence, Iran had tried to present the 'civil' side of Islam in calls for 'civil society' and 'religious democracy'. Even the Americans had somewhat acknowledged the development of 'positive trends' in Iran. For some time, Iran seemed even to have been accorded a slightly less belligerent status, at least in some US policy and media quarters, than Iraq and North Korea, which had been high on the list of Washington's 'rogue states'. But the bellicose US strategy has steadily created cause for Iranian Islamists to take a hard-line approach to the United States as a threat to both Islam and Iran. The appeal of Iranian Islamists to diplomacy, international law, human rights, peace, and dialogue since the American declaration of 'war on terror' has been focused on forming a united front of Muslims, both domestically and internationally, in opposition to US belligerence. The war in Iraq has certainly given the Iranian Islamists more reason to pursue this objective.

On the international scene, the task of forming a united front is made difficult by the divisions in the Islamic world. Iran's active politicking has been not only clearly aimed at overcoming the discord and disorientation on the domestic and international scenes, but also 'to make the threat into an opportunity'. Since the declaration of the 'war on terror', this has included intense lobbying in the Organization of Islamic Conference (OIC), and the convening of several conferences attended by politicians, religious leaders, academics, journalists, and activists from Islamic countries. Many other symbolic and political moves (at both state and public levels) could be added to this list. The initial results indicate both a further incorporation of 'Islamic Iran' into the Arab Muslim world and a relative pacification of the internal divisions.

Domestically, calls for a united front are advanced by the political and religious leaders of a nation divided by countervailing forces of militancy, associated with the traditional notion of 'religious honor' (gheyrat-e deeni), and resistance and détente, associated with the modern notion of national sovereignty and international law. The so-called conservative political faction that represents, broadly, the radical tendencies of political Islam in Iran, certainly advocates a militant posturing vis-à-vis the United States. This is certainly the position of the conservative-controlled media, including national radio and television, and the leaders of Friday prayer congregations nationwide.

The conservatives have practically gone on an offensive against the reformists, who present a less belligerent, if critical, view of US movements in the region. Accusations of complicity with the 'Great Satan' abound against the reformist journalists and activists, who until not long ago had been on a free ride of electoral wins at the expense of the unpopularity of the conservatives. But the aggressive US strategy has, surprisingly, not led to a tightening of the grip of religious and political hard-liners on power, nor even to a reversal of the calls for democratic reforms. If anything, the internal dynamics are weighing in the interest of further expansion of the public sphere in the interest of marginal and even critical voices of 'civil society'. The voices of warmongers on the Iranian side have been attracting diminishing public interest, while the presence of political analysts (advancing educated critiques of the US strategy) on the media scene (from the pulpit to the Internet) is on the rise.

An Iranian intellectual, Bijan Khajepour, told the Guardian in March 2002 that although President Bush's 'Axis of Evil' speech 'handed Iran's hard-liners a propaganda coup', the reformists did not lose the plot altogether, and even went on an offensive of their own in their calls for democratic reform. Ever since though, the reformist offensive have been effectively countered by the conservative invocation of 'resistance' to America's belligerence. But as already noted, the calls for democratic reform have not silenced.

Generally speaking, both over- and underestimation of the democratic claims of reformists could prove misleading not only for outsiders, but even for themselves. An Iranian reformist journalist and activist, Hamid Jalaipour, for example, was quoted by the Guardian in March 2002 as expressing joy with the endurance of his new newspaper Bonyan vis-a-vis conservative crackdowns 'Issue 26 and we haven't been closed', he said. Jalaipour was also quoted as saying: 'Iranian society has moved from a mass structure to a pluralistic one. The hard-liners don't have enough social ground any more.' But Jalaipour's joy did not last for long as Bonyan was in fact shut down in April on charges of subverting Islamic rule. Subsequent developments proved that the conservatives still commanded a powerful influence, but to the credit of Jalaipour, this was not powerful enough to stem the tide of the reform movement.

The main conservative ploy to rein in the reformist campaign for democracy has been to brand the reformists as allies of the United States. The US military attacks against Afghanistan and Iraq have provided ample opportunity for the conservative media to publish editorials condemning the emptiness of US claims to democracy and human rights, and question the support of local reformists for an US-type democracy. Nonetheless, the reformists keep insisting that the best way to counteract a possible US attack is 'to enhance the system's legitimacy by expanding democracy'.

Examples of real gains for the reformists are few, but significant. For instance, despite the attempts of the religious hard-liners to force Iran's National Security Council to declare a state of emergency vis-a-vis President Bush's threats against Iran in his

'Axis of Evil' speech, the Council drafted a (reformist-led) national plan for reconciliation. The reformists have also been trying ever since to revive a bill to give amnesty to all political detainees (who are predominantly reformists). Although this has not been successful and a few more of the reformist activists have since in fact been sent to jail on charges of threatening national security, the conservative judiciary has been under pressure to be more lenient than before in its treatment of the reformist activists.

The Bush 'Axis of Evil' speech has apparently not damaged the campaign for internal reform as much as first seemed likely despite repeated comments by US officials on the defeat of reforms in Iran, and discredited their anticipation of a radical popular turning against the conservatives in sympathy with the United States. In fact, both reformists and conservatives have played the US war threat in their own interests. For instance, while the reformists have been trying to justify negotiations with the United States as a move serving Iran's national interests, the conservatives have so far succeeded in pushing the desire for negotiation with the United States out the political agenda, calling it a threat to national security.

The issue of negotiation with the United States is a clear example of how local politics has been played out since the September 11 events. The issue came up seriously after the Bush 'Axis of Evil' speech in January 2002, and it has been a thorn in Iran's foreign policy ever since. Shortly after the US attack on Afghanistan, an editorial in the newspaper Azad emphasized 'the need for refraining from ruling out talks' with the United States. In March, the reformist-dominated Majlis (Parliament) followed the reformist press to seize the moment for establishing some sort of official contact with the US government by reacting positively to a proposal by a US Congressman (Joseph Biden) for talks between the Members of Parliament of the two countries. The debate over the relationship with the United States raged further when the results of an opinion poll indicated that a majority of the public would support contacts with the United States. But in May the Supreme Leader reserved no harsh words in dismissing any form of contacts. Ayatollah Khamenei came out in open and harsh attack against those who promoted official negotiations with the United States, accusing them of being devoid of 'religious honor'.

Although after this forceful dismissal the issue of negotiations with the United States was left in silence for some time in deference to the Supreme Leader, the US war on Iraq created a new opportunity to again raise the matter as an issue of national interest versus an issue of national security. Just before the US military operation against Iraq began, the powerful head of the Expediency Council, Ali-Akbar Hashemi-Rafsanjani, told in an interview with an academic journal that the issue of relations with the United States was not a matter of religious principle, as Ayatollah Khamenei had put it. He said rather that the issue was a matter of 'political expediency' to be decided either in a referendum or by the Expediency Council. Yet he was courteous enough to give the final approval to the Supreme Leader.

All things considered, despite the differences between the conservatives and the reformists, the increasing seriousness of the 'American threat' after the wars in Afghanistan and Iraq has pulled the two factions somewhat closer together in calling for the complete withdrawal of US troops from the region. Evidently, Bush's 'Axis of Evil' speech gave both sides of Iranian politics reasons for a kind of unity focused around the shared feeling of being insulted. Indications are that Iranians in general have also been outraged by the US threats although some of the fierce critics of the religious government still cherish crazy fantasies about the prospect of a US attack against Iran leading to the overthrow of the 'hated mullahs'.

The sense of public outrage was such that the organizers of the nationwide demonstration celebrating the anniversary of the Islamic revolution in February 2002 made an unconventional appeal even to the opponents of the regime to express solidarity with the nation against 'Bush's insult against the Iranian nation'. In response to Bush's statement whereby Iranian political authorities were categorically dismissed as 'non-elected' and 'unpopular', the Iranian officials went out of their way to emphasize the high place of the electoral process in Iran's Islamic politics. The continued US war threats created the right political atmosphere for yet another show of anti-American sentiments, which were expressed in the rallies on the anniversary of the revolution in February 2003 not long before the US military venture in Iraq began.

Iranian Islamists

The public reactions to the September 11 attacks were diversified in this nation of more than 70 million. On the official level, the reactions ranged from sympathy for the United States to sympathy for 'anti-American struggles of the oppressed'. The two main types of political Islam were in clear display here. Yet there were also spontaneous expressions by the secular middle class. In September just after the incident in the United States, a crowd that had gathered in one of Tehran's busy streets proceeded with a silent march holding candles in sympathy with the victims of the 'terrorist attack'. Meanwhile, an editorial in one leading reformist paper, Nowruz (run by the head of the National Security Committee of the Parliament, Mohsen Mirdamadi), brought the idea of an 'anti-terrorist coalition' into question, posing a number of what it called 'logical' questions:

What is the meaning of terrorism? Is the attack on the Pentagon a terrorist act? If so, then why are the attacks against the Palestinian institutions and the assassination of the Palestinian leaders (by the Israelis) not categorized as terrorist acts? Is terrorism a specifically American problem, or is it a problem of global proportions? If it is an American problem, then why should other countries be mobilized and pay for it? And if terrorism, like drug trafficking, is a universal problem, then why must America decide its course and destiny?

The editorial of one of the conservative papers (published by a group running a madrasa in Qom under the tutelage of the hard-line Ayatollah Mesbah Yazdi) was much harsher in its comments. The editorial of Feyziyyeh (entitled 'crime and punishment') said:

What for years Hollywood was trying to create in the genre of science-fiction movies in order to entertain the American people has now become reality in an ominous fashion. Yet there is a big difference between the fiction and the reality. In the Hollywood movies, some kind of superman would always come to the rescue in the last moment, unfolding the conspiracies and defeating the enemy; but in the real story neither the supermen, nor the high-tech intelligence and military machines, were able to even anticipate the enemy's operation. The American leaders whether they attribute this operation to elements beyond American borders, or to an internal conspiracy, will have to admit the beginning of the end of the myth of American invincibility. This audacious act was in fact a punishment for American crimes worldwide, in Hiroshima, in Vietnam, in the occupied Palestine, and in Iraq, the Sudan, Lebanon, Somalia and Iran.

In time, with the intensification of US threats against Iran, the Iranian officials took a tougher stance against the US government. In his tour of some European countries in March 2002, even the moderate outward-looking President Khatami took a strong position against the United States. He even went as far as predicting that 'America will one day include even Europe in its Axis of Evil'. Reuters (reporting on Khatami's European tour) cited President Khatami as calling for all foreign troops to withdraw from Afghanistan. 'A region in development does not need the presence of military forces. It needs solidarity,' he was quoted as saying. Khatami also said that the United States was using the war in Afghanistan to consolidate its position as the world's only superpower. He added:

After September 11, America is trying to use the situation to impose its own views and get rid of all obstacles in order to be the exclusive superpower. If this continues, America will include Europe in the 'Axis of Evil'. They will [also] add China and Russia [to the axis of evil] and the world will move toward a terrible war.

Nonetheless, President Khatami insisted repeatedly that: 'Iran is still committed to its policy of détente in the face of pending threats to the world from warmongers.' Actually, Iran had good reasons to be accommodating with regard to the US war in Afghanistan, as it has been with regard to the war in Iraq. If anyone apart from the Afghans and Iraqis themselves had a good reason to cheer the annihilation of 'the networks of terror' in Afghanistan, and the fall of Saddam in Iraq, it was the Iranians. After all, Iran was a primary victim of the Taliban's and Al-Qaeda's terrorism, and Iraq's weapons of mass destruction. Iran had not yet forgotten the massacre of its diplomats by the Taliban in 1998 in Mazar-Sharif, and the Iranian victims of Iraq's chemical weapons in the 1980s are still perishing by the day. Otherwise, there was little doubt about US involvement in the victimization of Iran. And if there were any doubts, the statements of a former Saudi diplomat in January 2002 washed them away. According to Mohammad Al-

Otaibi, a former Saudi ambassador to Afghanistan, in an interview with the London-based Arabic paper Al-Hayat (cited by the local press): 'Americans initially supported the Taliban in order to put Iran under pressure'. The Americans have also admitted that they had supported Iraq in its war against Iran in the 1980s because they saw a greater danger in the revolutionary Iran to US interests than in Saddam's Iraq.

Nonetheless, Iran played, in diplomatic jargon, 'a positive role' in the UN-sponsored conference in Bonn, Germany, which pieced together Afghanistan's post-Taliban government in early 2002, and followed up with concrete offers to help Afghanistan's reconstruction, to the tune of $600 million. Iranians have good reason to also contribute to peace and stability in Iraq, as they have repeatedly declared. As if all this was not enough to prove the goodwill of Iran toward American-controlled Afghanistan and Iraq, the Iranian government refrained from meddling with the internal affairs of these countries after their occupation by US forces. After the fall of the Taliban in Afghanistan, Iran even introduced visa requirements for the citizens of the Gulf states, ostensibly to prevent the entry of Taliban and Al-Qaeda members into Iranian territory, just as the United States had wanted. And after the launch of the US-led attack on Iraq, Iran did not allow the Iran-based Iraqi opposition armed forces to enter Iraqi territory, again just as the United States wanted. But the bellicose US strategy has not matched the Iranian official overtures. Certainly even ordinary Iranians, let alone the officials, expected a better deal from the United States.

The confrontational mood on the part of Iranians was shaped and nourished by the mediation of the American war rhetoric in a matter of few months. The commentaries in the press, which had been predominantly (but with few exceptions) critical of the attackers, calling them 'terrorists', began to blame the United States for what had happened there. The conservative commentators offered an analysis of the event whereby sympathy for the loss of human lives was overshadowed by conspiracy theorizing developed around two main themes. A grand conspiracy theory speculated that the whole project of the attacks had been designed either by domestic anti-state elements, or by an Israeli-American coalition. The other theme discounted the possibility of a premeditated design, but stressed the design of a contingency plan by the right-wing Jewish and American elements to take advantage of the situation for quelling radical Islam.

With regard to the US war threat, 'unity' and 'solidarity' were promoted as the official positions of all factions, as the opinion polls indicated the public preference for this option. According to opinion polls taken in March 2002, a majority of the residents of the capital city, Tehran, considered 'unity' and 'solidarity' as the most effective public response against a possible US military attack on Iran. These opinion polls also indicated an emphasis on 'the people's presence on the scene, resistance, and defense'. Interestingly, the citizens of Tehran were predominantly of the opinion that the best government response to American threats was 'to keep the citizenry happy' by adopting effective policies in addressing the social and economic problems of the people. Other solutions suggested by the public included establishing relations with the United States, and/or mobilizing resources to defend the country: 'Some 81 per cent believed that the people did not want to enter a war with the U.S. but, if such a war occurred, they would defend the country.' While the Tehrani citizens generally underestimated the possibility of the world community supporting the United States in any attack on Iran, they were confident that the Islamic countries would support Iran: 'About 68 percent of the respondents said that an American military attack on Iran would be a disaster. And some 81 percent suggested that the existing problems should be solved through political methods rather than on the battlefield.'

A reformist Member of Parliament, Majid Ansari, said that Iranians would close ranks to confront US threats if US leaders' aggressive overtures against the Islamic Republic take a turn for an attack. 'Our stance is based on restraint and détente, but if we are threatened by America, the Iranian nation will face up [to any attack] in an integrated rank,' he told a group of mourners at Ayatollah Khomeini's mausoleum in the south of Tehran. Meanwhile, a leading conservative cleric (addressing a crowd in the city of Isfahan) fended off President Bush's 'Axis of Evil' charge against Iran along with Iraq and North Korea. 'The Iranian people are not intimidated a bit by Bush's and American threats,' said Ayatollah Abolqassem Khaz'ali.

Several military chiefs also vowed strong resistance in the event of an attack amid US officials' accusations against Iran. A

Revolutionary Guard commander said that Iran would stand up to enemies with force and defend the country. 'We are not seeking a war, but we will stand up against the enemy should the need for defense arise,' the chief commander of the naval forces of the Islamic Revolution's Guards Corps, Brigadier-General Morteza Saffari, said in the ancient city of Shush in the oil-rich Khuzestan province.

The Iranian political and religious leaders and activists have, nonetheless, been careful not to antagonize the United States while maintaining their critical position vis-à-vis US support for Israel. Shortly after the inception of the US attack against the Taliban's Afghanistan, the Minister for Intelligence, Ali Younesi, announced in a speech to the seminarians in the Qom Seminary that Iran would not interfere with the US attack against Al-Qaeda and the Taliban, though he also requested the Americans to honor Iranian national sovereignty.

This careful politicking has also been the case with regard to the US attack against Saddam's Iraq. Not only did the Iranian leaders stand by their policy of not getting in the way of the Americans in Iraq, but they did not conceal their joy on the fall of Saddam, and understandably so. Yet even so, the Americans have not been satisfied and still accuse Iran of interference in both Afghanistan and Iraq. After all, without much effort, Iran wields astonishing political influence via religious influence in both countries - more so in Iraq than in Afghanistan due to the Shi'ite factor.

Given the economic significance of Iraq (based on oil) which Afghanistan lacks, the Iranian political and moral influence is understandably worrying for the United States even without Iran needing to rely on military intervention. The actual call by Iran for the withdrawal of the 'forces of occupation' from Iraq, echoed also by the Iran-based Supreme Council of the Islamic Revolution of Iraq (SCIRI), has risen also from Iraqi Shi'ite believers in their millions in peaceful religio-political anti-American rallies.

Much to the dislike of the Americans, with their fantasy of being cheered for liberating the Iraqi people from Saddam's dictatorial oppression, Iraqi Shi'ite believers gathered in Karbala in late April 2003 to express their resentment at the presence of infidel US troops on sacred Iraqi soil. Millions gathered from all over Iraq in response to a call from the leader of the SCIRI, Mohammad-Baqir Hakim, who came to Iran as an exile more than twenty years ago after his father, a high-ranking Iraqi Shi'ite scholar, was killed by Saddam for pro-Iran sentiments. They gathered to mourn the death of a celebrated Shi'ite immaculate imam chanting slogans in support of Islam and in rejection of both Saddam and US troops.

Iran's call for peace and democracy versus Bush's 'America is at war' message

The very claim of Iran's democratically minded Islamists (including President Khatami) is to create a different kind of (a truer) democracy, which cannot flourish unless it returns to a religious moral order. The idea is certainly less than novel. The liberation theologians (particularly of the Catholic persuasion) were the latest to criticize the irrationality of liberal claims to secular impartiality, and the disastrous moral consequences of the hypocritical claims of the modern secular state to defend 'freedom of conscience' and 'freedom of expression' as the main pillars of democracy. But the Islamist practical efforts in Iran at introducing democracy as a religious value are certainly novel. Particularly so, as the Islamic liberation theologians in Iran have, unlike their Catholic counterparts, had the opportunity to actually take charge of the management of a modern state. This is certainly a novel phenomenon, regardless of whether, or to what extent, the Islamist claims to democracy are genuine.

A comparative perspective of the contradictory quests of Iran and the United States for democracy was presented. 'If the recent U.S. threats and actions damage the development of new democratic structures in Iran,' he wrote, 'then it will not be the first time that Iranians' efforts to build a democratic system have been set back by foreign intervention'. Referring to the US-backed coup against the democratically oriented government of Mohammad Mossadegh in 1953, he questioned the sincerity of US claims to advancing democracy in other countries. Vaseghi noted:

It can be argued that Iran has a stronger claim to a democratically elected government than the United States. Iran's President Khatami has been elected by an overwhelming majority of Iranians for a second term. In contrast, there is some controversy on whether President Bush won a majority of the votes in the U.S. election.

The US consistent disregard for the authority of the United Nations and for international treaties, its 'terrorist' campaign against Nicaragua, its backing for undemocratic regimes in the Middle East, and particularly its support for Israeli atrocities against the Palestinians, were offered as examples of US double-standards. The author then went on to say:

Iran is now firmly on the learning path of development of democratic institutions and a pluralistic culture based on the realities and complexities of its own social traditions and political history. Iran has a long way to go, but it is on the right direction. In Iran there are passionate debates at all levels of the society, and most notably in the press, the parliament, and the government between various forces of conservatism and the progressive forces of modernization. These political forces happen to reflect the texture and the realities of the Iranian society. These debates are a necessary learning process as part of the development of a culture of pluralism and democracy in Iran, a process that was so often interrupted by those who do not consider a democratic Iran in their economic interests.

The contrast has become more salient as the US push to start a war in Iraq evidently diminished the trust of the world public, let alone the Muslim public, in the seriousness of the Bush Administration in promoting democracy in the world while crediting Iran's earlier allegations about American hypocrisy. As a result, the Iranian Islamists claim, Iran seems to have come out of the political wilderness enjoying the sympathy of the world's public opinion, while the United States seems to have been isolated and condemned for its defiance of 'collective wisdom'.

The combined anger and ridicule of the Iranian Islamists for what they call 'US double-standards' is difficult not to share when one takes note of American positioning with respect to the Israeli-Palestinian conflict, an issue highly sensitive to Iranians, and to Muslims in general. This is exacerbated even more since the United States claims to be playing the role of an impartial peace broker in this conflict. In late June 2002, for instance, President Bush, in his long-expected speech about the Israeli-Palestinian conflict, said that he did not trust the existing Palestinian leadership because it was 'compromised by terrorism', calling for a new leadership that was not 'compromised by terrorism'. But this meant, in both American and Israeli political language, a green light for the Israeli occupation of all that was earlier agreed even by the Israelis as Palestinian land. How could Palestinians get a new leadership that was not compromised by terrorism under the occupation of the Israeli troops, their imminent enemy, was a question that apparently never occurred to President Bush. Unless of course, he had complete confidence that only under such occupation can such a leadership take shape.

The situation was not much different in the aftermath of the recent war in Iraq. The American promise of a 'war of liberation', which was meant to bring to the 'oppressed Iraqi people' the chance of deciding their own political destiny, has met its logical, and yet hypocritical, conclusion. First a US military governor, and then an American civilian, were appointed to rule Iraq as long as necessary. Their main mission, according to Iranian Islamists, is to prevent the creation of another Iran. Iranians point to US claims to give Iraqis a chance to rule themselves while at the same time denying the Iraqis an immediate chance to decide their future. US political leaders would argue, of course, that the Iraqis are not yet ready to decide such a significant decision. Iranian leaders, on the other hand, point to the political maturity of the Iraqis, to a large class of learned scholars of religion with moral influence on the public, and to the vast number of highly educated middle-class Iraqis, as a reservoir of potential leaders of the future.

Iranians also point to orderly and peaceful religious ceremonies, held by the Shi'ite majority in the shrine cities of Najaf and Karbala. There, the demonstrators called for an immediate withdrawal of the 'forces of occupation', and for the formation of a 'popular government' via free and open elections. The position of the United States has been made more difficult as some Sunni religious leaders and even the Kurds, allied with the United States in the military phase of the operation 'Iraqi Freedom', have sympathized with the Iranian proposal. Iranians had also pursued diplomacy in unison with the world in order to prevent the outbreak of war in Iraq in the first place. They even worked with Muslim countries neighboring Iraq to find a peaceful solution to the Iraqi crisis, whereas the Americans defied the world by accepting no alternative to war.

On the international scene, such developments have made it possible for the Iranian Islamists to appear as advocates of 'true democracy' (i.e., a 'religious democracy') as against what they call the American 'hypocritical claims' to democracy. The now official policy line of 'dialogue between civilizations' found firmer ground when it was adopted as the theme of a joint gathering of the European Union and the OIC in Istanbul in the wake of George Bush's State of the Union address. President Khatami had already set the stage for the promotion of his idea of 'dialogue between civilizations' in an address to the General Assembly of the United Nations:

The day Iran proposed the idea of dialogue between civilizations to the General Assembly (in early 2001) few would anticipate that in such a short span of time this idea would become so imperative for world security, and so vital for saving the world from a terrible war.

Iran's propaganda against US disregard for human rights and international law, and condemnations of false claims to democracy, continued unabated, and even intensified with the start of the US-led military attack against Iraq. Iranian officials and most editorials in the press took heart from the anti-war and anti-American rallies worldwide to go as far as branding the United States the most dangerous terrorist power and the most frequent user of weapons of mass destruction.

Speculations about a Zionist plot

While speculations about the identity of the perpetrators of the September 11 attacks on the United States were going on, Iranian national television screened a local production in which the attack was portrayed as a 'Zionist plot'. The attack was seen as a ploy in order to create an environment for 'the brutal suppression of the Palestinian resistance against the Zionist occupation'. The film began with a scene of a UN-sponsored conference in Durban, South Africa, where, on September 3, 2001, the representatives of some 3000 non-governmental organizations from around the world signed a document declaring Israel a racist state with a record of 'war crimes, genocide, and ethnic cleansing'. Then after a dramatic turn of events, the film ended by revealing a grand conspiracy designed by the extremist Zionists and some ultra-right Americans to hit the United States, each for their own diabolical purposes.

The Zionists were placed at the center of the plot. Taken aback by the loss of the credibility of their claims to victimization, they plotted the September 11 attacks to achieve certain ends. First, they would shift the attentions of the world public from their crimes against Palestinians. Second, they would arrange the scene of their crime such that the Muslims would seem to be the culprits. Third, with the image of Muslims tarnished as a bunch of brutal terrorists, the Zionists would be given a free hand in doing what they wished with the Palestinians still resisting the occupation of their land. And finally, the Americans would stop putting pressure on the Zionists to make peace with the Palestinians, and would turn against the 'Muslim threat' thus making the world a safer place for Israel.

The film was only one example of a wide range of speculations among the public, and in the media, about an Israeli connection to the September 11 attacks. This was an added component to previous efforts at equating the strategy of Israel in repressing the Palestinian resistance and in dealing with its enemies, in general, to 'state-sponsored terrorism'.

Since 1948, the question of Palestine as a Muslim land, and its occupation by the Jews, has always raised sensitivity in Iran. But since the Islamic revolution of 1979, 'the need for the liberation of "the honorable Quds"' (as the place of ascendance of the Prophet Mohammad to heaven, or mi'raj), and the animosity toward the 'Zionists', have been commonplace. To that extent the Iranian Islamic revolutionaries who deposed the monarchic regime in the late 1970s have succeeded in time to make any talk of compromise with the Jewish State a religiously loaded political taboo. The intensity of 'anti-Zionist' propaganda was such that the moderate trends in Palestine (including even the Arafat faction) were denigrated for their preparedness to recognize the Jewish state (based on the 1948 occupation of Palestinian land) and for the return of not even the whole of the 1967 occupied territory.

It has become an entrenched tradition in post-revolutionary Iranian politics to see the ceding of even one inch of Palestinian territory, let alone recognition of the state of Israel on the Muslim territory, as a sellout of Muslim lands and a violation of Islamic values. Making a compromise decision over 'the sacred land' has thus been considered beyond the authority of Palestinians alone. The position of Iran was thus always too radical to allow for the recognition of the socalled peace negotiations between the

Palestinians and the Israelis. And its propaganda against the peace negotiations was always targeted at the sincerity of Israel in making a 'just peace', and at the eligibility of the United States as an impartial referee.

For the Iranian Islamists, since Ayatollah Khomeini called for the annihilation of the Jewish state after he took power in Iran in the late 1970s, Israel has been characterized as a 'cancerous tumor' and a 'source of corruption'. Moreover, it has always been the most important ally of the United States in the war for the destruction of Islam. But, interestingly, the public debates raised since the mid-1990s, and particularly since the 1997 elections, created an atmosphere in which alternative views about how to deal with the Israeli-Palestinian conflict could be raised, although very painfully and sometimes at high cost. The September 11 events made these talks even more open. In fact there arose three major points of view: the official view, the revisionist view, and the hard-line view.

The official view was expressed typically by President Khatami in an address to a conference on 'the media of the Islamic world in support of the Palestinian Intifada'. The main theme of this conference was to study the ways and means to give voice to the 'Palestinian resistance' against 'Zionist aggression' in the new conditions created in the aftermath of the September 11 attacks. The conference was thus aiming at counteracting the Western (and particularly American) media, which were believed to have sided with Israel in silencing the 'Palestinian voice'. In his address, Khatami called for the creation of a 'war crimes tribunal' in the occupied Palestine by the United Nations. He also called for a 'fund' set up by the OIC to finance the Intifada. According to Khatami:

The Intifada of the Palestinian oppressed nation is not to be characterized as violence and terror; for it is, in fact, a struggle against violence and terror; and for this it must be commended. The unity of the Islamic world is neither unrealistic, nor merely a matter of political expediency. It is rather a real, humane and moral affair, which will benefit the whole world. I declare here that every Muslim condemns violence, terror and violation of human rights, not least because he/she is a Muslim. Zionism has endangered peace and stability not only in the region, but also in the whole world. It has violated the basis of dialogue and understanding between nations and religions.

The revisionist view, on the other hand, was discussed at a conference on 'Palestine: an Iranian view' held in Tehran in December 2001. The young jurist Mohsen Kadivar's views (presented in a talk given to this conference) were typical of alternative views on how Iran should deal with the Palestinian question:

Our question today is whether or not some have made the support for the Palestinian cause a pretext for dampening the domestic problems. Only the Palestinian people can decide on their own destiny. If they decided on the Intifada as the way to liberation, we should support them; and if they chose the diplomatic option, we should support them all the same. We don't have the right to dictate our solutions to the Palestinian people, nor to make decisions on their behalf. We don't have the right to outpace the Palestinians in their struggle. The Palestinian question is first and foremost a national question. And religion is secondary to that. The first priority is the realization of security and the right to life for the Palestinians. The Palestinian question is a national question before it is a religious question. Over the past 23 years our view of the Palestinian question has been based on an ideological discourse. But considering the new developments in Palestine and the changes in the Palestinian people, we need to revise our view.

The hard-line view carried the core of typical conspiracy theories. An example of this was reflected in the views of the editor of a hard-line monthly Imamat in an interview published in the hard-line weekly YaLesrarat in late September 2001. Mohammad-Ali Ramin said in his analysis of the September 11 attacks:

The enormity and complexity of this event was such that one cannot pinpoint one or another renegade group as the only culprit. For one, the operation must have been carried out under the support and guidance of people with supreme intelligence on the American soil. For another, the perpetrators must have had insider information about the security services. The only elements in America capable of these are undeniably the Jews.

Asked how the Jews would undermine their staunchest ally, Ramin replied: 'There are historical precedents for such acts. For example, in the year 64 AD, the Jews, in their hostility with the Christians, convinced the Roman Emperor (Nero) to put Rome on fire and blame it on the Christians.' Asked about the motivations of the Jews in taking such an action, he retorted:

I see the Intifada as the source of all this. In the anti-racism conference in South Africa, thousands of NGOs condemned the Zionist regime and found Zionism tantamount to racism. This was unprecedented, as the Jews had previously attracted the sympathy of the world public opinion for their alleged victimization. The crimes of the Zionists against the Palestinian Intifada had finally begun to turn the tide of the public opinion against the Jews. Therefore, the explosions in America could serve as a distracter in the interest of the Zionists. Clearly today hardly anybody in the West takes a serious position against the Israeli crimes in Palestine. And meanwhile, the Jews sit back and watch the confrontation of Islam and Christianity.

The speculations about a self-hit involving 'the Zionist entity' came to a head with references by Iranian officials and the media to statements made by a US presidential hopeful, Lyndon LaRouche. An article posted on the web site of the weekly journal Executive Intelligence Review (founded by LaRouche) under the title 'Iran Blows the Lid off America's Reischtag Fire Lie' covered this development, and was quoted widely by the Iranian media and even some prominent politicians. As the article said:

Looks like Iran is the first country to formally start questioning the mysterious events of September 11, and hence of the real agenda behind America's War of Terror. And no amount of rhetoric about 'conspiracy theorizing' is going to silence this truth.

In 1999, LaRouche had already raised anger in some quarters in the United States when as a candidate running for the US Senate he said:

We are making a big mistake to think that the people out there hate us for our support of democracy and human rights. It will be a self-deception to ignore the lasting impressions of our crimes on the present generations of Japanese, Vietnamese, Iraqis, Palestinians and others.

The radio station Voice of the Islamic Republic of Iran (English language) went so far as to conduct a phone interview with LaRouche (on March 4). In it LaRouche elaborated in some detail his reading of the nature and significance of what he called 'the attempted coup d'état' of September 11. He even named some figures prominent in the faction around the former US National Security Advisor, Zbigniew Brzezinski, including the political scientist, Samuel Huntington, and the former Secretary of State Henry Kissinger. He was keen to add that these men 'are promoting a clash of civilizations'.

The interview was aired four times in one week (and a Farsi summary circulated throughout the press) both in Iran and internationally via satellite transmission. The story also appeared (on March 9) in the English-language daily Tehran Times (and in the vernacular print media), as well as on national radio and TV news programs. The Tehran Times web site reported:

A U.S. Presidential candidate in the 2000 [and 2004] election, Lyndon LaRouche, has said that the September 11 terrorist attacks had been organized by rogue elements inside the U.S., and were aiming to use the incident to promote a war against Islam.

In his interview with the Voice of the Islamic Republic of Iran, LaRouche claimed that the attacks on the United States (which claimed more than 3000 lives) were organized by American and Israeli elements (who were trying to promote a war). He also called the Israeli regime a dictatorial regime and said that Tel Aviv was prepared to commit Nazi-style crimes against the Palestinians.

Among top officials citing the LaRouche was Ali-Akbar Hashemi-Rafsanjani, formerly a powerful president of Iran and currently the Chairman of the Expediency Council. In fact, Rafsanjani used the occasion of Friday prayer congregation in Tehran to invoke LaRouche in support of his own speculation about the plans of the United States and Israel for expanding their dominance in Afghanistan, Central Asia, the Caucasus, and the Middle East. Noting the US attack on Afghanistan, he said: 'If the intention was to protect the Afghan people and to save them from poverty and misery, that would be a desirable thing; but all available evidence indicates that there are other objectives behind this presence' (Rafsanjani 2002). 'The objective is to pave the way for launching a war against Islam and Muslims,' he went on to point out.

But Rafsanjani, wise politician that he is, was keen in his sermon not to antagonize the United States. He said 'we are not at war with America. We hope that the Americans will not commit the blunder and get their hands stained in a war [with us],' he said, cautioning the Bush Administration that 'the outbreak of war in the region would not be of any benefit to the aggressor nor to the victim' (ibid.). He concluded by emphasizing the importance of the unity of all sectors of Iranian society, something that, as already noted, Bush's 'Axis of Evil' formulation had indeed assisted.

Another top official citing LaRouche was Hassan Rowhani, Iran's Secretary of the Supreme National Security Council. He was also an advisor to the President, a representative of the Supreme Leader, a member of the Expediency Council, and a member of the Assembly of Experts. In a keynote address delivered to an international conference convened in Tehran (on March 9), he referred to LaRouche's analysis to accuse the United States of moving in the direction of a new 'Roman Empire' (Rowhani 2002).

The conference was sponsored by the Institute for Political and International Studies (IPIS), a think-tank connected with the Foreign Ministry. The September 11 attacks were a primary topic of the speakers from the Persian Gulf and Asian countries. In his address to the conference, Rowhani noted that the September 11 attacks had initially produced a new picture of the American people, as 'a people that had been wronged', and expressed regret that this image did not endure due to the subsequent belligerence of the US government.

Rowhani said that the United States could have reacted by addressing the reasons for popular resentment around the world with respect to US policies; 'for example, by launching a new international Marshall Plan to eradicate poverty and injustice in the world' (ibid.). This would have won 'the hearts and minds of the populations of the world,' he added. The United States could also have taken legal steps to bring the perpetrators to justice, according to international law, by presenting evidence of the guilt of the accused; but 'when asked for evidence, President Bush said that now is the time for war, not evidence,' he noted. He then characterized a third option adopted by the Bush Administration: 'misrepresenting the act of terrorism in order to achieve the goals of a new doctrine of U.S. and Israeli dominance in the Middle East'.

Rafsanjani and Rowhani are two top Iranian officials who, in the past, had even been seriously concerned with improving relations with the United States despite Iran's long experience with US hostility. But like other Iranians, they had certainly sensed something fishy about 'the 9/11 scenario' right after it happened. Their invocation of someone like LaRouche in support of their premonitions could of course be for seeking allies at a time of increasing pressure from the United States. But they could have also sensed that September 11 was in fact the point of no return for the United States, and that its 'war on terror' was, in fact, the long-feared 'war against Islam'.

The Afghan and Iraqi Connections

There have been numerous speeches, commentaries, and policy statements reflected in the Iranian media since the September 11 attacks, mostly critical of the belligerent US strategy, and yet stopping short of inviting an attack. During the bombing of Afghanistan by the Americans, Iranian television was quick to send reporters to Afghanistan. This was the first time the Iranian media covered a war in another country. They covered, in particular, the destructive consequences of the air bombing for the civilian Afghan population in the cities and villages, some of which had been wiped out as a result of the US bombing campaign. A conference of Islamic media organizations was held to discuss the coverage of 'the Afghan plight'.

The coverage of the war in Iraq has been even more effective and wider in its scope. It has certainly been unprecedented in terms of the time allocated, the number of reporters sent to the location, and the number of analysts and experts interviewed. That the Iranian-sponsored satellite news network Al-Alam has made deep inroads into post-Saddam Iraq in terms of attracting a large audience has been acknowledged by a recent report in The New York Times. The intent of the Iranian media since the war in Iraq is to give voice to a looming 'anti-occupation movement' centered around Iraq's Shi'ite population, but including supporters and sympathizers from all other religious and ethnic persuasions. The main motive of this movement is said to be the protection of Iraq's independence, territorial integrity, and national, cultural, and religious interests. The programming for the domestic audience has been designed to raise social and political consciousness with regard to US threats to Iran after the United States is finished with the business in Iraq.

All in all, it is increasingly evident that the developments in Iran and their external influence have already created a new quandary for the United States in the Middle East, and particularly as far as Iran's influence on Afghanistan and Iraq is concerned. According to an article in the Washington Post published not long after the war in Afghanistan:

Viewed last fall as a potential ally in the U.S.-led war on terrorism, Iran is presenting an increasingly complex problem for the Bush administration's anti-terrorism policies in Afghanistan and the Middle East, according to U.S. officials and analysts. Iran's influence in Afghanistan has grown since President Bush said Tehran was part of an 'Axis of Evil', with senior U.S. officials charging that Iran is subverting the U.S.-backed interim Afghan government and providing refuge to Al-Qaeda and the Taliban fighters.

However, the Afghan President, Hamid Karzai, in his visit here in February 2002 thanked Iran's religious and political leaders for their humanitarian assistance, and signed agreements promising cooperation between the two countries. Iran has also been commended by the United Nations for hosting millions of Afghan refugees, who had fled 'the Taliban terror, for several years'. During Karzai's visit, Iran's president, responding to American accusations about Iran's sabotage of Afghanistan's security, said in no uncertain terms: 'Iran's national security is tied with a safe, peaceful and progressive Afghanistan'.

Given all this, it should be obvious what Iran would want in Afghanistan. A local journalist put the question 'What does Iran want in Afghanistan?' to the Iranian Deputy Foreign Minister, Mohsen Aminzadeh, in December 2001 by. He retorted:

We want peace in Afghanistan. What can secure our interests in Afghanistan is peace and security. Most of the security problems in our border provinces are associated with the problematic situation in Afghanistan. We are neighboring a land that had sheltered the most vicious outlaws one could imagine. Apart from this, there is the problem of refugees. Notwithstanding our humanitarian efforts to give refuge to 2.5 million refugees who have crossed to Iran as a result of Afghanistan's hostile environment, we cannot ignore the social and economic problems associated with accommodating such a huge population of foreign citizens. Therefore, we want a responsible government in Afghanistan, which is capable of governing this country in a way to improve the life condition of the

Afghan people. As long as the best standards of living in Afghanistan is worse than the worse standards of living in Iran, we will continue to have a refugee problem. We are after a sustained development in Afghanistan. An extremely poor neighbor is naturally a cause for insecurity, political instability and huge economic costs for our country. Thus, we have every reason to play an effective part in the economic, social and political development in Afghanistan.

The article in the Washington Post also noted examples of the complexities the Bush Administration has been encountering with regard to Iran's influence in Afghanistan:

One illustration of the complexities confronting the Bush administration as it considers Iran's role in Afghanistan involves Gulbuddin Hekmatyar, a onetime Afghan militia leader who is a vocal opponent of the U.S. presence as well as the Karzai government. The Iranians closed Hekmatyar's office in Iran, where he had lived in exile for five years, shortly before Karzai arrived in Tehran on Feb. 25, 2002. The Iranians then ordered him to leave the country. He reportedly tried to go to Iraq and was said recently to have crossed into Afghanistan.

Yet according to a senior US official, the Bush Administration was mixed in its view as to what the Iranians should have done with Hekmatyar. 'Some officials thought he should have been turned over to Afghan authorities, while others said it would have been better for the Karzai government if he had been kept in Iran, but under house arrest,' the article said. 'The administration's uncertainty over how to react to Iran's influence in Afghanistan - even when it is aimed at buttressing the Karzai government - and in the Middle East reflects a broader problem in U.S. relations with Tehran,' the Washington Post noted.

The same, if not more, complexity is a feature of Iran's influence in Iraq. The US authorities keep accusing Iran, this time, of subverting US military rule in Iraq, while the charges of backing terrorism and developing nuclear weapons have not abated. The US officials in the White House, the State Department, and the Pentagon also continue to accuse Iran of providing support, including arms transfers, to Palestinian rejection groups and Hizbullah of Lebanon. And this at a time when British Foreign Office officials have repeatedly praised Iran's role in the Iraqi crisis.

The real problem, though, may lie in the fact that the United States feels there is a serious challenge posed by Iran to its influence in both Afghanistan and Iraq. According to the Washington Post article, 'the Administration officials say Iran's growing influence could hinder U.S. efforts to stamp out terrorism and shape the country's post-Taliban direction'. The Director of the CIA, George Tenet, for example, said: 'The initial signs of Tehran's cooperation and common cause with us in Afghanistan are being eclipsed by Iranian efforts to undermine U.S. influence there.' But the Washington Post points to expert opinions whereby 'Iran's influence should come as no surprise, given that it shares a 600-mile border with Afghanistan and a long history of relations.' Moreover, the article cites some analysts who say, 'given the scale of Afghanistan's problems after more than two decades of war, the United States should not stand in the way of Iranian assistance'.

Similar arguments could be made in the case of Iraq, only more forcefully, given that there are more deep-seated historical, political, religious, and economic ties between Iran and Iraq. As to what Iran wants in Iraq, the answer may be even more clear cut than in the case of Afghanistan given the security threat that is still felt after the Iraqi invasion of Iran in the early 1980s, which developed in an eight-year war that was never officially ended. UN resolution 598 provided only for a ceasefire calling for further negotiations over the border disputes between the two countries, the issue of war reparations, the destiny of the POWs and MIAs, and other issues. None of these issues, except for the ceasefire that came into effect in 1988, has been ever resolved. Naturally, Iran would be concerned about the sort of government that would rule Iraq after Saddam given that, at the end of the day, the two neighbors will have to deal with these outstanding issues one way or the other.

The other main concern of Iran in Iraq pertains to the question of the vast Shi'ite population there, as well as the question of the management and upkeep of the Shi'ite shrines and madrasas in the cities of Najaf, Karbala, Samara, and Kazemain. There are naturally economic concerns as well pertaining most significantly to Iraq's oil, and particularly the impact of the flow of Iraqi oil onto the world markets on the price of oil on which Iran's economy is dependent. The remarks by some US officials about a plan for building a pipeline to take Iraqi oil to Israel, or about the possible withdrawal of Iraq from OPEC, are naturally sensitive for Iranians.

Summary

The American 'war on terror', not to mention the American so-called 'war of liberation' in Iraq, read (not only) by Islamists as 'America's war on Islam', could have only damaged the cause of democratic development in the Muslim world - though one finds no sensible argument against that fact that only such a development could provide the best guarantee of dealing with 'terrorism' at a fundamental level, or serve as a sound basis for political freedom.

'Axis of evil' or not, the Iranian nation consists of a diversified public whose opinions are increasingly affecting the course of political development here in the interest of democratic reforms. The American warmongering strategy has little to contribute to this process. If it was not for the powerful internal dynamics associated with the development of a public sphere, Bush's strategy 'to go to war for peace', combined with Sharon's strategy to 'out-terrorize the terrorists', would have even destroyed the whole process of democratization in Iran. This is a not too unfamiliar experience, given the history of the democratically oriented government of Mossadeq in the early 1950s.

The appeal of Iran's new religious intellectual movement to civil society and freedom of expression may in the last analysis be tied with political attempts to save the Shi'ite faith and its revolutionary-based political and public force from what is seen as the threat of secularist ideology. By turning the post-revolutionary religious culture into a public culture, the movement is seemingly trying to create a social space where religiously inspired republican virtues would produce a religious nation.

Prominent political and religious figures can invoke their scholastic background in Shi'ite jurisprudence and theology, as well as their background in modern science, to find religious legitimacy for the modern concept of civil society. It is hoped to be a public space where citizens of the Islamic nation can enjoy their 'natural rights' to 'freedom of expression' and 'equality before the law'.

Yet these innovative endeavors suffer from an inherent contradiction that is not unfamiliar to the Western tradition. On the one hand, these intellectual efforts involve incorporation of such secular concepts as civil society and democracy into the Islamic discourse and symbolism in order to give them religious legitimacy. Yet on the other hand, in order to avoid criticisms that point to the secularist consequences of their innovations, the religious intellectuals find it necessary to anchor these secular concepts in the imaginary of an Islamic nation.

This concept of Islamic nation is, at one and the same time, rooted in a religious history and symbolism that had characterized the original Islamic political community, and directed toward a universal political community (umma) that is to come with the return of the monji (savior) of the human world. And yet this concept is problematized when the reformist efforts to reconcile the religious history with the universal history of modernity is contradicted by the conservative guardians of the religious history who fear the loss of their religious-cultural identity to Western political and cultural hegemony.

The invocation of a religious nationalist rhetoric in reformist literature is what unites the reformists with the conservative ulama-in-power (who would find no better formulation for an Islamic umma than an Islamic nation). Yet the contradictory tendencies in this religious nationalism to either incorporate or resist the secular history of the nation, simply by claiming an Islamic history for the Iranian nation, have already become the source of serious religious disputes and political conflicts.

The source of the problem, as Asad has suggested, may lie in the fact that nationalism, despite its appeals to religious symbolism and ceremonials, is not formed by religion. Nevertheless, one may argue that modern nationalism is the consequence of the ultimate need of political communities in modern time to establish themselves within the structures of a modern state.

Despite its modernity, the modern state is anchored in the cult of community whose collective power it is to embody. And what feeds and nourishes this community cult better than a community religion? Thus while one could agree with Asad that nation needs a worldly history, one could also argue that a particular worldly history that could advance claims to truth is best fed by a religious tradition carried by a living religious community. Iran's living Shi'ite community cannot but have a worldly history, yet a history that often refuses to be presented as an appendix of Western modernity.

The revolutionary move of Islamists in Iran since the late 1970s to claim the whole of the public domain successfully, banishing the secularists from even insignificant public spaces, was a clear response to the secularist exclusionary enterprise of the previous decades. In its systematic secularization of the nation, this enterprise had denied the religious publics even a theoretical acknowledgement. Thus the construction of a Shi'ite Islamic national identity in Iran may be viewed as part and parcel of the process of redefining the boundaries of the public sphere.

It is in light of this mediated public experience of religion and politics that one could appreciate how a revolutionary movement in defense of religious traditions has contributed to the emergence of a public sphere, which is at one and the same time modern and traditional. One can also appreciate how the politicization (and popularization) of religion is shifting the boundaries between public and private, on the one hand, and state and society, on the other.

The shifts in the religiously inspired political discourse of the revolution have, in turn, contributed to the emergence of a democratic turn in how religion is understood and how power is exercised in tackling the problems of a modern nation-state in a global environment. Yet just as the appeals to nationhood have proved problematic even in liberal democracies due to the heterogeneity of the public, the process of 'nation-building' in Iran by Islamists has also had to deal with this 'notorious' diversity.

The examples of this diversity are reflected in the multiple expressions in the mediated public sphere. They range from the voice of a martyr-to-be (on an Internet site) who announces his readiness for Jihad to the voice of a religious reformist who searches (in his newspaper editorial) for the religious roots of democracy. In between there are other voices: the voice of a frustrated man (on a phone help-line) who wants to commit suicide due to acute depression, for example, or the voice of a woman who consults (on live television) a therapist about her problems with her husband and young children. There is also the voice of a Friday prayer leader who preaches (from the pulpit) about parental responsibility in controlling the sexuality of their kids, not to mention the voices in Diaspora (using the Internet) to promote the prospect of a secular Iran. Of significance here is the diversity and complexity of such expressions, and the attempts of all these people to extend their presence in the religious public sphere by appropriating Islam for their own purposes.

The transformation of Shi'ite Islam (as the faith of individual believers) into the main element of the cultural identity of an emerging nation-state has certainly had a transforming effect on the nature and functions of the faith, and the culture associated with it, in both doctrinal and practical terms. Moreover, this transformation is a product of a period which saw the doubling of the population and a staggering rise in education, information, and high-tech communication.

Yet Shi'ite Islam has certainly performed as more than a passive object of change. The rise of the Shi'ite ulama to political power and the transformation of Shi'ism from a community religion into a 'public religion' (equipped with discourses and institutions of power) have, in turn, played a significant role in dealing with the new economic, demographic, technological, and intellectual challenges. This process has involved the emergence of a public culture and a political environment where religion, nation, and state may after all strike a working balance.

My view of the role of a religious public sphere in Iran is shaped precisely by the new forms of public representation in a political context constituted by religious symbolism, which have emerged since 1997 in both affirmation and condemnation of political modernity. The characterization of the seemingly contradictory notion of 'religious public sphere' is the main focus of my thesis.

The believers have not stopped going on pilgrimages, to congregate in mosques for prayers, or to hold private religious sessions out of personal and private choice. But there has emerged a new powerful public element (with access to huge economic, political, institutional, and communicational resources), which has set out to bring religion to the people (no matter how willing or reluctant they are) via television, ceremonials, exhibitions, and all sorts of public enterprises.

Taking a comparative historical perspective, one cannot fail to recognize the imminent challenge of a Protestant-type reformation in the Shi'ite faith for its living representatives, i.e., the scholastic ulama, on the one hand, and the religious-reformist intellectuals, on the other. The emergence of a modern and young nation (and its very much 'secular' worldly desires) from a religious reformation is what makes the developments of Islam in Iran peculiarly similar to how the imaginary of nation was born in the Christian West.

Yet if it has become increasingly difficult to discern the roots of the modern 'secular' nation-state in peculiar codes of morality of particular religious communities, the living case of religious reformation in Iran displays the direct and indirect, open and secret, links between religion and nation. These links, though, are to be discerned in the context of a religious, and yet diverse and differentiated, public sphere.

Right before one's eyes, one has the case of a religion producing the secular as a condition of its own continued worldly significance. Yet it is, perhaps, in the nature of religions to provide a rationale for the existence of the secular, as it is in their nature to provide a rationale for committing sin. Obviously, the power of religious faith in enabling the 'true believers' (living in a 'sinful secular world') to restrain from committing sin is demonstrated fully only in a condition where the opportunity for committing sin is available; that is, the immediacy of a secular world is already taken for granted. Religion, as such, has already opened itself to the possibility of a sinful life in a secular world, because this also gives it its strength.

Faced with increasing and diverse populations of multiple and complex demands, the Shi'ite religious authority in Iran is increasingly forced to withdraw from certain important areas of social life (where it has performed miserably) without completely disappearing from the scene. It continues to exert influence; but in time it may have to do so through less open and often secret operations.

The significant characteristic of Protestantism, which gives it a universal aspect, intellectually engaging even after centuries for the protagonists of Islamic reformation in Iran (and, I suppose, elsewhere in the Muslim world), is its fundamental contribution to the emergence of calls for 'religious pluralism'. Religious pluralism, though, is not an external disinterested regulatory system that gives no religion a privileged position with respect to others. It is rather an internal system of balancing a plurality of moral claims, each with its own strict adherents or non-attached observers. In such pluralism, the constant tension between belief, secular reason, and sin is on full display in symbolic, or cultural, exchange at the social level.

In this sense, reading the religious intervention in political and public life in such a way as to have a case of confrontation between utilitarian rationality and religious irrationality is to impoverish our understanding of the (religious) sources of our modern secular way of understanding the world. I would argue (based on my observation of the development of Islam in Iran) that 'utilitarian worldliness' can live alongside religious standards of thinking and behavior, and even be enhanced by them.

It was once a truism that the modern secular nation-state was born out of free and open public debate in the context of a civil society from which religion was banished into the private space. A free and open public sphere and the banishment of religion to the private spaces of secrecy were the main elements of a political environment where public opinion could be presented as that of the nation. The consent of the nation to the disciplinary power of the state would then be considered indispensable for the legitimacy of power.

Yet this connection of state and nation in the public sphere of civil society often concealed the operation of another disciplinary power structure: that of religion. Despite its privatization (and perhaps because of it), religion has continued to play an underlying, but fundamental, part in shaping the imaginary of the modern nation. Secret pseudo-religious societies in Europe (e.g., the Freemasons) were no less fundamental in shaping the public opinion of national interests than the bourgeois intellectuals and their printed publications.

The emergence of a religious public sphere in Iran is a clear indication of the public and political role of religion in transforming an originally sectarian religious community into a national political community. It also displays both the open and secret influences of religious reform on the course of other main elements of political modernity: that is, the capitalist developments, the scientific and technological developments, and the educational and communicational developments.

Whereas the media (from the pulpit to the Internet) are increasingly shaping the expressions of the public (hence the sense of absence of a non-mediated public sphere), the exercise of power only partially relies on public opinion, represented (or made) by the media. Secret or obscure religious societies, associations, schools, and organizations, and even some private religious circles, families, and personalities, are fundamental in determining the overall moral order that determines, in turn, what is to be made public and what is to be kept secret.

But as we all are human (all too human), total control of us in all our diversity, complexity, and intrigue is as impossible in Iran's religious public sphere as it is in the Western liberal public sphere. In the West, the liberal advocates of secularism have had to allow the religious believers (who rely on their powers of persuasion alone) re-entry to the public domain. Just the same, the tolerant Islamists will be likely to open up the public space to the secularists (who accept not to transgress the 'red lines' of the public religious culture).

Surely, the challenge of religious reformation for the course of religious and national development in Iran has become public only since the late 1990s; nonetheless, it was always there in a secret, but tense, religious and political contest, between countervailing religious and political tendencies. Its development into a public matter of national interest has become possible only after the broad contours of the public domain, with its exclusion-inclusion criteria, were agreed upon; although this has remained subject to questioning, negotiation, bargaining, and manipulation.

Not unlike the Western bourgeois public sphere, the Shi'ite public sphere in Iran is a domain of public debate, which is neither completely free nor completely open, and yet capable of providing a space for the expression of a diversity of voices. Not surprisingly, some of these voices are heard to an effect, some are heard to little or no effect, and some are repressed.

A gathering of a group of Iranian writers and intellectuals on the Island of Kish in the Persian Gulf (off the coast of Iran) was an example of the peculiarity of the process of democratic reform in Iran. 'President Bush may list Iran as part of an "Axis of Evil", but writers and intellectuals on this dry and weedy coral island, 25 miles south of the mainland, say democracy may yet thrive in their country,' writes Andrew Lamb, a short-story writer for Pacific News Service.

Surely censorship is still in operation in Iran at various levels; so is secrecy and concealment of truths from the public. But this should not come as a surprise to the inhabitants of a liberal public sphere either, especially in matters of politics - though in the Iranian case matters of religion should also be added to this off-limit domain in the name of sanctity. Nonetheless, most of the thirty writers and intellectuals at the gathering in Kish agreed that 'recent years have delivered a strong and steady push toward social liberalization,' wrote Lamb (ibid.). Noting the disappearance and even murder of some Iranian poets and writers in 1998, a woman participant at the gathering was quick to say to the reporter: 'I hope you are going to say something nice about Iran. We are not evil.'

13

Response of the Jamaat-e-Islami Hind and Media

Introduction

The Issue of Terrorism: With Reference to the Country's Contemporary Situation'. The audience is unusually large - almost five times greater than the usual strength of its weekly meeting. There seem to be two reasons for this. First, it is obviously a hot topic after September 11. Second, the symposium is to be addressed, as stated in the invitation letter, by 'famous ideologues of the Islamic movement'. Maulana Yusuf Islahi, a national leader of the JIH, is the key guest speaker.

Maulana Islahi has the following position: the September 11 event is a wellplanned conspiracy to defame Islam. Muslims are being blamed for it without any evidence. Everyone knows who is the real culprit, Jews. Yet, the United States, the so-called champion of human rights and democracy, is targeting Muslims in Afghanistan and elsewhere. If the United States really believes in democracy, why is it supporting monarchy in Saudi Arabia? Hundreds of Islamic activists have been recently imprisoned there. The condition in Saudi Arabia is thus worse than in India. The United States has unjustly and arrogantly ruled the world for too long. Allah has destroyed that arrogance on September 11. God willing, this will also inaugurate the age of Islam the world over.

Before Islahi, Saud Alam Qasmi had made a passionate speech arguing that Jews, not Muslims, are terrorists. Jewish history is the history of terrorism. 'Jesus did not disappear, Jews killed him.' As for Islam, it is being forcibly linked with terrorism. It is indeed the religion of peace and divine truth. After September 11, the Italian prime minister said that Christianity would conquer Islam. But barely two weeks after his statement, the Italian Ambassador in Riyadh, Saudi Arabia, embraced Islam. In India also, says Qasmi, thousands of people annually convert to Islam even amidst bloody communal riots. Therein lies Islam's power and hope for a bright future.

A fortnight earlier, Syed S. Husaini, the national President of the Student Islamic Organization (SIO), the student wing of JIH, had expressed similar views in a lecture, held every Saturday in its Delhi-based headquarters situated on the bank of the Jamuna River. Speaking on The Course of Action for Muslim Ummah in the Global Context, he said that the West was really afraid of Islam's expansion. Hence its desperation to link it with terrorism. True, the United States is the military superpower and Japan the technological superpower. But let us not forget that Islam today is the ideological superpower. It is rapidly growing worldwide. Thousands have embraced Islam in the United States even after September 11. Islam indeed is the future and the future is Islamic. Given this, Muslims should ceaselessly do Dawah in India. 'Insha Allah,' he said, 'we will establish Islam's hegemony'.

What Husaini and the participants of the symposium said about September 11 is also broadly reflected in JIH's Urdu and English organs - Sehroza Dawat and Radiance. But before we content analyze them, it would be worthwhile to know, albeit briefly, the context of JIH's formation and its current position in India. As is well known, Jamaat-e-Islami was formed in undivided India in 1941 by Syed Abul Ala Maududi (1903-1979) to establish Hukumat-e-Ilahiya, God's governance. Maududi presented it as an alternative to both the Indian National Congress and the Muslim League, the two main parties dominating the political scene in the late 1930s. He rejected the Congress because under Congress-ruled India, he feared Hindus would absorb Muslims. He dismissed the League for its nationalism as a pale replica of the West. The League leadership, he felt, was not in the hands of righteous Ulema but the Western-educated individuals in whose scheme Islam as an all-inclusive ideology never figured. To be precise, the would-be Pakistan shall not be an Islamic state based on the Sharia but a mirror image of Godless, Western, secular democracy.

Barely six years after the formation of the Jamaat-e-Islami, India was partitioned. And in a volte-face of the first order, Maududi chose to be a citizen of the same Pakistan, which he had been ruthlessly condemning. After partition of the subcontinent into Pakistan and India, it was divided into two separate political organizations: Jamaat-e-Islami Pakistan and Jamaat-e-Islami Hind (JIH) respectively. The organizational division, however, did not lead to any substantive ideological shift. In India JIH described its goal as realizing Iqamate-e-Deen, the establishment of religion. Until 1952 JIH had a unit in Jammu and Kashmir, the only Muslim-majority state in India, that was constitutionally part of the former. Given the disputed nature of Jammu and Kashmir, however, in 1952 it decided to separate itself from its unit in Jammu and Kashmir. Since then Jamaat-e-Islami Jammu and Kashmir (JIJK) is separate from and independent of JIH. JIJK, unlike JIH, has participated in state elections. Right from the beginning it has questioned India's claim over Jammu and Kashmir and since 1989, when militancy began there, has been actively involved, directly or indirectly, in the armed struggle against Indian forces. In 1990, the Indian government banned JIJK for encouraging 'unlawful activities'.

The radically changed circumstances following partition in India excluding Jammu and Kashmir, nonetheless, required a different course for the JIH in India. Maududi left a blueprint, markedly different from that of its counterpart in Pakistan, for the JIH to follow. Given the numerical size of Muslims in post-1947 India, he recommended a four-fold action plan for the success of what he called the 'Islamic movement'. First, elimination of communal conflict that had gripped both Hindus and Muslims. Indian Muslims must not, as did the Muslim League before, raise any demand for representation in assemblies or government services. 'They should rather develop,' advised Maududi, 'indifference towards the new government and political system'. Second, Muslims should radically transform themselves in a manner such that non-Muslims begin to consider their religion and culture inferior to that of Islam. Third, all of their intellectual resources should be harnessed in the ceaseless propagation of Islam. Fourth, and following from the above, Muslims should readily learn the Indian languages to spread Islam far and wide. Their obsession with Urdu, he feared, would hinder the process of interaction with non-Muslims, the main target of JIH's mission. If the above steps were followed with zeal and conviction, predicted Maududi, in the future (he did not specify the time frame) the JIH will succeed in establishing an Islamic nation-state in India. The policies of the JIH since 1947 have been broadly in line with the original blueprint drawn up by its founder with one crucial and notoriously controversial exception.

Of Maududi's four points, the first one was not implemented quite fully. From the mid-1960s the JIH began to take an active interest in Indian politics. In line with Maududi's action plan, it had earlier asked its members not to vote in elections during the 1950s. Voting was considered Haram since the JIH regarded the Indian political system as ungodly and un-Islamic. However, after the emergency was imposed in June 1975 it lifted the restriction on its members temporarily and also campaigned for the victory of opposition parties. In 2002 state elections in the Uttar Pradesh state I witnessed it actively campaign against the communal, fascist candidates to ensure the victory of secularism and democracy. It has still not decided to field its own candidates either for the Assembly or for the Parliament, however. Obviously, this change was triggered by the growing militancy and anti-minorities policies of the currently ruling religious party, the Bhartiya Janata Party, at the center. This official move was contested by a significant number of its members, though. For them it was a stark deviation from the original line adopted soon after India's independence by JIH. (Non-)participation in voting is thus a major point of controversy within JIH.

Numerically speaking, the influence of JIH on Indian Muslims is not very significant. In 2000 it had no more than 5000 members, Arkaan, 25,411 workers and 270,146 sympathizers. It has contacts with 2769 non-Muslims. However, its influence is extremely strong among educated middle-class Muslims and its numerical size is not indeed the right barometer of its actual impact on Muslim society. Its chain of educational networks comprising nursery schools (67), primary schools (277), colleges (32), technical schools (6), adult education centers (288), religious seminaries of various standards

(234), libraries (1728), study circles (850), audio libraries (76), postal libraries (20), and social services such as hospitals (15), clinics (74), interest-free banks (378), Zakat centers (713), and Shariat Panchayats, Islamic legal courts, (72), is a very powerful and cohesive instrument through which it commands influence. It also publishes books, pamphlets, and newspapers, e.g., Radiance in Englishand Sehroza Dawat in Urdu, in almost all the important Indian languages. Its student wing, SIO, has grown quite strong in the last ten years. As of 2001 it had 3409 members and 40,546 associates. In north India, Aligarh Muslim University has the largest unit of SIO.

Now let us proceed to discuss how Sehroza Dawat and Radiance have read this monumental episode of the new millennium - September 11. Based on their analyses, the final section of the paper will attempt to raise certain theoretical issues emerging therefrom and the relation between the media and the public sphere. The analysis of Sehroza Dawat is drawn from issues published between September 16, 2001 and February 4, 2002, and of Radiance between September 16 and December 29, 2001.

Dawat in Urdu means what Dawah does in Arabic. It literally means 'invitation to faith'. In Urdu an invitation to dinner is also called Dawat. In the Indian context Dawat synoptically explains the method through which JIH seeks to achieve its goal of Iqamat-e-Deen, Islamic state. Its founder, Maududi, had predicted that an Islamic state in India could become a reality only through Dawat, first among Muslims and eventually among non-Muslims. The full name of the paper is Sehroza Dawat, three-day Dawat. Consisting of six pages, it is published twice a week and has a circulation of about 10,000-15,000. Originally it was launched as a weekly on September 13 in 1953. Around 1957 it was changed into a biweekly and remains so even today. Presently it is published from New Delhi. It has been regularly published since 1953 to date except during the emergency (1975-1977) when it was closed for two months.

An important point to keep in mind while dealing with the Urdu press is its historical specificity. There is a substantive difference between the content, readership composition, and editorial policy of Urdu and English newspapers or weeklies. Unlike the English press that reportedly addresses itself mainly to the English-educated 'secular' elites and upper middle class of varied faiths, the Urdu press in post-1947 India has come to be identified, ironically, with Muslims. It broadly caters to the lower classes of the Muslim majority, many of whom were educated in the traditional Urdu medium Madarsas or Maktabs. The news covered and issues raised in the Urdu press are thus predominantly related to Muslims. Exceptions to this general trend are, among others, two newspapers: Hind Samachar and Milap. The former is one of the largest selling newspapers in the Punjab. The latter is published from Delhi and Jalandhar. Very few Muslims read Hind Samachar and Milap, however.

Though the history of Urdu journalism is 182 years old - the first Urdu newspaper, Jaam-e-Jahan Numa, was launched under Munshi Sada Sukh's editorship in 1822 from Calcutta and it has a checkered history, some scholars believe that it has maintained continuity in terms of its basic feature. Maulana Wahiduddin Khan, a dissident of JIH and a noted Islamic scholar, argues that Urdu journalism indeed evolved as the journalism of protest and reaction. Its protest was directed chiefly at four enemies: the British government, Ahmadiyas-Arya Samaj-Christian Missionaries, Western culture, and Hindu communalism. Highly critical of this trend, Khan says:

The fundamental demerit of Urdu journalism is that it was born out of reaction against the tyranny of the enemies. The entire Urdu press, therefore, perennially suffers from a persecution complex. A person with persecution complex can never examine events objectively. He sees events not as a judge but as a partisan. This is the reason why reports in Urdu press are made either with one-sided orientation to Muslim emotions or generalizations are drawn from those partial or exceptional reports. Both these features go against honest reporting.

He continues: 'It is a fact that Urdu journalism Urdu journalism that is represented by Muslims in this country has been a product of reaction right from its beginning. All newspapers of Muslims have been started against some "enemies of Islam" or the other'.

Table 13.1 Regular items published in Sehroza Dawat

Items	Pages
Khabr-o-Nazr (News and Views)	1
Bela Tabsera (Without Comment)	1
Kisne Kya Kaha (Who Said What)	3

Mukhtasar Aham Khabren (Important News in Brief)	4
Deeni Tahriki Sargarmiyan (Religious Movement Activities)	4
Khutoot-o-Masaael (Letters and Problems; not regular)	5
Ads, mostly about its own publications(bottom half of the page)	6

Khan is not alone in articulating this viewpoint. Raisuddin Faridi too holds the same opinion though he expresses it in a more nuanced way. Most 'liberal' Muslim intellectuals that I met during my fieldwork in Aligarh also share Khan's viewpoint about the Urdu press. This liberal critique of the mainstream Urdu journalism is, however, considerably exaggerated, as it tends to simplify a rather complex story into a comprehensible whole. To say the least, it pays scant attention to other trends within Urdu journalism that were/ are no less significant.

Sehroza Dawat makes the first coverage of September 11 in its issue dated September 16. The column 'News and Views', written by the editor, first expresses surprise at the attack and wonders at the sheer inability of the US security system to pre-empt and check it. Then it speculates that those who carried out the attack must have strong grievances against the United States. And it is crucial to know them. However, the global media are not debating the reasons behind the attack. In other words, the United States ought to reconsider its policies. How correct is its unjust support of some countries and unreasonable hostility to others! It keeps on supporting its friends even if they indulge in crimes and opposes its 'enemies' who are not a threat to it at all but are rather its victims. It maintains a double standard on democracy: it is restless for its restoration in Burma but sternly opposed to it in Algeria.

In the end the column mourns the loss of innocent lives in the attack but with a subtle reminder. It says that it is painful to think about those killed and the sufferings of their dependants exactly in the same way when in the first Gulf War the United States killed 300 Iranians and again in the second Gulf War when it killed 400 Iraqis in a refugee camp in Baghdad - mostly the aged, women, and children.

Titled 'Attack on America', the editorial says that right from the first moment Western experts have pointed their fingers at Osama Bin Laden for the attack even though Bin Laden himself has denied it. So has the Taliban government. In fact the Taliban said that Bin

Laden did not possess such sophisticated technology and resources to carry out the attack. Yet, the whole Muslim world is being held responsible for it. Muslims are being projected as a militant, extremist, and conservative Ummah and as an enemy of the United States. Is it fair to label the entire Ummah as terrorist? As for the worldwide Muslim anger against the United States and celebration of the attack in some places by them, one ought to examine its reasons.

The same issue carries the statement - headlined as 'It is not Proper to Get Demands Conceded through Wrong Acts' - of the Deputy President of JIH, M. S. Monis. While condemning the attack, he says that governments are also doing injustice. They should act justly and people should put forward their demands properly and correctly. Referring to 'Islamic terrorism', he says that it is a misleading phrase. Islam means only peace. Those who commit wrongs in its name are not justified. At the same time such acts are happening everywhere.

They are happening in Sri Lanka as well. Is it because of Islamic terrorism? The next issue (September 19) has on its front page an article sans any byline - 'Events in America are not what is being Projected; Reality Seems to be Different'. According to this anonymous writer, in the absence of any evidence the West's insistence that Muslims should condemn this act is akin to sharing the blame. The West is creating a guilt complex in Muslims. The forces opposed to Islam have thus declared their judgment even before any inquiry. The column 'News and Views' comments on a piece by K. P. S. Gill published in the Delhi-based English daily The Pioneer (September 13). Gill asks: why is it that whenever a terrorist act is committed the world concludes that it is the handiwork of Islamic terrorists? The columnist answers that it is because of a deep-rooted conspiracy. Forces defending racism (to SD this means Israel) and the hierarchy do not want Islam's real face revealed. This is indeed a clash of civilizations as identified by Huntington. It is not a mere coincidence that after the attacks on New York and Washington, there is a frontal assault on Islam from all sides. It is indeed the outcome of decade-long efforts. These forces (enemies of Islam) first spread violence through their agents and then pass the buck onto Muslims. It is very likely that the same forces are behind September 11. Continuing the 'Jewish Hand' thesis, the issue dated September 22 carries a front-page story 'Attack on America has Sidelined Palestinian Issue: Was this its Objective?' The story details the history of Israel's illegal creation on the holy land of Palestine and how the United States, the former USSR, and Britain wholeheartedly supported this racist design. The creation of Israel, says the anonymous commentator, was itself an act of international terrorism. Of late, there has been a serious effort to resolve the Palestinian issue. The commentator indirectly suggests that the attack on America was meant to sideline it.

Another article - 'Objectives and Consequences of Attack on American Cities' - is more direct in blaming Israel, however. It says that no Muslim group in the world including Bin Laden has the resources and technology to cause devastation on such a big scale. Only Jews and the Israeli secret service, Mossad, have. In the United States Jews are the most powerful, organized group. Through them Mossad has also penetrated the US Administration. The reason why Jews could be behind the attack is because they are against a better alternative Islamic system emerging. In case it comes up, it will mostly harm the Jews who dominate the current world economy and are custodians of Israel. To tarnish the image of Islamic movements the Jews will go to any extent. For long-term objectives, they can even kill their own people as indeed they have done in the past.

In the issue dated September 25 half of the first page carries a story titled 'Why America is Fighting An Imagined Enemy, Not The Real One?' Like many other previous stories, this one is again anonymous. The commentator asks: does America really think that Bin Laden and Muslims are responsible for September 11? Is it innocent enough not to know the reality? The answer is no. According to the commentator, the United States knows too well that Muslims are not responsible for September 11 and that it is lying to the world. The reason for this is that if it tells the truth not only its economy but also its entire political system will collapse, because the forces actually responsible for the attack control almost every sphere of American life. In a way they have taken the United States as hostage. Who are these forces? They are none other than Jews who are taking revenge against the United States for some reason and inciting it to declare a war on Islam. The commentator offers four reasons for it.

First, in the last presidential election Jews had supported Al Gore because he had named a Jew as his deputy. By contrast, American Muslim citizens had supported George W. Bush and therefore he also had the moral support of the Muslim world at large. Second, Bush did not induct any Jew into his Cabinet. Third, Bush was taking the US economy in a direction detrimental to Jewish interests. Finally, the United States was seriously pressurizing Israel to resolve the Palestinian issue for good. For these reasons Jews were opposed to Bush. They have taken revenge against him through these attacks. The strongest evidence of their involvement is the fact that 4000 Jews working in the World Trade Center were absent on that fateful day. Yet, the entire global media are against Islam. Bush and his friends are well aware of these facts. However, since their life force is in the clutch of the Jews they are unable to tell the truth to the world and have instead launched a global war against an imagined enemy.

The subsequent issue, September 28, has an interesting commentary on Colin Powell's interview with the BBC in its column 'News and Views'. Powell says that the United States is committed to erasing terrorism form the entire world. He also mentions a few examples such as Kashmir, Northern Ireland, the Basques, and Colombia. Powell's list, says the columnist, is obviously not only incomplete but also unfair. Powell never said: 'America is against all kinds of terrorism'. He cannot say this. Because if he does, it would also include state terrorism. Powell speaks for democracy but refrains from saying any word about democratic voices that are being routinely hushed up in Egypt and Algeria. The biggest truth that he suppressed altogether is Israel's terrorism. He did not mention the tyrannical secret agency of Israel, Mossad, whereas the world knows that Israel is the greatest terrorist state in the world. It also knows who is its main patron.

Colin Powell, opines the columnist, may be satisfied with his clarification but he can no longer fool the whole world. The world is not blind anymore. It is another matter that it is not speaking out because of American supremacy and its civilizational glitter. However, the moment American magic vanishes it will begin to say that the United States itself and its unjust policies are responsible for September 11. It is a great irony that the United States is calling the terrorists terrorized and the terrorized terrorists. In reality, if any community in the world today is terrorized, 'it is the Muslim Millat' being attacked in various countries. And Muslims' only crime is that they are longing for a total Islamic system. In some other countries their crime is that they are resisting attacks on their religious identity. But the US government does not notice such terrorism against Muslims.

In the issue following September 28, there begins a series of articles titled 'Clash of Civilizations'. Published in three installments, it is written by a Canada-based author, Amar Sabit. Highly philosophical in tone, Sabit approvingly quotes Western authors like Bernard Lewis and Samuel Huntington. Sabit says:

The multi dimensional conflict between Muslim world and secular West can only be resolved at the foundational levels of faith and ideology. ... Western thought is informed by rationalism, ir-religiosity, democracy, freedom, capitalism and human values. This is its crux and fundamental civilizational identity. On the other hand there is Islamic world or Muslim Ummah that introduces itself as an Ummah whose foundation is based on revelation.

The variations in the nature of readership and language its presentation, styles and sources are different. Unlike SD, its audience is not mainly JIH's members/sympathizers. It is rather the liberal, broad-minded non-Muslims and perhaps the well-meaning as well as 'ultra secular' Muslims. According to a staff member of Radiance, a major chunk of its copies goes to Gulf countries. For the Arabic-speaking Muslim heads of government and influential individuals, it serves as the only source of information on Indian Muslims. Consisting of twenty-eight pages, it has been regularly published from Delhi since 1963. It is a weekly and has five regular columns - 'Wisdom from the Quran', 'Pearls from the Prophet', 'Ideology', 'From Darkness to Light (stories of conversion to Islam)', and 'Letters to the Editor'. Its full name is Radiance Viewsweekly.

Radiance covers the September 11 event first in its issue dated September 16-23. It publishes excerpts from an article - 'Who did it? The Israelis and American Zionists?' - by M. Amir Ali, Managing Director of the Chicago-based Institute of Islamic Information and Education. In Ali's view the air attacks required the latest technology, scientific know-how, deft coordination, and ample inside information. No Muslim group has those resources. Neither is it in their interest. 'The World has to come around,' he argues, 'to blame where the blame belongs - Israel'.

'Confusing Islam with Terrorism' is the cover story of the next issue. Calling the media's attempt to link terrorism with Islam 'mischievous', the author laments that no one is asking about the why and what of terrorism. If a survey were conducted vast section of Muslims would say that the tragedy that has struck the United States is the outcome of its own wrongdoings. If some people have rejoiced over the attack one should go into its reasons. The reason is that victims think that the United States should also taste what we have been tasting for long owing to its unjust policies. The author then tells readers who is responsible for the attack: 'Tel Aviv is the chief culprit. It is the Zionist influence on Western capitals that is playing havoc. Sooner or later, and sooner the better, at least now the needle of suspicion should turn towards Israel'.

Two other news items also suggest that it was the handiwork of Jews - 'Israeli Connection in Terror Attacks Revealed' and '4000 Israeli WTC Employees Absent on September 11'. In the same issue there are several pieces, most of them reproduced, critical of American policies: 'Defense is a Thin Cover for Militarization of Space' by Noam Chomsky, 'US Risks a Severe Miscalculation' by William Beeman (Brown University), 'Stop the Insanity Here' by Robert Jensen, and 'Our Hearts Call Out for Reconciliation, not Revenge' by David McRenolds.

The cover story of the next issue is 'Punish the Guilty, not the Suspect' by S. A. S. Vasfi. He says that despite Bin Laden's denial of non-involvement in the September 11 attack the United States seems to be hell bent upon punishing him. What is his crime? His only crime is that he disapproves of the US military's presence on the soil of Saudi Arabia, the nerve center of Islam. What does the US and its allies' insistence on punishing Bin Laden, then, mean? 'From this obduracy, we feel compelled to infer that it is a clash of faiths, not merely a clash of civilizations'. Vasfi is extremely critical of US-friendly Arab states which have mortgaged themselves to the United States and in so doing have humiliated Islam. Hence his appeal to Arab and Muslim states to uphold Divine Guidance and face the tribulations. In the subsequent issue the lead story is titled 'Muslim World Stands Immobilized'. It asks why Muslim Ummah is not activated for the future of Afghanistan. It offers two reasons: the inertia of the Islamic world and paralysis of will. Exhorting Muslims to rise, it warns them 'if they don't hang together today, they shall be hanged separately tomorrow'.

Bin Laden's innocence vis-a-vis the September 11 attack on the one hand and the Jewish Hand thesis on the other continue in both SD and Radiance even after the Americans released (on December 13) the videotape proving his complicity. Radiance does not even report the news of the videotape. Nevertheless, it persists with the Zionist conspiracy theory. Vasfi's article in the issue after December 13 asks: 'Is it not remarkably amazing that not a single Jew had been killed in the collapse of two towers where 4,000 Jews worked? What does it say?' (2001:39). His conclusion is straight and dead sure: Mossad and Jews are responsible for it. As proof he quotes Stern Intel that bases its opinion on American intelligence sources and sees Mossad's hand behind the attack. He also refers to Iranian President Khatami who echoes the Zionist design. The author does not find Mossad's involvement surprising. Zionists have done such acts repeatedly in the past. During World War II, says he, Zionists themselves sunk a ship carrying illegal immigrant Jews following Britain's refusal to allow them entry into Palestine. They did it in order to get world opinion on their side. In 1967 before the Israeli attack on Egypt they destroyed an American ship, the USS Liberty as it had monitored, well before the assault, Israel's readiness. They also destroyed Prince Edward Hotel in Baitul Maqdis (year of occurrence and other details are not given).

Unlike Radiance, SD covers the news of the videotape. Its response is along expected lines. Two weeks after its release, it carries a front-page story titled 'America's New Videotape Drama about September 11 Failed'. It does not have a byline. Neither is its source mentioned. The story begins with the comment that 'to justify and legitimize her attack on Afghanistan and prove Bin Laden as guilty, America released the videotape in Washington on December 13'. However, the world refuses to accept its authenticity. Those who are with the United States from day one are still supporting it whereas the unbiased and other circles see the videotape as a wholesale fraud. In electronic technologies voice can easily be changed. Moreover, if Bin Laden hatched the plan for September 11 why would he allow its recording to provide evidence? What is more, even if the tape is accepted as authentic, nowhere does Bin Laden accept the responsibility for the attack. And if the United States really has evidence why is it releasing it to the Jewish newspapers and TV channels rather than presenting it to a legal court? Sharing the doubt of Nasruddin Eisa, Secretary-General of Malaysia's Parti Islam SeMalaysia, the story ends by arguing that it is definitely forged through technological manipulation. Why did it take so long to release it after all?

One month later, SD reproduces a story from Al-Mujtama, an Islamic magazine published from Kuwait. The front page is titled 'Why Are The Real Culprits Behind Attacks on America Being Masked?'. It refers to Karl Cameroon's report on the web site of Fox News Channel in which the arrest of over sixty Israelis was reported. This report was soon withdrawn from the web site as it would have exposed the role of the Jewish lobby. In the report a Federal Bureau of Investigation official had stated: 'There is certainly some connection between the September 11 attack and the Jews. However, the evidence/argument is secret and I cannot make it public because it is absolutely secret'.

From the content analysis of SD in Table 13.1 and Radiance many interesting issues emerge for discussion. First, Muslims are portrayed as victims, not culprits. This is a picture that is radically at odds with the portrayal of Muslims by the mainstream Western media. In the reading of both SDand Radiance Muslims are not terrorists but terrorized. The West and the United States know too well that Jews are responsible for September 11, yet Muslims are being attacked and Islam's image smeared. And the reason for this Western hatred against Islam is that Muslims refuse to be assimilated into the West's cultural milieu. They desire instead an alternative Islamic system of their own. In Western perception this Islamic desire is a 'crime' and it therefore punishes Islamists. It has done so in Algeria and Egypt even though Islamists had won landslide victories in elections there. This shows how dubious is its commitment to democracy. It boasts of freedom and human rights but it denies them to Palestinians by blindly supporting Israel. Bereft of any principles, the West is thus presented as a hollow entity. It is no more than magic based on and sustained by sheer force. Islam is a superior alternative to it. Radiance's editorial contends:

Two very significant experiments have been made during the past century: socialism which has now become an insignificant footnote in history. Capitalism is being experimented in Europe and America today. Its fundamental point is: affluence would transform beast into man. Is it happening? See their crime rate, divorce rate and breaking of families because of prevalent promiscuity. Is there any ray of hope? ... Christianity, Judaism, Rationalism, affluence all seems to be admitting their failures. This fact devolves a greater responsibility on the shoulders of the Islamists who are in the possession of the last Divine Guidance. True the task is Herculean. But it is their moral, religious and human obligation. There is no short-cut to paradise.

It is this moral superiority of Islam that the West is afraid of. Because of its innate brilliance Islam is morally conquering people of all faiths worldwide. As Husaini and others say, thousands have embraced Islam even after September 11 in the United States, including the Italian Ambassador to Riyadh. Fearful of its expansion, the West is trying to halt Islam's onward march by linking it with terrorism. It is a Jewish design - pure and simple.

Second, many scholars explain, following Edward Said's groundbreaking work, religious revivalism in terms of orientalist construction. It is often argued that revivalists appropriate 'the other' even as they claim to reject it. Along the same line Huntington's clash of civilization thesis has been criticized at best as a Western construct and at worst as Western propaganda. Such criticism, though useful, loses sight of the agency of social actors. Every undesirable phenomenon cannot simply be dismissed as mere construct or as only ascription by 'the other'. The self-perception is no less significant (van der Veer 1994). As evident from articles in both SD and Radiance, JIH does think that Islam and the West are two competing, nay conflicting, worldviews - the former based on revelation and the latter on freedom and rationality. Both the papers have clearly endorsed Huntington's thesis of clash of civilizations/faiths.

Third, and finally, the issues raised in the two papers seriously call into question the very constitution, nature, and practice of the public sphere as theoretically conceived in Western scholarship. In his classic book The Structural Transformation of the Public Sphere, Jurgen Habermas argues that the public sphere in Europe historically emerged only with the disintegration of feudalism and near eclipse of religion. Their dissolution was rather a prerequisite for 'critical-rational public debate'. It was in principle inclusive and free from the considerations of status or rank. Further, he regards the press as the pre-eminent institution of the public sphere.

For both SD and Radiance Western media as the pre-eminent institution of the public sphere have been far from critical, rational, and inclusive in reporting September 11. They have instead worked as the mouthpiece of the Jews who, they think, control them. An article in Radiance argues how Jews are the culprits for September 11. The American establishment also knows it; yet Islam and Muslims are being blamed for it. This explains why:

They (Americans) are led by the nose by a media that is dominated by the Jews. CNN belongs to a Jew and Larry King is a hardcore Zionist Jew. There is hardly any independent media in the US. And even if there is what chance do they have to be really independent when even good old BBC succumbs to Jewish pressure?

It follows, then, that the public sphere is neither inclusive nor above status and necessarily critical. It is controlled and monopolized by a given category of people to meet and further its own set of interests - religious, not secular, as Habermas would have us believe. In the perception of JIH's organs media as a vital institution of the public sphere, e.g., CNN and the BBC, are so thoroughly dominated by the Jews that there is no space whatsoever for a Muslim viewpoint there. The public sphere is thus religiously exclusive rather than secularly inclusive.

What it also illustrates is that the public, in the reading of Radiance and SD, is not a homogeneous, undifferentiated whole but rather clearly split along religious lines - Jews and Muslims. Conceptually, this point has a larger implication. It means that if public and by extension society at large are hierarchical and socially differentiated in matters economic, religious, gender, and cultural it is only romantic to assume, as Habermas does, that these differences, cleavages, and hierarchies would simply evaporate in the public sphere and that the socalled critical and rational argument would remain untouched by their dynamics. This differentiated, hierarchical, gendered, and power-informed idea of society also implies multiplicity of public spheres. If a powerful group has its own public sphere and excludes its 'other', those excluded and rendered marginalized from it would necessarily forge their own public sphere. In other words, the idea of public sphere, argue Negt and Kluge, logically entails the notion of counter public sphere in the same fashion as 'nationalism creates other nationalisms - religious, ethnic, linguistic, secular'.

Habermas may explain JIH's criticism of the Western public sphere in terms of its refeudalization or degeneration as indeed the second half of his book exactly deals with this aspect. He may also explain this as undesirable intrusion of faith into it. For SD it is precisely the opposite, however. The column 'News and Views' of September 25 extensively comments on why Indian journalists are so hostile to Muslims and are following the United States in defaming Islam. They do so because they are bereft of faith, Imaan. And faith alone fosters honesty and true sense of justice. Where worldly success becomes the yardstick of human achievement there cannot be any honesty. And it is only Islam that infuses honesty and justice among its believers. For Habermas, whereas the public sphere and critical, rational debate develop and flourish on the ruins of religious edifice, for SD a truly just public sphere can grow and flower only on a religiously ethical foundation of Islam.

The above self-righteous posture of JIH raises a crucial question: Does its singular claim to honesty imply foreclosing of other sources of ethics and honesty? If the Western public sphere is biased in favor of the Jews and not independent, as so clearly argued by JIH, what is its own notion of public debate? Does it believe in the principle of open public discussion basic to liberal democracy? In the ultimate analysis, the answer is perhaps no. I say 'perhaps no' because it has not publicly debated this issue so far. However, if one were to infer from its position on other issues, it unambiguously shows that when in power it would barely allow freedom of debate or open profession and propagation of faiths - secular or religious. Many members of JIH and SIO believe that the Taliban government was right in preventing the missionaries in Afghanistan from propagating Christianity. But should not the Christian missionaries too have the right to propagate their religion in Afghanistan as Muslims have in India? No, they do not have. Their religion is false. A truly Islamic government, like the Taliban, therefore can never permit the propagation of falsehood. The word false includes every religion or worldview other than Islam - Islam as interpreted by them only.

In India JIH's position is markedly different, however. It is still far from its desired goal of Iqamat-e-Deen, which it seeks to bring about in a predominantly un-Islamic society through Dawat, ceaseless propagation of Islam among non-Muslims, which entails the processes of dialogue and public debate. As a matter of fact JIH employs exactly Habermas's phrase - public opinion - as the chief means through which it intends to achieve its ultimate objective. Its Constitution reads: 'and thus [Jamaat-e-Islami Hind] shall train public opinion in order to bring about the desired righteous revolution in the social life of the country'.

The world had witnessed tremendous, unprecedented changes. The war on Iraq by the US-led 'coalition of the willing' stands out as the most important one. How have JIH's organs responded to it? Is there any substantive change in their approach to the current world event when compared to September 11? The answer is a resounding 'No'.

As evident from the preceding pages, JIH sees the Western media and their public debate as biased in favor of the Jews and hostile to Muslims and Islam. Muslims are terrorized rather terrorists. It is Jews, not Muslims or Bin Laden and his network, who are responsible for the September 11 attack on the United States. The 'Jewish Hand' thesis does not change in case of war on Iraq. It remains. But now Christians are also held responsible as going the whole hog with the Jews and the Zionists. Colonial-imperial desire of the United States and Britain is also added to it. Indeed American colonial-expansionist design, almost under-discussed in its issues published soon after September 11, is highlighted.

In its issue dated March 2-8, 2003, Radiance carries Noam Chomsky's article 'Ruling by Force'. Derived from the talk the author gave at the World Social Forum in Brazil, Chomsky deals with the imperialist design of the United States and how it seeks to dominate the world by sheer force, unmindful of international laws and norms. It shows the double standard of the US policies. The second installment of Chomsky's article is published in the subsequent issue and elaborates the argument made in the first one. In its issue dated March 23-29, Radiance's editorial dubs the United States and Britain as 'neo-imperialists menacingly flexing their muscles'. In the same issue Stephen Gowans' article, 'UN Authorization cannot Make Rank Imperialism Just', is published.

The cover story of the issue dated March 30-April 5, 'The Moment of Untruth' by S. A. S. Vasfi, underlines US colonial motives behind its invasion of Iraq. Dismissing the charge of terrorism against Iraq and Saddam Hussain, Vasfi says that the original 'roots of terrorism lie in Tel Aviv'. 'Ugly Regime's Ugly War' by Stephen Gowans is another article in the same issue. In the following issue, the editorial 'Operation Iraqi Freedom or Enslaving Mankind' dwells on American 'naked aggression' of Iraq and its inherent nature of imperialism. The cover story by S. A. S. Vasfi deals extensively with the American invasion of Iraq. Titled 'Pax-Americana Starts from Iraq', he begins the story as follows:

The neo-imperialist attack on Iraq has four objectives: Dominance over the world, Erasal of Islam, Control over West Asian Leadership and Capture not only of the vast oil-reserves in the region, but those in the Central Asian Muslim states also. The brain behind this strategy is the Jews rather Zionism. The American President and the British Prime Minister are only tools meant for the implementation of the Zionist plan.

To make readers believe the seriousness of this Zionist design, he further says, 'Don't mistake this as a part of a Muslim's wishful thinking or a piece of the peculiar Muslim mindset that holds Jews responsible for each and every problem they face in their day-to-day life'.

In the next issue (April 20-26) the Jewish design against Islam is further laid bare in an article 'Israelization of the USA and Its Danger to Mexico' by Hector Carreon. It is as much about the US-Mexican relations after the Rancho San Cristobal Summit between George Bush and Vicente Fox Quesada, Mexico's President, as about the US approach towards Muslims and the role of Jews. It highlights the nefarious role of the 'Zionist Cabal' within the Bush Administration as the main architects of war on Iraq. 'Israel's 35-year occupation of Palestine', contends Carreon, 'enabled the Jewish state to perfect tactics that US troops needed in "house to house" combat in Baghdad (Iraq)'.

14

Future of Media and Experts Opinion on Terrorism

Introduction

All major leadership groups in the United States agree that the media have more influence than any other group in the society. Terrorists use the media to gain national and international attention. Student activists both in 1960s America and 1980s China spread, and knew they were spreading, their own message more widely than they could have thirty years earlier because of the impact of television.

Given the importance of the mass media, the question is now: Who shapes the news and according to what standards do they do so? Many radicals still insist that the media are biased in a conservative direction, while other commentators maintain that the various institutional checks created by media organizations insure fairness if not objectivity in describing world events. This chapter will offer evidence that both the nature of the mass media and the attitudes of journalists do affect the manner in which the media present the world, but in a direction rather different from that suggested by the radicals. I begin with a discussion of the general Weltanschauung of American journalists, and then show that they have come to determine what is news. This will be done primarily through two case studies media coverage of nuclear energy and media coverage of the IQ controversy which demonstrate that the generally liberal values of journalists can influence their presentation of reality to a wider public. I conclude with some brief reflections on some of the implications of these studies.

Changing Nature of the Journalistic Community

In the days of TheFrontPage, journalists, like most Americans, went to work after graduating from high school or even before. While some journalists and executives on leading papers were from upper middle-class backgrounds, journalism was most often a source of social mobility for working-class and lower middle-class youth. The generally Democratic sympathies of working reporters in the 1930s was partly a function of their class background.

This pattern changed after World War II. Increasing numbers of young men and women from upper middle-class backgrounds began to seek jobs in journalism and television as a way of partaking of an exciting and creative career and having an impact on society.

Journalists who work for the key national media today are far more likely than businessmen to have come from relatively affluent backgrounds, to have graduated from elite universities, and to be characterized by a liberal and cosmopolitan outlook. It was found that 45 percent of the staffs of leading media outlets remember their parents' income as above average compared to 31 percent of a sample of business executives at major firms. They were educated at elite universities, but are not scholars. Their careers, moreover, discourage scholarly activity. Operating under rigid schedules, and forced to deal with one breaking story after another, they do not have the time to investigate material in depth. Since they lack the time to read many books or to think issues through carefully (also partly due to temperament and choice), journalists' judgments as presented to the public are often based on a very shallow knowledge of the subjects with which they deal. They learn by reading newspapers and journals, and more importantly by picking the brains of those they interview, thus developing a superficial sophistication about various issues which face the country.

At the same time, journalists stand at the cutting edge of our loosely bounded culture. They are more likely to trust women who are feminist leaders than those who oppose the feminist agenda; they more often trust scientists who support environmental causes over those scientists who are skeptical about them (even if the latter are more representative of the consensus of the scientific community). Journalists' changing background and outlook has been accompanied by a shift in the structure of power in the major media. While many publishers are still fairly conservative, especially in the provinces, with some exceptions, publishers and even editors now give their reporters more or less free rein. We found it to be true in our study of national reporters, as did Stephen Hess in his analysis of the Washington Press Corps, and David Halberstam.

Advertisers also have less influence over the content of both newspapers and television than before. Increasingly, advertisers have come to believe with a few exceptions that they cannot and should not attempt to influence the content of news reporting. To sell their products, they must use those publications which reach the audiences they wish to reach. Indeed, during the 1960s many even advertised in counterculture journals which were quite hostile to the business community. Today, advertisers buy into programs on television which they are persuaded will attract mass audiences. They only refuse to buy time on given programs when they perceive it as possibly reducing the sales of the product they wish to sell.

Nor are publishers and advertisers the only ones at a loss. Even editors find that they can no longer fully control their staffs as much as they would like. The bright, young, well educated reporters see things in certain ways and insist on reporting them as they see them. And reporters are, by and large, more likely to view events from a liberal and cosmopolitan perspective.

Given their freedom from external control, and the manner in which they view the world, one might expect that the perspectives of both print and television journalists would enter into their descriptions of reality to at least some extent.

Journalists' Values and the News

It is my view that the better journalists do try to be "fair." The real question, of course, lies in determining what is fair. While equal coverage in a presidential election may constitute fairness, what about scientific controversies? Is it journalistic fairness to give equal time to those who believe that the earth is flat and those who believe that it is round? I very much doubt it, and, I suspect, so do most journalists.

A better test of the impact of journalists' ideology is probably "accuracy." How accurately do journalists describe events over the long run and what relationship does accuracy bear to journalists' world views? Most critics of the media (from both conservative and radical perspectives) claim that journalists do not describe events accurately. However, the critics' judgments are based on their own views of reality, which is precisely the question at issue. Critics - both conservative and radical and journalists thus talk past each other.

It was to overcome this difficulty that I and my colleagues developed the following techniques to determine the extent to which journalists' views affect their reporting. Assuming that on scientific issues accurate reporting will, by and large, reflect the consensus of experts, we first polled a random sample of experts on a particular issue, and then completed a content analysis focusing on how key national media outlets deal with the issue, and more importantly, how they characterize the views of the experts.

By using this approach, one can compare an expert assessment of an event with journalists' description of that event. One can then relate journalistic coverage to journalists' views on that specific issue and their broader political outlook, and even, with luck, measure the impact of the media on public opinion.

Decline And Fall of Nuclear Energy

The vast majority of Americans supported the development of nuclear energy. Today a substantial majority opposes the building of new nuclear plants. Completed plants have not been permitted to come on line, and in at least one case, voters have supported taking a plant off line which had been in operation for some years. Moreover, opposition is strongest among the most articulate and politically active segments of the population. While cost overruns and the abandonment of many partially completed nuclear facilities in the United States have probably played a role in the development of negative attitudes among various leadership groups, fears about safety among leaders and the public are far more important. The meltdown at Chernobyl accentuated fears to the point where nuclear development is not, at this time, a viable energy option in the United States. Public fears about nuclear energy, however, developed long before Chernobyl and even antedate the nuclear accident at Three Mile Island. Both these incidents took place within the framework of a climate of anxiety which had become widespread by the middle 1970s.

Scientific Community and Nuclear Energy

How do these estimates of nuclear safety by the public and various leadership groups accord with the scientific community's own evaluations? To find out, in 1980 we sampled 1000 scientists drawn randomly from American Men and Women of Science, supplemented by another sample of three hundred scientists who work in energy related fields. We defined the latter group broadly, including persons in fields such as atmospheric chemistry, solar energy, conservation, and ecology.

Scientists, especially those in energy related fields, regard nuclear energy as a necessary and relatively benign source of energy. Ninety percent of the random sample, and 95 percent of the energy expert sample believe that we should proceed with the development of nuclear energy. Seventy-six percent of the energy expert sample and 99 percent of the nuclear energy expert sample believe nuclear plants to be safe.

We administered a short form of the survey to the same respondents in 1985 with almost exactly the same results. A second replication of our study in Germany in 1985 revealed that German scientists agree with their American counterparts. A third replication of the study in the United States, one year after Chernobyl, again produced the same results.

Our findings of discrepancies between expert and public attitudes are not unusual. Slovic and others have discovered that the public's perception of danger does not correspond to the judgments of experts or to actuarial tables. Most significantly, they have found that the public rates nuclear energy as far more dangerous than any broadly verifiable assessment would support. Slovic and his colleagues suggest that the public is more concerned with possible major disasters than with more familiar everyday causes of injury or death, because the public perceives such megadisasters as far more disruptive, both socially and psychologically, regardless of likelihood of occurrence. In Slovic's et al. scheme, the public can accept with equanimity the greater number of deaths resulting from coal burning compared to deaths which might accrue from building new nuclear plants, because coal burning deaths have been part of the landscape for some time and do not call forth a grisly and apocalyptic scenario.

Their hypothesis, however, is not borne out by the evidence. As Richard Wilson, Edmund Crouch, and others have shown, people tend to ignore improbable, highly destructive potential disasters and live their lives as if these would not occur. The probability of a worst case nuclear meltdown is no larger than that of a large meteor striking a major city, a major earthquake in California, a massive flood disaster in other parts of the country, or the collapse of a major dam. Yet people not only live with these possibilities, they even ignore them, for example, by failing to take out flood insurance or by building on well-known fault lines. Such behaviors tend to suggest that the nuclear power issue has become part of a larger ideological perspective which cannot so easily be rationalized as a "natural" response to objective factors.

Journalists and Nuclear Energy

The scientific community is highly supportive of nuclear energy, regarding it as a relatively benign energy source to be tapped. Further, given that the public holds the views of independent scientists on environmental issues in relatively high esteem, one would expect both the public and other elite groups to follow the lead of the scientific community on this issue.

In fact, all the evidence shows that the public is relatively unaware of the views of the scientific community. In a 1984 national poll, almost six out of ten respondents expressed the belief that those scientists who are energy experts are evenly split as to the safety of nuclear energy, or that a majority of scientists consider nuclear energy unsafe.

The general public is not alone in these views. Most of the elite groups in our sample seriously underestimate scientific support for nuclear energy. For example, 85 percent of television producers, writers and directors believe that fewer than 25 percent of those scientists who are energy experts support the further development of nuclear energy. Indeed, like the general public, most of the leadership groups we studied perceive energy experts as sharply divided on the issue of nuclear energy, and this belief is associated with their views of nuclear safety. We found a high negative correlation between estimates of scientific opposition to nuclear energy and the belief that nuclear plants are safe.

Why should the general public and the leadership groups we studied be so misinformed on this question? Part of the reason for erroneous public perceptions of scientific views on nuclear energy lies with the manner in which information about those views is communicated to the public by scientists themselves. The scientific community as a whole does not often write for the general public. Rather, a somewhat smaller group of more visible scientists does most of that kind of work, and this group seems more supportive of the antinuclear position.

The relative skepticism of those few visible scientists who write primarily in popular journals may help explain why the public has a distorted view of the attitudes of the scientific community.

However, this cannot be the full story, since in absolute numbers, many more pronuclear than antinuclear scientists have published articles in popular journals. It is possible that antinuclear scientists publish in larger circulation periodicals, but our data points to another factor.

Elite journalists, including leading science journalists, are skeptical of nuclear energy. The most skeptical journalists of all are television commentators. On a "nuclear support" scale, constructed from several survey items whose scores range from minus nine to plus nine, scientists in energy related fields score 5.10, while television reporters and commentators score minus 1.89. Journalists employed by the national media are politically liberal, and their political ideology correlates with skepticism about the safety of nuclear energy. Most importantly, these attitudes seem to be reflected in news coverage. We analyzed news coverage of nuclear safety from 1970 through 1983 in the New York Times, the three major news magazines and the three commercial television networks (ABC, NBC, and CBS). Kepplinger found the same pattern of reporting on this and other issues in the German press. Other authors have documented the ideological aspect of the nuclear energy debate in America and the role of media coverage of nuclear energy in Sweden.

Our content analysis of national media coverage found that a distinct antinuclear tilt started in the early 1970s on television and the late 1970s in print. Overall, these major print and broadcast outlets failed to report accurately the views of the scientific community. Clearly antinuclear stories outnumbered pronuclear stories by two-to-one on television and in news magazines. Judgments of particular safety issues were primarily negative at all outlets, reaching a two-to-one margin on television. Among nuclear experts cited in news stories, critics outnumbered supporters by over two-to-one in news magazines and five-to-one on television.

Additional evidence is available from other sources. The Media Institute found that antinuclear experts and groups appeared on prime time TV newscasts during the 1970s about twice as often as pronuclear sources. By far the most widely quoted "independent expert" source on nuclear energy on television newscasts during the period of the study was the Union of Concerned Scientists, at that time an extremely small group very critical of nuclear energy.

The individual "expert" who received the most television exposure during the period of the Media Institute study was Ralph Nader, and the only academic scientific expert quoted in the aftermath of Three Mile Island was Dr. Ernest Sternglass, a strongly antinuclear radiologist held in quite low esteem by his colleagues. No pronuclear outside experts were among the ten most quoted sources in the eleven-year period before Three Mile Island nor during the month after. The only pronuclear sources in the top ten were spokesmen for utility companies and the nuclear industry. As we have seen, the public credibility of such organizations is quite low.

Many independent pronuclear scientists are available. Some of them, like Hans Bethe, are both well-known and active in scientific circles in their support of nuclear energy. The views of such people would have been far more representative of the scientific community than either those of the UCS or those of Dr. Sternglass. Journalists' decisions as to whom to interview on such issues should come as no surprise. When the elite journalists we surveyed were asked to list information sources they considered reliable on nuclear energy, they selected more antinuclear than pronuclear sources by a margin of over three-to-two. This would not be a large margin if the scientific community example were evenly split, but as we have seen, it is not. Even giving "equal mongers" when to be one runs counter to "progressive" views.

Elites and the Reliability of News Sources

It is hard to know precisely to what extent media coverage actually influences the views of the larger public. Our review of the evidence suggests that erroneous elite and popular perceptions of scientists' nuclear energy views could at least partly be ascribed to media coverage. Other evidence adds to the plausibility of this conjecture.

We asked our elite groups to rate the reliability of six national media outlets and six journals of opinion, allowing us to see whether the media outlets one trusts influences one's views on this subject. Our findings supported this hypothesis. For example, we found the belief in nuclear plant safety to be highly correlated with belief in the reliability of the National Review, a conservative journal which strongly supports nuclear energy development. On the other hand, we found the belief in the safety of nuclear plants to be inversely related to a belief in the reliability of public television. Commentators on public television were the most liberal and antinuclear group of reporters in our sample, scoring minus 3.25 on the nuclear support scale.

Of course, once perceptions of risk, distrust, and fears of new technologies become part of a "conventional wisdom," these arguments attract those who adopt the new conventional wisdom. Such is the case with nuclear energy. Any nuclear incident only further strengthens the belief that nuclear energy is too dangerous to use, even when no damage is done. While scientists seek "time" to the opposition views constitutes a revision of the facts about scientific opinion that our survey presents.

Combs and Slovic and Singer and Endreny argue that the media give far more play to "unusual disasters" (such as collapsing dams, tornadoes, or railroad accidents) than to daily occurrences which may kill or injure far more people. Indeed, journalists emphasize any disaster or potential disaster because that sells newspapers and increases ratings. They are professional purveyors of bad news. They are probably partially correct. However, their argument is not entirely persuasive. Journalists are probably no different from anyone else in one respect. They seek out sources they trust to help them understand issues which are both controversial and highly technical. And people tend to trust "experts" who share their own social outlooks.

The leading national media deferred to the views of the scientific establishment in ways that they no longer do. They more or less ignored those scientists who argued that fluoridation was potentially dangerous. (More recently they have behaved with exemplary caution in describing the Aids issue and have not catered to possible homophobia fears about the possible spread of the disease.) Certainly, reporters then were just as interested in disaster as they are now, and the science staffs of television or newspapers were neither larger nor better trained than they are today. Today, however, journalists regard "anti-establishment" scientists as rather more trustworthy than mainstream scientists. In short, journalists are not always disaster new ways of reducing the risks of accidents, much of the public, is no longer interested.

The problems which nuclear energy has faced in the United States cannot be laid entirely at the doorstep of the media, activist groups, or bureaucratic regulation. The nuclear industry itself is partly to blame, as are public utilities. Yet I believe their mistakes would not have destroyed the industry if the elite media had not played the role I have described. The elite media has played a similar role in the controversy over IQ.

Media and Public Policy

In a society where the demand for certain resources and opportunities outstrips their availability, tests of mental ability serve an important allocative role. In the United States today, intelligence and aptitude testing is prominent in elementary and secondary schools, in admissions to schools of higher education, and in employment. It has been estimated, for example, that the average public school student will take from six to twelve batteries of standardized tests between kindergarten and high school. While most of these will be achievement tests, many will be tests of intelligence or aptitude, designed not as measures of academic knowledge, but as tools for placing students in the most appropriate educational programs.

After World War II, the increasing reliance on intelligence and aptitude tests was generally considered progressive. Such tools would help people find their appropriate niche. Just as important, however, they would replace considerations of class and background by impersonal considerations of merit in university admissions, as well as in other spheres of life.

Attitudes began to change in this, as in so many other areas. As awareness of educational and economic inequities grew, testing opponents increasingly attacked intelligence and aptitude tests in the popular press and elsewhere as allocative tools helping to maintain the status quo. They criticized the tests as discriminatory and as poor measures of actual ability, while pointing out that psychologists could not even agree on the meaning of intelligence, much less test for it.

The IQ controversy reached a peak in the early to mid- 1970s, when the questions of racial and socioeconomic group differences in IQ dominated the scene. When the conflict was at its worst, those who argued that these differences were meaningful as anything but indicators of discrimination and biased tests were personally attacked. In a 1971Atlantic article, Harvard psychology professor Richard Hernstein argued that intelligence, as measured by IQ tests, is an important determinant of who gets ahead. Differences in intelligence, which have an hereditary component, therefore result in differences in socioeconomic status. Herrnstein was accused of being a racist by, among others, groups of student protesters who regularly disrupted his classes, and by the American Anthropological Association, despite the fact that he had never taken a position on the issue of possible ethnic or racial differences in IQ.

Though the late 1970s and 1980s have been rather more quiet, public criticism on IQ testing has continued. The NAACP and the National Education Association (NEA) have both called for a moratorium on standardized testing in elementary and secondary schools, charging that tests are racially and economically discriminatory, and that they are used to stigmatize low-scoring students. In several recent court cases, these and other groups successfully persuaded judges to strike down the use of intelligence tests for various educational purposes. In the most well-known of these, Larry P v. Wilson Riles, a California federal district court judge, Robert Peckham, barred the use of intelligence tests for the placement of black children into classes for educable mentally retarded (EMR) on the grounds that such tests discriminated against blacks.

The movement toward reducing the use of intelligence and aptitude tests is still gaining momentum. It is more or less a silent revolution, but if present trends continue, it is quite likely that the use of such tests will drop sharply in the future.

In order to obtain a clearer picture of informed opinion about the IQ controversy, we asked a sample of 1,020 testing experts their opinions on a wide variety of issues related to it. The expert population was purposely defined very broadly, so as to include not only those who primarily study educational testing, and who therefore might be accused of having a vested interest, but other psychologists or educational specialists who might reasonably be thought to have expertise about some aspect of mental testing.

We drew the sample randomly from various divisions of the American Psychological Association (APA), including Evaluation and Measurement, Educational Psychology, School Psychology, and Developmental Psychology, as well as from the American Educational Research Association and the National Council on Measurement in Education, and from more specialized groups like the Behavior Genetics Association and the Cognitive Science Society.

The questionnaire contained 35 testing-related questions, many with multiple parts, as well as demographic and background questions. Only some of the key findings are reported here.

Nature of Intelligence

The most basic and penetrating criticism made of intelligence testing is that psychologists and educators have no clear idea of what intelligence is, and therefore cannot possibly measure it. Critics thus claim that an IQ score tells us little about an individual's actual intelligence. We attempted to assess these claims by presenting experts with a list of thirteen descriptions of behavior widely used in defining intelligence, and asking them to indicate which, if any, they believed to be important elements of intelligence.

There is considerable consensus among experts sampled regarding both the important elements of intelligence, and that intelligence tests do an adequate job of measuring most of them. Experts generally agree about the important elements of intelligence, picking three attributes "abstract thinking or reasoning," "the capacity to acquire knowledge," and "problem solving ability" nearly unanimously. Sixty percent of the expert respondents also chose six others "adaptation to one's environment," "creativity," "general knowledge," "linguistic competence," "mathematical competence," "memory," and "mental speed."

We then asked experts to list other aspects of behavior that they felt should be included in definitions of intelligence. They suggested very few others, and none received more than minimal support.

The nature of intelligence, experts were next asked to indicate which, if any, of the important elements of intelligence are not adequately measured by the most commonly used intelligence tests. Once again, expert opinion runs counter to popular criticism. Of the ten descriptions believed by a majority of experts to be an important element of intelligence, only two "adaptation to one's environment" and "creativity" are thought by most experts to be inadequately measured.

We then asked our expert sample to give their opinions regarding the genetic basis of intelligence. Intelligence tests were once believed to be measures of innate mental ability, but not even testing's staunchest supporters would defend such a position today. Nonetheless, argument rages over the degree to which individual differences in IQ reflect genetic differences. Some critics of intelligence testing claim that all such differences reflect differences in upbringing and education, and that could they exchange environmental histories, the genius and the retardate would also exchange IQs.

The experts overwhelmingly disagree. Ninety-four percent of our sample indicate that there is a significant genetic component to individual differences in IQ, at least in the American white population (there have been very few relevant studies done in the black population). When asked to estimate what percentage of individual differences in IQ among whites are attributable to genetic variation, about half our sample give a mean estimate of sixty percent.

The other half of our sample do not feel there is sufficient evidence to do so.

Cultural Bias

A majority of expert respondents believe that some test bias against blacks and the poor exists, only about one-third describe that bias as moderate or worse. Moreover, 92 percent of experts sampled favor using intelligence tests in placing black children into EMR classes, further evidence that experts do not see racial bias as a major problem with intelligence tests. Whatever the merits of the judge Peckham's decision in the Larry P. case, it is quite clear that the experts do not agree with his ban on testing.

We should add that a slim majority of the responders (53 percent) believe that the roughly 15-point difference between blacks and whites must be explained by a combination of environmental and hereditary factors, only seventeen percent maintain that these differences are entirely the result of environmental variation. A measly one percent argue that the differences are entirely hereditary and 39 percent feel that they do not have enough data to decide the issues involved, or would not respond on other grounds.

Test Use and Misuse

The diversity of test usage in modern society brings with it an increased risk of test misuse, as tests may be misinterpreted or misapplied by those without adequate training in evaluation. Even those strongly in favor of test use complain about the uncritical manner in which student intelligence test scores are often treated -a sentiment reflected in our expert sample. More than sixty percent of our sample believe that the following three items are often or almost always present in test misinterpretation or misuse: improper comparison of test scores between students, improper comparison of intelligence and achievement test scores, and invalid use.

That tests are frequently misused does not mean, of course, that they are not valuable decision-making tools. We assessed expert opinion about test use by presenting respondents with a list of seven common test uses. Each item was rated on a 7-point scale as to the importance intelligence and aptitude tests should play in such decisions, relative to the role they now play: the number 1 represents a "severely reduced role," 7 is a "severely increased role," and 4 is "remain about the same." Despite the presence of substantial test misuse, experts believe intelligence and aptitude tests to be sufficiently useful to justify their continued use in elementary and secondary schools.

Critics have also charged that too much importance is placed on intelligence test scores, that IQ may be able to tell us who is most likely to succeed in school, but that it has little relevance in the real world. In contrast, proponents of testing have argued that intelligence, as measured by intelligence tests, is among the most important determinants of who gets ahead in our society. We asked experts to what degree they thought the average American's socioeconomic status (SES) is determined by his or her IQ. While only two percent of respondents indicate that IQ is the most important determinant of SES, 69 percent believe it is an important determinant. 25 percent believe IQ plays only a small role, and four percent believe it is not at all important.

Experts on intelligence and aptitude testing hold generally favorable views toward IQ tests. They believe such tests to be valid, generally unbiased indicators of what they purport to measure. They also believe that what intelligence tests measure is important to success in American society, and that a substantial portion of individual differences in intelligence is genetic in origin. Most importantly, experts favor the continued use of intelligence and aptitude tests in elementary and secondary schools, and in admissions to higher education, despite problems with test misuse in schools and the influence of nonintellectual personal characteristics on test performance.

How do we reconcile the generally positive attitudes of these experts with continued public assaults on testing? Is public opinion really at odds with that of the expert population, or do critics of testing represent only a small, but vocal, minority?

The maintenance of any public controversy requires the active participation of the news media. The IQ controversy is no exception. The news media did not invent the issues of cultural bias in intelligence tests, or the possible genetic basis of intelligence, but press coverage is critical in sustaining public concern. Intelligence and aptitude testing is an important element of public policy in many areas, most notably education and civil rights, and the media have a responsibility to keep the public informed. But this information is only as valuable as it is accurate.

That the news media are gathering expert opinion, but are improperly reporting it, or placing it in an inappropriate context, is one possible explanation for the disparity between expert opinion and the public controversy. To test this hypothesis we conducted a systematic analysis of news media coverage on IQ to see if this is true, and to get a clearer picture of how the media have handled these issues. Our procedures were similar to those we used in studying nuclear energy.

Media Coverage of the IQ Controversy

Our content analysis involved a study of key national media outlets. These consisted of the three major national news weeklies (Time, Newsweek, U.S. News and World Report), the three commercial television networks (ABC, NBC, and CBS), and three major newspapers (the New York Times, the Washington Post, and the Wall Street Journal). We systematically examined these outlets between January 1, 1969 and December 1, 1983. We included all articles and broadcast segments on the subject within each source. Standard content analysis coding procedures were used based on topics covered in the story segments. Coder reliabilities were in general .80 or better.

Extent of Coverage

The New York Times (NYT) and the Washington Post (WP) had the heaviest coverage of IQ testing and other related issues. The Wall Street Journal (WSJ) coverage was quite meager as was that of the major news magazines, which contributed a total of only 67 stories for the whole period covered. Television coverage was even more sparse. Only 65 broadcast segments dealt with the issues during the entire period. CBS contributed 68 percent of these.

The major media issues dealt with the nature of intelligence, intelligence test use and misuse, and IQ heritability and group differences. The media also paid a good deal of attention to the actions of and attacks upon Richard Herrnstein, Arthur Jensen, and William Shockley, a rather odd juxtaposition given their differences in training and background. Indeed the association of the three, given Shockley's lack of training in the relevant disciplines and his rather eccentric views, tended to undermine the credibility of the work of the other two members of the triumvirate.

Most stories appearing in both print and television were neutral in tone. However, those that were not tended to be hostile to testing and to take an environmentalist stance on the IQ issue. For example, 214 stories in the NYT were neutral; 35 were anti-testing, and only 18 were pro-testing in tone. The same pattern is to be found in articles on the relative importance of heredity and environment. Most stories in the NYT were neutral, but those which were not stressed environment and ignored the fact that most experts believe that both environment and heredity play a role in determining individual IQ.

The pattern is the same in most other aspects of the IQ controversy covered by the media. The media tended to dichotomize issues, to make simple errors, to sensationalize, and to erroneously characterize the views of experts in the field.

Nature of Intelligence

In contrast to expert opinion, the elite press generally portrayed intelligence as a poorly defined, poorly measured concept, and intelligence tests as narrowly focused, poorly developed measures of achievement. The following quote from an August 29, 1971 NYT feature article is typical:

There is little agreement among scientists as to what intelligence really is, and it is readily conceded by most psychologists that IQ tests measure a relatively narrow range of mental attributes.

The pattern of reporting on the news pages is a little better, though not completely accurate. Most stories which offer comment assume that IQ tests either measure test-taking ability or are measures of exposure to relevant environments (i.e., measures of achievement), not intelligence per se.

Only eight articles (five NYT and three WP) report something positive about the content of intelligence tests, stating that these tests measure abstract reasoning or problem solving. Arthur Jensen is the most common source of this opinion, accounting for half the attributions, despite the fact that eighty percent of our expert sample agree with Jensen.

Indeed, in those rare cases where positive statements about testing are made, the media almost always attributed them to Jensen, or, occasionally, Herrnstein. On the other side, one frequently finds such anti-testing psychologists as Leon Kamnin, Jane Mercer, Robert Williams and Jerome Kagen. Such a dichotomy, particularly when coverage of the latter group is predominant, is hardly representative of expert opinion.

The news magazines we studied were not very different from the newspapers, except that they were more likely to cite anonymous experts, with Jensen seemingly the only one differing from a broad consensus. TV coverage was too limited to draw firm conclusions, but the eight relevant television programs in our study were almost uniformly negative in coverage, describing intelligence as a concept with no meaning and thus nonmeasurable.

Most distressing about news media coverage on intelligence is not the amount of time or space given to criticism; journalists may feel that it is their obligation to report attacks on IQ tests in light of their importance. What is bothersome is the disproportionate media coverage given to such criticism and media misrepresentation of expert opinion. Experts do disagree about the nature of intelligence, and intelligence tests do not measure all important aspects of intelligence. But to stress these points repeatedly while giving virtually no coverage to the rough but important equation between IQ and intelligence is to do a great disservice to both experts and the general public.

Intelligence Test Use and Misuse

Discussions of the misuse of intelligence tests are even more prominently covered by newspapers than are discussions of the nature of IQ. Both the NYT and the WP (the WSJ carried very few stories on the issue) report a wide variety of test misuses. Jensen and Herrnstein are once again almost the only experts mentioned supporting the validity of tests.

While newspapers are willing to accept the notion that IQ tests may be decent predictors of academic success, or useful in discovering particular problems or talents, they worry constantly about their use in mislabeling students, especially those from poor backgrounds or minority groups. The most frequently cited sources for these stories are "critics of testing," or "minority groups" and the most cited experts are Jane Mercer and "many educators." From reading the NYT or WP, one would get the impression that test misuse is the norm in America, and that such misuse invalidates them.

News magazine and television coverage of test use and misuse are predictably less full than is newspaper coverage and, also predictably, take more or less the same line. The great emphasis is upon anecdotal evidence of test misuse which, as in newspapers, makes it seem the norm.

Heritability and Group Differences in IQ

Newspaper reports on the heritability of IQ tend to present the issue in polar terms more frequently than would experts, i.e., that the source of intelligence lies either in heredity or the environment. Physicist William Shockley, and psychologists Arthur Jensen, Richard Herrnstein, Cyril Burt, and Hans Eysenck are most often the cited sources for believing in total IQ heritability. Many journalists are, of course, aware that Jensen and most other "hereditarians" believe in an interaction between environment and heredity, although this fact is often ignored by newspapers.

Of course, the relationship between heredity and IQ has become even more volatile, given the differences in scores between blacks and whites. On this issue, the press couples Jensen most often with Shockley. They also imply that a belief in group differences follows all but inevitably from the belief that individual IQs have a hereditary component.

In explaining the difference in the IQ scores of blacks and whites, the media most often cite the cultural biases of IQ tests, and imply, if they do not state explicitly, that the great majority of experts or "critics of IQ tests" assert such views.

In general, reading or watching the major media would lead the public to conclude that most experts believe that intelligence cannot be defined or measured, that tests are administered badly, and that group differences in test scores are due to weaknesses in the test. As we have seen, the portrait is not an accurate one. Experts do disagree on these issues, but a majority support all the views which the media suggest they oppose.

The issues are presented in the media in the fashion described partly because of the temper of the times and the unwillingness of journalists to alienate large groups in the society. The history of racism and racial discrimination in the United States, Nazi racial doctrines and, more recently, the rise of feminism have led to strong criticisms of any statements which suggest that individual or group differences have an hereditary component. However, journalists' views are not without importance. For this study we polled a new sample of national journalists. Predictably, they are more likely than our expert sample to believe that black-white differences in IQ scores are entirely due to the environment (34 percent of journalists as against 17 percent of the expert sample). Surprisingly, while the expert sample exhibits a somewhat wider spread of views than journalists, they are as politically liberal as members of the media, and are more likely to strongly support affirmative action for blacks than are journalists.

Summary

The issues discussed in this essay were not necessarily chosen because of their intrinsic scientific interest, but rather because they more easily permit one to judge the relationship between the ideology of journalists and the accuracy of their description of reality. Other public policy scientific issues, such as views on pesticide use and other environmental sources of cancer, could have been chosen with similar results. Whatever else journalists might say about nuclear energy or the IQ controversy, most, I believe, would agree that it is their job to report the views of experts accurately. Our evidence indicates that they do not.

Above all, this essay has stressed two themes: first, that the mass media exert increasing influence upon public opinion in general and even that of other elites. Indeed, the media are probably the single most influential institution in the United States in terms of shaping public opinion. Journalists thus are among the more important leadership groups in our society.

Second, the social and political views of journalists influence how they perceive the world and how they describe it to others. Since American journalists tend to be both liberal and cosmopolitan, news presentation tends to take on that kind of cast in the long run.

I need not rehearse the implications of the increasing power of the media for the maintenance of successfully functioning democratic institutions. These implications are certainly mixed, though in my view more negative than positive.

A final word should be added. To a larger extent than hitherto, issues that intersect science and public policy are becoming more central to the political process. Whether we are concerned with the "greenhouse" effect, energy sources, acid rain, IQ testing, nuclear power, or the use of therapeutic drugs, a range of issues has emerged which journalists generally are ill equipped to handle, for most journalists are quite ignorant of scientific issues and find it very difficult to deal with them accurately. This only increases the tendency for ideology to play a role in determining how the public comes to view these problems. Insofar as decisions require that the public be adequately informed, the mass media have not and are not making as positive a contribution as they might.

Bibliography

Abu-Lughod, J. (2001) 'After the WTC disaster: the sacred, the profane, and social solidarity'. Online. Available HTTP: (accessed: March 2002).

Ajami, F. (2002), 'What the Muslim world is watching', *Transnational Broadcasting Studies*, 8, (originally published in *New York Times Magazine*, 18 November 2001).

Aksoy, A. and Robins, K. (2000) 'Thinking across spaces: transnational television from Turkey', *European Journal of Cultural Studies*, 3, 3, 345-367.

Alexander Yonah, and John Gleason, eds. *Behavioral and Quantitative Perspectives on Terrorism*. New York: Pergamon Press, 1981.

Alexander Yonah, and Seymour Maxwell Finger, eds. *Terrorism: Interdisciplinary Perspectives*. New York: The John Jay Press, 1977.

Alexander Yonah, David Carlton, and Paul Wilkinson, eds. *Terrorism: Theory and Practice*. Boulder: Westview Press, 1979.

Alexander Yonah, ed. *International Terrorism: National, Regional and Global Perspectives*. New York: Praeger Publishers, 1976.

Allen, C. (2001) 'Islamophobia in the Media since September 11th', Paper presented at Conference on Exploring Islamophobia: Deepening our Understanding of Islam and Muslims, University of Westminster, 29 September.

Alternet.org (2001) 'The War for Public Opinion', December 10. Online. Available HTTP: (accessed March 2002-May 2003).

Anderson R. H., and J. J. Gillogly. *Rand Intelligent Terminal Agent (R.I.T.A.): Design Philosophy*. Santa Monica: Rand Corporation, R-1809-ARPA, 1976.

Andropov Yuri. *Speeches and Writings*. Trans. by *VAAP Moscow*. New York: Pergamon Press, 1983.

Anzovin Steven, ed. *Terrorism. The Reference Shelf. 58*, no. 3. New York: H.W. Wilson Company, 1986.

Arendt Hannah. *On Violence*. New York: Harcourt, Brace and World, 1970.

Aron Raymond. *Peace and War*. London: Weidenfeld and Nicolson, 1966.

Ayad Abu. *Le'lo Moledet*. Jerusalem: Mifras, 1978.

Barron John. *KGB: The Secret Work of Soviet Secret Agents*. New York: Bantam Books, 1974.

Bassiouni M. Cherif, ed. *International Terrorism and Political Crimes*. Springfield, Ill.: Charles C. Thomas, 1975.

Baudrillard, J. (1991) *La Guerre du Golfe n'a pas eu Lieu*. Paris: Editions Galilée.

Bauman, Z. (1989) *Modernity and the Holocaust*. Cambridge: Polity Press.

Bryson Lyman, ed. *The Communication of Ideas*. New York: Cooper Square, 1964.

Central Intelligence Agency, National Foreign Assessment Center. *International Terrorism in 1977: A Research Paper*. Washington, D.C.: Government Printing Office, RP-78-102554, 1978.

Chandra M. (1987) *Islamic Resurgence in Malaysia*. Petaling Jaya: Fajar Bakti Press.

Crozier Brian. *A Theory of Conflict*. London: Hamish Hamilton, 1974.

Das, V. (1995) *Critical Events: An Anthropological Perspective on Contemporary India*. Delhi: Oxford University Press.

Dayan, D. and Katz, E. (1992) *Media Events: The Live Broadcasting of History*. Cambridge. MA: Harvard University Press.

Eckstein Harry, ed. *Internal War*. New York: Free Press of Glencoe, 1964.

Enloe Cynthia. *Ethnic Conflict and Political Development*. Boston: Little, Brown and Company, 1973.

Epstein Edward. *Between Fact and Fiction: The Problem of Journalism*. New York: Vintage Press, 1975.

Esposito John. *Islam and Politics*. Syracuse, N.Y · Syracuse University Press, 1984.

Esposito, J. L. (1992) *The Islamic Threat: Myth or Reality?*. Oxford: Oxford University Press.

Eulau Heinz. The Behavior Persuasion in Politics. New York: Random House, 1963.

Evans Ernest. Calling a Truce to Terror: The American Response to International Terrorism. Westport, Conn.: Greenwood Press, 1979.

Eveland, W. C. (1980) Ropes of Sand: America's Failure in the Middle East. New York: W. W. Norton.

Friedlander Robert. Terror--Violence: Aspects of Social Control. New York: Oceana Publications, 1983.

George Alexander, and Richard Smoke. *Deterrence in American Foreign Policy: Theory and Practice*. New York: Columbia University Press, 1974.

Gitlin, T. (2002) 'Cranking the "axis of evil"', *OpenDemocracy*, 13 February.

Goodnight, G.. T. (2003) 'Finally, a Picture that Justifies War', April 10. Online. Available HTTP: (accessed April 24, 2003).

Grice, A. (2001) '"Parallel lives" of blacks and whites blamed for riots', Independent, 11 December.

Guardian (2001) October and November issues.

Guggenberger Bernd. "What Motivates the Urban Guerrilla?" German TribunePolitical Affairs Review 28 (3 October 1976): 16.

Gurr Ted Robert. Why Men Rebel. Princeton: Princeton University Press, 1971.

Hackett, B. (2001-2) 'Covering (up) the "war on terrorism"', *Soundings*, 19, 46-53.

Harakah (2001) *Tangkapan KMM di bawah ISA: Usaha PM Ambil Hati Amerika*, August 16-31.

Harkabi Y. *Fedayeen Action and Arab Strategy*. London: Institute for Strategic Studies, 1968.

Hayakawa Samuel. *Language in Thought and Action*. New York: Harcourt, Brace, Jovanovich, 1972.

Heitmeyer, W., Schröder, H., and Müller, J. (1997) 'Desintegration und islamischer Fundamentalismus: Über Lebenssituation, Alltagserfahrungen und ihre Verarbeitungsformen bei türkischen Jugendlichen in Deutschland', *Aus Politik und Zeitgeschichte*, 7-8, 17-31.

Higham, N. (2001) 'Media Confronts a New World', September 25. Online. Available HTTP: (accessed October 2001).

Hull Roger. *The Irish Triangle: Conflict in Northern Ireland.* Princeton, N.J.: Princeton University Press, 1976.

Ingraham Barton. *Political Crime in Europe: A Comparative Study of France, Germany, and England.* Berkeley: University of California Press, 1979.

Institute for the Study of Conflict. *Annual of Power and Conflict: 1978-79.* London: Institute for the Study of Conflict, 1979.

Jensen, R. (2003) 'Images We Choose (To Ignore)', April 10. Online. Available HTTP: (accessed April 14, 2003).

Karakullukçu, E. (1999) 'Çifte vatandaþliði sirtindan vuranlar', *Hürriyet* (European edition), 11 February.

Kessler, C. (1992) 'Archaism and Modernity in Contemporary Malay Political Culture', in J. S. Kahn and F. L. K. Wah (eds.) *Fragmented Vision: Culture and Politics in Contemporary Malaysia.* ASAA Southeast Asia Publication Series, Sydney: Allen and Unwin.

Klute, E. (2002) 'Tuning in to diversity', , 31 January.

Mackinlay, J. (2001) 'Tackling bin Laden: lessons from history', *Guardian*, 28 October.

Mahathir M. (2001) *The Challenge of Global Terrorism*, Keynote speech delivered at the Conference on Terrorism organized by the Institute for Strategic and International Studies (ISIS-Malaysia), Kuala Lumpur, November 17.

Morley, D. (2000) *Home Territories: Media, Mobility and Identity.* London: Routledge.

Robins, K. and Aksoy, A. (2001) 'Abschied von Phantomen: Kulturelle Identitäten im Zeitalter der Globalisierung', in B. Busch *et al.* (eds.). *Bewegte Identitäten: Medien in transkulturellen Kontexten.* Klagenfurt: Drava.

Scannell, P. (1989) 'Public service broadcasting and modern life', *Media Culture and Society*, 11, 2.

Shawcross, W. (2001) 'Stop this racism', *Guardian*, 17 September.

Taher, A. (2001) 'Goodness gracious me, 3m Asians loyal to Britain', *Guardian*, 23 November.

The Economist(2003) 'The Changing of the Guard: A Survey of Malaysia', April 5.

Waters Harry. "Gomorrah Revisited." Newsweek, 5 April 1976, 61.

Weinberg Leonard, and William Eubank. The Rise and Fall of Italian Terrorism. Boulder: Westview Press, 1987.

Welch Susan, and John Comer. Quantitative Methods for Public Administration: Techniques and Applications, 2d ed. Chicago: The Dorsey Press, 1988.

Wilkinson Paul. Political Terrorism. London: MacMillian, 1974.

Young, H. (2001) 'A corrosive national danger in our multicultural model', *Guardian*, 6 November.

Index